HERITAGE TOURISM IN SOUTHEAST ASIA

HERITAGE TOURISM
IN SOUTHEAST ASIA

Edited by
**Michael Hitchcock, Victor T. King
and
Michael Parnwell**

University of Hawai'i Press
Honolulu

Published in North America by
University of Hawai'i Press
2840 Kolowalu Street
Honolulu, Hawai'i 96822
www.uhpress.hawaii.edu

First published in Europe by
NIAS Press
Nordic Institute of Asian Studies
Leifsgade 33
2300 Copenhagen S, Denmark

Library of Congress Cataloging-in-Publication Data

Heritage tourism in Southeast Asia / edited by Michael Hitchcock, Victor T. King
and Michael J.G. Parnwell.
   p. cm.
  Includes bibliographical references and index.
  ISBN 978-0-8248-3504-0 (hardcover : alk. paper) -- ISBN 978-0-8248-3505-7
(pbk. : alk. paper)
  1. Heritage tourism--Southeast Asia. I. Hitchcock, Michael. II. King, Victor T.
III. Parnwell, Mike.
  G155.S644H47 2010
  338.4'79159--dc22

  2010022209

Printed in Singapore

CONTENTS

Figures

Tables

Preface and Acknowledgements

The lengthy lead in time of this volume on heritage tourism in Southeast Asia requires a word of explanation. Several of the chapters that comprise this collection were originally scheduled to be part of our edited volume, *Tourism in Southeast Asia: Challenges and New Directions* (NIAS and University of Hawai'i Press, 2009), but the manuscript ended up being unwieldy and the publishers asked us to prune it. It was a dilemma that had a happy outcome since the publishers agreed to consider a second volume based around the four chapters on heritage tourism in the original manuscript. These chapters were sufficiently interconnected and coherent that they could be lifted out to form the core of a second volume, to which new papers were added. The first volume could then be published with much less difficulty.

In this regard we are endlessly grateful to those who agreed to accept a delay in the publication of their papers until we could assemble a companion volume and who permitted us, at relatively short notice, to transfer their work to the heritage tourism book. We have to bear in mind that we began the whole process of assembling and editing the long-awaited sequel to our *Tourism in South-East Asia* (1993) as long ago as 2005; the delay in publishing the four heritage papers has therefore been considerable. Our sincere thanks must therefore go to Gywnn Jenkins, Mark Johnson, Keiko Miura and Nick Stanley for being so cooperative in allowing us to address our dilemma and in helping us embark on what we believed to be the most constructive way forward.

Having said this, and in duly recognizing the obvious delay in publication, the heritage volume is not without a certain rationale and in the event, in our view, the enterprise has proved to have turned out very successfully indeed.

Two of the co-editors (Hitchcock and King) had already edited a special issue of the journal *Indonesia and the Malay World* (IMW) (2003a) on the theme of what we, and Ian Glover, referred to then as 'discourses with the past', and it seemed to us that we could develop several of the issues which had already been raised and debated in that publication. We therefore had the basis for a much more extended and detailed consideration of the political, economic and socio-cultural contexts within which heritage and the tourism activities associated with it have been developing in the region. More especially what had become very clear to all three co-editors in preparing the first volume was that we needed to devote much more attention to the significance for Southeast Asian governments of UNESCO World Heritage Sites (WHS) and the conflicting pressures, interests and agendas which were being brought to bear on these sites, as well as on the ways in which heritage, whether recognized by UNESCO or not, was becoming a very central element in the promotion of tourism in the region and in the construction and transformation of identities (national, ethnic and local). Three of the four papers which we transferred to the heritage volume focused on globally significant UNESCO sites: Johnson on Hue, Miura on Angkor and Jenkins on the recently designated historic centre of George Town on Pulau Pinang (which along with Melaka was designated as Malaysia's third WHS in 2008). Incidentally Gwynn Jenkins had also contributed a co-authored paper on George Town to our special journal issue of 2003.

Our earlier foray into heritage studies in Southeast Asia has also enabled us to develop a network of researchers, some of whom we could call on at short notice to provide chapters for our new volume. We therefore commissioned and edited several new papers for this second book in addition to writing an extended editorial introduction and an accompanying conclusion, a process which has taken us well over two years to complete. Two of the co-editors stepped in to write chapters afresh in *Heritage Tourism*: Mike Parnwell has contributed a chapter on natural heritage sites by comparing the WHS of Ha Long Bay in northern Vietnam with a similar but non-designated site, Phang Nga Bay, in southern Thailand, and Mike Hitchcock along with fellow researchers Nguyen Thi Thu Huong and Simone Wesner, who had worked with him on a field project in northern Vietnam, have given an overview and analysis of some of their fieldwork findings on handicraft industries and tourism in Hai Duong. Some colleagues who had contributed to our 2003 special issue also came forward with chapters for this current book: Nigel Worden kindly agreed that we could include his previously published paper on the theme of heritage tourism in Melaka and Malay-Malaysian national identity (with some revisions and updating by Victor King); Can-Seng Ooi who has been working on the role and use of museums in the construction and reconstruction of Singaporean national identity stepped in at very short notice; and Kathleen Adams has provided us with a substantially revised and updated chapter, based on her 2003 publication, on the local political issues surrounding moves to secure UNESCO World Heritage listing for the Toraja hamlet of Ke´te´ Kesu´ and the wider Torajaland.

We were also able to call on fellow researchers who had worked with us before and who had contributed to the conference (and the book which emerged from it) which was organised by the three co-editors and Janet Cochrane of Leeds Metropolitan University in June 2006 in Leeds (see Janet Cochrane, *Asian Tourism: Growth and Change*, 2008, Oxford and Amsterdam: Elsevier Ltd). Drawing on this circle of contacts we asked Wantanee Suntikul (with Richard Butler and David Airey) to offer us a chapter on the recent work that they had completed on Vietnamese heritage in Hanoi. Finally, and at a very late stage in the editing process, Geoff Wall enquired whether we would be interested in seeking a publisher for a study which one of his postgraduate students, Mami Yoshimura, had undertaken on the cultural heritage of the Atayal of Wulai in Taiwan, a minority group with cultural affinities to Southeast Asian populations. We took advantage of their generous offer and invited them to submit a co-authored chapter.

Aside from this current edited book, another positive result of the collaboration on heritage tourism in Southeast Asia which will carry forward some of the issues raised in this volume is the recently launched British Academy-funded three-year research project (2009-2011) undertaken by the three co-editors and Janet Cochrane on 'The Management of World Heritage Sites in Southeast Asia: Cross-cultural Perspectives'. Examining eighteen sites across Thailand, Vietnam, Laos, Malaysia, Indonesia and the Philippines, the research team will address several major research questions which, among others, focus on the different perspectives on these sites held by the different users and stakeholders, the problems and opportunities involved in managing and developing WHS, and the impacts on them and local communities of increasing tourism pressures.

A further word of thanks is due. Of course it goes without saying that we are most grateful for the patience and understanding of our contributors and the very constructive way in which they have supported us in bringing this volume to press. But we would also like to express our special thanks to Gerald Jackson and his team at NIAS Press for the extremely positive and helpful approach they have adopted in ensuring that both our tourism volumes have at last appeared in print. They have gone beyond the call of duty. From what started as a proposal for one 'longish' book we have managed to achieve much more in producing two volumes. But because the second edited collection was conceived in and was born and grew from the first we hope that readers will appreciate that there is advantage in considering them 'in companionship' as a two-volume set. Despite the enormous effort and time expended by all concerned in producing these two books we think that it has been worth while bringing into the public domain a wide range of established, ongoing and recent research on tourism in Southeast Asia and setting out several potential research agendas for the next decade. Not least we hope that we have demonstrated the advantages of examining and understanding tourism in a region-wide framework and across disciplinary boundaries. We fully intend to continue our research in this collaborative spirit.

Contributors

Kathleen M. Adams is Professor of Anthropology at Loyola University, Chicago, and an Adjunct Curator of Southeast Asian Ethnology at Chicago's Field Museum of Natural History. She is the author of *Art as Power: Recrafting Identities, Tourism and Power in Tana Toraja, Indonesia*, University of Hawai'i Press, 2006, which won the 2009 Alpha Sigma Award. Her articles on cultural representations, tourism, ethnic relations, museums and the politics of art have appeared in various edited volumes and journals, including *American Ethnologist, Ethnology, Museum Anthropology, Annals of Tourism Research*, and *Tourist Studies*.

David Airey is Professor of Tourism Management at the University of Surrey, where he has also served as Pro-Vice-Chancellor. His current research interests include tourism education, tourism policy and organisation. He was co-editor of the first book on tourism education and is recipient of the UNWTO Ulysses Award for his services to education.

Richard Butler is Emeritus Professor in the Strathclyde Business School, University of Strathclyde, Glasgow. Trained as a geographer, his main research interests are in destination development, tourism in islands and remote locations, and its relationships with local residents. He continues to work on the Destination Life Cycle model (1980, 2006) and also on tourism and indigenous peoples (2007).

Michael Hitchcock is Academic Director and Dean of Faculty at the IMI University Centre, Luzern. He was formerly Deputy Dean for External Relations and Research in the Faculty of Business, Arts and Humanities at the University of Chichester. Between 2000 and 2008 he was a Professor and Director of the International Institute for Culture, Tourism and Development at London Metropolitan University. His recent publications include *Tourism in Southeast Asia: Challengers and New Directions*, NIAS/ University of Hawai'i Press, 2009 (ed. with Victor T. King and Michael J. G. Parnwell) and *Tourism, Development and Terrorism in Bali*, Ashgate, 2007 (with I Nyoman Darma Putra).

Gwynn Jenkins trained as a 3D designer and moved to live and work in Penang, Malaysia, in 1995. After 11 years of pioneering heritage conservation with a Penang architectural practice and gaining a PhD in Social and Cultural Anthropology supported by the University of Hull, UK, Gwynn continues to live, research, conserve and write from a restored Chinese shophouse in the heart of the old city.

Mark Johnson is Senior Lecturer in Social Anthropology at the University of Hull. His research interests are in gender, sexuality, heritage, landscape, environment, migration and diaspora. He has conducted research in the Philippines, Vietnam, Costa Rica and most recently Saudi Arabia. Recent publications include 'Both "One and Other": Environmental Cosmopolitanism and the Politics of Hybridity', *Nature and Culture*, 3, 1, 2008 (with S. Clisby) and 'Naturalising Distinctions: Contested Fields of Environmentalism in Costa Rica', *Journal of Landscape Research*, 34, 2, 2009 (with S. Clisby).

Victor T. King is Professor of South East Asian Studies and Executive Director of the White Rose East Asia Centre, University of Leeds. His research interests are spread widely across the sociology and anthropology of the region, with a particular focus on change and development. His recent publications include *The Sociology of Southeast Asia: Transformations in a Developing Region*, NIAS/Hawai'i Press, 2008, and (with William D. Wilder) *The Modern Anthropology of South-East Asia: An Introduction*, Routledge, 2006 (reprint).

Keiko Miura is Lecturer (part-time) in the School of Letters, Arts and Sciences, Waseda University, Japan, and also Research Fellow in the Cultural Property Research Group, University of Göttingen, Germany. Her research interests include heritage conservation, tourism development and local ways of life. Recent publications include 'Needs for Anthropological Approaches to Conservation and Management of Living Heritage Sites: From a Case Study of Angkor, Cambodia', in E. A. Bacus, I. C. Glover and

P. D. Sharrock (eds), *Interpreting Southeast Asia's Past: Monument, Image and Text,* National University of Singapore, 2008, and 'Conservation of a "Living Heritage Site": A Contradiction in Terms? A Case Study of Angkor World Heritage Site', *Conservation and Management of Archaeological Sites (CMAS),* 7, 1, pp. 3–118, James & James, 2005.

Nguyen Thi Thu Huong graduated from Hanoi Architecture University in 1993 and worked as an architect in the Ministry of Construction in Hanoi. In 1998 she completed a Master's Degree in Urban Planning at the Catholic University of Leuven, Belgium. Since then she has executed various development projects for different international NGOs and donors. In 2002-2004 she worked as project manager and ran the Handicraft Centre in Hai Duong under the EU Asia-Urbs framework, and at the same time prepared two research papers about handicraft production in Northern Vietnam for the International Labour Organisation. She lives in Munich and is undertaking a second Master's course in land management and land tenure in the Technical University, Munich.

Can-Seng Ooi is an Associate Professor at Copenhagen Business School. His research centres on cultural tourism in Singapore and Denmark. Currently, he is leading a team of researchers looking at 'new heritage' or contemporary art in these two countries, and also in China and India.

Michael J.G. Parnwell is Professor of South East Asian Development in the Department of East Asian Studies at the University of Leeds. He has a wide range of research interests, including sustainable development, sustainable tourism, heritage management, social capital, localism, Buddhism and alternative development. He has undertaken field-based research in Thailand, Malaysia, Indonesia, Vietnam and China.

Nick Stanley is Leverhulme Research Fellow at the British Museum and the University of Cambridge. Professor Stanley was formerly Director of Research and Chair of Postgraduate Studies at Birmingham Institute of Art and Design. He has worked on collections and display within museums of Oceanic materials both in Melanesia as well as Europe and North America. His current work is on the artistic production of the Asmat people in West Papua.

Geoffrey Wall is Professor of Geography and Environmental Management at the University of Waterloo, Canada. He is interested in the implications of tourism of different types for destinations with different characteristics, and the planning implications of these relationships. He has explored these themes particularly in Indonesia, China and Taiwan. He is the author, with Alister Mathieson, of *Tourism: Change, Impacts and Opportunities*, Pearson, 2006.

Wantanee Suntikul is an Assistant Professor at the Institute for Tourism Studies in Macau. She gained her PhD in Tourism Studies from the University of Surrey. Her core research interest and expertise are in politics, heritage, social and environmental aspects of tourism and tourism's potential for poverty alleviation. Her recent publications are mostly about tourism in Laos and Vietnam.

Simone Wesner is a Senior Research Fellow at the International Institute for Culture, Tourism and Development at London Metropolitan University. Her research focuses on historical interpretations of cultural values and their impact on current arts and heritage policy development in Europe and Southeast Asia. Recent publications include Hitchcock, M. and S. Wesner (2009) 'Neo-Confucianism, Networks and Vietnamese Family Businesses in London', *Asia-Pacific Business Review*, 15, 2, pp. 265-282.

Nigel Worden is Professor of History at the University of Cape Town. His publications include work on Cape slavery and its Southeast Asian and Indian Ocean context as well as public history and heritage in these regions. His current research focuses on the construction of social identities among the underclass of eighteenth-century Cape Town.

Mami Yoshimura moved back to Japan in 2007 upon completion of her MA degree in Geography from the University of Waterloo, Ontario, Canada, and has worked for an international NGO (EDF-Japan) as a programme officer. She will now begin a new career as a gender programme officer for UNDP in Riyadh, Saudi Arabia. Her research interests lie in the areas of gender, colonialism, and indigenous tourism.

CHAPTER 1

Heritage Tourism in Southeast Asia

Michael Hitchcock, Victor T. King and Michael J. G. Parnwell

WHAT IS HERITAGE?

This book focuses on disputes and conflicts over what heritage is, what it means and how it has been presented, re-presented, developed and protected, set against a back-drop of the demands, motivations and impacts of heritage tourism. This involves examining the different agents or actors involved in encounters and contestation, drawing in issues of identity construction and negotiation, and requiring the contextualization of heritage in national and global processes of identity formation and transformation (also see Hitchcock, King and Parnwell, 2009). Melanie Smith (2003: 103) usefully summarizes a set of key issues pertaining to heritage, which we shall also revisit in the book; these comprise questions about the ownership of heritage, its appropriate use, access to it as against conservation needs, heritage as a commodity, as entertainment and as an educational medium, and finally the interpretation and representation of heritage forms.

The book explores Southeast Asian heritages, their conceptualizations and representations, set against relationships between culture, nature, tourism and identity. The book arises from and develops a previous contribution to the relation between tourism and heritage which two of us presented in a special issue of the journal *Indonesia and the Malay World* and which explored a variety of cases of the appropriation, creation, presentation and developmental significance of cultural heritage, principally in Indonesia, Malaysia and Singapore, with additional case material from mainland Southeast Asia and Taiwan (Hitchcock and King, 2003a). That collection of essays, covering diverse examples of heritage (e.g. cultural parks, temple complexes, archaeological sites, museum exhibitions, 'living cultural landscapes', cultural performances), was designed to demonstrate how local communities with varied interests and perspectives interact dynamically with national and global actors, who themselves carry and promote different expectations and images of heritage and the past. One theme in that collection examined the ways in which heritage has been subject to selection, construction and contestation in the context of more general processes of local and national identity formation (Hitchcock and King, 1993b: 3–13);[1] that theme is pursued in much more detail in this current book through a range of examples of World Heritage Sites and the presentation of diverse aspects of cultural and natural heritage.

Having proceeded boldly to state what we intend to do, we have to accept that heritage is a concept which is difficult to define. Indeed, David Herbert suggests that it is 'among the undefinables', though he categorizes heritage into three broad types: 'cultural', 'natural' and 'built environments' (1989: 10–12). In a narrow and simple sense heritage is literally 'what is or may be inherited' (*Little Oxford English Dictionary*, 1996: 294), or 'something other than property passed down from preceding generations: a legacy; a set of traditions, values, or treasured material things' (*Reader's Digest*, 1987: 721). Melanie Smith, taking the meaning somewhat further and emphasizing human agency, proposes that heritage, as distinct from but related to 'the past' and to 'history', is 'the contemporary use of the past, including both its interpretation and re-interpretation' (Smith, 2003: 82). In introducing the notion of interpretation, which suggests that heritage is created, given meaning and imbued with significance, we move into a much broader conceptualization which pertains to notions of local identity, ethnicity and nationalism, and even global identity. In this latter sense heritage is presented and re-presented as something which relates to the past and which is in some way given special value or significance as 'treasure' or 'legacy'. Therefore it is constructed through processes of selection and elimination, appropriated by the state and its agents, then objectified to become worthy of political, economic and 'touristic' attention. The concept of heritage thus refers to tangible and concrete elements of the past (buildings, monuments, artefacts, sites and constructed landscapes), as well as to those aspects of culture expressed in behaviour, action and performance (usually referred to as 'intangible cultural heritage') which are interpreted, valued and judged to be worthy of our attention and protection. David Harrison has also argued that what is considered to be 'heritage' more generally is in any case a form of performance, display and exhibition; it is an imaginative construct (2004: 281–290; and see Ooi, 2002b: 44).

'Heritage tourism' has also proved difficult to define and categorize. Melanie Smith remarks that terms such as 'heritage tourism', 'arts tourism', 'ethnic tourism' or 'indigenous tourism' are often used interchangeably (2003: 29–44). However, she prefers to classify them, along with 'urban cultural tourism', 'rural cultural tourism', 'creative tourism' and 'popular cultural tourism', as separate sub-types of a broad category of 'cultural tourism', recognizing that cultural tourists as a highly differentiated category consume not just the cultural products of the past but also a range of contemporary cultural forms (ibid.; Clarke, 2000: 23–36; Hughes, 2000: 111–122). Cultural tourism is therefore no longer seen, as it was in the past, as 'a niche form of tourism, attracting small [sic], well-educated and high-spending visitors' (Smith, 2003: 45). Heritage tourism therefore comprises that part of cultural tourism which, according to Linda Richter, is 'applied by some to almost anything about the past that can be visited' (1999: 108). Tourism in this case becomes a 'history-making business' or at least an activity which commercializes the past (Shaw and Williams, 2002: 203).

Heritage is also contested and transformed not only by representatives of the state but also by global actors, including representatives of international organizations such as the United Nations Educational, Scientific and Cultural Organization (UNESCO), researchers and foreign tourists, as well as domestic tourists, local communities and their neighbours. It has therefore become a highly politicized project concerned with constructions of identity and conflicts over its character and trajectory (ibid.: 37–38). Black and Wall state appositely that 'the sites selected to represent the country's heritage will also have strong implications for both collective and individual identity and hence the creation of social realities' (2001: 123). In this connection Ian Glover observes, in his examination of the political uses of archaeology in Southeast Asia, that governments 'attempt to create discourses with the past in order to legitimize and strengthen the position of the state and its dominant political communities' (2003: 16–17).

In newly independent or post-colonial developing states this is an even more urgent task and the need, in Benedict Anderson's terms (1991: 178–185), to 'imagine' the nation leads to the selection and deployment of archaeological finds and heritage sites to present images of national resilience, unity and innovation, often in the context of an 'imagined' golden or glorious age of endeavour and achievement which was subsequently eclipsed by colonialism (Glover, 2003: 17). Glover also notes that Anderson traces this appropriation of such elements of heritage as 'the great monuments of decayed Indic civilizations' to the late colonial period 'to give added legitimacy to colonial rule'. He continues: '[s]ubstantial resources were put into clearing, excavating, and restoring great temples', and, paraphrasing Anderson, 'old sacred sites were incorporated into the map of the colony, their ancient prestige draped around the mappers' (ibid.; Anderson, 1991: 181–182). In this respect post-independent governments have often had to reposition their archaeological sites to express indigenous achievement and demonstrate the legitimacy conveyed by ancient genealogy as against Western interpretations of the sites as evidence of indigenous failure, inertia and neglect, and which have been rescued for posterity by discerning and civilized outsiders who recognize the value of this cultural legacy.

It was the western colonial powers which played a significant part in fostering a sense of states' historical identity among their dependent populations. This identity was created not simply in opposition to 'a colonial other' but also out of the colonial desire and need to delimit, control, administer and defend their possessions, and to differentiate their territories from other neighbouring states, which were in turn invariably in the possession of other competing colonial powers. This process of identity construction involved, among other things, the study and preservation of local heritage, particularly where the colonial administration relied on the traditional authority of royalty, nobility and aristocracy, usually in systems of indirect rule, in order to buttress their political position (Long and Sweet, 2006: 463).

A useful starting point in the search for the detailed meanings associated with the concept of heritage is UNESCO's World Heritage Centre based in Paris and its associated Committee, which designates World Heritage Sites as of either 'cultural' or 'natural' or 'mixed' (both cultural and natural) importance, and more particularly as sites of 'outstanding universal value' (http://whc.unesco.org/en/; and see Adams, 2003: 91–93; Hitchcock, 2004: 461–466; Long and Sweet, 2006: 445–469; Smith, 2003: 38, 105–116). Since the late 1960s, heritage has been internationalized by such bodies as UNESCO, which has 'helped to generate a new set of understandings of culture and built heritage' (Askew, 1996: 184). The *Convention Concerning the Protection of the World Cultural and Natural Heritage*, which was instituted to protect global heritage, was adopted by UNESCO in 1972, and the recent 'criteria for selection' of sites to be included on the World Heritage List provide us with a combination of 'cultural' and 'natural' criteria. Until 2004 these sites were selected using six cultural and four natural criteria, but since then they have been brought together in revised guidelines to comprise a composite list of ten criteria displayed on the Centre's web-pages under the title 'The Criteria for Selection'. As one would expect the list is sprinkled with superlatives: the first is 'to represent a masterpiece of human creative genius', another 'to bear a unique or at least exceptional testimony to a cultural tradition or to a civilization which is living or which has disappeared', another 'to be an outstanding example of a type of building, architectural or technological ensemble or landscape which illustrates (a) significant stage(s) in human history', and another 'to be an outstanding example of a traditional human settlement, land-use, or sea-use which is representative of a culture (or cultures), or human interaction with the environment especially when it has become vulnerable under the impact of irreversible change'.

Interestingly one of the 'cultural' criteria in the World Heritage Site list (Criterion VI: 'to be directly or tangibly associated with events or living traditions, with ideas, or with beliefs, with artistic and literary works of outstanding universal significance') has been given something of a dependent or complementary status, in that the Committee considers that it is not free-standing and that it 'should preferably be used in conjunction with other criteria'. Heritage using this concept of culture corresponds more or less with a broad anthropological definition. More recently in its *Convention for the Safeguarding of the Intangible Cultural Heritage* (2003), UNESCO has affirmed the importance of culture as expressed in oral tradition, performing arts, social practices, rituals, festivals and traditional craftsmanship. Finally, there is a criterion (Criterion II) that partly overlaps with notions of traditions, ideas and beliefs, but which addresses the dimension of cultural exchange and dynamic process within the context of broader cultural regions, that is: 'to exhibit an important interchange of human values, over a span of time or within a cultural area of the world, on developments in architecture or technology, monumental arts, town-planning or landscape design'. In sum, UNESCO's concept of cultural heritage is extraordinarily broad, but, given those cultural sites currently on the World Heritage List, the emphasis is still on groups of buildings, monuments and settlements which require some form of protection, conservation and preservation for posterity, and therefore tend to be tangible sites of historical, aesthetic, artistic, architectural, archaeological, scientific, technological or ethnological value rather than a 'living tradition'.

'Natural heritage', on the other hand, refers to areas which embody outstanding physical, biological and geological features and those which have significance in terms of their uniqueness and their importance in the evolution of the natural world. They may 'contain superlative natural phenomena' or be 'areas of exceptional natural beauty and aesthetic importance'. They may be 'outstanding examples representing major stages of earth's history' or 'representing significant on-going ecological and biological processes in the evolution and development of (...) ecosystems and communities of plants and animals'. Finally, there is emphasis on the importance of natural habitats where biological diversity needs to be conserved, particularly where there are threats to 'species of outstanding universal value from the point of view of science and conservation'. It is interesting in the Southeast Asian context just how many of the designated World Heritage Sites are 'natural', including national parks, as a proportion of the total number of sites; in fact, almost half (see Table 1.1). As of 7 July 2008 the World Heritage Committee had 878 sites on its list; of these 679 (77 per cent) were cultural, 174 (20 per cent) natural and twenty-five (3 per cent) were mixed sites; thirty (3.4 per cent) were also placed on an 'in danger list' including the rice terraces of the Philippine Cordilleras. In the Asia Pacific region the majority of the sites are to be found, not unexpectedly, in China, India and to a lesser extent Japan.

In Southeast Asia there are twenty-nine World Heritage Sites; seventeen (59 per cent) of these are cultural and twelve (41 per cent) are natural. They are distributed between Indonesia which has seven, the Philippines, Vietnam and Thailand with five each, Malaysia with three (the recently inscribed 'historic cities of the Straits of Malacca' in fact includes two sites, George Town and Melaka, both of which are featured in this book), and Laos and Cambodia with two each (Table 1.1). Certain of the cultural sites so designated are perhaps unsurprising: Angkor in Cambodia; Luang Prabang and Vat Phou in Laos; Hue, Hoi An and My Son in Vietnam; Ayutthaya, Sukhothai and Ban Chiang in Thailand; Borobodur, Prambanan and Sangiran in Indonesia; and Baroque Churches and Vigan Town in the Philippines. Bearing in mind Southeast Asia's rich early, classical and colonial history one might have expected the designation of many more historical and cultural sites, but the process of selection and approval is a highly politicized one at the national and international level, and many of the proposed and potentially designated sites in Southeast Asia, which have not made it on to the UNESCO list, have suffered from the depredations of modernization and development, particularly in such places as Singapore, where most of the built forms of the past have been demolished and replaced with a high-rise, glass and concrete cityscape. It is interesting to note, again perhaps not unexpectedly given the country's recent turbulent history, that there are no designated sites in Myanmar, but nor are there approved cultural sites in Brunei, and only a handful in the remaining Southeast Asian countries. Southeast Asia is also home to at least one grassroots rebellion against the creation of a World Heritage Site: the sacred temple complexes of Besakih in Bali (I Nyoman Darma Putra and Hitchcock, 2005: 225–237).

Here we need to emphasize the major preoccupations of those international organizations which focus on Southeast Asian heritage and which attempt to set a global heritage agenda. Organizations like UNESCO (and its regional office in Bangkok), the World Monuments Fund, the International Council of Museums (and its Asia Pacific Organization), the International Council on Monuments and Sites (ICOMOS), The Getty Conservation Institute, and, at the regional level, the Southeast Asian Ministers of Education Organization (SEAMEO) and the Southeast Asian Regional Centre for Archaeology and Fine Arts (SPAFA), invariably stress the concepts of 'tradition', continuity and 'unchangeableness', expressed particularly in built heritage and material culture, which needs to be designated and given special attention, managed, monitored, conserved and protected (http://icom.museum/; http://www.getty.edu/conservation/; and see Vines, 2005). This perspective, which is also expressed in the heritage tourism industry, tends to indulge in nostalgia for the past and in the presentation of the exotic and an idealized and 'essentialized' Orient (Kennedy and Williams, 2001), and also a 'pristinized' nature.

It is also worth noting here that such bodies as UNESCO usually emphasize the importance of continuity in the original fabric of buildings and other physical structures in defining the authenticity of built heritage. Conversely, in East Asian cultures, as expressed in *The NARA Document on Authenticity* (1994) which originated in Japan, the stress is on the continuity of use in heritage buildings rather than structure and materials, because their fabric is usually periodically renewed and refurbished (Long and Sweet, 2006: 447).

Table 1.1 UNESCO World Cultural and Natural Heritage Sites in Southeast Asia

	World Heritage Site	
CAMBODIA		
Angkor	Cultural	1992
Preah Vihear Temple	Cultural	2008
INDONESIA		
Borobudur Temple Compounds	Cultural	1991
Komodo National Park	Natural	1991
Prambanan Temple Compounds	Cultural	1991
Ujung Kulon National Park	Natural	1991
Sangiran Early Man Site	Cultural	1996
Lorentz National Park	Natural	1999
Tropical Rainforest Heritage of Sumatra	Natural	2004
LAO PDR		
Town of Luang Prabang	Cultural	1995
Vat Phou and Associated Ancient Settlements within the Champasak Cultural Landscape	Cultural	2001
MALAYSIA		
Gunung Mulu National Park	Natural	2000
Kinabalu Park	Natural	2000
Melaka and George Town, Historic Cities of the Straits of Malacca	Cultural	2008
PHILIPPINES		
Baroque Churches of the Philippines	Cultural	1993
Tubbataha Reef Marine Park	Natural	1993
Rice Terraces of the Philippine Cordilleras	Cultural (in danger)	1995
Historic Town of Vigan	Cultural	1999
Puerto-Princesa Subterranean River National Park	Natural	1999
THAILAND		
Historic City of Ayutthaya	Cultural	1991
Historic Town of Sukhothai and Associated Historic Towns	Cultural	1991
Thungyai-Huai Kha Khaeng Wildlife Sanctuaries	Natural	1991
Ban Chiang Archaeological Site	Cultural	1992
Dong Phayayen-Khao Yai Forest Complex	Natural	2005

VIETNAM

Complex of Hue Monuments	Cultural	1993
Ha Long Bay	Natural	1994, 2000
Hoi An Ancient Town	Cultural	1999
My Son Sanctuary	Cultural	1999
Phong Nha-Ke Bang National Park	Natural	2003

*Source: UNESCO World Heritage Centre, World Heritage List April 2009 (http://whc.
unesco.org/en/list)*

In this connection a major concern of international heritage organizations
during the past decade, expressed in a number of international workshops,
conferences and training initiatives, has been the theft, looting and the
illicit trade in the cultural heritage of Southeast Asia, as well as the impact
on heritage sites and on local cultures of rapidly expanding tourism activity
and globalization. Particular concern has been raised in international
organizations about the systematic looting and sale of artefacts from
Cambodia, Laos, Vietnam and Myanmar, which are often traded across
national borders into Thailand. The blame is placed at the door of transnational tourism, local poverty, the internationalization of the art market and
global capital flows (see, for example, Galla, 2002; Bradford and Lee, 2004).

Concerns and anxieties about the possible debasing of culture and
ethnicity, the decontextualization of culture through its 'simplification',
'distortion', 'fabrication', 'fragmentation' and presentation as 'a global
product', the need to make culture 'better than reality' in the interest of
tourism promotion, and the process of 'cultural colonization' and tourism
as 'neo-colonialism' are presented forcefully by Boniface and Fowler (1993:
2–4, 7, 11–13, 20, 152–162; Ooi, 2002b: 67, 123–138). Indeed, a considerable
emphasis in the literature on heritage is the commoditization and
'falsification' of the past, and the consequences of these processes (Smith,
2003: 82; and see Harrison, 2004: 283–286). Ooi argues that sometimes
such cultural intermediaries as tour guides have an important role in this
process in that 'they teach tourists to consume authenticity' (2002b: 159).
And in this regard Walsh takes an uncompromising stand in his criticism
of the heritage industry when he says, 'History as heritage dulls our ability
to appreciate the development of people and places through time.' It has
an 'unnerving ability to deny historical process, or diachrony. Heritage
successfully mediates all our pasts as ephemeral snapshots exploited in
the present' (1992: 113, 149; and cited in Smith, 2003: 82; and see Watson,
2000: 450–456).

In this edited book we are mainly concerned with cultural rather than natural heritage, although one of the co-editors provides a comparative chapter on natural heritage management. We focus on cultural forms as heritage because governments, in promoting tourism in particular, tend to focus on those elements which are immediate, accessible, distinctive, impressive, colourful and visible to the 'tourist gaze', and whose meanings and significance can be more easily constructed, shaped, changed and controlled (Wood, 1997: 10). Some of these forms comprise World Heritage Sites (as in Angkor, Vat Phou Champasak, and Hue), but others are either much more deliberately constructed or modified forms displayed in museums, cultural parks and urban areas or are intimately interrelated with cultural expressions devised for the purposes of tourism promotion. Because of their unstable and contested characters, these forms enter into the arena of cultural politics and identity. In this exercise, in which international and national players seek to define and control the meaning of a site, landscape, artefact or cultural display and performance, they may seek to disregard or re-define local cultural meanings and perspectives (Adams, 2006; Black and Wall, 2001: 124, 132; Askew, 1996: 203–204). Heritage sites are therefore designated as significant in some way; and their meaning and significance are interpreted and explained by various actors, often with different interests and views.

Heritage then becomes a political tool in negotiations over identity, but it is also part of an 'industry' – a heritage, tourism and leisure industry – which generates employment, income and development (Herbert, 1989: 12–13; Richter, 1999: 108). History is therefore translated into a marketable commodity and heritage comprises 'the commodified cladding of symbols of antiquity' (Boniface and Fowler, 1993: xi; Rahil, Ooi and Shaw, 2006: 161–163). Heritage therefore has various functions and is often the focus of struggle, debate and dispute over its use or uses and what it expresses or represents, a struggle in which those who have more power and authority usually have a more influential say. In his study of the plans to redevelop and rehabilitate Rattanakosin Island, the old inner royal precinct of Bangkok, Askew (1996: 203–204), for example, identifies several key national players in the debates about the character of a re-constructed historical space: purist and elitist architect/landscape planners, the Thai royal family, state agencies interested in tourism development, and national and metropolitan planners concerned to promote Bangkok's capacity as a generator of national income. These are essentially members of the political and bureaucratic elite and to avoid an overly elitist view of this historic core of Bangkok, Askew calls for a greater involvement of local activists, academics and conservation professionals to draw attention to 'the ordinary spaces of commerce and residence, of the structures of the older communities now in decline and of some of the typical features of the built environment' (ibid.: 204).

The concept of heritage as used in this book shades into the concepts of culture and tradition; it embodies competing notions of the unchanging and authentic past and the consciously constructed and transformed present and future; and it is bound up with issues of local, ethnic, provincial, national and global identities. However, as we shall see, even the natural environment can be defined and sanctioned as heritage and moulded in particular ways for the tourist market, although it is usually presented and given meaning, as is cultural heritage, as pristine, enduring, authentic and connected to the distant past. Primeval jungles which are preserved and organized in the form of national parks and nature reserves, provide one of the best examples of the deliberate creation and appropriation of nature, usually in the context of ecotourism. Harrison makes the important point, which confirms our view expressed here (and see Parnwell, Chapter 12), that '[t]here is nothing "natural" in our appreciation of landscape. We learn to appreciate it through our backgrounds and socialization, but the socialization of the expert may differ from that of the layman, and thus interpretations of what is natural will vary' (2004: 282). Just like other examples of heritage, landscapes are multivalent, and are sites of dispute, debate and shifting interpretations.

HERITAGE AND IDENTITY

The study of the construction, presentation, negotiation and transformation of heritage and our understanding of the politics of heritage owe much to the work of Robert Wood (1984, 1993, 1997) and Michel Picard (1996; and see Picard and Wood, 1997a; and Michaud and Picard, 2001) on the relationships between tourism, identity and the state. In their co-edited book on cultural and ethnic tourism in Asian and Pacific societies, they focus on the relationships between tourism and the state on the one hand and race, ethnicity and identity on the other, and specifically the ways in which identities are commoditized for the purposes of tourism development (Picard and Wood, 1997a). The major question which they address is 'How are ethnic divisions, symbolized by ethnic markers selected for tourism promotion, reconciled with national integration and the assertion of a national identity?' (Picard and Wood, 1997b: ix). The state, and particularly the state in the developing world, enters into the relationship between tourism and identity because both are seen to require state-directed political action. Developing countries promote tourism as an increasingly vital sector in strategies for economic growth and development, and they do this on the basis of such resources as their heritage and more widely their culture, or cultures. They also use these resources in the process of creating national identities and 'to reconcile ethnic diversity and modern nationhood' (ibid.).

Suharto's New Order government in Indonesia did precisely this in the interests of 'nationalist ideals' and 'the exigencies of economic development'; it 'defined the boundaries of acceptable ethnicity, simultaneously celebrating and subjugating indigenous groups' (Morrell, 2000: 257; and see Pemberton, 1994; Picard, 1996, 1997, 2003). In this exercise cultural differences were 'often reduced (...) to a superficial promulgation of traditional costume, architecture, dance and other art forms' (Morrell, 2000: 257). Richter also points to the profoundly political character of state-directed and state-sponsored tourism in the Philippines under President's Ferdinand Marcos's martial law (1996: 233–262) and the more general 'battle over power and resources' involved in heritage development (1999: 108). In another example, the government of Singapore had to create an identity for this small city-state after its departure from the Federation of Malaysia in 1965. An important dimension of this identity construction has been heritage and history, though Singapore has no World Heritage Sites and indeed has radically transformed, redeveloped and modernized the cityscape (Saunders, 2004). The government has deliberately constructed a heritage industry (and an identity) and promoted cultural and educational tourism based on its multi-ethnic population, its history, its broader Asian identity, and its strategic gateway location within a wider Asian region (Ooi, 2002b: 214–228).

The relevance of these issues to the construction and representation of heritage is obvious: considerations of ethnicity, identity and heritage are combined in the encounter of representatives of the state with local people (Henderson, 2003). Picard and Wood (1997b: viii) observe that '[w]ith the proliferation of ethnic tourism, of ethnic museums and theme parks around the world, and of ethnic artefacts consumed not only by tourists but also by members of ethnic groups as assertions of their ethnic identities, ethnicity itself has become increasingly commoditized in specifically touristic ways'. In this arena of national image-making and local constructions of identity the subject of heritage, conceptualized as a tangible and accessible representation of the past and of established tradition, plays an important role (Askew, 1996: 187–191). It is also part of the more general process undertaken by those who hold political power to legitimize and authorize their political position (and see Richter, 1989, 1996, 1999; Rahil, Ooi and Shaw, 2006). This action in turn encourages local communities to contemplate, discuss, debate, negotiate and contest their identities in the face of the attempts by the state to intervene, manipulate and control them. As Wood says '[t]he contradictory interests of the states, partly rooted in their desire to promote ethnic tourism, provide room for creative manoeuvre by local ethnic groups, and produce complex forms of mutual accommodation' (1997: 15; and see Shaw and Jones, 1997). A good example of these processes is that of the hybrid 'peranakan' and Eurasian communities of Singapore and the multiple identities and perspectives involved in the promotion of ethnic heritage for tourism purposes there (Henderson, 2003; Shaw and Rahil, 2006). What is also especially interesting in more recent heritage tourism activities is the increasing trend 'to remember *marginalized groups*', 'the powerless' and 'the overlooked' (Richter, 1999: 115, 122, italics in original).

Heritage sites, which are tangible expressions of identities, therefore provide excellent laboratories to explore the meaning and constructions of 'place', particularly 'historical places' and the identities which are often associated with or claimed for particular locations (Askew, 1996: 184). As Han has proposed, in an interesting study of the construction of images of colonial Singapore, specific places are imbued 'with an identity, spirit, and personality'; they are sites in time where 'collective histories and personal biographies' intersect (2003: 257–258). But there is usually no one image which prevails, rather images and meanings which define and characterize particular sites are conflicting and overlapping; they express relations of power and resistance and competing goals, interests and expectations on the part of those who inhabit, are in some way associated with, or who gaze on a site (and see Yeoh and Kong, 1995, 1996; and Yeoh, 1996). Heritage sites provide opportunities for different ways of 'seeing and valuing' (Askew, 1996: 186; Boniface and Fowler, 1993: 20, 152). They are also 'rarely unchanging embodiments of tradition' (Adams, 2004: 433).

CONTESTATION AND AGENCY

The crucial issue of the 'invention' and 'imagination' of tradition, or heritage, is hardly a new one (Hobsbawm and Ranger, 1983; and see Hitchcock, King and Parnwell, 1993b: 8–16). Culture, heritage and identity are not passed on in an unchanging fashion from one generation to the next; they are not fixed but rather are 'constantly reinvented (…) reimagined (…) symbolically constructed, and often contested' (Wood, 1997: 18). Richter reinforces this point in her observation that '[e]ven the very substance of a heritage is a political construction of what is remembered – different for many groups in society' (1999: 109). Social science studies of tourism have been engaged in the examination of the processes of cultural construction and transformation for over thirty years, especially in the context of debates about whether or not tourism undermines, contaminates or destroys previously 'authentic' or 'real' cultures, and what 'authenticity' means (Cohen, 1996: 90–93, 97–98, 105–107; Crick, 1996: 40–41; Ooi, 2002b: 21–31; Richter, 1999: 118–122; Smith, 2003: 20–23). However, attention has increasingly been devoted to the ways in which cultural phenomena are deployed to make statements about identity.

As Adams (2006) has observed recently in her detailed and subtle analysis of the 'politics of art' among the Toraja of Indonesia, items of material culture are 'imbued with emotional force'; they embody multiple meanings and ambiguities, and they express meanings in symbolic form. These meanings can be manipulated, transformed and contested and they can also influence particular directions of action and behaviour. Art objects, used to express particular identities, also serve as an appropriate medium for encapsulating conflicting and contradictory narratives. Adams's apposite remark on the character of art can be applied more generally to heritage in that it comprises 'a complex arena encompassing contending discourses concerning identity and hierarchies of authority and power' (ibid.: 210). One of our major tasks is to examine and understand the different 'heritage narratives' which are being selected and promoted for tourism and other purposes (Boniface and Fowler, 1993: 11); and to understand the ways in which sites become designated as worthy of heritage celebration (Harrison, 2004). As Harrison observes 'there is nothing intrinsically sacrosanct about any building, any part of nature, or any cultural practice' because 'as one class or pressure group takes ascendancy over another, new perceptions, new views on the past and what was of *value* in the past, also take over' (ibid.: 287, italics in original).

Another important analytical focus in some recent studies of cultural politics and the relationships between identity, tourism and the state is that of human agency. As Wood has remarked, in drawing out underlying themes in his co-edited book, 'nowhere have local people been powerless or passive' (1997: 15). To be sure they operate within particular frameworks of constraint, and some states are more interventionist and control and regulate their citizens more tightly, but even then there is evidence of local resistance, 'subtle manipulation', rivalry and conflict, and the exercise of options and choice (ibid.: 15, 18–24). The contestation over the temple and religious complexes of Pura Besakih in Indonesia and the local opposition to its World Heritage Site designation is an excellent case in point (I Nyoman Darma Putra and Hitchcock, 2005).

Tourism, therefore, tends to encourage the intervention of the state, but it also provides people with 'new resources for pursuing their own agendas' (ibid.: 21). In this connection, 'local cultures develop during the dynamic process of making use of tourism to re-define their own identities' (Yamashita, Kadir Din and Eades, 1997: 16). The situation in a tourism context is also complex because a range of actors are involved – tourists, tourism intermediaries, local people and state agents in particular. For these reasons state policies on tourism development and identity formation may lead to consequences which they did not intend or foresee. The strong tendency of international and national agencies to plan and manage heritage sites in a top-down manner is inevitably countered by local communities and their representatives, although there are many examples, too many, of the failure to consult these communities, and of the experience of displacement and disenfranchisement (Hitchcock, 2004: 463–465; Lask and Herold, 2004: 399–411; Wall and Black, 2004: 436–439).

GLOBALIZATION

Finally, certain of the more recent studies of culture, identity and tourism have also turned their attention to issues of globalization, regionalization and cultural hybridization in situations where culture becomes subject to various interacting trans-national forces and 'inter-country collaborations' (Yao, 2001; Ang, 2001; Teo, Chang and Ho, 2001; Rahil, Ooi and Shaw, 2006). Globalization as a phenomenon of increasing importance in cultural construction, heritage and identity formation, and in tourism development, has been much more explicitly theorized during the past decade or so.

More particularly the dialectical relations between the global and the local ('glocalization') and between local and global forces which act both to homogenize and to differentiate local cultures and identities have been examined in some detail (Appadurai, 1990: 295; Meethan, 2000: 196; Smith, 2003: 4–7, 11–16, 99–116). As Kahn has said, in his recent work on changing Malay identities in Malaysia, 'globalization is as likely to generate difference, uniqueness, and cultural specificity as it is to produce a genuinely universal or homogeneous world culture' (1998: 9; Boniface and Fowler, 1993: 145–146, 162). But specifically in relation to heritage, Wall and Black have argued pertinently that 'World Heritage sites constitute extreme examples of global-local interactions' (2004: 436).

Within this context of globalization, governments play key roles in regulating capital and markets, in sponsoring and shaping tourist assets, in controlling and promoting the movement of tourists, and in presenting certain images of the nation and its constituent populations both to its own citizens and to international tourists (Hall, 2001: 18–22). In the hands of government, heritage therefore becomes 'officially sanctioned brand identities and their storylines' (Ooi, 2002b: 155). Although we have stressed processes of contestation in relation to heritage, which seems to us to be a more general feature of heritage construction, we should note that in certain cases, at certain times and for certain actors there may be compromise or agreement over the use and meaning of a site. Long and Sweet, for example, have observed, in their recent examination of the World Heritage Site of Luang Prabang in the Lao PDR, that there can be a marked *convergence* between the heritage interests of international bodies like UNESCO and, in this case, the Lao authorities. The Lao government has been anxious to present a particular vision of national identity by the selective recognition of certain historic locations (2006). UNESCO and national governments sometimes have to reach an accommodation, although their agendas are ostensibly quite different. UNESCO has to work through national governments on national and international projects in order to achieve its universal objective of establishing uniformity in standards of protection and management of its designated heritage sites (Long, 2002). It has to be careful not to infringe national rights and sovereignty. On the other hand, national governments often need international finance, support and expertise; UNESCO recognition of a heritage site also lends prestige to a particular country and provides the opportunity to develop international tourism. There are therefore pressures on both parties to reach an accommodation, and, in the case of UNESCO's and the Lao government's approach to the interpretation and management of the World Heritage Site of Luang Prabang, there is a 'shared commitment to the preservation of certain aspects of the Lao past' (Long and Sweet, 2006: 468).

UNESCO wishes to preserve the integrity and historical importance of a particular site but each national government as the 'states party' to the World Heritage Convention (Hitchcock, 2005: 181) is usually concerned to present its national heritage in the interests of national goals of identity and unity. What is emphasized in Luang Prabang is Buddhism and its manifestation in temples, the legacy of royalty, the harmonious intermixture of colonial French and indigenous Lao architecture, and that this apparently unchanging urban settlement is 'a repository of particular Lao essences' (ibid.: 469). Long and Sweet argue that this site has been 'idealized' and 'Orientalized'; it is not, in this representation, a living, breathing, functioning urban area, or a vibrant cultural landscape, but rather it is presented as timeless, and authentic, the location of 'a passive visitor experience' and 'a large-scale museum display' (ibid.: 454, 455). Luang Prabang therefore gives expression to an unchanging past, whilst, in contrast, it is the capital city of Vientiane which is presented as the modernizing, fast-changing focus of the Lao nation. However, we suspect that if Long and Sweet had probed a little more deeply they would have discovered alternative discourses, often generated at the local level, about the position and role of Luang Prabang in the Lao consciousness. They might also have discovered different perspectives on the part of international tourists who increasingly visit and gaze upon this royal and sacred capital.

Another World Heritage Site, Angkor in Cambodia, which Keiko Miura examines in detail in this book, has also been the site for the interplay of global and national forces, and as Winter (2004: 333) has observed, in his insightful analyses of Angkor, it has provided a national focus for debates about Cambodian identity. Here we can witness considerable differences in the meaning of Angkor for different constituencies so that even global or international actors can differ significantly in their interests and perspectives. Re-discovered and fashioned by the French as an invaluable part of the national heritage of its Indochinese protectorate and as part of their civilizing mission in the East, the 'once glorious Angkor' has been used by successive post-independent Cambodian governments to express their changing visions of the nation and its history. Yet in the case of Angkor it is also the site for the imaginings not just of UNESCO experts, national politicians and ordinary Cambodians, but also of international tourists, some of whom will have seen Angkor as the re-created and stereotyped site of an ancient civilization in the Hollywood movie, *Tomb Raider* (2003). Hardly a neutral, abstract, objective, unchanging, traditional site of historical interest, Angkor embraces a range of meanings and significances: for UNESCO experts notions of architectural and archaeological conservation; for ordinary Cambodians its importance as a living cultural landscape; for political leaders its role as part of an ideology of national revival, power and identity; and for some international tourists at least, Angkor's post-modern representation as 'a culturally and historically disembedded visual spectacle' (ibid.: 66).

Another interesting UNESCO World Heritage Site in Southeast Asia from the perspective of global–local interactions is that of Borobodur, a historic Buddhist temple complex, which is situated on a small hill in the Kedu Plain, north-west of Yogyakarta in Central Java. It has not been the subject of detailed primary research but Black and Wall, in their brief comparative study of the UNESCO sites of Borobodur, Prambanan and Ayutthauya, propose that the 'values which local people attach to a [sic] heritage are different from, though no less important than, the values ascribed to it by art historians, archaeologists and government officials' (2001: 121). According to Black and Wall the planning process and the evaluation of the importance of these heritage sites of international importance have tended to be formulated in a top-down fashion without meaningful consultation with the local inhabitants. In consequence local cultural meanings and interpretations have tended to be disregarded and local cultural participation in, for example, presenting dance and drama performances for visitors and in interacting with the site have not been encouraged (ibid.: 132–133).

An overriding factor in this disregard for local contributions has been the strong commitment of international conservation and heritage agencies to the 'freezing' or preservation of a site from outside interference rather than permitting or encouraging local encounters with it. A further consequence of this is that local people are not made to feel that they are stewards of a site or that they have significant cultural and historical connections with it. The perceived authenticity of a site often depends precisely on denying its status as 'living' or 'lived' cultural heritage. Indeed, when a site is fenced off to help protect it but at the same time visitors pay for the privilege of viewing it the local communities are usually deliberately excluded from it, and, in the case of Borobodur, they have been resettled at a respectable distance from the temple complex. Interestingly, the need for conservation is also often in tension with the need of national governments and tourism agencies to generate revenue. In the case of Borobodur the site has been developed to meet tourist needs in such a way that it has taken on elements of a theme park with tour buses and large car parking areas, fenced off zones, ticket booths, kiosks, vendors, touts and market stalls, security huts and wardens, loud-speakers, and artificially landscaped gardens (Steels, 2007).

There is another sense in which national and international interests and perspectives exclude local ones. In the case of Borobodur it has become an instantly recognized national symbol of Indonesia, though it is promoted not as a religious monument in predominantly Muslim Indonesia, but as a cultural monument. It still happens to be a focus of domestic and international Buddhist pilgrimage, but for the Indonesian government it is overwhelmingly a cultural heritage site for the promotion of domestic and international tourism. In her recent study Steels (2007) also reveals that the tourists with whom she spoke were not especially preoccupied with its authenticity or with local meanings or indeed with the concerns of the international heritage agencies. They had very little if any notion of what an 'authentic Borobodur' would have been like or should resemble other than that for the international tourists they disliked being harassed by market vendors. For the majority it was a major site on the tourist circuit which they had to gaze upon and at which they wanted to be seen and photographed. It was quite simply a 'must' place to visit associated vaguely with a forgotten and romanticized past (ibid.).

A major task in the global heritage industry is to create cultural otherness and distinctive tourism products that stand out in the marketplace to present a unique and special national identity. In this connection Sofield has said of tourism that it 'creates or even re-creates difference, aggressively re-imaging, re-constituting and appropriating heritage, culture and place, pursuing localisation in marked contrast to its globalising influence' (2001: 104). It does this in its encounter with local communities which are pursuing their own cultural strategies and agendas in order to direct tourism to meet their own needs and interests (Erb, 2000: 710). Local communities in turn operate within particular international parameters, contexts and service standards so that generally tourists can move with relative ease, comfort and safety whilst experiencing otherness, and whilst moving between the familiar and the unfamiliar (Urry, 1990; Lee, 2001). Yet, as we have seen, in the global heritage industry international tourists are but one of the interested parties.

SUMMARY OF THE CHAPTERS

This book contains twelve substantive chapters based on empirical research which examine the interface of heritage and tourism in Southeast Asia from a variety of perspectives and set in a diversity of contexts. The overall aim of the book is to help with understanding how the notion of heritage is formed, constructed and operationalized, what conservation measures have been put in place and who the self-appointed custodians of natural and cultural heritage are, what tourists are looking for at heritage sites and how this dovetails or conflicts with local needs and interests, and how the tension between the protection and mobilization of heritage resources is rationalized. The chapters address issues of agency, competing discourses, local level interactions, identity, socio-cultural change, and cultural invention.

Kathleen M. Adams explores the politics of heritage in upland Sulawesi, Indonesia, which is the homeland of the Sa'dan Toraja people, known for their elaborately carved ancestral houses and spectacular burial cliffs. Drawing on long-term anthropological field research that was initiated in 1984 during the heyday of Indonesian tourism, the chapter examines Toraja's re-framing of heritage in the post-touristic era, specifically the historical, economic and personal dynamics underlying Tana Toraja's emergence as a potential World Heritage Site. These are used to illustrate how so-called 'heritage landscapes' are, to some extent, products of local responses to and engagements with regional, national and global political, cultural and economic dynamics. Heritage is not only about individual and collective identity, but it is also entwined with economics and with symbolic power. In today's world of global migrants and international bodies such as UNESCO and NGOs, 'heritage' is rarely of merely local or domestic concern. Heritage must be understood in terms of layers of local, national and international romances and rivalries. What many have underscored regarding contemporary tourism sites, Adams points out, is equally true of heritage locales: in seeking to understand the dynamics at play in such sites, we must be attentive to the theme of 'contested heritage', and engage not only with local structures and rivalries but also with international relations and global organizations and markets.

Mami Yoshimura and Geoffrey Wall focus on the reconstruction and reconfiguration of the cultural heritage of the Atayal in Wulai, Taiwan, an ethnic group with strong cultural affinities with Southeast Asia. The Atayal are an indigenous people who have experienced both colonialism and tourism development. During Japan's occupation, the Atayal were forced to abandon their most important socio-cultural activities: facial tattooing, head-hunting and weaving. The Atayal lost most of their original textiles because many of them were taken to Japan. Today, these textiles are preserved in a few Japanese museums. The Atayal's textiles are now being reconstructed by indigenous women in Wulai who weave primarily for museums. Others weave for domestic tourists although they have little success in competition with less expensive Han Chinese factory-made woven products. The reintroduction of weaving has required the Atayal to retrace their weaving history and to revive lost skills. It has also opened up an opportunity to create new motifs with imported looms. However, the meaning of weaving has changed from being a representation of the Atayal women's gender identity alone to the representation of the Atayal's collective ethnic identity and heritage. It has become an ethnic symbol and a tourism product but the indigenous residents of Wulai are now barely involved directly in tourism businesses, even though symbols of their identity are used to promote tourism.

Michael Hitchcock and Nick Stanley also touch on the theme of 'living cultural heritage' as seen through the institution of the outdoor ethnographic museum (and see Hitchcock, Stanley and Siu, 1997; Hitchcock, 1998). Using comparative studies from Taiwan and Indonesia they explore the ways in which such museums – which tend to adopt a primordial view of ethnicity and traditional culture – have been used as a means of communicating narratives of nation-building, nationalism and national conscious-raising, and of smoothing the rough edges of inter-ethnic relations. In the main they present their constituent ethnic groups in an idealized manner that has little bearing on modern twenty-first century reality. While the ethnographic museum format remains little changed from its early nationalistic origins, both the context within which it is placed and the audiences to which it reaches out have changed significantly. Nowadays their educational role seems much diminished and their entertainment (and touristic) function is greatly enhanced – creating an awkward amalgam which the authors, following the industry, term 'edutainment'.

Can-Seng Ooi examines the ways in which museums in Singapore are used to construct and present identities. He argues against the notion that the West 'Orientalizes' and dominates Asian cultures (and see Ooi, 2002b). He states, contra Edward Said, that the 'so-called Orient is not naïve nor necessarily helpless'; neither is it 'passive', 'docile' and 'submissive'. In the case of the Singapore National Heritage Board, which presides over the three major museums in the city-state (the National Museum of Singapore [NMS, formerly the Singapore History Museum], the Singapore Art Museum [SAM] and the Asian Civilizations Museum [ACM]), different kinds of identities are presented in a process of 'self-Orientalization' or 're-Asianization', to address the needs of tourism and nation-building in Singapore. Museums operate as 'contact zones' between tourists and local identity constructions, and Singapore is presented as a unique 'Asian' society which combines modernity and tradition, as well as vernacular notions of the East and West. The NMS presents an image of a 'unique Asian entity' which has its own identity and history. The SAM, in turn, provides Singapore with a regional identity; it is a 'cultural centre' of Southeast Asia, which in turn is characterized as an 'aesthetic entity'. Finally, the ACM relates the broad ethnic categories (Chinese, Indian and Malay Muslim) – devised by the government as part of the process of national identity formation – to the great cultural traditions of China, India and the Middle East. In sum, the museums separate and interrelate various dimensions of Singaporean identity promoted by the government, but that identity is 'essentially Asian and is still exotic'.

Keiko Miura draws on several years' experience of working at the UNESCO World Heritage Site at Angkor in Cambodia, the country's principal tourism destination, to trace evolving attitudes and policies towards the people and communities whose homes and livelihoods are constructed in and around this globally important heritage site. Historically, conservation and preservation efforts have led to local people being largely excluded from the land they occupied and resources they utilized prior to heritage conservation becoming a national and global concern. But more recently there has been a move to nurture 'living heritage sites' where, still within quite strictly controlled parameters, communities can maintain their livelihoods whilst providing a back-drop of human interest and context to the refurbished stone structures of cultural heritage. Even as democratization and participation are being advocated by the international heritage conservation community, particularly in the shape of UNESCO, as a means of ensuring local communities benefit more substantially and directly from heritage tourism development, their translation into effective action at the local level is shown to be severely constrained by prevailing political and personal power structures. Nonetheless, by comparing the Angkor complex with the Vat Phou heritage site in the Lao PDR, Miura suggests that, in relative terms, some progress has already been made with creating a living heritage site at Angkor. Nonetheless, she concludes by advocating a more radical community-based approach to the management of heritage sites, based on the recent experience in Phrae and Nan provinces of Thailand.

Nigel Worden looks at national identity and heritage tourism in the historic city of Melaka, which has become a major site of international and domestic tourism, and is represented in Malaysia's tourist and heritage industries as the place 'where it all began', the very source of the cultural and political values and institutions of the Malays and of a Malay-dominated Malaysian nationhood. The chapter examines the meaning of this slogan in the context of the cultural policies of the Malaysian state in the late twentieth century, when constructions of the political and religious traditions of the pre-colonial Melakan Sultanate were presented as emblematic of the *bangsa melayu* or Malay nation. An emphasis on ethnic Malay heritage was accompanied by an indigenization of other Melakan inhabitants, such as the Portuguese Eurasians and the long-established hybrid Chinese Peranakan, whilst largely ignoring the heritage of the majority Chinese and Indian immigrants who arrived later. The chapter details the various buildings, sites and performances, some real, some imagined and some invented, which collectively make up Melaka's cultural heritage, and which are presented to tourists in part as a political project of ethnic representation. It also discusses some of the pressures and transformations that have been created by modern developments which have eroded the city's historical character and integrity, and which were largely responsible for UNESCO's refusal to grant Melaka World Heritage status until very recently. The chapter ends by considering the impact since the mid-1990s of a new Malaysian national identity that stresses a multi-ethnic *bangsa Malaysia* in a more globalized context.

Gwynn Jenkins looks at the conservation of the rich and diverse urban cultural heritage of the historic port city of George Town, in the Malaysian state of Penang, as part of wider cross-regional moves to arrest the rapid decay and decline of the historical quarters of the classical 'Asian city'. She reveals a strong underlying tension between the visions and efforts of the authorities and other stakeholders, who appear committed to promoting new developments in the interests of urban renewal and economic regeneration, including the expansion of tourism, and both the communities themselves and the advocates of sympathetic heritage preservation who promote a vision of living cultural heritage which not only allows continuity in the functions and interconnections of the various ethnic communities which make up the cultural mosaic of George Town but which also offers a more 'authentic' cultural resource for consumption by both domestic (the greater segment of the tourism sector) and international tourists. Using two contrasting case studies, Jenkins shows how different the trajectories and impacts of heritage conservation and associated tourism development can be depending on whether they are community-focused and community-driven, or dominated by external influence and interference. She concludes that the latter threatens the very soul of the city – 'the connectivity between community, space, place and cultural practice' – and the very basis of 'authentic' touristic experience. George Town, its colonial heritage and its ethnically diverse urban landscape are now under threat from commercial developers and it remains to be seen whether or not the conservation movement and local communities can counter the encroachment of poorly planned new build and renovation. George Town is on the World Monuments Fund 'watch list' as a site of global significance whose heritage is in danger, though its recent listing as a World Heritage Site may give some room for optimism.

Mark Johnson's insightful study of the Imperial City of Hue in central Vietnam, a UNESCO World Heritage Site, explores the role of tour guides and conservators/researchers in the making and (re)presentation of Vietnam's heritage for the 'tourist gaze' (Urry, 1990) – what Johnson describes as the 'carefully ordered and orchestrated process of selective representation inherent in touristic encounters'. Although tourism is presented as an important factor in the dynamics of heritage conservation, the focus in Johnson's chapter is not on the tourists and their orchestrated readings of heritage and culture, but on certain of the agents of representation – the motivations, interpretations and agendas that lie behind their narratives of place. Johnson echoes some of Ooi's concerns in his exploration of cultural mediators in Singapore (2002b). Using a case study of the Hue Monuments Conservation Centre, and some interesting qualitative data, Johnson examines not only the interface of tourism development and heritage conservation within the more tolerant and catholic environment of post-reform Vietnam – drawing parallels between the country's imperial history and current processes of 'bureaucratic imperialism' within the official structures of heritage preservation – but also the ambivalent relationship of guides and researchers to the history of the Hue site and in their representations of the site to tourists. Johnson also usefully explores the 'tourist gaze' from the perspective of domestic tourists, and reveals a sharp contrast in the knowledge, enthusiasm, attitudes and behaviour of tourists from northern and southern Vietnam towards their country's cultural heritage.

Wantanee Suntikul (with Richard Butler and David Airey) examines three different types of heritage sites in Hanoi (the Ancient Quarter, the Hoa Lo Prison and the Ho Chi Minh Mausoleum) and the relationships which Vietnam has with its history in selecting and marketing its heritage as a tourism commodity. Wantanee draws attention to the role of heritage as a 'cultural anchor', particularly in a period of economic and cultural transition, and the competing forces at work on those elements which are being subjected to tourism. Many agree that the Hanoi Ancient Quarter should be preserved, but such work would require inhabitants to be relocated to alleviate overcrowding and to enable restoration; the area is also subject to the pressures of modernization and commercial development. Of concern is the danger that, like Luang Prabang in the Lao PDR, it would become 'frozen in time' and thus presented as an exotic 'Orientalized' spectacle. On the other hand, Hoa Lo Prison stands as a reminder of foreign intervention, serving as the place where 'Vietnamese nationalists, communists and peasant fighters' were incarcerated, and where American prisoners of war were detained during the Vietnam/American War. Like the Ho Chi Minh Mausoleum, the Hoa Lo Prison Museum expresses a strong sense of Vietnamese patriotism, and both are sites of domestic and international tourist interest. Wantanee concludes her investigation with the view that the three sites mediate between different interests involved in heritage tourism – between the domestic and the foreign, the past and the future, economics and ideology, and the individual and the collective.

Michael Hitchcock, Nguyen Thi Thu Huong and Simone Wesner take up the theme of heritage as a developmental issue in a case study of Hai Duong, a city lying at the heart of northern Vietnam's zone of rapid industrialization. A visitor passing through Hai Duong on the main highway linking Hanoi to the port of Hai Phuong might be surprised to learn that the city has any heritage at all, surrounded as it is by gleaming new factory units and other symbols of modernity. The heritage here is not so much the buildings but rather the important handicraft centres that lie in and around the urban areas; these provide employment for large numbers of people and constitute an essential part of the history and identity of the region. Moreover they are an important material and symbolic expression of mainstream Vietnamese culture, which is often overlooked by researchers and tourists more interested in the material culture of the country's minority populations.

Michael J. G. Parnwell's chapter explores the notion of 'natural heritage', and the power relations that lie behind this concept. He uses the examples of Ha Long Bay in Vietnam and Phang Nga Bay in Thailand to compare and contast coastal natural heritage management efforts within and outside the framework of UNESCO World Heritage designation and protection. These two broadly similar drowned karst landscapes have become globally well known (in the case of 'James Bond Island' in Phang Nga Bay, as with Angkor Wat and *Tomb Raider*, this is because of the filming of *The Man with the Golden Gun* in 1974) for their spectacular limestone towers, islets and both intact and collapsed cave systems (*hong*). Both locations have come under intensifying pressure from both tourism and other forms of modern development, which have threatened both the aesthetic and intrinsic values of these distinctive landscapes. The chapter traces the responses of various stakeholders to the imperatives of landscape, ecosystem and nature preservation, and identifies a degree of convergence in the strategies adopted by the two countries, despite their obvious political, historical and developmental differences. Movement towards holistic, integrated and community-focused approaches to economic and environmental management can be identified in both contexts, reflecting more general trends in resource conservation which in Thailand substitute for, and in Vietnam are promoted through, heritage management under the auspices of UNESCO.

Finally, the editors round off the discussion by drawing out some common themes from the empirical chapters. We reflect on the way that the notion of heritage has been discursively created and developed, allowing considerable scope for politics and political agendas, both internal and external, to become suffused within national projects of heritage promotion. An outside–inside tension is also evident in policies and methods of heritage management, with competing agendas and competitive positioning in the tourism market-place often getting in the way of effective international communication of best-practice. The question is raised as to whether it is both possible and desirable to have a universal model or principle of heritage protection given the huge diversity of contexts to which it must be applied. To what extent do the ways that the territories, structures and practices that constitute Southeast Asia's cultural and natural heritage have unique meanings, importance and significance to local populations that are at odds with the vision that transnational bodies (such as UNESCO) seek to engender globally? We address such questions in the conclusion by outlining a tentative agenda for future cross-disciplinary and comparative research – in terms of impact mitigation, ownership, inclusion, participatory democracy and the convergence of external and internal conservation agendas – through which a fuller picture of the factors contributing to successes and shortcomings in Southeast Asian heritage management can be generated.

NOTE

1   This theme of the politics of heritage has also been taken up in a much more wide-ranging way by Michael Hitchcock in a co-edited volume with David Harrison; they include case material from Singapore, Indonesia, Vietnam and Cambodia, as well as from other parts of the world (Harrison and Hitchcock 2004 [2005]).

CHAPTER 2

Courting and Consorting with the Global

The Local Politics of an Emerging World Heritage Site in Sulawesi, Indonesia[1]

Kathleen M. Adams

INTRODUCTION: LONGING FOR A GLOBALLY-ACCLAIMED TORAJA

October 2006 marked the launch of a much-publicized Toraja Culture Festival, a ten-day event that was to attract upwards of 30,000 visitors to the Toraja homeland in the highlands of Sulawesi, Indonesia, to celebrate Toraja heritage. Touted as 'Toraja Mamali' or 'Longing for Toraja', the event was heralded as a homecoming festival for Torajas living around the globe, a time for all those of Toraja ancestry to return to their homeland and strengthen Toraja unity and pride, nationally and internationally (www.torajamamali. com). Planned to coincide with Tana Toraja Regency's fiftieth anniversary year, organizers envisioned the festival as an occasion for overseas Torajas to return and demonstrate their commitment to developing the tourism, educational and agricultural realms in their ancestral homeland. As the Toraja organizers explained on the bilingual 'Longing for Toraja' web page:

> Toraja is renowned for having maintained its traditional culture, from the unique funeral ceremony (*rambu solok*) to the distinctive handicrafts, also (...) the elegant and inspiring traditional dance and music. Life goes on as it has for centuries, carrying the rhythms of ritual, creativity and culture

as precious inheritance for the present generation and the generations to come. It is to continue and pass down this precious inheritance between the sweeping tides of [the] modern world that the Toraja Mamali was announced, forming up to be an act of concern [sic] in making Toraja a world class cultural centre as well as making Toraja a leading region in the sector of education, technology and agriculture. (www.torajamamali.com, accessed 28 February 2008)

Tens of thousands of Torajas and over 8,000 foreign tourists made the journey to upland Sulawesi for the 'Longing for Toraja' festival. Over the course of the festival these visitors, along with thousands of local residents, witnessed and participated in water buffalo pageants, model village competitions, healthy child contests, as well as the rehabilitation of 'tourist objects', schools, major infrastructure arteries and a traditional market. The pinnacle festival day drew 125,000 spectators and was officially opened by Indonesia's Vice-President Jusuf Kalla beating one of the 300 drums that had been transported from throughout Indonesia for the occasion. On this day Toraja heritage was showcased in a grand carnival fashion, with a parade of traditionally clad Torajas and decorated water buffalos, as well as a traditional musical instrument performance. Official speeches and the unveiling of a spectacular and enormous new monument to Toraja freedom fighters were overshadowed by the long-awaited 'Mamali Dance', performed by 2,000 local dancers. As a number of Torajas proudly recounted when I returned in 2008, the size of this traditional dance performance broke all Indonesian records and was widely covered in the Indonesian media.

Reflecting on the Toraja Mamali festival, Tana Toraja's Regent (*Bupati*) elaborated, 'Tana Toraja was in need of a trigger to jumpstart it out of its lassitude. We hope that the "Longing for Toraja" festival will be the embryo that revitalizes Tana Toraja' (quoted in Palar, 2006: 1). While some Torajas were sceptical, for a number of Toraja cultural and political leaders the festival was an opportunity to restore to Toraja what it had been poised to attain a decade earlier during the heyday of international tourism, prior to the current tumultuous era of 'Indonesian crisis', when the steady flow of tourists to the region fell to a trickle. That is, the festival carried the twin hopes both of revitalizing much-needed tourism revenues and of reasserting Toraja's place as a 'world-class' culture. In many ways, the 'Longing for Toraja' festival was an attempt to rekindle a courtship with the global that had gone badly astray. Just a few years earlier, when Tana Toraja had been nominated for inclusion on the UNESCO World Heritage List, this romance appeared poised to blossom into a long-term relationship. But after several years of little attention and scant visitor revenues, in the minds of some Toraja leaders it was time to call for the reanimation of the heritage-themed courting of overseas Toraja migrants, tourists and international bodies such as UNESCO.

This chapter is broadly concerned with the politics of heritage in upland Sulawesi. As the staging of the Toraja Mamali festival suggests, heritage is not only about individual and collective identity, but it is also entwined with economics and with symbolic power. Moreover, in today's world of global migrants and global bodies such as UNESCO and NGOs, 'heritage' is rarely of merely local or domestic concern. Heritage must be understood in terms of layers of local, national and international romances and rivalries. What many have underscored regarding contemporary tourism sites is equally true of heritage locales: in seeking to understand the dynamics at play in such sites, we must be attentive to the theme of 'contested heritage', and to engaging with not only local structures and rivalries but also international relations and global organizations and markets (Teo, 2002: 460; Teo, 2003a; Hitchcock, 2004: 463; Burns, 2006: 18–20).

More specifically, in this chapter I draw on the case of the emergence of Tana Toraja as a potential World Heritage Site to illustrate how so-called 'heritage landscapes' are, to some extent, products of local responses to and engagements with regional, national and global political, cultural and economic dynamics. While there are undeniably certain indigenous Toraja ideas about the meaning and manifestation of heritage,[2] these conceptions of heritage are also, to some degree, a colonial and post-colonial product. My aim is to problematize representations of such sites as pristine embodiments of local tradition. I suggest that World Heritage Sites are seldom simply the newly-threatened landscapes of tradition they are imagined to be. Rather, they are the products of a long interplay between the local, the national and the global.[3]

In chronicling the emergence of a potential World Heritage Site, I am particularly interested in illustrating how transformations of dynamic local places into fixed 'heritage sites' is not a 'natural' process but rather a political process that can be fraught with calculation, collusion, conflict, collaboration and co-optation. Recently, researchers have begun to push for more attentive analyses of the process of cultural objectification. Writing on the process of reactive objectification, Nicholas Thomas has observed, 'If conceptions of identity and tradition are part of a broader field of oppositional naming and categorization, the question that emerges is not how are traditions invented? But *against what* is this tradition invented? Or, in general, how does the dynamic of reactive objectification proceed?' (Thomas, 1997: 190). In a similar vein David Harrison observes, 'Whatever elements of the past are presented as heritage (...) they have already passed through a complex filtering process whereby someone, or some group, has *selected* them. Nothing – but nothing – is automatic heritage material' (Harrison, 2004: 285; also see Hitchcock, 2004: 463–464). Turning a more refined lens to the history of one locale currently on the Tentative List of Indonesian World Heritage Sites enables us to gain a more nuanced perspective on the politics of the process of cultural objectification, and to better appreciate the complicated roles of local and international agents and agencies in 'fixing' dynamic locales. My use of the term 'fixing' here is deliberate and meant to evoke the multiple meanings of this word – in the sense of rendering something dynamic into something lifeless and immobile, as well as in the senses of renovating and repairing, and arranging and organizing. As I suggest, we can learn from this case study, for in today's globalized world even hinterland heritage sites are shaped by multiple forces, actors and agencies from within, around and beyond the nation.

I begin this chapter with a vignette concerning the events that led to the selection of a particular Toraja hamlet (known as Ke'te' Kesu') for tentative inclusion on UNESCO's List of World Heritage Sites. In this portion of the chapter I also unpack some of the local reactions to this selection, and contrast these reactions with an analysis of UNESCO conceptions and assumptions pertaining to World Heritage Sites, many of which are entwined with romantic assumptions about ancient life-ways under siege by the contemporary world. I then turn to trace the history of Ke'te' Kesu', from its colonial roots to the present, illustrating how the birth of this hamlet as well as its rise to pre-eminence was part and parcel of colonial and post-colonial dynamics. Finally, I turn to address how local contestations over whose heritage was to be elevated to fame ultimately fuelled a re-framing of the World Heritage Site nomination, such that Ke'te' Kesu''s nomination was broadened to all of Tana Toraja. Finally, I close with a discussion of the broader lessons emerging from this case study.

UNESCO ENCOUNTERS KE'TE' KESU' AND TANA TORAJA: THE MULTIPLE AND SHIFTING MEANINGS OF HERITAGE SITES

In April 2001 there was cause for jubilation in the highland Toraja village of Ke'te' Kesu' on the island of Sulawesi. Residents had just learned that their rural hamlet was poised to achieve international fame and reverence, on a par with Borobodur or the palaeolithic caves of Lascaux. For their village had just been officially selected for consideration as a World Heritage Site by the Southeast Asian members of UNESCO. Over the previous week Southeast Asian delegates and UNESCO representatives had gathered in Tana Toraja Regency to attend a UNESCO Global Strategy meeting devoted to nominating and reporting on Southeast Asian World Heritage Sites. The selection of Tana Toraja Regency as the venue for this meeting was far from haphazard; it was, in part, the culmination of years of lobbying by local Toraja cultural activists and Indonesian politicians. At the official opening ceremony of their gathering in Tana Toraja, UNESCO delegates were regaled with Toraja dances and ritual processions set against the backdrop of the finely carved ancestral houses that form the core of the hamlet of Ke'te' Kesu'.[4] These UNESCO delegates toured the area in their leisure hours, becoming acquainted with the cultural richness and natural beauty of the region. Ultimately, a UNESCO team appraised the touristically touted Toraja village of Ke'te' Kesu', determining that it satisfied many of UNESCO's criteria for World Heritage Sites. According to Indonesian news reports, Sulawesi government officials and locals were optimistic that Ke'te' Kesu' would soon join the ranks of official Southeast Asian World Heritage Sites (Hamid, 2001).[5]

UNESCO has a clearly articulated definition of what constitutes a World Heritage Site. The groundwork for UNESCO's role in determining, preserving and protecting World Heritage Sites was established at the 1972 UNESCO General Conference in Venice. At this meeting, UNESCO delegates ratified the World Heritage Convention. As decreed by this convention, UNESCO would embark upon compiling a 'World Heritage List', registering unique sites of supreme universal value. The convention stipulated that the governments of UNESCO member countries could nominate sites for inclusion on the World Heritage List. If it is determined that a nominated site meets the established criteria for inclusion on the list,[6] it could potentially merit resources for its protection and preservation. In short, the underlying motivation for creating the World Heritage List was the notion that certain locales embodied properties of 'outstanding universal value' and deserved international conservation efforts. Today, in keeping with the 1972 Convention, *cultural, natural* and *mixed sites* are included on the World Heritage List. *Cultural heritage sites* are monuments, groups of buildings or locales with historical, archaeological, aesthetic, scientific, ethnological or anthropological value. *Natural sites,* in contrast, are locales that embody outstanding examples of the earth's history, biological or ecological evolution, habitats of biological diversity or threatened species, and exceptional natural beauty. Finally, *mixed sites,* also termed *cultural landscapes,* 'encompass both outstanding natural and cultural values that illustrate significant interaction between people and their natural environment over a period of time '(Villalon, 2001: 1).

The Toraja hamet of Ke'te' Kesu' was nominated for inclusion on the World Heritage List as a *mixed site* or 'living cultural landscape'. Located on the Indonesian Island of Sulawesi, four kilometres southeast of Rantepao (Tana Toraja Regency's main town and tourist base), the hamlet of Ke'te' Kesu' has long been a magnet for anthropologists, historians, architecture students and tourists. With such local celebrity, it seemed fitting that Ke'te' Kesu' would also capture the fancy of the Southeast Asian UNESCO meeting delegates. Heralding the traditional ancestral houses (*tongkonan*) that comprise the heart of Ke'te' Kesu', one of the attendees at the UNESCO meeting commented,

> The tongkonans [ancestral houses] of Tana Toraja are living heritage in the true sense. They go beyond the sense of 'home', being regarded as living symbols of local families who insist on maintaining their religious, cultural and environmental traditions. The tongkonan does not exist in isolation in the Tana Toraja landscape. The vista of Tana Toraja villages – sweeping roofs of parallel rows of tongkonan built at the foot of a hill where ancestors are buried and surrounded by communal rice fields – shows the long interaction of the local population and their environment. The landscape demonstrates a deep relationship with nature that has existed for generations. Preserving the *genius loci* of Tana Toraja villages goes beyond protecting the unique architecture of the dwellings. It means preserving a total lifestyle while attempting to make the traditional lifestyle, severely threatened by 21st century influences, continue to be relevant (Villalon, 2001: 3).

As this commentary underscores, 'preservation' is a key theme in the UNESCO World Heritage Site designation. In tandem with this preservationist orientation is the attendant assumption that the 'traditional' is under assault by contemporary '21st century influences': The Toraja village of Ke'te' Kesu' is celebrated as a utopic[7] and quintessential ancestral 'home' where humans live as they always have, in harmony with the environment. However, as the UNESCO narrative suggests, this idyllic Eden is endangered, warranting the protection of World Heritage Site designation. Ironically, as this chapter illustrates, the very globalizing forces that prompted Ke'te' Kesu''s discovery by UNESCO (tourism and accelerated discourse with the outside world) are now deemed threats to its *'genius loci'*.[8]

When I first learned of UNESCO's interest in this Toraja hamlet, I shared in some of the jubilation of Ke'te' Kesu''s inhabitants. In the mid-1980s, while conducting research on Toraja art and identity, I resided in this highland Sulawesi village for twenty-two months and have made frequent return research visits in subsequent years. While mulling over the implications of Ke'te' Kesu''s candidacy as a World Heritage Site, I received a call from a Toraja friend who had been a young boy during my initial research in Ke'te' Kesu'. My friend was now based in Florida and employed by an international cruise ship line. His income from his job had enabled him to erect a spacious new home with an electricity supply for his mother on a hilltop above Ke'te' Kesu' village. My friend's cruise ship position afforded him regular opportunities to tour celebrated World Heritage Sites and I was anxious to hear his reflections on Ke'te' Kesu''s candidacy. Expressing his delight at the designation, my friend immediately underscored that the new status promised to revitalize lagging tourist visits. As he lamented, recent political violence and economic instability in Indonesia had eroded tourism to Tana Toraja, resulting in economic difficulties for village souvenir sellers. With World Heritage Site designation, residents' livelihoods (now largely dependent on tourism revenues) would be reassured, enabling Ke'te' Kesu'ers to pay off debts, stage long-postponed mortuary rites, and modernize their homes. The more we talked, the more apparent became the disjunction between his conceptions of the meaning and value of heritage and those of UNESCO. Whereas my Toraja friend stressed the changes and affluence this new status would bring, UNESCO's emphasis was on the preservation of an imagined past that would stave off modernizing influences. Subsequent conversations with other Ke'te' Kesu'ers revealed similar disjunctions. Several residents noted that becoming a World Heritage Site would affirm for the world that the Toraja could no longer be dismissed as a backward hill people: now they would become world stars. For this group of Ke'te' Kesu'ers, World Heritage Site designation was not about the preservation of an imagined past, but rather about *amplification*, be it amplification of wealth for some, familial prestige for others, or ethnic identity for still others.

Some time later, I had the opportunity to talk with several Toraja acquaintances in Jakarta about Ke'te' Kesu''s new-found fame. These acquaintances, whose ancestral villages were in other regions of Tana Toraja, had markedly different reactions from those of my Ke'te' Kesu' friends. As one declared to me, more heatedly than I'd anticipated, 'I'm all in agreement with Tana Toraja being a World Heritage Site, but Ke'te' Kesu'? I don't agree! That is a political play, not heritage (...)' While his comments suggested that heritage and politics were separate realms, the more we talked, the clearer it became that he and his friends were willing to do their own political lobbying to ensure that Ke'te' Kesu'ers could not hijack the fame that was due to all of Toraja for themselves.

As the above vignette suggests, ideas about the meaning and value of World Heritage Site designation are multiple and variable. Hobsbawm and Ranger (1983), Keesing (1989), Linnekin (1990, 1991) and others have adeptly illustrated how ideas about 'tradition' and 'heritage' are infused with the politics of the present. Building on their foundational work, this chapter argues that today, as in the past, heritage sites are stages on which various groups and actors inscribe competing and commingling histories and meanings. In the context of globalization and international tourism, 'heritage' and 'tradition' become all the more intensely rethought, rearticulated, recreated and contested, both by insiders and outsider packagers, politicians and visitors. Tourism does not simply impose disjunctions between the 'authentic past' and the 'invented past', as earlier researchers suggested, but rather blurs these artificial lines, creating new politically-charged arenas in which competing ideas about heritage, ritual and tradition are symbolically enacted (cf. Hitchcock, King and Parnwell, 1993a; Wood, 1993; Adams, 1995, 1997a, 2006; Bruner, 1996, 2001; Picard, 1996; Picard and Wood, 1997a; Erb, 1998; Cartier, 1998).

I turn now to trace the politics, rivalries and colonial and post-colonial forces behind the rise of Ke'te' Kesu', from obscurity to touristic fame to its (ultimately temporary) status in 2001 as one of the newest sites on Indonesia's Tentative List of World Heritage Sites.[9]

The Toraja village of Ke'te' Kesu': from colonial heritage to 'tourist object'

What is thought of as Ke'te' Kesu' today consists of four stately ancestral houses (*tongkonan*), an imposing museum shaped to resemble a traditional house, and numerous carved rice granaries and souvenir and handicraft stands. Around the fringes of the plaza are homes of local residents, some Bugis-styled on stilts, others of wood or bamboo, and still others of concrete. A footpath behind the central ritual plaza of the village winds down through a bamboo grove to cliff-side graves. Here visitors can gaze upon ancestral skulls, weathered wooden effigies of the dead, carved sarcophagi, and more recently erected ornate cement tombs. A hundred years ago, this village, as such, did not exist. In stating this, however, it is *not* my intention to suggest that Ke'te' Kesu' is a spurious pretender to World Heritage Site status. In fact, I would emphatically champion Ke'te' Kesu''s inclusion on the list of World Heritage Sites, as it is very much a landscape upon which ancestral memories have been inscribed and enacted.

At the turn of the century, the four ancestral houses, or *tongkonan*, that comprise the heart of Ke'te' Kesu' were scattered on various peaks, some miles from the current site. It was the advent of colonialism that triggered the birth of Ke'te' Kesu' village. Prior to the 1906 arrival of Dutch colonial forces, kin groups lived in scattered mountain top settlements, maintaining ties through an elaborate system of ritual exchanges (Nooy-Palm, 1979, 1986). The *tongkonan* played (and continue to play) a central role in these inter-group relations. In recent years, Toraja has been discussed as a 'house society' in that it is challenging to fully comprehend its cognatic kinship system without an understanding of houses as the orienting point of this system (Waterson, 1990, 1995: 47–48).[10] In short, the *tongkonan* is more than a physical structure: it is a visual symbol of descent and a key marker of heritage for most contemporary Torajans (Adams, 1998a).[11] At various *tongkonan*-centered rituals,[12] histories of the founding ancestors and their descendants are carefully recounted and all who trace their descent to the *tongkonan* being fêted are expected to contribute financially or materially to the ritual expenses. Just as *tongkonan* are closely tied to ancestry, they are also linked to ideas about rank. Elaborately carved *tongkonan*, such as those found in Ke'te' Kesu' today, were associated with the elite. Commoners and (former) slaves were traditionally barred from embellishing their ancestral homes with such ornate carved motifs. Affiliation with an older named *tongkonan* established by early, elite ancestors carries more prestige than affiliation with a more recently established splinter-group *tongkonan*.

Tongkonan Kesu', from which Ke'te' Kesu' takes its name, is one of the older, most prestigious *tongkonan* in the region. In the early part of the twentieth century, the leader of this *tongkonan* was a politically astute member of the elite named Pong Panimba. Observing that Dutch authorities conferred leadership roles on the nobles located closest to Dutch headquarters in the Rantepao valley, Pong Panimba sagely perceived the disadvantages of his *tongkonan*'s remote hilltop location. Recognizing that propinquity to Dutch headquarters was a key ingredient for one's continued authority in the new era of Dutch colonialism, Pong Panimba had his home and seat of authority *(Tongkonan Kesu')* relocated from its remote mountaintop site to the valley, clustering it with several other family *tongkonan* *(Tongkonan Tonga, Tongkonan Sepang and Tongkonan Bamba)*. Since fathers buried the placentas of newborn children adjacent to their *tongkonan*, these ancestral houses become closely tied to the lands on which they were constructed. Thus, in general practice *tongkonan*s were not to be moved, as their physical sites took on added importance with each generation.[13] The decision to break the tie between site and structure would have weighty, requiring lengthy discussions amongst all those affiliated with the ancestral house. Pong Panimba would have had to exercise all of his political skills to grease the path for the move. No doubt, the exigencies of the colonial era made what may well have been a controversial relocation decision more viable – especially since, during this period, Dutch officials began forcing some Toraja families to relocate into the major valleys for administrative convenience (Bigalke, 1981). According to my Toraja mentors, ritual prescriptions were followed that enabled the relocation of this celebrated ancestral house.[14]

Tongkonan Kesu's new site was strategically selected, for it was not only physically lovely, but it was also a mere four kilometres from the Dutch colonial headquarters. The move, completed in 1927, proved to be a successful scheme for currying authority in the new colonial context. Pong Panimba was soon named the second head of the colonial 'Kesu' District'.

By the 1940s, however, the Second World War, the Japanese occupation of Indonesia, and Indonesian independence posed new threats to the family's security and standing, as well as reinvigorating old rivalries between competing Toraja elites. In the late 1940s, when the newly independent Indonesian government established the government seat far from the Kesu' District in the southern city of Makale, near the Sangalla *adat*[15] region of Tana Toraja, Ne' Reba Sarungallo[16] (Pong Panimba's grandson and then-leader of *Tongkonan Kesu'*) became concerned. As the new *Tongkonan Kesu'* leader, Ne' Reba observed that rival Sangalla nobles and Sangalla *adat* were threatening to overshadow those of the Kesu' area. Ne' Reba's misgivings cemented in 1950 when, following independence, the subdistricts of Tana Toraja Regency were formally established: a Sangalla District (*kecamatan*) was delineated, but no provisions were made for a Kesu' District. Ne' Reba astutely recognized that with this new political geography, the name Kesu' would be lost, as would Kesu' heritage, traditions and the authority of the Kesu' nobles. If Kesu' were to survive in the new post-colonial order, a strategy was needed. However, the 1950s and 1960s were tumultuous times in South Sulawesi (as Muslim insurgencies and secessionist movements posed constant threats to Toraja highlanders), and it was not until the late 1960s when the region was calmed that possibilities to reinvigorate Kesu' heritage presented themselves.

As the first off-the-beaten-track tourists began to trickle into his hamlet in the late 1960s, Ne' Reba perceived an avenue for ensuring that the name Kesu' lived on. Drawing on his authority as an elected politician, aristocratic leader and Dutch Reformed Church elder, as well as his substantial charisma, Ne' Reba lobbied local government authorities to declare his hamlet the first official 'tourist object' (*obyek wisata* or *obyek turis*).[17] Significantly, the name he proposed for this 'tourist object' was Ke'te' Kesu'. In 1974, Ke'te' Kesu' was officially recognized as a 'tourist object', along with two other sites (Londa and Lemo, both burial sites rather than villages). This was prompted, in part, by a PATA (Pacific Asia Travel Association) conference held in South Sulawesi that year. South Sulawesi police and government officials were drawn upon to promote Tana Toraja and to transport PATA delegates interested in touring the region. The PATA tour featured the three newly-designated 'tourist objects'. At Ke'te' Kesu', delegates admired well-rehearsed dance performances, carving demonstrations and weaving displays. They also listened raptly as Ne' Reba recounted the history of the development of *tongkonan*, and the significance of those found in Ke'te' Kesu'. The tour and Ne' Reba's lesson on *tongkonan* heritage were deemed a success. PATA delegates returned home and began promoting the region as a pristine and fascinating destination for foreign tourists. In these early promotions, as in current-day advertisements, the 'traditional village' of Ke'te' Kesu' was prominently highlighted.

THE POLITICS AND PRACTICALITIES OF PROMOTING HERITAGE

Around the same time that tourists were discovering Tana Toraja, so were anthropologists and historians. As the reigning Kesu' noble and as an exceptionally knowledgeable elder, Ne' Reba was increasingly sought out by foreign and domestic researchers. By the 1970s and 1980s, Sulawesi scholars were making routine pilgrimages to Ke'te' Kesu' to interview Ne' Reba. These scholars later returned home and chronicled Ne' Reba's accounts of Kesu' heritage in their English, French, German, Japanese and Indonesian books and monographs. In this fashion, Eastern and Western academics and their institutions were entwined with the cementing of Kesu' heritage and the concomitant growing celebrity of Ke'te' Kesu'.[18]

After successfully enshrining the name Kesu' on the touristic and anthropological map of Tana Toraja, Ne' Reba produced a written history of *Tongkonan Kesu'*, and began to offer lectures at tourism, architectural and university seminars on the historical significance of Kesu'. By the mid-1980s, Ne' Reba was one of the key lecturers at training sessions for local tour guides and in 1985 he was ceremonially recognized by Indonesian government officials as the 'founding father' of Tana Toraja. When Ne' Reba passed away in 1986, Indonesian dignitaries who had met him on prior trips to the highlands returned for his elaborate pageantry-filled funeral at Ke'te' Kesu'. A foreign ambassador, several governors, four Indonesian Cabinet Ministers and thousands of guests converged on Ke'te' Kesu' for the ten-day ritual. The funeral received ample coverage on national television, radio and in newsprint, and was also documented by several anthropologists, further propelling Ke'te' Kesu' and the Kesu' story on to the national and global stage.[19]

Following Ne' Reba's death, it was unclear who was to succeed him in his role as maintainer of Kesu's prominence. His brother, Renda Sarungallo, inherited his position as *Tonkonan Kesu'*'s elder, but he resided in Jakarta, too far away actively to serve as a local promoter of Kesu' heritage, identity and authority. Those of Ne' Reba's sons still living in Ke'te' Kesu' were either too young or reluctant to compete with one another for the role of 'local authority'. All agreed, however, that although tourists still flooded to the village, without Ne' Reba to promote the kin group's heritage, the family's continued prestige was in jeopardy. Once again, they risked being overshadowed by other elites with competing ideas about the meaning of Toraja heritage and competing claims to ancestral glory.

Initially, Ne' Reba's surviving siblings and children decided to pursue the traditional avenue to reaffirm the kin group's status: they opted to stage a re-consecration ritual (*mangrara tongkonan*) for their ancestral *tongkonan*, *Tongkonan Layuk* at Ke'te' Kesu'. Typically, for Toraja such rituals are visual affirmations of the glory of the kin group affiliated with the *tongkonan* being celebrated. All members of the kin group associated with the *tongkonan* are expected to contribute to the ritual, lending their energy, savings, raw materials, construction skills, vehicles and livestock to the cause. After several years of planning and fund-gathering, the family staged the ritual on 20 January 1990. The event was deemed a magnificent success, drawing thousands of guests, tourists, and even the Jakarta media. A two-page article on the ritual, illustrated with colour photographs, appeared in *Kompas*, the nation's premier newspaper. Also, with the aid of local and Jakarta-based sponsors, the family published a 50-page booklet detailing the meaning of the *mangrara* ritual and the history of the *tongkonan* at Ke'te' Kesu' (Panitia Mangrara, 1990). Published in Indonesian, the booklet not only offered anthropological accounts of the buildings, but also listed the names of the elites currently playing leadership roles in each of the Ke'te' Kesu' *tongkonan*. Today, the booklet is offered to visiting researchers and was most likely circulated as part of the lobbying effort to secure the attention of UNESCO.

In addition to staging the *tongkonan* consecration ritual, the family devised other plans for their re-emergence on the local political stage. In the late 1980s, the family embraced a new avenue to regain their ebbing authority: the institution of a museum. The urban Jakarta kin were well aware of the political role of museums in Indonesia and elsewhere, particularly as the 1980s were a decade of museum mania in the country (with new museums opening on a regular basis). Likewise, propelled by the touristic celebrity of Ke'te' Kesu', several of Ne' Reba's son's had spent time overseas, carving traditional houses in museums in Japan and elsewhere. On these trips, they had gained a fuller appreciation of the heritage promotion potential of museums. At the time, the only existing museum in Tana Toraja Regency was a small museum in the Sangalla district, run by a competing elite family. As the Sarungallo family recognized, with Ne' Reba gone and with no museum of their own, they would be disadvantaged in their ability to receive the same level of recognition as these local rivals. By 1988, the Sarungallo family had opened the Indo' Ta'dung Museum in one of the ancestral *tongkonan* in Ke'te' Kesu'.[20] The museum was named after Ne' Reba's deceased sister, who had sold Toraja sculptures, antiques, trinkets and textiles out of her home in Ke'te' Kesu' until her death in 1985. The core of the museum collection had come from her inventory and the family felt it fitting to honour her memory with the museum. Indo' Ta'dung had been a popular local figure, with a surplus of humour, charisma and some claim to local fame. Not only had she been married to a Toraja freedom fighter during the revolutionary struggle against the Dutch, but she was recognized as the first courageous Toraja to raise the Indonesian flag in Rantepao following Indonesia's 1945 declaration of independence. This original flag was still amongst Indo' Ta'dung's belongings and was envisioned as a cornerstone of the future museum's collection.

Initially, the museum space and displays were simple, comprised largely of traditional eating utensils designed for elites, ancient knives, relics, and prized ritual textiles. By the mid-1990s, however, the vision expanded. Renda Sarungallo had received an unexpected windfall from an Indonesian cabinet minister to help fund a new museum and '*bibliotheek*'[21] structure in the heart of Ke'te' Kesu'. By my 1995 visit to Ke'te' Kesu' construction of the new, expanded museum was well under way. The new museum was designed in the shape of an oversized *tongkonan* and dominated the hamlet's plaza. The first floor was to be devoted to displays of Kesu' heritage objects and the lofty second floor was envisioned as the library and future headquarters for research on Toraja culture and heritage. Here would be housed a collection of scholarly books and manuscripts concerning Toraja culture. In short, as family members told me, the library would ensure that, even though knowledgeable elders such as Ne' Reba were now deceased, people would continue to perceive Ke'te' Kesu' as a source of ancestral knowledge (a legacy no longer embodied in a person, but now in a library and museum structure). That is, the borrowed institution of the museum was to become the font of Toraja culture and heritage.

In the spring of 1998, just prior to the collapse of Suharto's New Order, the Sarungallo family plan appeared to be poised for success. The construction of the new museum was nearly complete and the building was slated to open the following year with a grand traditional *mangrara banua* ritual (a *tongkonan* consecration ritual). However, the vision was derailed by the Asian economic crisis and Indonesia's decline into political turmoil. International and domestic tourist flows to Ke'te' Kesu' abruptly dwindled to a trickle and villagers whose livelihood had come to rely heavily on tourist expenditures were increasingly anxious about their futures. On my most recent visit, Ne' Reba's eldest son, a quietly reflective middle-aged man, voiced not only his concerns about Toraja's future economic livelihood, but also his fears that, without village-based tourism revenues, the young generation of Ke'te' Kesu'ers would come to view their culture and heritage as irrelevant. As he confided,

> I worry that my children's generation isn't going to be interested in their heritage any more. They will see our cultural problems and traditional etiquette as ancient and old-fashioned. Yet, I *know* that out of ten ancestral Toraja regulations (*aturan Toraja*), at least five of them are always going to be relevant, no matter when. I am sure of that. What is the proof? The proof is in our architecture. Our *tongkonan* are held up as examples by people who are not even Toraja – Europeans, Japanese. Even in your Pasadena Rose Bowl parade a few years back, remember, it was the float modeled after a Toraja *tongkonan* that won the first prize. This shows that Toraja culture is relevant to the rest of the world. We should all be proud of our heritage, and of those accomplishments.

As a twin-pronged approach for tackling the economic and heritage-confidence challenges of the post-New Order era, Ne' Reba's son had been training young Ke'te' Kesu'ers to carve utilitarian objects embellished with Toraja designs for export to both the domestic and international market. As he explained to me, in carving utilitarian objects such as coffee tables, clocks and Kleenex boxes embellished with traditional Toraja designs, these young people would discover that their heritage still has value and is still valued in the world. In addition, they would one day take pride in seeing these Toraja-produced objects in homes throughout Indonesia and the world.

The penultimate chapter in this saga is the 2001 UNESCO nomination of Ke'te' Kesu' as a World Heritage Site. By late 1998, Ne' Reba's son had become increasingly concerned about what he perceived to be cultural slippage, as he observed that the new generation was paying less heed to Kesu' and Toraja traditions. Given the trends he was observing, he feared that Kesu' and Toraja would soon be lost to new buildings and new people, with traditions and heritage paved over and forgotten. He reflected on how best to convey to his own people as well as to the world that their 'cultural heritage was a form of wealth that could not be measured in rupiah (...) and that the Kesu' and Toraja way of life should be preserved'. Drawing on all of his political skills, he slavishly lobbied various ambassadors and politicians, eventually gaining the moral support of the Indonesian

Directorate of Culture and earning the assistance of the Japanese Cultural Center. Eventually he and his growing chorus gained the ear of Indonesia's Minister of Tourism, who then invited the UNESCO Conference for the Asia–Pacific Region to convene in Tana Toraja Regency. As a result of this meeting, through the efforts of Ne' Reba's son and others, Ke'te' Kesu' was registered for candidacy as a World Heritage Site (receiving registration No. C1038). This designation promised not only renewed celebrity and respect for Kesu' heritage, but also suggested a timely infusion of financial capital into the village. Initially, the publicity surrounding the UNESCO nomination as well as Indonesia's enhanced political stability with Megawati Sukarnoputri's installation as President prompted a resurgence of tourism to Tana Toraja Regency and gave the residents of Ke'te' Kesu' reason for optimism. However, following the aftermath of the Islamist suicide aeroplane hijackings and crashing of 11 September 2001 and the Islamist bombings in tourist enclaves in Bali in 2002 and 2005, the short-term future of tourism in Indonesia began to look precarious.

'FIXING' WORLD HERITAGE

By 2004, Ke'te' Kesu''s trek to global celebrity had ended. Apparently, the core issue that toppled the hamlet's candidacy for World Heritage Site status centred on the thorny concept of authenticity. Although it is possible that local Toraja rivalries and resentments over the hamlet's rise to UNESCO celebrity were also at play in Ke'te' Kesu''s derailing,[22] the Regional Adviser to UNESCO for Culture in the Asia Pacific does not acknowledge these issues. Rather, he summarizes why the hamlet was removed from consideration as a World Heritage Site as follows:

> Both the tourism industry and the heritage profession risk becoming confused about what is real and what is fake. A nomination for World Heritage inscription of the Tana Toraja homeland was put forward recently to the World Heritage Committee, prepared by the Ministry of Culture and Tourism (which at that time were part of the same ministry). However, and in spite of the rhetoric about the importance of protecting the cultural landscape and traditional practices, when the nomination maps were closely examined it was clear that the area that was in fact nominated for protection under the World Heritage Convention was limited to only five structures in the compound of the local tourist office, one of which was a totally new construction in modern materials made to look like a traditional house, while the other four were moved from their original location and

rebuilt to the tourist office premises, with considerable alteration to their form and material – and a complete loss of original function. The rejection of this nomination by the World Heritage Committee caused consternation among both the tourism industry and the heritage management office, neither of which understood what was inappropriate about the nomination – a circumstance which demonstrates just how confused the heritage tourism industry has become about what is real and what is not. Local inhabitants, however, welcomed the rejection of this nomination and took advantage of the confusion caused by this so-called 'set-back' to heritage tourism to retake control of how – *and even if* – Torajan heritage is to be shared with visitors (Engelhardt, 2007: 6).

Striking about this summary is the assumption that the movement of the ancestral homes almost 100 years ago, the more recent attempts by local tourism agencies to improve the village by adding features such as sidewalks, as well as one local family's addition of a museum in the form of an ancestral house all added up to what this UNESCO adviser deemed to be 'fake'. That the ancestral homes continue to be the centre of local ritual activities, that the village has long been home to multiple families and that these families themselves were responsible for many of the village's transformations did not enter into this particular UNESCO consultant's calculus of Ke'te' Kesu''s authenticity. For him, the yardstick of authenticity had been fixed at some imagined point in the distant past. As he went on to conclude, this was an instance of 'staged authenticity' which 'is always inappropriate and culturally unacceptable' (Engelhardt, 2007: 6). While Ke'te' Kesu'ers would be the first to acknowledge that they are savvy players in the game of cultural politics, they would be startled by this characterization of their ancestral hamlet as an inauthentic fiction rebuilt to tourist office specifications.

Ultimately, as Engelhardt alludes to in the above quote, other Torajas 'took advantage of the confusion' to navigate for a broader conception of the entire region as a heritage site. In June 2005, Indonesian authorities submitted a draft nomination of all of Tana Toraja for consideration as worthy of inclusion on the World Heritage Site List. However, the region still sits on the sidelines awaiting global recognition, as UNESCO deemed its documentation incomplete and advised authorities to finalize it for re-submission (Feng Jing (UNESCO official), personal communication 7 March 2008).

As the Tana Toraja case study illustrates, the emergence of heritage sites is not a 'natural' process, but rather one born out of complex exchanges, competitions and collaborations between local groups, as well as national and international entities. While there are important 'Toraja' indigenous ideas about heritage inscribed in the *tongkonan* that comprise the village of Ke'te' Kesu' (cf. Adams, 1998a, 2006), the hamlet itself is also very much a product of the Dutch colonial past. Moreover, in the course of its evolution over the past century, Ke'te' Kesu' has been shaped by other processes and institutions that stretch far beyond the local. While local actors and rivalries between local elites are salient to understanding Kete' Kesu's trajectory to candidacy as a World Heritage Site, as well as to understanding its replacement on this list with the broader category of 'Tana Toraja', a more informed analysis requires situating this particular cultural landscape into a larger national and global context.

As we saw, the mid-twentieth century uncertainties of Indonesian national independence were not without ramifications for Ke'te' Kesu', as local districts were reshaped and renamed by new government bureaucrats. This threat of administrative erasure of the Kesu' name prompted Kesu' elites to search for alternative means to ensure the longevity and prestige of their heritage. International tourism and foreign and domestic social science researchers became avenues for Ke'te' Kesu''s survival. In a similar vein, as Kesu'ers gained in experience outside the region, the western institutions of museums and libraries were embraced as supplementary avenues for fortifying Kesu' heritage. Finally, as the Asian economic crisis reached Tana Toraja and Indonesian political stability eroded in the late 1990s, Kesu'ers explored new non-touristic avenues to promote their economic survival and simultaneously their heritage. Through marketing modern utilitarian wooden objects embellished with carved Toraja motifs nationally and internationally, Kesu'ers' livelihood and involvement in producing traditional symbols was assured. In short, while certainly a '*genius loci*', Ke'te' Kesu' is not the static and unchanging embodiment of tradition imagined by UNESCO. And, in fact, when UNESCO advisers became aware of the broad strokes of Ke'te' Kesu's history, it was promptly discarded as a candidate for World Heritage Site status, ultimately to be replaced by the broader (and less rivalry-inciting) site of Tana Toraja.

The Tana Toraja's Tentative World Heritage Site status is the product of a long interplay between the local, the national and the global. As we have seen, Ke'te' Kesu'ers were reshaping and rethinking their notions about heritage, as they encountered multiple forces from within, around, and beyond the nation. Examining Ke'te' Kesu''s derailed ascendance to candidacy as a World Heritage Site, and the shift to the broader category of 'Tana Toraja', offers insights into the process of cultural objectification, as we come to appreciate better the complex roles of local and international players in 'fixing' and promoting this dynamic locale. Moreover, it is highly probable that the case of Ke'te' Kesu' hamlet, and ultimately Tana Toraja, is not a unique tale in the annals of UNESCO World Heritage Sites. Rather, it would seem that most locales that successfully gain candidacy for UNESCO World Heritage Site status are places that have undergone similar trajectories, where local, national and international forces have conspired, wittingly and unwittingly, to project these 'endangered' sites on to the global stage.

NOTES

1   This chapter is a revised and up-dated version of 'The Politics of Heritage in Tana Toraja, Indonesia: Interplaying the Local and the Global', originally published in *Indonesia and the Malay World* in 2003 (a condensed version of that earlier article also appeared in Current Issues in Tourism in 2004).

2   Here I do not mean to reify the sense that there is a universal 'Toraja' perspective on the meaning of heritage. Clearly, ideas about heritage vary between different sectors of the population (elites and those of 'low' ancestry, urban Toraja and hinterland villagers, etc.) and also vary regionally.

3   Moreover, it may well be the case that it is precisely this history of overlooked discourse with the wider world (and the concomitant notion of newly-arrived endangerment from the wider world) that enables heritage sites to gain UNESCO pre-eminence.

4   For a brief video clip of this opening ceremony, see the 'Global Meeting' section of the web page http://jakarta.unesco.or.id/prog/clturetoraja.html.

5   As of 2008 the World Heritage Committee had 878 sites on its list; of these 679 were cultural, 174 natural and 25 were mixed sites, and only 29 are located in Southeast Asia (see introductory Chapter 1 and Table 1.1). As some Asian observers have noted for some time, the Asian sites have been under-represented (Villalon, 2001: 1). Calling for 'brotherhood despite diversity' some Southeast Asian cultural observers have urged that Southeast Asian Cultural Heritage site nominating should not be done in isolation, but rather Southeast Asian sites should be proposed strategically with an emphasis on selecting sites that 'identify the common cultural thread uniting Asians despite their differences' (Villalon, 2001: 2).

6   Among the criteria for inclusion of cultural properties on the World Heritage List are the requirements that the nominated site, '(i). represent a masterpiece of human creative genius; or (ii) exhibit an important interchange of human values, over a span of time or within a cultural area of the world (...); or (iii) bear a unique or at least

exceptional testimony to a cultural tradition or to a civilization which is living or which has disappeared; or (iv) be an outstanding example of a type of building or architectural or technological ensemble or landscape which illustrates (a) significant stage(s) in human history; or (v) be an outstanding example of a traditional human settlement or land-use which is representative of a culture (or cultures), especially when it has become vulnerable under the impact of irreversible change; or (vi) be directly or tangibly associated with events or living traditions, with ideas, or with beliefs, with artistic and literary works of outstanding universal' (http://whc.unesco.org/opgutoc.htm#debut, downloaded 21 May 2002). Criteria for inclusion of natural properties include the following: That the sites '(i) be outstanding examples representing major stages of earth's history (...); or (ii) be outstanding examples representing significant on-going ecological and biological processes in the evolution and development of terrestrial, fresh water, coastal and marine ecosystems and communities of plants and animals; or (iii) contain superlative natural phenomena or areas of exceptional natural beauty and aesthetic importance; or (iv) contain the most important and significant natural habitats for in-situ conservation of biological diversity, including those containing threatened species of outstanding universal value from the point of view of science or conservation' (http://whc.unesco.org/opgutoc.htm#debut, downloaded 21 May 2002).

7   See Andrew Causey (2003) for a stimulating discussion of the concept of utopics in contemporary tourism practices and fantasies.

8   Bruner's observations that tourism has recuperated the major binary oppositions such as 'traditional–modern' long since discarded by anthropology appears to apply to international heritage organizations as well (Bruner, 2001).

9   Because of limitations of space, this chapter's discussions of Toraja conceptions of these matters concentrates primarily on Ke'te' Kesu' elite perceptions and their representations of heritage.

10   In recent years there has been much discussion of the idea of the house as a specific form of social organization. This proposition has captured the attention of many Austronesianists, as it appears to have a great deal of explaining power for many dimensions of kinship practices and orientations. See Claude Lévi-Strauss, 1983, 1987; Waterson, 1990, 1995; Fox, 1987, 1993; Carsten and Hugh-Jones, 1995, and Erb, 1999 for further explorations of this concept.

11   Waterson notes that the salience of the *tongkonan* may well have grown in recent years, as tourism and cultural efflorescence have become increasingly important in Indonesia (1990). Architecturally, *tongkonan* structures have become more exaggerated over the past two decades, with the rooftops of newer *tongkonan* flaring ever-higher and Toraja families incorporating *tongkonan* motifs into their homes (cf. Kis-Jovak, Nooy-Palm, Schefold and Schulz-Dornburg, 1988).

12   Such as the *mangrara tongkonan* ritual.

13   As Waterson notes, 'Some origin-houses associated with very important ancestors have in fact long ceased to exist, but their sites are still well remembered and in theory if the descendants willed it, they could be rebuilt' (Waterson, 1997:65). Indeed, friends who traced their ancestry to *Tongkonan* Kesu' always pointed out its original site when we found ourselves in its vicinity.

14   I was told that certain highly symbolic pieces of the *tongkonan* would be relocated in such a move, but that generally the entire house is not dismantled and relocated (although this is done with Toraja rice barns, when circumstances call for their move). Beyond this, my mentors did not provide further clarification on the physical logistics of the *tongkonan* relocation process. Given that it is common practice for Toraja families to completely rebuild *tongkonan*s that fall into disrepair on the same site, using new wood, new carvings and new roofs, I can only conclude that this was what was done with *Tongkonan* Kesu'.

15   The term adat is ubiquitous in the Malay world and carries complex multiple meanings. Generally translated as 'custom', 'customary law', 'tradition' or 'behaviour', numerous writers have explored the nuances of this concept. C. van Vollenhoven published one of the early texts on adat in the Netherlands Indies in 1918, establishing the foundation for subsequent works on the topic. Drawing on ethnographic research, he created classifications for various adat or customary law regions in the Netherlands Indies (1918). Contemporary scholars have turned their attention to examining subjective dimensions of the concept of adat and to chronicling its political manipulations. Zainal Kling, for instance, defines adat as the 'indigenous body of knowledge and law of the Malay world' (1997: 45) and discusses adat as the folk-model whereby Malay self-identity is maintained. Ultimately, he suggests that adat is most aptly understood as 'the subjective understanding of the Malay society of their cultural formations and cultural constructs' (1997: 46).

16   In previous writings I have used the pseudonym Ne' Duma. However, he is now deceased and his descendants have expressed their desire to have his memory and contributions better known, be it through anthropological writings aimed at the English-speaking world or via more Toraja-oriented memorials.

17   Wisata translates as 'tour', and obyek wisata can be translated as 'tour object' or 'tourist object'. The Indonesian government has promoted the use of these expressions as part of its tourism development project. The very use of these terms suggests a reconditioning of the local gaze, as village inhabitants come to perceive their homes as 'objects' for tourists.

18   See Adams 1993a, 1995 for further elaboration of the role of foreign researchers in amplifying particular versions of Toraja heritage and identity.

19   On the final day of the funeral, Ne' Reba's body was enshrined in an enormous and spectacular modern cement tomb behind the village by the cliff-side graves. Today, almost twenty years later, guides still pause by his tomb to recount the story of this Kesu' elder and his final send-off.

20   For a more detailed discussion of this museum, as well as the museum in Sangalla, see Adams, 1997b.

21   It is noteworthy that in describing his vision to me, Renda Sarungallo chose not to use the Indonesian term for library (*perpustakaan*) but rather the Dutch term. As a Dutch-educated Torajan whose first wife had been Dutch, Renda Sarungallo was clearly inspired by this European institution.

22   As noted earlier, people in other regions of Tana Toraja felt their own villages were equally deserving of World Heritage Site recognition and were irked by Ke'te' Kesu'ers' attempt to grab the limelight for themselves.

CHAPTER 3

The Reconstruction of Atayal Identity in Wulai, Taiwan[1]

Mami Yoshimura and Geoffrey Wall

INTRODUCTION

Cultural expressions come in both tangible and intangible forms, with associated stories and interpretations. Selected cultural expressions may be commodified as heritage and sold to tourists, and in the process their meaning and significance may be changed. This chapter addresses both the heritage of the Atayal in Taiwan, parts of whose cultural activities were suppressed by colonial powers, and their attempts to reconstruct their culture, identity and heritage within the context of tourism. The contribution addresses questions concerning the changing relationships between culture, identity and tourism as this indigenous people strives to recover from a marginalizing situation that has resulted from colonialism and neo-colonialism.

The Atayal are one of thirteen officially-recognized indigenous groups in Taiwan. Although Taiwan is not a Southeast Asian country, the Atayal are speakers of an Austronesian language with many affinities to Southeast Asia. They have experienced both colonialism and tourism development. During Japan's occupation (1895–1945), they were forced into village settlements and were required to abandon certain socio-cultural activities: facial tattooing, head-hunting and weaving. The Atayal lost most of their original textiles because, during the Japanese colonial period, many of them were taken to Japan. Today, these textiles, most of which are in storage, are preserved in a few Japanese museums, and are brought out only when special exhibitions are held by the museums. Now, in Taiwan, the Atayal's textiles are being reconstructed by the hands of some indigenous women in Wulai (Figure 3.1), a town about a one-hour drive from Taipei and which has become a tourism destination based on both natural and cultural resources. It is important to note that most of these women weave primarily for museums, using as their models a handful of remaining traditional clothes as well as Japanese books that describe the textiles and provide very detailed pictures of the originals; they reconstruct replicas as well as new works based on the remaining originals and the pictures. Other artisans weave for domestic tourists but they have little success in competition with less expensive Han Chinese factory-made woven products.

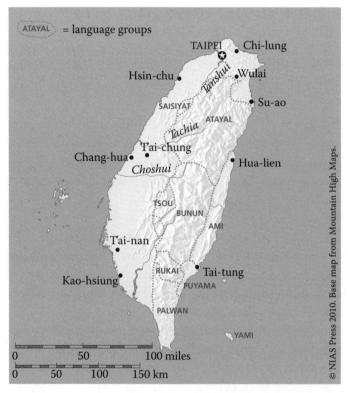

Figure 3.1: Map of Taiwan showing location of Wulai

After the mid-1960s, when tourists started visiting their village, the indigenous residents of Wulai generated most of their income though international tourism (Hitchcock, 2003). However, since the mid-1990s the number of international tourists has declined. The end of the 'golden era' of international tourism in Wulai began in part because of the opening up of China as a competitive alternative destination. Unlike many other parts of Southeast Asia that the Chinese authorities approved as tourism destinations, the political situation has meant that Taiwan has yet to benefit from the growing number of tourists emanating from mainland China. In the face of a reduction in the number of international visitors, Wulai's indigenous residents have gradually relinquished their tourism jobs. Some of them have left for Taipei or Sindian to search for new employment. Others have stayed in Wulai where they try to make ends meet. In 1997 some indigenous women who had left their jobs in tourism started to revitalize Atayal weaving. The reintroduction of weaving not only required the Atayal weavers to retrace their weaving history and to reconstruct and revive lost skills but also opened up a novel opportunity to create new motifs with western looms imported from Sweden and New Zealand and to earn income through weaving.

The weaving is authentic in that it is undertaken predominantly by Atayal women by hand in their homes, albeit with a modified technology. However, authenticity is a slippery term and, as will be seen, the context in which the weaving is undertaken and the meanings attached to the product have changed. Furthermore, cheaper machine-made, broadly similar products are produced by machine by majority Han entrepreneurs that undercut the hand-woven textiles that require more skill and time to make. This has greatly reduced the ability of Atayal weavers to create textiles as a commercially viable tourism product.

The reintroduction of weaving has had multiple effects on the Atayal community. Weaving has changed from being a symbol of the Atayal women's gender identity alone to a representation of the Atayal's collective ethnic identity as a whole. Now the Atayal proudly claim their weaving culture as a part of their ethnic identity. It has also become an ethnic symbol and a tourism product, although most of the current domestic tourism market is satisfied by machine-made products.

Having experienced sixty-two years of inactivity as a result of traditional Atayal weaving culture being banned by the colonial Japanese from the mid-1930s until its revival in 1997, why did the Atayal decide to weave again? How has weaving contributed to Atayal identity formation? Focusing on facial tattooing, head-hunting and weaving as an entry point for the exploration of changes in Atayal culture, this chapter will demonstrate how the Wulai Atayals' multiple identities have been changed through their experiences of the post-colonial history of Taiwan and the contemporary history of tourism development.

HERITAGE AND IDENTITY

Heritage and identity are closely related concepts and they both occur along a scale-gradient. While the United Nations recognizes special places with universal value, many such places will be unknown to many, or perhaps most, people who may not readily identify with them. At the other end of the scale, individuals have personal heritages and identities. In between there are national and regional heritages and identities, and these may be contested and malleable. The following discussion is concerned with the heritage of an indigenous group and how a particular aspect of that heritage has been variously viewed as a symbol of identity from perspectives that are both internal and external to the group.

In recent years, the notion of identity, and with it identity politics, has become relevant within a variety of social sciences discourses (Holloway et al., 2003). But what is identity? There are three main ways to understand identities. First, identities are understood by comparing and contrasting the Self with the Other. The construction of the Other is often characterized by the establishment of dualisms or binary opposites (Aitchison, 2000; 2001), although such a process may result in the simplification and stereotyping of the Other. Gregson et al. (1997: 84–85) defined a dualism as follows:

> A dualism is a particular structure of meaning in which one element is defined only in relation to another or others. Dualisms thus usually involve pairs, binaries and dichotomies, but not all pairs, binaries and dichotomies are dualisms. What makes dualisms distinctive is that one of the terms provides a 'core', and it is in contrast to the core that the other term or terms are defined. Thus dualisms structure meaning as a relation between a core term A and (a) subordinate term(s) not–A.

By defining cores and peripheries, norms and deviants, centres and margins, the powerful and the powerless, the process of Othering defines the Self as possessing greater power and status than the Other (Aitchison, 2000). In other words, the idea of Othering suggests that our sense of who we are is not based on a wholly internal process but relies on an external reflection of power relationships between us and them (Crang, 1998). Holloway and Hubbard (2001: 77) also asserted that:

Your identity – the way you think about yourself and the ways others think about you – is defined not just by what you are but also what you are not.

Indeed, we make sense of ourselves by identifying differences between ourselves and others. Adams (1996) suggested that all identity is constructed across difference, and that identity politics are rooted on the politics of difference. It is hard to contest that these differences are important to understanding society (cf. Swain, 2002). The concept of the Other provides a useful vehicle for examining power relationships among people at different places and times (Aitchison, 2001). Thus, the concept of the Other and the process of Othering are important to the understanding of identity formation.

Second, our identities are not static but relational. The Self and the Other are produced though social relations of identification and differentiation. Hubbard et al. (2002: 89) also described identity as follows:

> Human identity is endlessly complex and fluid, and (...) the placing of people into particular pigeon-holes or categories is dependent on the discursive regimes (and power relations) that dominate at any one moment.

Our identities are socially constructed and changeable over time. Holloway et al. (2003: 252) has argued that all societies are relational in that 'they are always constructed and understood in terms of their sameness to, and difference from, others'. Thus, difference is a relational concept that we experience in terms of discrimination, inequalities of power and domination over others. In other words, identity formation stresses differences between others and the self as they change over time. This is important when considering aspects of heritage for it may be valued and interpreted differently by members of a group and outsiders, and these values and interpretations may change over time. Symbols of identity may be invented, as in the case of bagpipes in Scotland, and they may be reinvented, once lost, as in the case under consideration below.

Third, our identities are not singular but are multiple. Drawing upon the work of Ewing (1990), Gombay (2005) argued that our identities are not singular but are multidimensional, and these multifarious, inconsistent selves are context-dependent and can shift rapidly. Gombay (2005: 425) further argued that:

Identity exists at many levels. It exists in private and in public. It is attached both to individuals and to collectives. It varies according to context and scale (...). The composition of identity reflects such things as people's history, social experiences, and development.

Gombay (2005) called this perspective 'multiple identities' and also pointed out that the composition of identity reflects social experiences, historical context and origins. By understanding the elements that constitute identity, the socio-cultural and political-economic processes that have affected people can be better understood.

CONCEPTUAL FRAMEWORK: SHIFTS IN IDENTITY FORMATION

To understand how the Atayal's multiple identities have changed, a diagram has been created that can be used as a conceptual framework for displaying changes in multiple identities (Figure 3.2). The darker centre of the diagram shows elements that constitute a group's multiple identities (e.g. culture, ethnicity, race, gender and place). On the other hand, on the outer ring of the diagram the symbols that represent each identity are shown. Symbols are important identity markers (Schermerhorn, 1974; cited in Ashcroft et al., 2000), therefore a loss or replacement of a symbol affects the construction of the multiple identities and, thus, leads to shifts in identity formation. This diagram is used to highlight how the indigenous peoples' multiple identities have been modified through their colonial experiences. The diagram can be applied at a variety of scales from the individual to collectivities to illustrate visually how multiple identities have been changed through particular events. The diagram as used here encompasses indigenous, Japanese, and even Han, perspectives on identity. These differ but they are not entirely separate for one informs the other in reciprocal relationships. In future research, such a diagram could be applied to different groups or individuals in the exploration of changes in identity formation and, thus, is viewed as having wide applicability.

Study site description

GEOGRAPHY AND PEOPLE OF TAIWAN

Taiwan is a mountainous country, located 160 kilometres off the southeast coast of China (Munsterhjelm, 2002). It is a small island that is 377 kilometres long and 142 kilometres wide (Cauquelin, 2004). More than

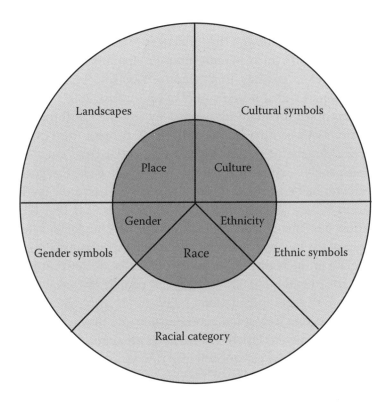

Figure 3.2: Diagram to represent shifts in multiple identities

two-thirds of Taiwan's surface is covered by mountains (Copper, 2003) and this is where the majority of indigenous people now live.

In terms of population, there are close to twenty-three million people in Taiwan (ibid.). Although there is disagreement about whether the term 'ethnic' accurately describes different social groups in Taiwan, Taiwan's people are commonly described as being in four major groups: (1) the indigenous peoples; two groups of native Taiwanese ((2) Fukienese or Hoklo, and (3) Hakka); and (4) mainland Chinese (ibid.: 68). The indigenous peoples are usually seen as being ethnically distinct from the other three groups, and they have been broadly defined into two groups: (1) the lowland and (2) mountain indigenous peoples (Copper, 2003). In this chapter, the indigenous peoples that are referred to are those in the mountains. Many lowland indigenous peoples were either killed or assimilated by the Chinese over a long period of time and it is, thus, difficult to trace their indigenous identity. On the other hand, mountain indigenous peoples still maintain their distinct indigenous identity, although their culture has been considerably modified through the influences of their colonial encounters.

As of January 2007, thirteen indigenous groups are officially recognised: the Atayal, Taroko, Saisiyat, Thao, Bunun, Kavalan, Amis, Tsou, Rukai, Puyuma, Paiwan, Yami and Sakizaya (*The China Post*, 2007). These official classifications were originally developed by Japanese anthropologists in the early twentieth century, when indigenous peoples were divided into nine groups (Munsterhjelm, 2002; Hitchcock, 2003). In recent years, some indigenous people such as the Taroko have challenged the government of Taiwan who had continued to use the schemes based on the Japanese classification system (Munsterhjelm, 2002). The result is that the official classification has changed accordingly and is still under debate. While the number of the indigenous peoples recorded by the census might be an underestimate of the reality (Allio, 1998; Arrigo et al., 2002), it is believed that there are roughly 400,000 indigenous people; they constitute only two per cent of the total population of Taiwan (Munsterhjelm, 2002). The Atayal are the second largest indigenous group and they mostly live in the northern part of Taiwan (Hsieh, 1994). Based on linguistic differences, the Atayal people are further categorised into three sub-groups: Atayal proper, Tseole and Sedeq (Hsieh, 1994). While there are common cultural features among the three Atayal groups, there are also regional differences.

THE WULAI ATAYAL

Wulai is located 27 kilometres south of Taipei city (Hsieh, 1994). The indigenous people of Wulai are considered to be one of the sub-groups of the Atayal proper. The 2004 census showed that Wulai had 767 households and 2192 residents, including 851 indigenous people and 1341 Han Chinese (Wulai Township Office, 2004). The Township of Wulai consists of five villages: Jhongjhih, Wulai, Sinsian, Siaoyi and Fushan. During Japan's occupation, the Japanese relocated the Wulai Atayal to the five villages to consolidate their administration (Wulai Township Office, 2004). This had many implications for their lifestyles and, consequently, their heritage. Except for Wulai or '*Ulay*' which means hot spring in the Atayal language, the other villages now hold the Chinese names given by the government (Hsieh, 1994). In Wulai, along the Nan Shih River, there is a natural hot spring that people come to enjoy and, in walking distance, there is the tallest waterfall in Taiwan.

Methods

Following the identification of Wulai and the Atayal as a potential research opportunity by the second author in 2005 and the establishment of local contacts, library research was conducted, initially in Canada and later in Taiwan and Japan, to explore relevant concepts and the documented history of Japanese–Atayal relationships. Field research was conducted for fourteen weeks in Wulai in summer 2006 primarily by the first author with some assistance from Taiwanese colleagues and students. During this period she lived with the most accomplished weaver, interacted with all other weavers in the community on many occasions, participated in many community events, and interviewed numerous officials and other informants, both in Wulai and Taipei. Being fluent in Japanese and English and being able to read some Mandarin, many conversations were conducted in Japanese, particularly with older informants; interviews with officials were sometimes conducted in English. An interviewer/translator was used occasionally when it was necessary to converse in Mandarin, particularly in the early part of the field investigation.

Facial tattooing, weaving and head-hunting

BEFORE 1895

Prior to colonization by Japan, the Atayal held traditional religious beliefs called *gaga* (Figure 3.3). For their place identity, the Atayal saw the mountains in which they lived as an identity marker. The Atayal also spoke their own language, Atayal. Their language and facial tattoo patterns showed regional characteristics; therefore, they were important identity markers for the Atayal to determine who belonged to which group (identified in the outer ring of Figure 3.3).

Prior to colonization, the Atayal men and women got their facial tattoos at the age of fifteen to sixteen when they were ready to get married. The Atayal men got tattoos on their foreheads and chins, in two separate short vertical bold lines, when they proved themselves to be accomplished head-hunters (Wiedfeldt, 2003). Once the men were tattooed, they were eligible to get married (Yamamoto, 1999; 2000). Women, on the other hand, had to be meticulous and accomplished weavers before they got their tatoos (Wiedfeldt, 2003): a bold line on their foreheads and cheeks (Figure 3.4) and a wide line from one ear, across the cheeks, through the lips to the other ear, making a V shape (ibid.). Like Atayal men who took many heads, Atayal women who were recognized as great weavers were allowed to have tattoos

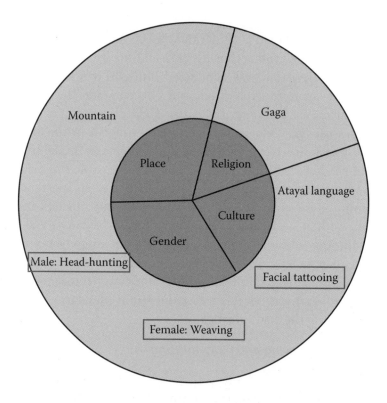

Figure 3.3: Determinants of the nature of the Atayal's multiple identities: before 1895

on other parts of their bodies, such as palms and legs as well as special tattoos on their foreheads (Yamamoto, 1999).

In Atayal society, successful male head-hunters were considered to be brave men and their accomplishments were marked by the chin tattoo. Thus, head-hunting was a particularly important ritual for the Atayal men to show their adulthood. According to Yamamoto (1999; 2000), the qualification to have facial tattooing for men changed over time. Originally, only those who succeeded in head-hunting were allowed to have a facial tattoo on their chin (Yamamoto, 1999; 2000). Later, regardless of success in head-taking, Atayal men were allowed to have facial tattoos if they touched the head of a nobleman taken by their father or a sibling (Yamamoto, 1999; 2000). At any rate, head-hunting was a symbolic activity for Atayal men and was required to obtain facial tattooing, and the relationship between facial tattooing and head-hunting was inseparable for the Atayal to define

Figure 3.4: An Atayal woman with facial tattoo

Source: Mami Yoshimura: photograph of part of an exhibit in the Shung Ye Museum of Formosan Aborigines, Taipei, Taiwan.

their gender identity as Atayal men. Although head-hunting is no longer undertaken, hunting for game is a respected male activity.

Similarly, becoming an accomplished weaver was crucial for the Atayal woman as it promised her a successful marriage with a strong, skilful Atayal man. Traditionally, the Atayal women used backstrap (body tension) looms to weave. The weaver sat on the floor, straightened her legs, put a strap on her back to keep the tension of the warp threads, and then wove a piece of cloth by running the weft into the warp. To make the threads, the Atayal women planted *noka* or ramie, cut the ramie plant, peeled it, and separated the bark into pure fibres with toothed bamboo tools (Okamura and Zhang, 1968: 31). With regard to weaving motifs, the Atayal women mainly wove plain and twill. The former weaving technique allowed them to make stripe line motifs. The latter allowed them to engage in more complicated motifs such as rhombus patterns, which were the most popular motif woven by them. In terms of colours, white and dark orange were the Atayal's two most traditional colours for weaving. The Wulai Atayal also used indigo blue because of the widespread availability of the indigo plant in the region.

Because a woman's acquisition of weaving skills was directly related to her ability to get a facial tattoo and then to get married, the Atayal mother passed down her weaving skills only to her own daughters. If someone came to their house when she was weaving, she hid away her looms and any materials related to weaving, including yarns and weaving pieces. It was important for the Atayal women to keep their skills within their family. Once they got their facial tattoos and married, they then wove fabrics to store away for their daughters' trousseau when they were due to be married. Thus, the Atayal men's head-hunting and the Atayal women's weaving represented their gender identity and, in turn, were closely connected to facial tattooing and their cultural identity.

JAPANESE COLONIZATION (1895–1945)

After China's defeat in the Sino–Japanese War, Japan officially annexed Taiwan, the Pescadores Islands, and the Liaodong Peninsula via the Treaty of Shimonoseki in 1895 (Tipton, 2002). Japan then attempted to establish its own empire in Asia and the Pacific, hoping to achieve equal status with the Western nations. Japan's war victory against China certainly brought Japan into the Western nations' consciousness as an 'Asian imperialist' (Tipton, 2002: 76). However, despite increased recognition from Western nations, Japan was forced to abandon its claim to the Liaodong Peninsula via the Triple Intervention made by the Russian, German and French governments (Tipton, 2002). This situation was resented in Japan which was well aware of its position as the first non-Western state to join the ranks of the nineteenth-century colonial powers (Wong, 2004). The Japanese government was certain that Japan's colonial practices in Taiwan would be compared to European colonial rule in other parts of the globe; thus, they

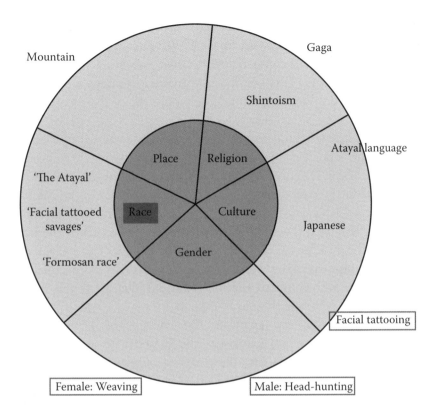

Figure 3.5: Shifts in the Atayal's multiple identities: after Japanese colonization, 1895–1945

determined that Taiwan should become a model colony (Tsurumi, 1977; Lin and Keating, 2005). Accordingly, Japan tried to follow in the footsteps of the West and to exercise its colonial power based on the notions of Enlightenment.

Due to Japan's occupation, the Atayal's multiple identities were forced to change, at least superficially, to meet the expectations of the Japanese and their anthropologists (Figure 3.5). First, the colonial state of Japan imposed Shintoism as a state religion on the Atayal. The Atayal were forbidden to practice *gaga*, their own belief, and thus their religious identity was buried (represented by its placement outside the outer ring in Figure 3.5). In terms of cultural identity, the Atayal also learned to speak Japanese as the authorities educated the indigenous children in this language. Facial tattooing was banned by the colonial government to prevent the Atayal from engaging in head-hunting, for these practices were closely linked

(Yamamoto, 1999). Women's weaving was banned after Japan initiated its 'Holy War' against the West in the 1930s. Because facial tattooing was closely connected to the construction of the Atayal's gender identity, the ban severed the links between facial tattooing, marriage and weaving for women and head-hunting for men, helping to bury the Atayal's cultural gender identity.

During Japan's occupation, a new identity was also imposed on the Atayal: they were racially categorized as an inferior 'Formosan' race (Harrison, 2003: 345) and named the 'facial tattooed savages' because of their facial tattoo practices (now placed in the outer ring in Figure 3.5). According to Atayal informants, 'Atayal' only meant 'human being' in the Atayal language (Personal communication, 2006). Until the Japanese classified the indigenous peoples into nine groups, the Atayal did not consider themselves as the 'Atayal tribe' (ibid.). In other words, the Japanese were the ones who imposed the idea of tribal identity as the 'Atayal' on those indigenous people (Hsieh, 1994).

For the colonial-era Japanese, the concept of a savage/civilized dichotomy was important (as it was the Western norm), defining other peoples as inferior, different, deviant and subordinate in Eurocentric epistemologies and imperial/colonial ideologies (Ashcroft et al., 2000). Like other colonial empires in the West, the Japanese wanted to show themselves as the 'saviours' of the indigenous peoples to legitimize the occupation of Taiwan (Stainton, 1999: 30). Thus, the production of the colonial Other – the indigenous peoples as savages – was essential for the early part of Japan's colonization to suggest that Japan was leading the savages towards civilization.

The colonial state of Japan separated the colonized people into two groups, Han Chinese and indigenous peoples, to prevent them from co-operating to fight against the Japanese. They classified Han Chinese as 'common people' and the indigenous peoples as 'savages'. The effects of this may linger today as the indigenous people are minorities with lower living standards and life opportunities and they are regarded as inferior by many Han. Furthermore, the indigenous areas were segregated by fortification lines and the indigenous peoples were required to have minimum contact with the outside world. This categorization between Han Chinese and the indigenous peoples, and the segregation of living places between the two groups, promoted linked ideas of place and racial identity. Ashcroft et al. (2000: 26) noted that 'perhaps one of the most catastrophic binary systems perpetuated by imperialism is the invention of the concept of race'. By ignoring the cultural specificity of the indigenous peoples of Taiwan, including the Atayal, Japan's imperialism placed the concept of race into a simple binary that reflected its own logic of power.

Based on linguistic differences, the indigenous peoples were further categorized into nine tribes and the Atayal were recognized as one such by the colonial government of Japan (Harrison, 2003). Finally, the Japanese colonial government forced the Atayal into village settlements (Hitchcock, 2003) and, thus, the Atayal had to modify their mountain life based on shifting cultivation. The colonial government was particularly interested in the Atayal's area of habitation because of its rich camphor plantations. The ban on head-hunting was also a step in forcing the Atayal men to engage in farming, which had previously been Atayal women's work.

NATIONALIST CHINA'S COLONIZATION (1945–1987)

After the Second World War was over in 1945, Japan's fifty years of occupation also ended. At the same time, Nationalist China's colonization started. With the Cairo Declaration, Taiwan was placed under the rule of mainland China (Cauquelin, 2004). Chiang Kai-shek and his Nationalist Party, the Kuomintang (KMT), saw their retreat to Taiwan in 1949 as a temporary setback until they could return to mainland China (Cheng, 1994; Manthorpe, 2005). Thus, it was important for the KMT to govern Taiwan as if it were mainland China (Manthorpe, 2005). This mentality led to the Sinicization of Taiwan. To redefine people's identity and ideology in Taiwan, Chiang Kai-shek's central government rigorously implemented an entire 're-Sinicization policy' (Cauquelin, 2004). As a part of this policy, it was made compulsory to teach Mandarin in schools and to use Mandarin in the media (ibid.). For the indigenous people of Taiwan, including the Atayal, this transition meant becoming more Chinese, and their multiple identities needed to be shifted again. Particularly in the case of the Atayal in Wulai, the ways in which the Wulai Atayal reconstituted their multiple identities were greatly affected not only by Nationalist China's colonization but also by the forces of international tourism development.

After Japan's occupation was over, Christianity began to be introduced to the indigenous people of Taiwan, including the Atayal (Figure 3.6). In the case of the Wulai Atayal, missionaries from Canada rigorously converted the Atayal to Presbyterianism. Later, Australian missionaries also successfully converted many Atayal to Catholicism (Wen and Xiao, 1997). After their

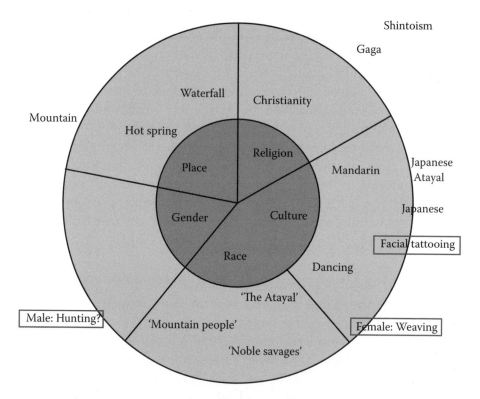

Figure 3.6: Shifts in the Atayal's multiple identities: after tourism development, 1945–1990

conversion to Christianity, their own belief (*gaga*) and Shintoism were quickly erased from their religious beliefs (represented as lying outside the outer ring in Figure 3.6).

In terms of their linguistic identity, the Atayal had to learn a third language: Mandarin. When in 1949 the Nationalist KMT government occupied Taiwan, the Atayal were fluent in Japanese, and had even integrated some Japanese words into Atayal, but the Nationalists forbade the Atayal to speak their hybrid language. All instructions in schools were conducted in Mandarin, and the young Atayal eventually lost their ability to speak their own indigenous language.

International tourism development in the Wulai Atayal area encouraged the speaking of Japanese. After 1956, when Chiang Kai-shek established a new tourism policy, the growth rate of the tourism industry exceeded more than 23 per cent annually for two decades (Copper, 2003). The tourism industry became a major source of income – foreign exchange – and provided significant employment opportunities in Taiwan, including nearby Wulai. In 1964, the Administrative Office of the Wulai Scenic Area was founded (Hsieh, 1994). The number of tourists coming to Wulai was estimated to average about 3,000 per day from the mid-1960s to the early 1990s (ibid.). The Japanese constituted the largest number of visitors to the area. During this period, tourism revenues became the most important economic resource for local residents (ibid.).

It had been a generation since the Wulai Atayal attached the traditional meanings to their facial tattooing rituals, head-hunting and weaving, but it did not take long for them to reinvent their traditions. Tourism was not the major catalyst in reinvigorating their heritage but it played a part in influencing outcomes and meanings by creating a changing market for textiles. The older Atayal women with facial tattoos became photo subjects for the Japanese who came back to Taiwan not as colonisers but as tourists. Meanwhile, young female Atayal wore costumes and danced for Japanese tourists because it was easier for them to earn income by dancing than to weave, which was very time-consuming. The Atayal men were largely absent from the tourism scene, and tourism jobs placed more emphasis on the Atayal women, once again shifting the gendered division of labour among the Wulai Atayal. The Atayal men are believed to have been engaged in some animal-hunting activities, not head-hunting; however, their voices were not collected directly in this research and thus this cannot be confirmed.

The Atayal were still categorized racially as 'Atayal', but their naming had shifted from 'facial tattooed savages' to 'noble savages' and from 'Formosan Race' to 'Mountain People' in the eyes of the Japanese (Figure 3.6). In tourism brochures, the Wulai Atayal were described as 'simple, wild, healthy and passionate'. According to Jahoda (1999: 11), during the Enlightenment period the idealized noble savage represented a 'state of closeness to nature, simplicity, freedom and robust health as a counterpoint to what were felt by some to be the evils of a corrupt civilization and lack of liberty'. During the Japanese colonial period, the indigenous people were portrayed as uncivilized, barbaric savages. They were represented as colonial Others who were the subject of Japan's civilizating and modernizing mission. After Japan's colonization was over, the Atayal were idealized as noble savages with a strong heritage who were close to nature. Those images were created to manipulate the desires of Japanese tourists who were in search of exotic Others.

In terms of their place identity, Wulai's unique landscapes, with the hot spring and waterfall, were commodified for the Japanese tourists. While the Han Chinese dominated the lower hill of Wulai, the Atayal were displaced to the upper hill of Wulai. After the development of international tourism occurred, the segregation of residential areas between Han Chinese and the indigenous residents became clearer as wealthier Han Chinese were able to purchase land in the valley bottom and gained profits through tourism businesses. Thus, the Atayal were further marginalized within their own community, both spatially and economically.

THE RISE OF DEMOCRACY AND THE DECLINE OF INTERNATIONAL TOURISM (1987–PRESENT)

After the lifting of martial law in 1987, the Progressive Democratic Party (DPP) was created as the first opposition party in Taiwan (Cauquelin, 2004). In 1996 Lee Teng-hui organized Taiwan's first free and fair presidential election (Manthorpe, 2005). Lee's victory in the 1996 democratic election was the sign of the complete transition to democracy in Taiwan (ibid.). In 2000 Taiwan organized the second presidential election. The presidential candidate of the opposition DPP, Chen Shui-Bian, broke the KMT's 55-year monopoly on state power in Taiwan (Simon, 2002). During his presidential campaign, Chen had placed indigenous rights at the centre of his platform. His election was clearly a victory for the native Taiwanese majority and for the forces advocating Taiwanese independence (Arrigo et al., 2002). Meanwhile, the indigenous rights movement was by this time active around the globe. In Taiwan, two organizations, the Alliance of Taiwan Aborigines and the Presbyterian Churches in Taiwan, were organized to promote this movement (Allio, 1998; Stainton, 2002).

At the same time, the Wulai tourism enterprise changed its emphasis from international to domestic and cross-Straits tourism. Due to China's entry into the global tourism market as well as Chiang Ching-kuo's lifting of martial law, the market trend favoured China over Taiwan in the late 1980s. With shifts in the market, the number of Japanese tourists declined and some indigenous female residents in Wulai left their jobs in tourism. With the advance of democracy, the rise of Taiwan's independence movement, the growth of the global indigenous rights movement since the late 1980s and the decline of international tourism in Wulai, the Wulai Atayal experienced another big change in their life.

During the 'golden era' of international ethnic tourism development in Wulai from the mid-1960s to the early 1990s, the indigenous residents of Wulai were represented as 'noble savages', and in fact this image continues today. By portraying the indigenous residents as 'classic people' who do 'classic works', the tourism brochures still construct the image of the Atayal as noble savages. Although this English term is not used specifically, the Atayal are described as being brave, honest, simple and in harmony with nature in tourism brochures and are similarly romanticized in Japanese travel writing. Since the Taiwanese-led government positioned the indigenous peoples as a crucial icon of Taiwan's national identity, the diversity in cultures has been celebrated (Arrigo et al., 2002) and the indigenous people have been encouraged by government policies and funding to 'reinvent their traditions'. In the case of Wulai, the Atayal women's weaving culture was selected as a way to promote their indigenousness. As noted above, until Japan banned the Atayal from getting facial tattoos, weaving was a symbol of women's gender identity. Sixty-two years later, weaving was revitalized, but its meaning has changed for some Atayal: weaving now represents the collective ethnic identity of the Atayal (Figure 3.7 overleaf). In Wulai, all junior high school students are now encouraged to learn the Atayal language and to learn traditional culture. Traditionally, weaving was considered to be strictly a woman's task, but now all students are free to learn how to weave regardless of their gender. One of the weavers who is in favour of this change expressed her opinion that 'if we stick to our tradition too much, we will not have enough weavers in the future, and our skills will eventually be diminished'. On the other hand, others are strongly against men weaving, since as we have seen there has been a clear gendered division of labour in the Atayal's traditional society.

For the Atayal males who have difficulty in accepting men's involvement with weaving, their gender identity can still be constructed through men's game-hunting activities. Atayal men who go game-hunting were not interviewed directly for this chapter, so this interpretation of contemporary men's perspectives on the construction of their gendered identity has yet to be confirmed.[2] Nevertheless, some evidence gathered via participant observation suggests that this might be the case: although head-hunting is no longer practised, the Atayal men constitute their gendered identity by game-hunting (Figure 3.7).

Facial tattooing is still an important symbol of the Wulai Atayal. In Wulai, objects depicting tattooed faces are found in various artistic forms:

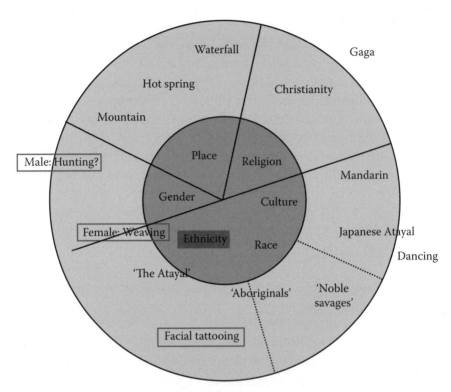

Figure 3.7: Shifts in the Atayal's multiple identities: after the rise of democracy in Taiwan and the decline in international tourism in Wulai, 1990–present

murals, totem poles, tapestry, paintings, framed pictures, business cards and, of course, weavings. The Wulai Atayal have also found a new way instantly to revive the facial tattooing culture by means of stickers; during the festival season, a number of Wulai Atayal men and women decorate their faces temporarily with artificial tattoos (Figure 3.8).

In addition, the indigenous residents have been encouraged by the national government to speak their indigenous language again. However, because the tourism development favoured Mandarin and Japanese over the Japanized Atayal language, the Wulai Atayal have struggled to revitalize their own language (Figure 3.7). The Wulai's hot spring and waterfall are still important landscape features for tourist consumption but most of the supporting businesses are now run by Han people. The fact that entrepreneurs from elsewhere run the businesses associated with the heritage of minorities is a common theme in the tourism literature.

Figure 3.8: Atayal women and a Han Chinese man with facial tattoo stickers
Source: Mami Yoshimura

Furthermore, the segregation of places between Han Chinese and the indigenous residents has deepened since the promotion of domestic tourism in Wulai. Some indigenous weavers have attempted to sell their hand-made weaving products, but they have had little success in competition with the factory-made weaving brought in by Han Chinese entrepreneurs. On the upper hill of Wulai, the Wulai Church symbolizes the Atayal's place and religious identity. The elder Atayal now try to teach *gaga* to the younger Atayal (at present it still lies outside the outer ring in Figure 3.7), but their religious belief is still very much influenced by Christianity.

CONCLUSION

This chapter has explored the Wulai Atayal's heritage and changing identity and how these have been modified through the experiences of the post-colonial history of Taiwan and the contemporary history of tourism development. The construction of the dichotomy between the civilized and the savage by the colonial state of Japan and its modification to 'noble savage' for Japanese tourists has also been discussed. Until the Japanese banned facial tattooing among the Atayal, cultural identity was constituted by the Atayal themselves on the basis of their facial tattoo patterns. These functioned as the Atayal's identity markers to distinguish who belonged to which communal group, until they were buried by the Japanese colonial regime about 100 years ago. After Japan's occupation was over, the Atayal's facial tattooing culture was appreciated as 'Other' culture only in the context of tourism. Today, the Wulai Atayal proudly speak of their facial tattooing culture, but using removable stickers, they temporarily reclaim and exhibit their culture only on special occasions (although in 2008 Shayun Foudu, a 33-year-old woman, became the first Atayal woman in 100 years to get her tribe's traditional facial tattoo: http://www.culturalsurvival.org/images/atayal-woman-taiwan, accessed 24 August 2009).

Once forbidden from doing so, the Atayal now celebrate their facial tattooing as well as weaving as a part of their ethnic identity. In the past, facial tattooing, head-hunting and weaving signified their gendered cultural identity, and today they have reconstructed their weaving using imported western equipment and have simulated facial tattoo practices as identity symbols. While it is unclear the extent to which the Atayal men's hunting activity in the mountains, albeit for different quarry, remains an important identity marker for their construction of place and gender identity (this needs to be further investigated by collecting the voices of the Atayal men), what is clear is that Atayal culture is being modified to meet contemporary values, such as is seen in the commercial production of traditional motifs on tee-shirts and machine-made cloth.

Although colonial discourse is produced within the society and the culture of the colonizers, their situated knowledge also becomes how the colonized see themselves. It creates a deep conflict in the minds of the colonized people as it is not consonant with their other knowledge about the world. The 'weaving for the Atayal's collective ethnic identity as the Atayal' is a good example to highlight the conflicts that the colonized people have experienced. Once weaving represented women's gender identity. Now, regardless of gender, weaving has been promoted as an Atayal 'ethnic symbol' by the Han Chinese government. Some Atayal have accepted the changes in the meaning of weaving but others still struggle to accept them.

Atayal heritage has been commodified and has become a tourist attraction, albeit one among a number in Wulai. It is ironic that the Japanese banned facial tattoos but returned as tourists to photograph elderly women who retained this feature. Textiles, which were once also banned, have been revived and have become a part of the heritage tourism product of Wulai but in two forms: a high quality hand-made product which is essentially a labour of love and, being relatively expensive, does not sell well to a domestic market; and a machine-made product made and sold by Han entrepreneurs who benefit financially from an appropriated and modified expression of Atayal culture.

All heritage and identity are constructed through the recognition of differences. Identities are relational and dynamic: they are socially constructed and change over time. Moreover, identities are not singular but multiple. In discussion of the relational construction of identity, Gombay (2005) argued the importance of examining why an identity was invented or adopted by individuals or groups. In the case of the Wulai Atayal, their indigenous identities were also relational, primarily with respect to the attributes of the colonizers, and made up of multiple components such as place, religion, ethnicity, race, culture and gender. These have evolved over time in response to Japanese colonialism, post-colonialism, Han neo-colonialism and tourism. The Wulai Atayal's multiple identities are intertwined and their reconstruction of multiple identities is an on-going task as their struggles and resistance against powerful 'Others' continue.

NOTES

1   Funds for research in summer 2006 were provided under a grant obtained by Geoffrey Wall from the Social Sciences and Humanities Research Council of Canada. We thank all Atayal and other residents of Wulai, Taiwan. Particularly, we owe a debt of gratitude to Sa-yun, Alice Takewatan and Philip and Tammy Diller for their great hospitality and friendship. We would also like to thank Janet Chang, Penny Fang, Sally Weng, Yu-Hsin Liao, David Ma, Jenn-Yeu Yang, Tw-Wen Wei, Masaharu Kasahara, Katsuhiko Yamaji, Maoko Miyaoka, Naoki Ishigaki, Taira Nakamura, Yuka Sugino from the Tenri Art Museum, Scott Simon and Jody Decker.

2   It is worth examining how the Atayal men have pursued their gendered identity as male Atayal but this is beyond the scope of this chapter.

CHAPTER 4

Outdoor Ethnographic Museums, Tourism and Nation Building in Southeast Asia

Michael Hitchcock and Nick Stanley[1]

INTRODUCTION

Outdoor ethnographic museums in Southeast Asia enjoyed huge popularity in the late twentieth century, not only with tourists – both domestic and international – but also with the governments that were involved in their inauguration. These developments were often linked to international tourism projects involving EU and UNESCO consultants. The creators of these 'living museums' did not simply rely on an established format, but often synthesized different and sometimes antithetic approaches, often without clear acknowledgement of their sources. On the one hand they drew some of their inspiration from the world fair or exposition style, which emerged in the nineteenth century and continues today in international trade fairs, while on the other the readily detectable concern with education and entertainment – or 'edutainment' – that is widely associated with Disney (Kalakota and Whinstone, 1997: 264) harks back to both the Skansen-style folk museums of Europe and the Disney-style world showcase displays (Hitchcock, Stanley and Siu, 1997). The Southeast Asian open-air museums are laid out in outdoor village style, but differ from their European antecedents in distinct ways. The European Skansen-style museums usually comprised conserved and relocated original dwellings, whereas the Southeast Asian displays are largely based on reconstructions.

In short they are Asian hybrids, part open-air museum and part theme park, that serve a multiplicity of audiences, neither strictly academic nor overtly popular, for which Hendry has adopted the Japanese rendition, *tēma pàku*, or theme park (Hendry, 2000: 19).

A recurring theme, however, in these Southeast Asian ethnographic displays is the role played by nationalism, often of the Herderian kind, in binding together amalgams of diverse peoples. These structures often provided showcases for national construction and national consciousness projects and thus may be understood as forms of codification that express the realities of emergent nations (Hefner, 1994: 94) and the statements of the officialdom that either built them or encouraged their development (Anderson, 1973). It is this latter usage that has attracted the attention of Western analysts (e.g. Anderson, 1973; Pemberton, 1994; Wood, 1997; Hitchcock, 2003), but what this chapter addresses is whether or not these didactic approaches exert much influence on the twenty-first century audiences for whom the priorities of late twentieth century governments in Southeast Asia, many of which were authoritarian at the time, are a thing of the past. The Sarawak cultural village in Kuching, however, remains an interesting exception because the Malaysian government, in order to emphasise its plurality, deliberately privileges Dayak cultures over others at Damai Beach as a mark of a loose federal unity. Within this it also privileges certain Dayak communities at the expense of others. The Chief Minister, as a Melanau, has ensured that the Melanau longhouse towers over others and dominates the site. The point is that this is a state-led rather than a federal-led enterprise, so that Kuching can privilege its own communities.

NATION-BUILDING PROJECTS

Like older established countries, the new nations of Southeast Asia have in the twentieth century looked to exemplary pasts to construct narratives justifying their birth and continued existence. Much has been written about the role of 'invented traditions' (Hobsbawm and Ranger, 1983) and 'imagined communities' (Anderson, 1983) in the evolution of the modern nation state. Diverse and locally bound cultures in these new nations are superseded by standardized cultures, usually carried by literacy (Anderson, 1983; Gellner, 1983). Choices made by the state are embodied in state-supported productions such as the construction of national monuments (Wood, 1984: 366). National identities may be expressed in diverse ways, some of the commonest being: the launching of a flagship carrying airline; the construction of grand capitals laid out according to symbolic principles; the inauguration of schools and universities bearing the names of illustrious national ancestors (Hitchcock, 1998).

The open-air village museum that has attracted the most academic scrutiny in this regard is arguably Indonesia's Taman Mini (*taman* = garden; *mini* = miniature) or Taman Mini Indonesia Indah (*Indonesia indah* = beautiful Indonesia) to give it its full title. Taman Mini serves as a showpiece of the state philosophy of *Pancasila* (five principles) and may be understood as a kind of codification, involving new forms of expression to address the realities of an emergent nation (Hefner, 1994: 94). Visited by both foreign and domestic tourists, Taman Mini represents the past as an integral part of the future, and serves as a tangible expression of modernization. Anderson argues that the Taman Mini project in particular was intended to make Indonesia known to tourists and to raise national consciousness (Anderson, 1973: 65). Tourism would provide a source of foreign revenue, enhance Indonesia's international reputation and would serve 'as a strategy for fostering domestic brotherhood' (Adamsf 1997c, 156–157). State propaganda combined with Taman Mini encourages domestic tourism as a means of consolidating national cohesion (Wood, 1997: 20).

The situation in Taiwan is somewhat different since, although its indigenous population may be regarded as culturally Southeast Asian, the island is deemed to be an inalienable part of China by the government of that country. The Japanese legacy to the Taiwanese, however, was the development of the South Country characterized by 'local colour' (Liao, 2002). Both of these developments lead the Taiwanese to self-exoticize as 'tropical people' with a distinct identity which indigenous Austronesian inhabitants served to underscore (see also Chapter 3). Taiwan's open-air village museums therefore could not be conceived as part of a nation-building strategy without offending its more powerful neighbour, though they share many features with those of the ASEAN region. Interestingly, the open-air ethnographic museums of China, which are often concerned with minorities that have ties with Southeast Asia, might helpfully be seen at least partially as an attempt at national consciousness-raising, since China's policies involve the incorporation of diverse ethnicities into a Chinese-dominated but also internally diverse majority population.

The Taiwan Aboriginal Cultural Park (TACP) and the Formosan Aboriginal Cultural Village (FACV) may also be likened to Taman Mini in their approach to questions of national and ethnic identity. Their overviews of Taiwan's ethnographic heritage are set within a narrative that smooths over the rough edges of real inter-ethnic relations. What also needs to be borne in mind is the intrusion of tourism into arenas usually associated with nation-building. An interesting issue is raised by MacCannell (1992: 158–159), who tries to distinguish the tourist's approach to ethnicity from earlier ethnological and colonial perspectives; he goes on to suggest that in certain cases, which he does not specify, tourism superficially resembles the behaviour of ethnic separatist movements.

The political context is, however, changing as the 'Taiwanese' and younger 'mainlanders' increasingly emphasize their separateness from China. These changes may be detected in attitude surveys of Taiwanese visitors to the National Palace Museum, particularly among younger age groups (Wu, 1998). Visitors continue to enjoy the splendour of the salvaged heritage of China, but increasingly expect a more explicit Taiwanese focus.

MEDIATION OF ETHNICITY

In order to appreciate how ethnicity is presented in Southeast Asian open-air village museums it is also helpful to consider the so-called 'primordial' and 'situational' or 'instrumental' approaches to ethnicity (Rex, 1986: 26–27). The first of these perspectives, the 'primordial' view, sees ethnicity as dependent on a series of 'givens': by being born into a particular community, by adopting its values (e.g. religion) and speaking its specific language, or even dialect of a language, and following a set of cultural practices that are associated with that community (Geertz, 1963b: 109). Generally speaking, Skansen-type museums are constructed on Herderian lines and tend to interpret ethnicity in primordial terms.

In contrast, the situational or instrumental perspective offers a more dynamic view that places emphasis on ethnicity as a set of processes and social relations, which may be invoked according to circumstances. The latter approach places emphasis on ethnicity as a set of social relationships and processes by which cultural differences are communicated and maintained. In order that an identity may be understood, it has to be constantly invoked through intentional agency and it may be argued that the open-air museum comprises such agency. The social communication of cultural difference may be observed and described, though these activities are elusive and difficult to quantify analytically, not least because ethnicity cannot be reduced to a fixed system of signs (Eriksen, 1991: 130).

The Taiwanese open-air museums differ in some important respects from those of Southeast Asia because classificatory systems adopted by Japanese anthropologists during the Japanese occupation (1895–1945) continue to be used in their layout and interpretation, though no Taiwanese anthropologist has defined the term 'ethnic group' (Hsieh, 1994: 185). Like the Japanese, the Taiwanese recognize certain attributes – common language, customs or social organization – as markers of ethnicity, but do not appear to have subjected the ethnic names themselves to great scrutiny. The open-air ethnographic museums of Taiwan provide particularly interesting venues to analyse these processes at a time of change.

In view of the on-going commercial and cultural ties between Japan and Taiwan, it may also be helpful to draw a parallel with the Japanese movement known as *muraokoshi*, which made widespread use of tourism to revitalize rural villages. This approach involved various efforts by villagers and local government officials to revive village economy and society in the face of out-migration, economic stagnation and population aging (Moon, 1997: 182). It is also worth noting that the *muraokoshi* type of tourism development is often associated with a search for local identity; in many village re-vitalization movements special effort has been made to recreate or rediscover the unique features of local culture that sets the destination apart from what are regarded as the internationalized or bland characteristics of metropolitan culture (ibid.: 183). In many cases what is perceived to be local culture has been reconstructed through careful study and investigation, often with the aid of volunteer groups that were formed to recover forgotten local history and to reconstruct extinct local cultural traditions (ibid.). The resurgence of folklore studies (*minzokugaka*) in the late 1960s and 1970s paved the way for the development of folk museums, and by the late twentieth century there were more than 200 of them throughout Japan, reflecting the endeavours of numerous amateur local historians and ethnologists (ibid.).

The open-air museums of Taiwan stick in the main to the classificatory systems used by the Japanese and do not, with one exception, question their applicability. As Hsieh (1994) has argued, however, the indigenous people were virtually created as distinct groups by the Japanese occupation's ethnographers. For example, the existence of the Atayal (in the official phonetic spelling) or T'aiya (in the romanization of Chinese pronunciation), the second largest indigenous group, may be dated from 1898 when they were first identified as such by Japanese ethnographers. As Hseih points out the Atayal are a diverse group distributed over eight counties, who may be further sub-divided into three smaller groups: the Atayal proper, the Tseole and the Sedeq. This distinction is based on linguistic evidence, though Taiwanese scholars maintain that a common set of cultural features exist among these scattered people (Hsieh, 1994: 186), though why the ethnonym 'Atayal', the name of one of the groups, should be used as the over-arching term remains unclear. Similar observations can doubtless be made for the other eight or nine indigenous groups of Taiwan. To complicate matters the managerial concerns of the state also cut across these issues since the Taiwanese government recognizes 30 *shan ti hsiang* (mountainous administrative units) for the *shan ti jen* (literally 'mountain people').

Another problem with the presentation of identity is that few, if any, of Taiwan's indigenous people still live in the manner suggested by the reconstructed displays, as is also the case in many parts of Southeast Asia. With regard to the Taiwanese system, the Atayal maintain some traditional features in order to distinguish themselves from the Han and to glorify the culture inherited from their ancestors. 'Traditional culture' for them comprises items of material culture and observable activities such as the celebration of the harvest festival (ibid.: 193).

What is significant, however, is that the Atayal – who speak Mandarin, live in concrete multi-storied dwellings and who wear the same clothes and share the same values as the Han – still differentiate themselves from the majority (see also Chapter 3). They refer to themselves as Daiyan as opposed to the Mugan (Taiwanese), Kelu (Mainlanders) and Kelang (Hakka) (ibid.). The term Daiyan is said by some Atayal to mean 'human' and is a name for themselves alone, whereas others maintain that it is a general name for all the aboriginal people of Taiwan. Hsieh argues that the two separate meanings allow the Atayal simultaneously to claim Atayal and pan-aboriginal identities. Ethnicity in this context may be seen as an adaptive strategy to cope with a complex environment in which the Taiwanese control access to many economic and political resources, especially tourism. Hsieh argues that, in the absence of many of the cultural symbols commonly associated with ethnicity, ethnically oriented tourism fills the gap (ibid.: 196–197). His perspective resembles MacCannell's observations on the similarities of identities constructed in tourism to those advanced by ethnic separatist groups (Hitchcock, 2003).

EDUTAINMENT IN TAIWAN

The Formosan Aboriginal Cultural Village (FACV) in Nantou County, which was completed in the late 1980s, comprises three distinct areas: an Amusement Isle with theme park rides, shows and shops; a European Palace Garden with restaurant, coffee shop and miniature railway; and the Aboriginal Sights and Villages comprising collections of reconstructed buildings representing the nine indigenous peoples. The latter area invokes academic authority through the use of plaques bearing the names and other cultural details of the nine peoples, but confuses the issue with a display area dedicated to 'Indian Totem Poles' comprising copies of carvings from the America's North-West Coast as well as a Maori post from New Zealand.

The material culture buildings combine originals and reproductions, and the layout follows the fieldwork (1938–1943) and plans of the Japanese ethnographer Chijiiwa Suketaro. Not all the work is attributed to the Japanese, however, since the men's house in the Puyuma village is based on research conducted by Wei Hui-lin in 1954. Costumed interpreters drawn from the indigenous people are on hand in the houses to welcome visitors and explain the displays, and to demonstrate crafts and cooking skills. The Naruwan Theatre has a seating capacity of 2,000 and visitors are entertained by 'the FACV Youth Troupe, made up of enthusiastic and talent [sic] young people from each tribe'. The shows follow the Polynesian Cultural Centre format with a pageant of canoes, dances and games of daring involving the audience. The FACV employs an artistic director, and a backstage team looks after costume repairs, props and make-up. Cloth woven by employees is used both for costumes and for souvenirs, and a sign in the Atayal compound advertises 'Rent clothes'.

In comparison with the FACV, the Taiwan Aboriginal Cultural Park (TACP) in Pin-dan County, which was founded in 1986, has sought a 'purist' approach (Stanley, 1998: 76). Built on a steep hillside overlooking a river, the park follows the cultural village format with compounds of houses representing the nine indigenous groups. Visitors enter the TACP via a courtyard containing shops selling indigenous handicrafts, and a museum that displays photographs relating to research by Japanese ethnographers in the late 1890s. The exhibitions cover the material culture of the indigenous people in detail, and there are reconstructions of ritual events such as the canoe launch. The interpretation in the reconstructed dwellings is detailed with maps, diagrams and text in both Chinese and English.

The text acknowledges the contribution of the Japanese, but does not shy away from some of the more controversial aspects of the occupation. The Atayal, for example, are said to have lived a more independent existence prior to the arrival of the Japanese, who forced them into village settlements. What is hinted at is that the village format may reflect Japanese imposed norms, though how settlements were organized before this period remains unclear. The text also reflects on the sub-divisions within the different groupings, and mentions cultural exchanges between the Han and the indigenous peoples. The interpretation includes a great deal of botanical information and the TACP's general impression is more scientific and academic than the FACV's. There is another exhibition hall within the park that has slide shows on indigenous culture, displays on aboriginal life and narrative boards devoted to Bunun pictographs. A medley of indigenous song and dance performances can be watched in the theatre, which holds around 2,000, and audience participation is encouraged, particularly with regard to the Taiwan custom of catching a soft ball on a long spiked pole.

EDUCATION AND RECREATION IN TAMAN MINI

Taman Mini's visitors may be divided into two categories: students and school children who come for educational reasons and those that visit for recreational purposes. There are around four million visitors a year and despite attempts to market the museum internationally, overseas visitors have declined in response to the various crises that have engulfed Indonesia since the fall of President Soeharto in 1998. The site is complex with only the central area being devoted to the collection of traditional houses for which Taman Mini is renowned. The museum's educational role is largely focused on raising awareness of Indonesia's arts and cultural heritage, though there is also provision for undertaking environmental studies in the related sites containing the Aquarium, Insect Museum and Bird Park. To reach out to those who are not engaged in educational activities, the museum endeavours to create a recreational atmosphere that will draw the visitors into educational activities that are regarded as enriching.

The visitors may be divided between those with leisure or educational expectations, but there would appear to be a considerable overlap between what motivates them. According to a study produced in 2005, 62.07 per cent of all visitors expected to learn about Indonesian art and culture during the course of their visit, with only 33.79 per cent expecting fun and entertainment (Wulandari, 2005: 36). Recreation featured strongly (52.41 per cent) in the reasons for visiting as compared with only 13.79 per cent wishing to learn about Indonesia's diversity and another 12.41 per cent wishing to learn about Indonesian culture.

The study is indicative and not definitive, but the results are nonetheless intriguing since they seem to indicate a mis-match between what is desired and expected by visitors in the twenty-first century and what were the original intentions of the founders, former President Soeharto and the late Mrs Tien Soeharto. In the presidential address that was published in the first official guide, Soeharto makes it clear that 'By visiting this Park we will know ourselves better, we will know our nation better and we will love our motherland more' (Soeharto, 1975b: 9). The museum's nation-building mission may be lost on what appear to be the majority of contemporary visitors and perhaps never was immediately apparent to visitors right from the outset, but another of the founders' initial motives appears to have stood the test of time. In the official guide, Mrs Tien Soeharto discusses the importance of using Taman Mini to stimulate and develop regional handicrafts to 'encourage communications, mutual knowledge and understanding among nations' (Tien Soeharto, 1975a: 13), and according to Wulandari's study this is pretty much what the contemporary visitor expects today.

Wulandari's study may indicate some of the enduring features of Taman Mini, but she cautions against being overly optimistic about the role of traditional culture in twenty-first century Indonesia, and points out that that the young are more interested in modern technology and Western products than out of date and unfashionable Indonesian traditions. Her conclusion is that the young are not readily receptive to didactic attempts to interpret Indonesian culture, and that they expect to learn in ways that interest them and without any hint of compulsion (2005: 57) and that whatever the founders' intentions, Taman Mini seems to be heading down the route of edutainment.

Interestingly, what seems to have become more explicit in recent years, though it was apparent in the original foundation, is the link between Taman Mini and tourism. The main focus for this is the original pavilions representing traditional houses from each of Indonesia's provinces, though there is considerable variety in how they manifest themselves. Some pavilions seem to have little connection with the promotion of tourism, whereas others appear to be acutely conscious of the need to use the facilities to promote tourism and other trading activities. One province in particular, Lampung, seems to be making a determined effort to utilize its pavilion to promote its cultural attributes and developmental potential, complete with its own illustrated guidebook, written in Indonesian and English, and an actively engaged pavilion manager. The pavilion is well staffed, well maintained and organizes a busy cultural programme, a complete contrast to some of the other pavilions that appear to be in a state of advanced neglect. Since the fall of Soeharto, Indonesia has embarked on a programme of decentralization, and this may explain Lampung's enthusiasm to promote itself, though why some of the other regions seem to be less engaged remains unclear.

The Irian Jaya pavilion has yet to be renamed and there are still Asmat carvers (and non-carvers) regularly decorating it rather than carving in the enclosure. Following the devolvement of centralized decision-making to numerous Kabupaten (Regencies/Districts) in the provinces and the prospect of the division of Irian Jaya into two provinces, the whole premise of Taman Mini is likely to be thrown into further dramatic disarray. Taman Mini does, however, have some adaptive capacity as is exemplified by the pavilion of the breakaway former province of East Timor, which has become the 'Museum of East Timor', a memorial to the period of Indonesian rule.

CONCLUSION

Taman Mini, Indonesia's renowned open-air museum, and its counterparts in Taiwan struggle to make sense of some complex and messy ethnographic realities on behalf of their respective audiences. The issues to be juggled include: contemporary re-evaluations of the work of earlier researchers, notably in Taiwan; a lack of coherence between administrative and ethno-cultural boundaries; the need to be educational while simultaneously being entertaining; competition from other sources of information that can often offer more fun; and changes in the political landscape, particularly the move away from overtly authoritarian rule and the tendency to be didactic on behalf of the national interest.

Certain themes endure and appear to have contemporary resonance, notably the use of handicrafts as enhancers of cross-cultural communication, but these open-air museums or *tēma påku* (theme parks) in Taiwan and Indonesia are starting to look dated in the twenty-first century. Measured alongside Butler's renowned 'Tourism Area Life Cycle Model' (1980), the graph that plots numbers of tourists against time, these museums appear to have passed the consolidation phase at the top of the curve, but whether they will rejuvenate or decline remains a moot point. Not only do both destinations have to contend with declines in international tourist interest, but their local markets have also become re-orientated, especially among the young with their lack of sympathy with pedantic attempts to interpret cultural heritage. Both might benefit from interpretative democratization offering alternative perspectives, not least a history of ideas that shows the circumstances in which they evolved. They might become venues for more serious inter-cultural dialogue using heritage to interconnect different communities and to move beyond national narratives that show a consistent and homogeneous view of history. Such approaches might lead to fresher visions of where they might be going and what issues are at stake – a kind of heritage future as it were.

NOTE

1   The authors gratefully acknowledge the support provided by the South-East Asia Committee of the British Academy, and would like to thank Ariel Wu and Anak Agung Ayu Wulandari for their help with this research.

CHAPTER 5

Histories, Tourism and Museums
Re-making Singapore[1]

Can-Seng Ooi

At one level, some see Singapore as a developed country. It has developed itself into an economic powerhouse in Southeast Asia since the 1950s, and like many other Asian cities it aims to be the financial and cultural capital of the region. At another level, Singapore is perceived by some as an authoritarian state (Chua, 1995; Ooi, 2005) yet one that is still exotic and part of the romantic Orient. Such conflicting images of Singapore have allowed its governmental authorities to re-imagine and re-market Singapore strategically in the world, so as to attract tourists, foreign direct investments, and talented foreign workers. As I will show in this chapter, in the context of tourism, Singapore attempts to self-Orientalize itself to attract more tourists, and at the same time to re-define many of the Oriental images in order to social-engineer its society and also to assert its dominance in the region.

Many researchers are interested in the social impact of tourism. There are at least three broad and interrelated streams of research in this area. The first is the most common. It addresses issues related to problems such as crowding of heritage sites, trinketization of local crafts, commodification of native social practices, sensationalization of indigenous folklores and even price inflation and traffic problems (Cohen, 1988; Philo and Kearns, 1993; van der Borg, Costa and Gotti, 1996; Watson and Kropachevsky, 1994). Some people even see tourism as a form of colonization and treat tourism as 'whorism' (Mathews, 1975). But not all social impacts of tourism are negative; studies have shown that over time seemingly alien cultural effects of tourism are welcomed and eventually appropriated into the destination (e.g. Boissevain, 1996; Erb, 2000; Martinez, 1996; Ness, 2003; Picard, 1995). Many researchers are thus advocating a balanced and sensitive approach to the management of tourism development (Chang, 1997; Jenkins, 1997; Newby, 1994; Teo and Yeoh, 1997).

A second, related, stream of research addresses the political dimensions in defining and managing the so-called sensitive and balanced approach to tourism development. While few researchers and practitioners disagree on the need for such an approach to tourism development, how is this need translated into practice? For instance, in using Giddens' 'Third Way', Burns (2004) paints a bipolar view of tourism planning. The first – 'leftist development first' – view focuses 'on sustainable human development goals as defined by local people and local knowledge. The key question driving development is "What can tourism give us without harming us?"' (Burns 2004). The second – 'rightist tourism first' – view aims to 'maximize market spread through familiarity of the product. Undifferentiated, homogenized product dependent on core [elements] with a focus on tourism goals set by outside planners and the international tourism industry' (Burns, 2004: 26). The Third Way brings different interests together and aims to generate consensus. Burns' Third Way remains conceptual. Different host societies have found their own ways to bring about sustainable tourism. Comparing Denmark and Singapore for instance, the Danish tourism development strategies aim to protect Danish society from the social impacts of tourism, while in Singapore the impacts are actively absorbed and appropriated into the social engineering programmes of the destination (Ooi, 2002a). Both the Danish and Singaporean authorities claim that their own tourism programmes are well balanced and sensitive to both tourism and local needs (Ooi, 2002a). The definition of a balanced approach is determined within the social and political contexts of the host society. The political process eventually decides which interest groups and lobbies have more influence and say.

The third stream of research on tourism impact relates to how the 'West' imagines less developed, non-Western destinations. Western imaginations are seen to affect these host societies and bring about another form of colonization. Except for a few studies, such as from Morgan and Pritchard (1998), Ooi, Kristensen and Pedersen (2004), Selwyn (1996) and Silver (1993), this area of research has received limited attention. This chapter is but a small contribution to this stream of research. Studies of this sort tend to examine the insidious effects of destination images on host societies. Not only are the images superficial and caricaturized, but these images are being imposed upon and reified in the host societies, resulting in the so-called West dominating the less developed host communities. Such studies draw inspiration from Edward W. Said's critique of Orientalism (Said, 1979; Leong, 1997; Ooi, Kristensen and Pedersen, 2004; Selwyn, 1996). The domination of the Orient by the West is the main focus in such studies; I propose a more nuaunced understanding of the Orientalization processes. The so-called Orient is not naïve nor necessarily helpless; the Orient can snap back and even become a colonizing master. This seems to be the case in Singapore.

This study compares the three main museums run by the Singapore National Heritage Board (NHB) – the National Museum of Singapore (NMS) (formerly the Singapore History Museum), the Singapore Art Museum (SAM) and the Asian Civilizations Museum (ACM). These museums present and assert various Asian identities of Singapore. This is part of the self-Orientalization process in the city-state. Western tourists have come to place demands on a destination like Singapore to become more Asian. The Singaporean tourism authorities and government attempt to Orientalize Singapore through these national museums, so as to serve the needs of tourism and nation building. This article will question the Saidian-inspired focus on how the Occident dominates the Orient; host societies can and do appropriate and re-invent Orientalist images for their own identity projects. The Orientalism debate should not just be about how the Occident dominates the subservient Orient; powerful groups in host destinations may adopt and revise Orientalist images to draw benefit from the tourism industry and to reconstruct local and regional identities. The Orientalization of host societies must be understood within the local social and political context.

In the next section, I elaborate on tourism as a form of domination through a Saidian framework. Subsequently, I present the case of the three national museums of Singapore. These museums were founded by the Singapore Tourism Board (STB) to make Singapore more Asian. The NMS establishes Singapore as a unique country in Southeast Asia, the SAM asserts Singapore as the cultural centre of Southeast Asia and the ACM traces Singaporeans' ancestral roots to China, India and the Middle East. The section that follows discusses how each of these museums Orientalizes Singapore, and how they each introduce new narratives to shape both tourist and local imaginations. These presented narratives nevertheless must be understood within the social, cultural and political circumstances of Singaporean society. The concluding section summarizes the arguments and advocates a more nuanced understanding of tourism as a form of domination in tourism and heritage research.

TOURISM AND ORIENTALISM

Following the critical footsteps of Foucault (1972), Said (1979) interrogated and challenged Orientalist studies. Said entwined political and cultural imperialism and argued that Orientalists – 'Western' writers and academics who study the 'Orient' – have misrepresented, and still misrepresent, the Middle Eastern Islamic world in a manner that has eased the way for the West to dominate the Orient. Said argued that Orientalism is not only an academic discipline but an ideological discourse inextricably tied to the perpetuation of Western power. Said reasoned that many Western scholars who study the Orient present and distribute particular images of the Orient, centred on the distinctiveness of the Oriental mind, as opposed to the Occidental mind. Such images create, essentialize and caricaturize the Orient, and the images do not correspond to empirical reality and reduce the significance of the varieties of language, culture, social forms and political structures in the so-called Orient. Hidden in the ideological underpinnings of Orientalism, the Orient is often imagined as inferior, despotic and uncivilized.

The logic and premises behind Said's attack on Orientalism have inspired many scholars to think critically about how people imagine other societies, and how people inadvertently disperse particular geopolitical messages in their activities. Orientalist debates have been extended to the study of places like Africa (Jeyifo, 2000; Mazrui, 2000), East Asia (Clarke, 1997; Dirlik, 1996; Hill, 2000; Hung, 2003) and Eastern Europe (Ash, 1989; Kumar, 1992; Ooi, Kristensen and Pedersen, 2004). Orientalism has also inspired scholars to look at how discourses have come to misrepresent and caricaturize the Other with regard to sex and gender (e.g. Albet-Mas and Nogue-Font, 1998; Lewis, 1996; Mann, 1997; Prasch, 1996), race and ethnicity (e.g. Jeyifo, 2000; Mazrui, 2000) and religion (e.g. Amstutz, 1997; Burke III, 1998; Kahani-Hopkins and Hopkins, 2002; Zubaida, 1995). Similarly, the North–South, Rich–Poor divides are seen as parallels to the Orient–Occident dichotomy. As a result, tacit and biased discourses are highlighted by many anti-globalization lobbies as they protest against the political, economic, social and cultural domination of the West (Chua, 2003; Klein, 2000; Shipman, 2002). Tourism researchers like Clifford (1997), Echtner and Prasad (2003), Morgan and Pritchard (1998), Ooi et al. (2004) and Silver (1993), have also drawn inspiration from Said.

Said's challenge against Orientalism is critical and political. Such a critical perspective identifies who benefits, who is subverted, who disseminates the Orientalist discourses, how the discourses are disseminated and the consequences of reifying the discourses. This approach thus identifies the messages transmitted and the embedded ideological meanings. In this perspective, all messages are seen as constructs that carry unequal relationships between the party that misrepresents the Other and the Other itself – words are chosen to load the presented messages, meanings are accentuated, while other meanings are selectively ignored. So for instance, in referring to the manner Singapore was presented in the British Broadcasting Corporation's *Holiday Programme* series, Morgan and Pritchard (1998: 225–228) show how Singapore's exoticism was selectively constructed with reference to its romantic colonial past, its Chinese medicine (dried lizards, seahorses and scorpions) and its autocratic rule. The programme did not mention that the current government was one of the parties who drove the British colonial masters out in the 1950s, that few Singaporeans use Chinese medicine as the first choice of cure today and that many of the so-called strict rules and regulations are also common in other countries, including in the UK. Implicit in the messages are: Singapore is a successful colonial legacy (thanks to the British); Singapore is still an exotic Asian destination; and Singapore is not a democracy. Viewers will get to experience Britain's colonial heritage in Singapore, see how those Asians heal themselves and experience life in an autocratic regime. Such types of images and messages enthuse certain viewers and help to sell destinations, but also caricaturize host societies.

> Such images are Orientalist in character. Firstly, the images are superficial and based on misinterpretations but are presented with authority and as factual. Secondly, the caricatures presented aim to reaffirm widely accepted views of the Other. Thirdly, the misrepresentations are systematically and institutionally disseminated, including through the mass media, tourism promotion activities and everyday hearsay. Fourthly, the messages construct the Other through the viewpoint of modern Western societies and, inadvertently or otherwise, judge the Other through the eyes of the West. Let me elaborate.

It is a challenge for foreign tourists to know the host society because their visits are relatively short, they lack local knowledge and they rely on filtered information from tourism mediators (Causey, 2003; Ooi, 2002b). A large majority of tourists have shallow, stereotypical and essentialized images of foreign destinations because their images are built from sources, including travel reviews, news stories, guide books and tales from family and friends, many of which are not reliable. For instance, movies help generate interest and create narratives for the consumption of places. Popular movies such as Braveheart and The Lord of the Rings have respectively promoted Scotland and New Zealand as tourist destinations. Not all movies-promoted narratives and images are positive and accurate. The Hollywood blockbuster, Tomb Raider, which is partly set in Angkor Wat (Cambodia), makes references to (non-existent) secret passageways, Egyptian hieroglyphs (in a Buddhist complex!) and subservient natives (submitting to the bad guys). To many conservationists, such references create new narratives for tourists that undermine the efforts to conserve the ancient Buddhist temple complex and introduce a more serious and historically accurate form of cultural tourism. (Winter, 2003)

While Western tourists harbour Orientalized images, these images are also being institutionalized and promoted by the non-Western destinations themselves. That is partly because the large numbers of affluent Western tourists are important for the local tourism industry. And these tourists' preconceptions have to be factored in when promoting the destination. For instance, Singapore is found to be clean, developed and efficient by most tourists, but promoting such modern achievements alone will not persuade Western tourists to come (Ooi, 2002b). While these modern-day comforts are important, Singapore, like many other Asian destinations, still needs to percolate and distil its Asian essence into tourist-friendly products to attract Western tourists. The Asian images constitute Singapore's unique selling proposition to the West; the modern comforts are essential but not unique selling points (Ooi, 2002b: 127). Many Western tourists are still drawn to exotic places that are different and relatively untouched by modernization (Errington and Gewertz, 1989; Jacobsen, 2000; MacCannell, 1976; Silver, 1993; Sørensen, 2003). And many of the promoted images feed into the 'Western consciousness' (Silver, 1993).

Besides providing the images Western tourists want, tourism promotion agencies also know that tourists' preconceptions affect tourists' experiences. Tourists seek out and affirm their preconceptions during their travels (McLean and Cooke, 2003; Prentice, 2004; Prentice and Andersen, 2000). Western tourists do not constitute a monolithic entity, and neither do they have a single Orientalist tourist imagination, thus tourism promotion agencies have to figure out and imagine what Westerners generally want from their destinations. These agencies – by frequently employing the help of major advertising companies based in Western cosmopolitan centres, as observed by Pritchard and Morgan (2000) – attempt to meet the various demands of Western (and also non-Western) tourists; they not only present Orientalist images of themselves, they also reify those images. As a result, 'authentic' cultural products are also created and staged for tourists. These products range from 'Voodoo' shows in Haiti (Goldberg, 1983) to selling Jewish 'religious' objects (such as skull caps and candles) in Israel (Shenhav-Keller, 1995) to visiting an 'original' Manggarai village in Indonesia (Allerton, 2003). Many exotic images freeze the host society in the past and ignore the changes and developments that the society has achieved. These images and reifications feed into the Orientalist tourist imagination. Therefore, researchers such as Echtner and Prasad (2003) and Silver (1993) have suggested that Third World representations in tourism foster a particular ideological position that places developing countries in an inferior position. These places are seen as backward, the natives eager to serve and the destination just a cultural playground.

Even museums, which are often institutions of authority and scholarship, have come to perpetuate the Orientalist imagination. Museums function as 'contact zones' (Clifford, 1997). Contact zones are sites where geographically and historically separate groups establish on-going relations. Clifford (1997) examines the ways 'primitive' societies are represented in 'civilized' museums, which reflect an on-going ideological matrix that governs how 'primitive' societies respond to and are perceived by 'civilized' people through these museums. Museums construct the Other under their own assumptions and worldviews, and the Other re-imagines itself in, and responds to, the exhibitions. Museums have become sites for people to reflect on who they are, and the ideological matrix behind the identities presented is partly shaped by the imagination of the Other (Ness, 2003).

In sum, researchers have argued that tourism can be a form of domination, not just in terms of tourists' presence and meeting tourism demands. Tourism can also transmit a set of inaccurate discourses and misrepresentations to less developed and non-Western countries (Morgan and Pritchard, 1998; Ooi, Kristensen and Pedersen, 2004; Selwyn, 1996; Silver, 1993). As a result, 'tourism marketing is one of the many forms of Third World representation that, in sometimes subtle but nonetheless serious ways, serves to maintain and reinforce colonial discourse and the power relations and ideology it fosters' (Echtner and Prasad, 2003). Inadvertently or otherwise, these caricaturized images may form the basis for non-Western destinations to imagine, re-invent and transform themselves (Morgan and Pritchard, 1998; Ooi, Kristensen and Pedersen, 2004).

In considering tourism as a form of imperialism, there is a tendency to focus on how tourists dominate the destination as if the host society is passive and submissive. The view of a docile and submissive host society is not correct, as I will show in how the museums in Singapore Orientalize the city-state.

MAKING SINGAPORE MORE ASIAN

In 1995, while facing fierce competition in the tourism industry, the Singapore Tourist Promotion Board (STPB) (present-day STB)[2] and the Ministry of Information and the Arts (MITA) released a blueprint to make Singapore into a 'Global City for the Arts'. Among other things, Singapore was to have the NMS, SAM and ACM (Chang, 2000; Chang and Lee, 2003; Singapore Tourist Promotion Board and Singapore Ministry of Information and the Arts, 1995; Singapore Tourist Promotion Board, 1996). These three museums were to showcase the island's unique Asian identities. From the late 1980s, Singapore began to find its modern and efficient image less attractive, as tourists flocked to more exotic destinations in Southeast Asia (Singapore: National Tourism Plan Committees, 1996). Singapore was being perceived as just another modern city.

The thrust of the tourism strategy since the mid-1990s has been to communicate the image of Singapore as a destination where the modern blends with the old; the East blends with the West (Ooi, 2004). So despite the city's ubiquitous modern manifestations, the STB tries to show that aspects of the exotic East are actually embedded in Singapore's development and progress. For example, tourists are told that many skyscrapers in Singapore are built with the ancient Chinese practice of geomancy in mind, that there are many restaurants serving international western dishes with Asian spices and that most Singaporeans are able to speak their own version of English (known as Singlish) besides standard English. Other attempts at making Singapore more Asian include conserving and enhancing Chinatown, Little India and the Malay Village, selling tour products that highlight the Asian soul in the city-state's modern settings and producing souvenir products that accentuate Singapore's Asianness (Chang and Teo, 2001; Ooi, 2002b). The creation of the three museums, all managed by the National Heritage Board (NHB), is yet another attempt to make Singapore unique and more Asian. These museums tell locals and foreigners about Singapore's 'Asianness', with each museum constructing, interpreting and asserting different Asian identities for the city.

The museums took on an even more significant role in the Singaporean economy when, in 2000, the MITA pushed the 1995 initiatives further and envisaged Singapore as a 'Renaissance City' (Singapore: Ministry of Information and the Arts, 2000). Building and expanding on the 2000 Renaissance City report, the government-commissioned Economic Review Committee–Services Subcommittee Workgroup on Creative Industries (ERC–CI, 2002) produced the most ambitious and comprehensive blueprint yet on the creative economy, which includes explicit and specific plans to develop Singapore into a creative economy. The arts, culture, heritage and tourism are considered central in Singapore's emerging creative economy. The NMS, SAM and ACM feature prominently in this scheme of things. These museums are part of a stock of icons indicating that Singapore is culturally vibrant and creative, and will help drive Singapore's fledgling creative industries and tourism needs.

THE NATIONAL MUSEUM OF SINGAPORE

The NMS, housed in a purpose-built neo-classical museum building, has had a chequered history since its founding in 1887. It underwent dramatic changes and was named the National Museum in 1965, after Singapore became independent. It then became the Singapore History Museum in 1996. In December 2006, after the building was expanded and renovated, the museum became the National Museum of Singapore.

The NMS will have none of any generalized images people may have of Singapore as just another Asian country. It aims to showcase trends and developments that have characterized and influenced Singapore, highlighting the emergence of contemporary Singapore (Singapore Tourist Promotion Board and Singapore Ministry of Information and the Arts, 1995). In its new permanent exhibition on Singapore's past, it starts with Singapore as a fishing village known as Temasek some 700 years ago, then moves to Singapore's colonial past (from 1819 to 1963). The visitor is shown how, during Singapore's colonial period, the island went through difficult times: poverty, social problems, racial conflicts, the Second War World, the struggle for self-rule and the communist threat. Then in 1963 Singapore became part of Malaysia, but that merger ended dramatically in 1965. Fortunately, the viewer is told, economic successes came soon after Singapore's independence in 1965, thanks to the actions of the efficient and effective People's Action Party government. One has to use an audio guide to get through the exhibition because the exhibits are labelled only with numbers. The emphasis is on story-telling. There are many video presentations – interviews, reconstructions of accounts and documentaries – to enliven the stories.

The basic message from this Singapore history gallery is that Singapore is not British, nor is it Japanese or Malaysian; Singapore is a unique Asian entity. Since its independence in 1965, the People's Action Party government has promoted a 'Singaporean Singapore' policy. This policy aims at giving equal treatment to all citizens regardless of their ethnicity. Singaporeans of different ethnic groups are encouraged to interact.

In sum, the NMS story tells visitors that Singaporeans have their own identity. The Singapore history gallery is complemented by the 'Singapore Living' permanent exhibitions, which focus on Singaporean lifestyles in the past, including women's fashion, the local film industry, early family structures and food cultures. The permanent exhibitions challenge any simplified preconceptions that Singapore is like its neighbours in Southeast Asia. A distinctive Singaporean identity has been actively engineered and has now emerged. The Singapore population may have started with migrants from the region but Singapore is now a unique country and society.

THE SINGAPORE ART MUSEUM

In contrast to the NMS, the Singapore Art Museum (SAM) presents a Southeast Asian regional identity for Singapore. The museum opened in January 1996 and showcases contemporary Southeast Asian visual arts (SAM, 2007; www.nhb.gov.sg/SAM/Information/AboutUs/AboutUs.htm). It is one of the first art museums with international standard museum facilities and programmes in Southeast Asia. Dedicated to the collection and display of twentieth-century Singaporean and Southeast Asian modern and contemporary art, the SAM joins a league of new-generation museums around the world with well-executed exhibitions and community outreach programmes. It houses the national art collection of Singapore and has the largest collection of twentieth-century Southeast Asian art owned by any public institution.

The SAM plays a big part in the programme to develop Singapore into an internationally acknowledged arts city and the cultural centre of Southeast Asia. Besides the SAM, the newly opened Esplanade–Theatres on the Bay (a gigantic complex by the sea and right in the city centre) also play a significant role in promoting Singapore as a contemporary art destination, but by offering visual art performances.

In contrast to the NMS's message that Singapore is unique in Southeast Asia, the SAM presents Singapore as having strong and closely intertwined relationships with Southeast Asia. Singapore was a founding member of the Association of Southeast Asian Nations (ASEAN), along with Indonesia, Malaysia, the Philippines and Thailand, in 1967 as an anti-Communist political alliance. Other countries have since joined: Brunei, Burma (Myanmar), Cambodia, Laos and Vietnam. The current ten member states adhere to different religions, speak different languages and were colonized by different foreign powers in the last centuries. Some were even recent enemies; for example, Vietnam occupied Cambodia between 1979 and 1989, and was a Cold War adversary of the original ASEAN members. The SAM bundles Southeast Asia into a single aesthetic entity; perhaps because the area's countries are geographically close, the countries are also assumed to be culturally similar. Despite the fact that Southeast Asia is heterogeneous and does not have a clearly distilled identity, the SAM nevertheless builds on the perception that many people around the world conceive Southeast Asia as a region. The SAM has now formulated yet another Southeast Asian identity, as an aesthetic region.

The SAM acknowledges that the artistic communities in Southeast Asia and their experiences are diversely rich (Sabapathy, 1996). Thus the museum employs a harmony-in-diversity strategy to affirm Southeast Asia as an aesthetic entity. Common themes are used to bring disparate works of art together: 'Nationalism, revolution and the idea of the modern', 'Traditions of the real', 'Modes of abstraction', 'Mythology and religion: traditions in tension', 'The self and the other' and 'Urbanism and popular culture'. The SAM's curators are constantly reminded by their bosses that they have to maintain their museum's unique proposition by presenting a Southeast Asian identity in their exhibitions.

The construction of such an aesthetic region is however politically sensitive despite pronouncements of close friendship amongst ASEAN members. For instance, ASEAN foreign ministers declare that '[w]hile fully respecting each member country's sovereignty and national property rights, ASEAN recognizes that the national cultural heritage of member countries constitute the heritage of Southeast Asia for whose protection it is the duty of ASEAN as a whole to cooperate' (ASEAN, 2000: point 1). But the SAM's actions to identify themselves as the exhibition centre of the area are perceived as signs of Singaporean cultural imperialism by other Southeast Asian countries. Individual countries want to keep their national art treasures at home. Other Southeast Asian countries want to be the contemporary art centre for the region too.

THE ASIAN CIVILIZATIONS MUSEUM

> The Asian Civilizations Museum (ACM) is the first museum in the region to present a broad yet integrated perspective of pan-Asian cultures and civilizations. As one of the National Museums of Singapore under the National Heritage Board, we seek to promote a better appreciation of the rich cultures that make up Singapore's multi-ethnic society. (ACM, 2007a: www.acm.org.sg/themuseum/aboutacm.asp)

The first wing of the ACM opened in April 1997 in the former Tao Nan School building on Armenian Street. It expanded in March 2003 to include the 14,000 square metre Empress Place colonial building next to the Singapore River, in the heart of the financial district.

> While Singapore's forefathers came to settle in Singapore from many parts of Asia within the last 200 years, the cultures brought to Singapore by these different people are far more ancient. This aspect of Singapore's history is the focus of the ACM. The Museum's collection therefore centres on the material cultures of the different groups originating from China, Southeast Asia, South Asia and West Asia. (ACM, 2007a: www.acm.org. sg/themuseum/aboutacm.asp)

Besides being Singaporean, every citizen of Singapore has been assigned an ethnic identity. They are boxed into the Chinese, Malay, Indian and Others (CMIO) ethnic model – 99 per cent of the Singaporean population are considered either Chinese (77 per cent), or Malay (14 per cent), or Indian (8 per cent). There is also the miscellaneous category of 'Others' (1 per cent). The CMIO model is politically defined, and is central to the state's nation building and social engineering programmes (Benjamin,

1976; Chua, 1995; Pereira, 1997; Rudolph, 1998; Siddique, 1990). The an-
cestries of the Chinese, Malay and Indian communities are officially
broadly defined as from China, Malaysia/Indonesia and the Indian sub-
continent respectively. This model over-simplifies the immigration patterns
and cultures of Singaporeans' forebears. These three countries/regions are
not homogeneous within themselves, and the ACM acknowledges, but does
not dwell on, the diversity. For instance, in the case of China, Confucianism
is simply epitomized as Chinese society (ACM, 2007b: www.acm.org.sg/
themuseum/galleries4.asp):

> In Chinese society, the patriarchal system, based on Confucianism, placed
> the father at the head of the family, just as the emperor was the head of state.
> Great care was taken to respect and look after one's elders and ancestors.
> Many stories were written to eulogise exceptionally filial acts.

With the emphasis on the broad concepts of being Chinese, Indian-
Hindu or Malay-Muslim, the museum suggests that Singaporeans should
be proud of their ancestral pasts because these pasts are the sources of
Singaporeans' Asian ethnic identities. In contrast to the NMS, which shows
that Singapore is a relatively new country, the ACM reclaims historical
links to China, India and the Middle East. While Singapore is in the middle
of the Malay-Muslim world in Southeast Asia, the ACM chooses to trace
the Singaporean Malay-Muslim population to the Middle East. Malaysia
and Indonesia are Singapore's immediate neighbours. The accentuation of
Singaporean ethnicities via other countries' pasts is a double-edged sword.
While Singaporeans are asked to associate themselves with the pasts of
other countries, they can also easily associate themselves with the present
social and political situations in these same countries. Since Malaysia
and Indonesia are Singapore's immediate neighbours, the Singaporean
government officially acknowledges that Malay Singaporeans are at a
greater risk of split loyalty if Singapore has conflicts with either of its two
neighbours (Ooi, 2003: 82–83). Since almost all Malays are also Muslims,
the ACM concentrates on the Muslim aspects of the Malay Singaporean
population and links this group's heritage to the Middle East.

Despite the difficulties in acquiring precious artefacts for its own
collection – as governments in other countries jealously protect their own
heritage – the ACM is still able to bring together priceless material heritage
from the above-mentioned places (apart from Malaysia and Indonesia),
offering visitors a sweeping view of Singaporeans' 'ancestral heritages'

(Singapore Tourist Promotion Board and Singapore Ministry of Information and the Arts, 1995). Through loans, acquisitions, donations and travelling shows, some of the spectacular exhibits include items like eighteenth-century calligraphic implements from Iran and Turkey, seventh-century Tang dynasty sculptures from China, and eighth-century architectural fragments from nagara temples in India. To promote the museum, it organizes so-called blockbuster exhibitions to attract even more visitors; these exhibitions include Buddhist artefacts from Indochina and treasures from the Vatican.

The ACM is a site that shows off the glorious heritages of old Asia. The grandeur and glory of Singaporeans' ancestors are celebrated, and the values embodied in the artefacts are said to be internalized in Singaporeans today. Unlike the NMS, in which Singapore's identity is accentuated by the country's differences from its neighbours, and the SAM, in which Singapore is said to represent Southeast Asia, the ACM asserts Singaporean ethnic identities by claiming ancestral links to selected historical periods of particular Asian countries and communities. These links are the deep roots of Singapore's Asianness.

TOURISTIFICATION AND ORIENTALIZATION PROCESSES IN CONTEXT

The NMS, SAM and ACM are national institutions that assert Singapore's Asianness. They not only play a part in the social engineering programmes, but also play a central role in making Singapore more Asian for western tourists. As mentioned earlier, Singapore has developed into a modern city and the STB realizes that Singapore has lost the exotic Oriental charm that many western tourists expect and demand. The museums are attempts to re-Orientalize and self-Orientalize Singapore.

Adorno and Horkheimer (1972) argue that there is a tendency for the culture industry to systematically insert secondary meanings, replacing original meanings in cultural artefacts. The self-Orientalization processes in the national museums of Singapore can be understood in this context. Let me explain. In museums, stories are presented and meanings are added to artefacts. New interpretations and meanings are often inserted into the exhibits. For example, the Museum of Scotland tells stories and stages myths of Scotland in the context of contemporary political and cultural understandings of the country (Cooke and McLean, 2002; McLean and

Cooke, 2003; Newman and McLean, 2004). Meanings and contexts behind the exhibits are inevitably modified too; for example, scholars such as Hudson (1987) and O'Doherty (1986) point out that an exhibit, such as an old painting or a piece of sculpture, usually has an original functional setting in a church, temple or home, which encourages a mood of relaxation and contemplation, but when it becomes an exhibit in a museum it is uprooted into a 'neutral, unnatural atmosphere, where it has to compete for attention with many other works of art. In these circumstances, the emotions become anaesthetized, the intellect takes over and museums become temples of scholarship' (Hudson, 1987:175). Museums used as spaces for representation inevitably interpret and re-contextualize the exhibits. The NMS, SAM and ACM have created and inserted stories and narratives into their exhibits. These stories constitute part of the self-Orientalization of Singapore.

There are however variations to the Orientalization process in these museums. First and foremost, the SHM, SAM and ACM are engaged in the 'reasianization' process (Hein and Hammond, 1995). This process is not unique to Singapore. The process of reasianization is found among many Asian countries trying to seek and re-establish their relations with their Asian neighbours (ibid.). Particularly in the 1980s and 1990s, when the Asia-Pacific region was economically vibrant, many Asian countries, like Japan, Malaysia and Singapore, tried to assert their dominance. Many scholars and researchers also predicted then that many far eastern economies would eventually overtake western economies. Such a view inspired the reasianization process, as many Asia-Pacific countries thought that they would collectively dominate world economics and politics in the twenty-first century.

Alongside the reasianization process was the process of 'reverse Orientalism' (Hill, 2000). This process entailed the attribution of a set of cultural values to East and Southeast Asian societies by Western social scientists in order to contrast the recent dynamic progress of Asian development with the stagnation and social disorganization of contemporary Western economies and societies. The contrast provided legitimation for some of the nation-building policies of political leaders in such countries as Singapore and was incorporated in attempts to identify and institutionalize core values.

Many people saw the economic success of the Asia-Pacific region as stemming from Confucianism. Confucian values, as supposedly practised in Japan and the Asian tiger economies (namely, South Korea, Taiwan, Singapore and Hong Kong, and now China), offer a set of work ethics –

hard work, collective mindedness, thriftiness – that has an affinity with capitalism (Hofheinz and Calder, 1982; Kahn and Pepper, 1979; Vogel, 1979). Suddenly Confucianism and Confucian values were seen as positive by many inside and outside the region. Previously they had been seen as anti-progress and anti-development (Hill, 2000). In the 1980s the Singaporean government started to celebrate Singaporeans' Asian roots and began the reverse Orientalism process (Hill, 2000). That process has not stopped. Confucianism has since developed into another strain of Orientalist discourse (Chua, 1995). Confucian values have equivocally come to mean Asian values in Singapore, tending to privilege the Chinese and marginalize the Malays and Indians. Regardless, the Singapore government has embarked on a social engineering programme that has been Confucianized, so that Singaporeans will learn about social discipline, social solidarity and community responsibility (Chua, 1995; Hill, 2000; Lam and Tan, 1999). The pride in being Asian has also been translated into tourism, with Singapore branding itself 'New Asia' in 1996 (Ooi, 2004). That brand and the current brand, 'Uniquely Singapore', communicate the idea that Singapore is in an economically, socially and culturally dynamic region (Ooi, 2004).

The NMS, SAM and ACM are part of the reasianization process to celebrate the expected rise of Asia. Singapore proudly self-Orientalizes itself because the images that the world has of Asia are changing for the better. The Singapore government could even use the positive parts of the Orientalist discourses to engineer and persuade Singaporeans to be hard-working and authority-respecting subjects (Chua, 1995). But there are different Orientalization strategies used in the three national museums of Singapore.

While celebrating Singaporeaness, the NMS attempts to *de-Orientalize* visitors' perceptions of Singapore. As presented earlier, the images that the NMS presents of Singapore are specific and detailed. The NMS asserts Singapore's uniqueness in Southeast Asia; Singapore is very different from its immediate neighbours. The NMS gives historical examples of how Singapore, Malaysia, Indonesia and other neighbouring countries disagreed and had violent conflicts. There are also exhibitions to show the distinctiveness of various Chinese communities in Singapore, showing that the Chinese in Singapore speak different languages and have different customs, beliefs and practices. Furthermore, Singapore is shown to be special because it has become an economically developed society due to good government, unlike most of its neighbours. In other words, Singapore is both Asian and modern but in its own way. The NMS challenges Orientalist images visitors may have of Singapore as just another Asian country. It boasts of the city-state's economic and social successes despite the strife and challenges facing an unstable Asia.

In contrast, the SAM creates a new set of Orientalist discourses on Southeast Asia. It *re-Orientalizes* Singapore and the region. It firmly asserts Singapore as leader in Southeast Asia and constructs a set of Orientalist narratives about Southeast Asia as an aesthetic region. As mentioned earlier, the region is diverse: it has more than 500 million inhabitants, officially made of 11 different countries, and within most of these countries there is a variety of languages and cultural differences. In terms of contemporary art, there is a wide variety, ranging from Chinese ink paintings to Javanese batik, Vietnamese impressionism to Singaporean abstract sculptures. It is a difficult task to construct a Southeast Asian art genre, but the museum honestly tries to do so by presenting the diversity of visual art forms from the region and then creating themes to connect the works. The SAM celebrates the diversity of Southeast Asia but claims that the region is a somewhat artistically unified region. This unity invents yet another Southeast Asian regional identity. Effectively, it introduces a new set of Orientalist discourses on how to view the region. The promoted narrative firmly places Singapore as the art centre of the region. Therefore, the SAM is trying to replace the old Orientalist view of Southeast Asia that ignores the art in the region with a new view of Southeast Asia that makes Singapore the art and cultural centre. It re-Orientalizes Singapore and the region with its own narratives.

The ACM *reaffirms* certain Orientalist views of Asia, having even bigger ambitions than the SAM, in the sense that it is presenting the material cultures of the major ancient Asian civilizations. It does not attempt to claim common roots with China, India and the Middle East. Instead, the museum works within the confines of common views of China, India and the Middle East. These places are perceived as homogeneous social and cultural entities, and Singapore is constructed as a site where all these cultures influence the modern city-state. The fact that the long histories of these civilizations have been chequered with political revolutions and social evolutions is not emphasized. For instance, the vast differences between dynasties, between Chinese languages and between communities are glossed over by the idea of a single Chinese civilization. The one-China culture impression is not only held by most people in the world but is also actively promoted by China; Singapore also takes the view of a single Chinese culture in its ethnic engineering programme (Leong, 1997). The ACM reaffirms the generalized ideas of Chinese, Indian and Islamic civilizations. In other words, like the SAM advocating Southeast Asia as a somewhat homogeneous bloc, the ACM reaffirms the view of Asia in terms of dominant clusters of civilizations. While the curators know that the situation is much more complex, the messages they communicate are basically that Asia is culturally rich and diverse along certain pre-defined boundaries of civilizations.

Table 5.1 The Orient responds through the National Museums of Singapore: de-Orientalism, re-Orientalism and reverse Orientalism

	NMS	SAM	ACM
The main messages	• Singapore has its own cultures and identity • Singapore is distinct from other countries in the Southeast Asia	• Singapore is part of Southeast Asia • Southeast Asia offers a unique genre of art • The SAM is the place to experience Southeast Asian art	• Singapore is Asian • Asia is exotic and rich in history • Singapore society has deep Asian roots
Type of Orientalization processes	It de-orientalizes any simple images people may have of Singapore as just another Asian country	It re-orientalizes Southeast Asia by presenting a Southeast Asian art genre	It affirms Orientalist images that Asia is made up of clusters of civilizations
Ways to attract more tourists to Singapore	• Celebration of Singaporean society • Singapore is a 'Global City for the Arts' • Experience Singapore as a unique country in Southeast Asia	• Celebration of Southeast Asian art and culture • Singapore is a 'Global City for the Arts' • Experience the best in Southeast Asian art and culture	• Celebration of ancient Asian civilizations • Singapore is a 'Global City for the Arts' • Experience different, exciting and rich ancient Asian heritages
Role in social engineering and nation-building	• Reverse Orientalism: be proud of Singapore • For national education • Singapore has a difficult history and the current government has brought about stability and prosperity	• Reverse Orientalism: be proud of Southeast Asia • To promote art among Singaporeans • Singapore is the cultural capital of the region	• Reverse Orientalism: be proud of being Asian • Singaporeans should know their roots and they can see their ancestral pasts in the ACM • Encourage Singaporeans to accept prescribed 'Asian values'

The three museums present Singapore and the region differently. These different messages and strategies are developed out of the needs of tourism and nation-building. Table 5.1 summarizes the arguments that I have put forward on the different forms of Orientalization in the national museums of Singapore.

Indeed, while serving the tourism functions, these museums have also become platforms for the Singaporean authorities to re-Orientalize and reverse Orientalize the city-state. Despite being visibly modern and developed, Singaporeans are reminded that they are Asian with good work ethics and high moral values. Tourists are shown that Singapore is essentially Asian and is still exotic. The Orientalist discourses that the museums have developed also allude to Singapore's superiority to its neighbours. Singapore has inadvertently become the imperialist in the region.

CONCLUSIONS

The comparison between the three national museums shows how Orientalist discourses can be subverted, reclaimed and celebrated. Orientalism is not just about the Occident misinterpreting and controlling the Orient. It goes further, suggesting that the Orient can manipulate notions of itself with caricaturized images. The SAM has created another set of Orientalist narratives for Southeast Asia, a set that celebrates contemporary art from the region with Singapore in the centre. The ACM celebrates Asia not by inventing a new set of Orientalist discourses for Asia but by affirming the Orientalist imagination of Asia as being divided into sets of ancient civilizations. The NMS contrasts with the SAM and the ACM by celebrating Asia but also arguing that Singapore is different from other Asian countries, emphasizing the fact that Singapore is doing much better economically and socially than its neighbours.

New and secondary meanings can be easily added to cultural products. Therefore, in the context of the national museums of Singapore, that which has been presented and articulated must also be understood within the context of use. All knowledge is created within its age and is necessarily contingent, no knowledge can be unaffected by the circumstances under which it comes to be (Burke III, 1998). With this holistic approach, presented stories and histories must then be read and understood as constructions by museum mediators within the contexts in which the stories function, rather than as objective and unadulterated accounts of reality. This chapter has read the main stories of the three national museums of Singapore within the tourism and local social-engineering context.

The Singaporean identities constructed are meant to attract tourists, assert Singapore's role as a cultural centre for the region and generate pride in Singaporeans' ancestral pasts. In that process, Singapore has become more Asian, and has created a domineering presence in the region by claiming cultural spaces from around the region. The ambition to become the cultural capital of the region will undoubtedly be challenged by Singapore's neighbours for decades to come.

NOTES

1   Data for this empirical study were collected between 1997 and 2006. Besides visits to and documents amassed concerning the museums, interviews and discussions were held with top officials in the ACM, SAM, NMS, National Heritage Board and STB.

2   The Singapore Tourist Promotion Board (STPB) became the Singapore Tourism Board (STB) in November 1997.

CHAPTER 6

World Heritage Sites in Southeast Asia
Angkor and Beyond

Keiko Miura[1]

INTRODUCTION

Since the inception of the World Heritage Programme in the 1970s, popular destinations of nature and culture tourism considered to have 'outstanding universal value' have been nominated as World Heritage Sites. By mid-2008, 878 properties had been inscribed on the World Heritage List: 29 are found in Southeast Asia,[2] all of which have been put on the list since 1991.[3] This rather recent special branding of heritage sites has added a considerable boost to the development of Southeast Asian economies and prestige, primarily through increased tourism revenue. At the same time it has led to tensions at different levels within the communities concerned as well as rapid socio-cultural changes.

World Heritage Sites have become a new genre of community, both imagined and real. A new community entails a new social space, new values and borders, which are often contested among stakeholders. This new genre has become an important subject matter of study requiring multidisciplinary approaches. Comparative studies are also considered highly beneficial to our understanding of the nature of such communities. As compared to the rapidly growing number of nominated Sites and the enormous problems which accrue from nomination, there has been little comprehensive research conducted on the processes of change before and after nomination. An urgent matter is to examine what emerges upon creating a new community or demarcating a certain area as such, and what it implies to have such a site for the various interacting communities concerned, both geographical and professional. The former category includes the interplay of local, provincial, national, regional or international communities, as well as processes taking place within the respective communities themselves, while the latter category includes the interactions between experts on conservation, tourism and community development. In other words, the study of World Heritage Sites provides us with fairly clear evidence of 'knowledge interfaces between local communities (their practices and discourses) and external agents of change, who have their own practices and discourses' (Pottier, 2003: 2). As Pottier assumes, nevertheless, there is no clear-cut distinction between 'local community' and 'external agents'. The production of knowledge is embedded in social and cultural processes imbued with aspects of power, authority and legitimation: the act of producing knowledge involves social struggle, conflict and negotiation (ibid.: 2).

This chapter is therefore not a straightforward study of tourism in Southeast Asia, but of the complex social, cultural, economic and political ramifications and dynamic processes of change surrounding the designation of certain areas as World Heritage Sites. My particular concern here is sites with resident populations, the so-called 'living heritage sites'[4] – another new category of community. The main issues at such sites are often antagonistic triadic concerns and discourses about conservation, tourism and local ways of life. Even though a balance between the three elements is emphasized, the reality often proves to be far from ideal. Local ways of life tend to be subordinated to concerns about conservation and tourism development. Tensions among various stakeholders become more intense in developing countries due to the limited economic resources available. In other words tourism in World Heritage Sites cannot be discussed in isolation, but must include reference to discourses about the conservation of monuments and sites and the maintenance of local ways of life.

This chapter attempts to study various constructions of the image of the heritage site, in the minds of local people, experts, policy-makers and national authorities, set against the reality – the institutional and legal frameworks – as well as the contestation over conservation, tourism and local ways of life. It also intends to show that in a given span of time the stakeholders modify their approaches as a result of interaction and negotiations among them. By demonstrating the nature and the processes of contestation, I wish to highlight the complexities and diversities in understanding heritage, tourism and site management, as well as the educational values and social benefits that accrue from such contestation and negotiations. As is shown later, negative consequences developing at the sites are becoming lessons to be learnt by policy-makers and various authorities, who are reformulating and modifying their policies and strategies in managing the sites so as to make them acceptable to a wider community. This only confirms their mutual dependence, reciprocity and influence, reflecting rapidly interacting world communities. World Heritage Sites with high profiles have undoubtedly become political and economic icons of hope, prestige and capital for Southeast Asian countries.

Two case studies are presented here to highlight the main issues, namely, of the Angkor World Heritage Site in Cambodia (hereinafter called Angkor), inscribed on the World Heritage List and the List of World Heritage in Danger at the same time in 1992, and of the Vat Phou[5] and Associated Ancient Settlements within the Champasak Cultural Landscape (hereinafter called the Vat Phou site)[6] in Laos, which was included on the List in 2001. The choice of these sites for discussion is to do with my own involvement with the work of the Culture Sector of the United Nations Educational, Scientific and Cultural Organization (UNESCO) in Cambodia for nearly six years from November 1992 to August 1998, and two following years of doctoral fieldwork in Angkor, together with the familiarity and availability of relevant data for the Vat Phou site.

The study begins with a brief examination of shared issues across the regional sites. It is followed by an analysis of the significance of Angkor as a turning point from former approaches towards the concept of heritage and site management by international conservation agencies and specialists. Case studies of Angkor and the Vat Phou site are then introduced, first with reference to socio-cultural resources and the management framework of the sites and the significance of the sites in the minds of people at various levels, and second with an illustration of the tensions among the three main concerns: heritage conservation, tourism development and local ways of life. Finally, recent policy emphases concerning the human dimension of heritage values and the effective use of heritage are discussed. The conclusion highlights the importance of *negotiating* conservation, tourism development and local ways of life, which may assist with the democratization processes in countries with World Heritage Sites in the region.

SHARED ISSUES

At the time of inscription on to the List, the criteria for inclusion and the socio-political and economic frameworks show considerable differences among the sites with resident populations. There are, however, shared issues: tensions around the universal values of cosmopolitanism (vis-à-vis the local and the national); discourses of ownership and management; tensions between conservation, tourism development and local ways of life; patterns of exclusion; and the symbolic meanings attached to these sites (cf. Bianchi and Boniface, 2002: 80). The gap between the policies and practices of site management is another salient issue across heritage sites. The notions of heritage and tradition are selected, constructed and represented by various actors, including the state, international agencies and local communities in the context of nation-building and tourism development (cf. Hitchcock and King, 2003b: 6), and conservation and community development. Questions of authority, authenticity and aesthetics are closely tied up with the notions of heritage and tradition (Hitchcock and King, 2003c: 163);[7] authenticity and aesthetics are particular concerns of conservators and visitors.[8]

The significance of Angkor as a turning point

Before the inscription of Angkor as a cultural World Heritage Site in 1992, the management approach of earlier nominations, such as Sukhothai and Ayutthaya in Thailand, and Prambanan and Borobudur in Indonesia, was to remove the local residents from the sites to conserve and recreate them as historic parks, primarily for tourism. Black and Wall (2001: 129–130) mention the negative impact of removing the local residents from the sites, especially in Borobudur and Prambanan where local people's spiritual and emotional ties with the monuments and the land around it are weakened because of relocation and the erection of fences around the monuments. It also entails the reduction of economic opportunities. As a result, 'the relationship between residents and government officials was adversarial, tense and sometimes violent' (ibid.: 129).

By learning from negative past experiences, the inscription of Angkor as a World Heritage Site showed a stark shift in policy-formulation from that used for earlier cultural heritage sites. The clear shift can be seen in the underlying criteria, which have moved from just preserving the monuments and sites as representing a 'frozen idealized past' devoid of people, except tourists and conservators, to making the site 'living' and more integral with local people who are therefore not to be resettled. Nevertheless, we have seen unfortunate official responses at both Angkor[9] and Vat Phou: internal marginalization, restricted movement and restricted access to erstwhile cultural and socio-economic resources, and visible and invisible 'barriers' erected as new boundaries. The situation at the two sites has made tense the relationship between the local community and the incumbent authorities. Conflicts between conservationists and tourism promoters are also severe, for the former consist of international conservation agencies and experts in conjunction with a minority of local experts, while tourism promoters represent local governments and business-oriented groups, both local and international. The local governments are also divided into various groups, and there are individual players, all of whom strive for more personal economic and political gains over the control of the sites. On the one hand, there is a high-level contestation over access to and control of cultural and natural resources at the sites; on the other hand there is little concern about the lives of local populations, who tend to be restricted in their access to 'their' heritage sites, or who become a neglected community.

Since 2004, however, the situation has seen some improvement in Angkor, for the Cambodian government finally publicly acknowledged the rights of local villagers whilst prohibiting any illegal activities by various state authorities or private individuals. What is happening in Angkor also reflects the democratization process that is taking place in Cambodia in general, on which the presence and voices of the international community have had a strong bearing. For the situation of the Vat Phou site, we will have to wait and see whether or not the same trend is to come soon. There are nonetheless strong possibilities that Angkor will serve as an iconic site to influence the ways by which other World Heritage Sites in the region are managed and represented.

Cultural landscape

Sites nominated on the basis of 'cultural landscape' criteria began to emerge from 1992,[10] in respect to the human–nature interactions that have led to the creation of such landscapes (UNESCO–World Heritage Centre, 2008: 14, 86–87). Angkor was not designated as a 'protected cultural landscape', though the areas along rivers such as the Siem Reap River and Puok River are included in a zone of 'protected cultural landscapes' (cf. Autorité pour la Protection du Site et l'Aménagement de la Région d'Angkor/APSARA, 1998: 192–196, 213).[11] Whether nominated with reference to the criteria of cultural landscapes or not, sites that include local inhabitants are regarded as 'living heritage sites'.

An example in the region of a living heritage site, referred to as a 'living cultural landscape', is the rice terraces of the Philippine Cordilleras, inscribed on the World Heritage List in 1995 (Reyes, 2005: 48).[12] The issue of the local Ifugao population here is not to do with exclusion, but more to do with the negative impact of tourism development or difficulties in managing economic life there, including the deterioration of the meaning of traditional rites and dance performances for the local population, the lack of strong economic benefit from tourism to the local community, the degradation of natural resources, consequential shortages of water for farming (ibid.: 48–50), inaccessibility to modern equipment due to the narrowness and steepness of the rice terraces (Engelhardt, 1997: 3), and the outflow of younger inhabitants as economic migrants to urban areas, leading to a decrease in the number of original inhabitants willing to continue farming. This critical situation of conserving Ifugao rice terraces was taken seriously by UNESCO, which designated it as a World Heritage Site in Danger in 2001.[13]

Using a more comprehensive approach to give protection to the site as well as local ways of life is a large step forward to improve the ethical dimension of managing a living heritage site. As demonstrated briefly above, however, designation alone is not enough to make the ideal become a social reality. There are complex ramifications surrounding what is available and desirable to local inhabitants to achieve their objectives, which at times may conflict with the expectations and needs of the state and/or the international community.

Angkor: its socio-cultural resources and its management framework

The most outstanding of Angkor's socio-cultural resources are no doubt its numerous monuments and sites produced during the Angkor period of the Khmer[14] civilization, a period that developed extensively from the ninth to the fifteenth centuries CE. Angkor refers to this period and is used as a general term for the monuments and sites built during that time. There is however a prevalent confusion between Angkor and Angkor Wat. The latter was created in the first half of the twelfth century CE and is at the centre of Angkor. It is also the largest religious monument in the world.

Angkor itself was one of the most powerful and advanced civilizations in mainland Southeast Asia, which was ruled by deified kings with a pronounced hierarchy, extensive irrigation systems, and a programme of temple building. At its height, the kingdom stretched from the vicinity of Vientiane in Laos to much of the Malay Peninsula and from the southern part of Vietnam to the borders of Pagan in Burma.[15] In the mid-fifteenth century CE Angkor was sacked by the Siamese and was under Siamese influence or control until 1907 when Siam ceded Angkor to the French. The French recognized the immense value of the Angkor heritage, and several missions, both official and private, were organized to investigate the scale, condition and quality of the monuments and sites, as well as to bring back to France a number of artefacts from Angkor even prior to 1907. While some temples such as Angkor Wat and Bayon had apparently been used for worship by the local population, the monuments and sites in general were full of rubble, destabilized walls, and lichens, and nature was taking over the structures (cf. Dagens, 1995: 48–114).

Angkor's legacy is not only historical buildings and infrastructure, but also socio-cultural traditions, including dance, theatre, games, beliefs, rituals and ways of life. Paying attention to the monumental heritage alone, Angkor Park was established in 1925 (Tashiro, 2005) and opened in the next year as a kind of open-air archaeological museum, which was managed by French conservators as such until 1972. Aesthetically pleasing cultural traditions had been appraised and promoted by the French, but not certain other aspects of local practices such as resin-tapping and logging, as shall be discussed later.

The World Heritage nomination brought about the segmentation of the site according to various aspects of protection. It has created confusion and contestation over whose heritage Angkor is, what to protect and to what extent local practices should be allowed to continue.

The area designated as the World Heritage Site covers 401 km², centring on the heart of Angkor civilization. The Site is separated into three areas: Roluos, Banteay Srei and Angkor (including Angkor Wat[16] and Angkor Thom – the large city or capital built from 1190 to 1210 CE). Five zones were created: Zone 1 – Monumental Sites; Zone 2 – Protected Archaeological Reserves; Zone 3 – Protected Cultural Landscapes; Zone 4 – Sites of Archaeological, Anthropological or Historic Interest; and Zone 5 – The Socio-Economic and Cultural Development Zone of the Siem Reap/Angkor Region.

By the early 1990s not only had two decades of war damaged the monuments and sites, but long negligence of management had caused them to fall into alarming conditions of destabilization and decay. They had also been subject to rampant destruction, theft and illicit traffic of artefacts. Following the nomination of Angkor as a World Heritage Site, the Tokyo Conference in October 1993 created an international framework for managing the monuments and sites, i.e. the International Co-ordinating Committee for the Safeguarding and Development of the Historic Site of Angkor (ICC) . It was decided then that Japan and France would co-chair and UNESCO act as the standing secretariat. ICC was mandated 'to meet periodically to set priorities and monitor the conservation work on the site as well as to mobilize the necessary funds'. Angkor was then (and probably is still now) considered as one of the largest conservation workshops in the world. Tourism and conservation were in the mind of UNESCO and the international community initially, but more to use tourism revenue for the conservation of the monuments and sites (cf. UNESCO, 1993: 15) and also to prevent excessive and rapid tourism development.

As a national body responsible for the management of Angkor, the APSARA Authority (hereinafter called APSARA) was established in 1995. A special police corps for the protection of cultural heritage (the so-called 'heritage police') was established in 1997. By 2004 Angkor was considered not to be at risk any longer and was removed from the World Heritage List in Danger.[17]

While Angkor has steadily made progress in establishing the management framework required through the World Heritage nomination, it has been perceived differently by different groups of people, even though its outstanding socio-cultural value has been reconfirmed by all.

Angkor as imagined

The nomination of Angkor as a World Heritage Site has led people of various social levels from diverse social backgrounds to consider and reconsider what Angkor means to them, the local communities, the nation and the world, while taking into consideration what has happened to Cambodians over the last three decades. On pondering the historical experience of Cambodians, Azedine Beschaouch, UNESCO's former Scientific Advisor for Angkor, said:

> The last 25 years have been a period of intense philosophical reflection for the Cambodians. They have asked themselves whether the decline of the Angkor Empire (...) signalled the end of a Cambodia that was peaceful and highly cultured, and whether they themselves were part of another Cambodia, one which is destructive and barbaric. Angkor above all allows

them to be reconciled with their own history: aligning themselves to this great civilization allows them to draw a line under the barbaric times (UNESCO/Boukhari, 2002).

For Sok An,[18] Minister in Charge of the Council of Ministers and the Chairman of the National Tourism Authority of Cambodia, Angkor is the national legacy par excellence, so that 'in all services from those of the airport, visitor accommodation, tourist sites and departure points from Cambodia, workers, all levels of relevant officials and people in general should behave well, [and] use proper language and decorum, displaying the Khmer national identity that is a legacy of the glorious generation of the Angkor era' (Sok, 2001: 3).

Sok's emphasis on the national importance and pride surrounding Angkor was shared with the then heritage police chief. For the latter, Angkor is the unique legacy of their ancestors that can give them great pride not just locally, but internationally. He said, 'How could the Khmer act in an appropriate way in order to respect the honour of Angkor, which does not only belong to a few people? We have to know how to give honour to our ancestors. If the Khmer had no Angkor, nobody would recognise us.'[19]

For this French-educated Khmer anthropologist and former director of the Heritage and Culture Department of APSARA, 'Angkor is a living heritage site: it has not only ancient temples, but also villages that have existed from the past until the present. The Angkor heritage is not only the temples, but includes monks, rich people and poor people (...) I would not actually move villagers from the site where they have been living. I just wish them to live in balance with the environment.'[20] He also emphasized the emotional and healing dimension of heritage elsewhere, saying that 'in times of despair, Angkor is the only reference point' (UNESCO/Boukhari, 2002).

Many local villagers seem to find it difficult to express their overwhelming feelings towards Angkor. The words of a Buddhist monk from the village in front of Angkor Wat gave the author the feeling that the most powerful presence of Angkor is in one's mind: 'I have lived all my life seeing Angkor Wat. I cannot imagine living in a place without it.' Angkor for him is a homeland, inseparable from his life and everyday living.

As is clear from the above, Angkor is imagined and valued in a variety of ways in the minds of all concerned. In reality, however, the significance of Angkor for local inhabitants has been little considered. They have never been invited to the ICC and have rarely been provided with other venues to voice their concerns; rather, they have been given orders or criticism from above. Very little was known about what they considered 'their' heritage to be or how their lives have been interwoven into the site.

Local inhabitants and their heritage

According to the survey of the United Nations Transitional Authority in Cambodia (UNTAC), the entire population of Zones 1 and 2 was estimated at approximately 22,000 in 1992. This figure is unreliable, for many areas then had land mines, and the security of the area had not been safe enough to conduct an accurate population census. Nonetheless, we see a sharp increase in the population in the space of six years. The national population census of 1998 states the population at 84,000. In 2005, the number had reached 100,000, including 18,500 households according to the survey of APSARA. The two zones consist of five districts, 19 communes and 102 villages (Khuon, 2005).

Most inhabitants are rice farmers, though they consider themselves as 'forest' people, or people who dwell in the forest region and depend on forest products for subsistence. They have traditionally owned certain lands within the temple sites as well as made use of natural resources within the Angkor complex. In the compounds of Angkor Thom and Angkor Wat they have an ancestral heritage of rice fields in the form of ponds, lakes and the moats of Angkor Thom. Likewise, parts of the large temple sites such as Ta Prohm temple have been cultivated by local villagers through several generations. Trees, especially those yielding resin or fruits, are owned by certain villagers, who care for them. Resin provides an important supplementary income for them as well as being used to make torches for both home consumption and sale. Logs not only provide firewood, but are also utilized to make charcoal for domestic use and the market. Other forest products constitute an important subsistence economy in terms of food and craft materials.[21] Temple compounds where forests are not dense provide cows with grass to graze. Moats, ponds and lakes are bathing places for water buffaloes.

International restoration and conservation teams have provided labour opportunities for local populations since the late 1980s, as had the French conservators since the early twentieth century. In the Guidelines for Management Article 17 local residents are mentioned: 'Give residents of the protected sites priority of employment in the matters of site management and preservation work' (APSARA, 1998: 218). Based on this, APSARA has also provided jobs in site maintenance, initially as part of the food-for-work project of the International Labour Organization (ILO), and it later created jobs for temple guards recruited from local villages. Some local residents also produce handicrafts, mainly woodcrafts, and/or sell souvenirs or drinks in Angkor.

Since the end of the Pol Pot regime in 1979 local villagers, in particular the followers of the eight precepts, started voluntarily to take care of Buddha and Hindu statues in the temples. Some of the Hindu statues have been venerated as powerful local tutelary spirits called *neak ta*. The most powerful *neak ta* in the region is called Neak Ta Ta Reach (royal *neak ta*) in the form of Vishnu guarding the western gallery (the west is the front) of Angkor Wat. During the war-time in the 1970s local villagers fled to Angkor Wat and Angkor Thom to avoid shelling from the Lon Nol side in Siem Reap, when the Angkor area was occupied by the Khmer Rouge guerrillas. Angkor monuments thus not only provided local inhabitants with spiritual and moral protection but also physical shelter. Generations of local inhabitants have established close relationships with the monuments, in terms of constructing original buildings, conserving and maintaining them, and keeping the site vital by continuing to live and work there and believing in its sacredness and its symbolic values. The temples also provide them with spaces for praying, learning, merit-making, meeting people, protection and artistic performances.

Prior to the establishment of schools in the villages, Angkor Wat monasteries were the only places where boys could be educated and become monks to learn about Buddhism. Since 1979 seven monasteries have been created on the ancient temple sites in Angkor Thom. Many of the monks of the monasteries in Angkor Thom and Angkor Wat are from local villages. Among them many abbots and senior monks had been restoration workers during the French management of Angkor. The monasteries have also served as culture centres where people from other communities can meet, and exchange news and knowledge. In particular, Angkor Wat has seen the highest level of national (and international these days) artistic performances, and been the place for traditional New Year games[22] for people in the Angkor area. Local villagers also have their ancestors' ashes housed in the stupas or buried in the compound of Angkor Wat monasteries.

In short, Angkor is closely linked to the everyday life of local villagers as well as to their memories and to their ancestors' practices. It is their homeland and an integral whole; religious life and socio-economic life are inseparable. Both the continued relevance of the site to local villagers' everyday living, and its symbolic and inspirational importance for the nation, make the site 'a living heritage site'. This is not just because Angkor has continued to be a worship-site. It is essential to understand that it has long been safeguarded by local inhabitants as their personal and national heritage, which is now considered a world heritage.

ANGKOR: CONSERVATION, TOURISM DEVELOPMENT AND LOCAL WAYS OF LIFE

Local inhabitants of Angkor have had a close association with the sites for generations. At the international level of discourses over 'Save Angkor', the issue of local inhabitants has been little discussed. While it is true that their contribution as a valuable labour force for restoration and conservation work is usually mentioned, the main focus of discussion is on the conservation of the Angkor monuments and tourism development. The year 2001 saw a significant change in the political atmosphere vis-à-vis Angkor, when the Cambodian government voiced its strong concern over speeding up the promotion of tourism development in Angkor.

Conservation versus tourism development

The primary interest of the international community has been with the restoration and conservation of the monuments and site, whereas the main concern of the Cambodian government since the late 1990s has clearly been with tourism development, in particular with the profit from tourism to be used to overcome the political and socio-economic ills of the country. The difference in priority envisaged by the two camps was clear from the outset, and has been proved by subsequent words and actions.

At the beginning, the ICC was busy co-ordinating international restoration and conservation teams' projects, reporting periodically on the progress made as well as setting technical standards and ensuring international co-operation rather than competition.

Tourism development was slow in comparison because of the prevalence of land mines, occasional incursions of Khmer Rouge guerrillas into the Angkor area, and the general insecurity of the site after dark. Meanwhile, the Cambodian government agreed a contract for collecting entrance fees charged to visitors with a private company called the Sokha Hotels Company (more popularly known as Sokimex) – one of the largest private companies in Cambodia. The company has a close association with the ruling Cambodian People's Party (CPP).

UNESCO and the international community initially envisaged that the entrance fees[23] collected from visitors would be used for conserving and managing the site. This situation became a salient point of dispute between the two camps at ICC. The Japanese government was especially critical and voiced its disagreement with the system since it is the largest donor country to Cambodia. Even though severe criticism could not completely change the situation, partial distribution of royalties to APSARA has gradually been achieved. In April 1999 US$1 million of annual revenue was distributed to APSARA. Between 1 September 2000 and 31 December 2000, the distribution of royalties to APSARA and the Sokha Hotels was set at 70 per cent and 30 per cent respectively. Since 2001 APSARA has arranged to receive 70 per cent of the profit if the total revenue exceeds US$3million, 50 per cent if less (APSARA, 2000: 2–3). The contract was renewed in August 2005 and runs until 2010 (De Lopez et al., 2007: 7).

Apart from entrance fees, ICC has also had to deal with a number of covert agreements made between the Cambodian government and entrepreneurs, or proposed schemes from the latter to the former. Prominent examples include a sound and light show scheme by a Malaysian company, YTL, in Angkor Wat in 1996;[24] the construction of hotels in the protected zone; and several private karaoke establishments[25] within Zone 2: at least one was established by a high-ranking military officer. The sound and light show, private karaoke establishments, and a lift in Angkor Wat were cancelled. The scheme for a sound and light show in Angkor Wat has resurfaced recently, as have new projects for moored Sokimex hot-air balloon flights over the site near Angkor Wat and the construction of a cable car to Phnom Bakheng (cf. ICC, 2001: 32–34). The air balloon scheme was permitted and can be seen to the west of Angkor Wat.

While zoning boundaries had been unclear to most social actors until lately, some clearly exploited the situation and began to build or plan to build hotels within the protected zone. One hotel was built, partially blocking an ancient canal which was discovered when the construction was nearly completed. After serious criticism was levelled, all such plans were reviewed. Consequently some plans were scrapped, while it was requested that other architectural plans be modified in order to restrict the number of rooms and keep the height below that of the Grand Hotel d'Angkor at the centre of Siem Reap town.

In addition, APSARA had long been ineffective because of internal political strife, inadequate financial and human capacity, and relative isolation from other well-established Cambodian authorities, who tend to see APSARA as a development impediment and often ignore its authority. A crucial point was reached with the dismissal by the cabinet in 2001 of the Director-General of APSARA, who was a confidant of the former king, Norodom Sihanouk, and also a staunch French-educated architect and conservationist. He was replaced by his deputy, and Sok An, Vice-Minister, became the Chairman of APSARA.

Within two months of the dismissal of the Director-General, a National Seminar on Cultural Tourism took place in both Siem Reap and Phnom Penh, in which the author participated. At the opening speech in Phnom, Sok An (Sok, 2001), then as the Minister in charge of the Council of Ministers and the Chairman of the National Tourism Authority of Cambodia, expressed the government's intention and determination to promote 'cultural tourism' more effectively and expressed his hope that 'the strategy to develop cultural tourism can be given even greater impetus'.

At the session in Siem Reap, a representative of UNESCO emphasized the need for the conservation of historical monuments to be carried out in harmony with the development of Angkor: Angkor was a 'human heritage'. He recommended to the national authorities that the tourist development action plan take 'quality of life' into consideration. As some of the priorities for consideration he mentioned communications, comfort (service facilities), entertainment, culture, place, tradition, and the sensitization of the local community to ensure that they should participate in the tourist development and profit from it.

Local ways of life

Through the ICC, UNESCO has repeatedly emphasized the human dimension of Angkor heritage and stressed that the revenue from tourism development be fairly shared with the local community. On the part of the Cambodian government, their emphasis on urgency in tourism development was claimed as necessary to provide more employment opportunities to the rural poor and as a pre-requisite to the alleviation of poverty throughout the country.

Local villagers, however, have not gained much from tourism development. For instance, positions in hotels are mostly taken by urban and better-educated people who know English or another foreign language and have connections to recruiters or owners. A lack of formal education and connections to 'the rich and powerful' means that rural people often end up working at construction sites with highly exploitative working conditions. Some work as gardeners for large hotels, others are fortunate to be recruited for free skills-training programmes to produce silk or cotton textiles, wood- or stone-carving, lacquerware, or carpentry. Yet others are studying English or other foreign languages to become unofficial tourist guides.[26]

Although they have largely been ignored in policy-making and re-presentation in the international forum of discussions over Angkor, this is not the most serious predicament to befall the local villagers. The nomination of Angkor as a World Heritage Site has become a convenient excuse for the many representatives of the national authority to demand that the local villagers stop their traditional socio-economic practices in Angkor. Many traditional practices have been banned by the heritage police under the Ministry of Interior since April 2000, without prior consultation with APSARA. This ban includes cutting trees, collecting forest products such as resin, the cultivation of rice, grazing cattle, killing birds, entering the forest, bringing cutting instruments or firearms inside Angkor Thom, and the increase of land cultivation within the Angkor complex. Releasing water buffaloes into the moat of Angkor Wat and releasing cattle on its banks have also been banned on grounds of sanitation and aesthetics (Kingdom of Cambodia, 1999). No compensation or alternatives were provided in the course of imposing the ban, which narrowed subsistence options for local villagers. Many are now obliged to seek temporary wage labour in hotel construction or other work that provides no security and is highly exploitative in most cases.

Even before the ban was imposed, the local villagers were exposed to the abuse of power by the heritage police. It is widely known that the heritage police have been exacting money from Cambodians working in Angkor, regardless of whether they are vendors of souvenirs or drinks, caretakers of religious statues, collectors of edible ants' nests, beggars or rice cultivators.

Many of Angkor's large trees, especially Yeang[27] trees which yield resin, have been logged illegally since 1979. This was especially severe during the Vietnamese occupation of Cambodia from 1979 to 1989, when extensive logging took place in Angkor by both the Vietnamese and Cambodian military. The then heritage police chief, himself a native of Angkor, however, blames the destruction of forests on the local villagers, whilst admitting that some of his men have also collaborated with them.

Because of the increase of antagonism which had developed between the local villagers and the heritage police, a meeting was organized at Ta Nei temple by APSARA in July 2000. It invited major stakeholders of the site, including representatives of local authorities, the then heritage police, Buddhist monks, village chiefs and vice-chiefs, representatives of a local NGO, international organizations and researchers. At the meeting the then heritage police chief threatened local villagers with arrest, imprisonment, and the death sentence for many of the illegal activities, but finally compromised on the collection of firewood. The then chief, nonetheless, declared that the site was for the world, not for some local families. In his mind local heritage was unimportant; it should be subordinated to a higher cause and wider concerned parties.

The then heritage police chief quoted laws and regulations that concerned the protection of the national cultural heritage, promulgated prior to Angkor's world heritage nomination. These are based on the old conservation philosophy and policies of freezing the past, almost completely eradicating human interactions in the monumental zone. While some representatives of the local authorities demonstrated a certain degree of sympathy towards the local villagers, they mostly went along with the heritage police ban. Only the representative of the local Department of Forestry strongly challenged the stance of the heritage police chief. NGO workers and international researchers also voiced their support for the continuation of rice cultivation on the site because some families have no other rice fields or any immediate alternatives for survival. Both the national and international sector of forest conservation and management have emphasized the importance of incorporating local participation in their tasks; their appeals have largely been ignored by other sectors of the Cambodian authorities.

It was not the first time that local practices in Angkor had been restricted. Upon creating the Angkor Park in 1925, the French (although not of one view as regards local inhabitants) tried to restrict resin-tapping and tree-cutting, but enforcement was not strict. While the people living within the sites of Angkor Wat and Angkor Thom were moved outside the moats, they were nevertheless allowed to cultivate rice and to continue the collection of forest resources other than resin. The French authorities proposed removing the monks from Angkor Wat, too, but reconsidered because the name of Angkor Wat would be meaningless without monks, according to a local *achar* (ritual officiant).

The ultimate French exclusion of local inhabitants from and the restriction of their practices on major monumental sites has been emulated by the Cambodian authorities at various stages in the past and today with more intensity and cynicism, though local inhabitants cannot be physically removed from the residential areas now because of the government decision in September 2004 (APSARA, 2005).[28] An order promulgated by the government in the same year confirms that some of the bans delivered by the heritage police continue to be effective, including resin-tapping and releasing cattle in the Angkor site (ibid.).[29]

Irregularities occurring at Angkor and conflicts between various levels of the national authorities and local communities have recently been taken seriously by the government. It has issued several official documents, which clarify and endorse the exclusive authority of APSARA in the management and development of the site and in matters of land use. At the same time, the government has, for the first time, clarified some of the rights of the local villagers such as residential rights and rights to manage the land inherited from ancestors, while strictly prohibiting land transactions with outsiders or for establishing service sector facilities (ibid.). This is a favourable change for the local community, but its implications and implementation are as yet unclear.

THE VAT PHOU SITE

The Vat Phou site shares several characteristics with Angkor. Firstly, both sites are credited to Khmer kings for the construction of the monuments. Secondly, the areas designated within the World Heritage Site are large and are inhabited. The important linking point of the two sites is that the zoning of the Vat Phou site and the criteria for its nomination reflected the lessons learnt from the shortcomings found in Angkor, particularly the failure to designate the entire site as a cultural landscape. Yet, the problems that have occurred after nomination have turned out to be similar, i.e. the marginalization of local inhabitants and the subordination of local ways of life to the needs of various levels of national authorities.

Socio-cultural resources

The main inhabitants of the Vat Phou site[30] are Lao people,[31] but the site is mainly associated with the Khmer. The present residents however make use of the site as a sacred place and, at the same time, as a place for living.

According to a Khmer inscription at the site, it was the heartland and the sacred site of the pre-Angkor kingdom of Chenla (sixth to eighth centuries CE) (Ishii and Sakurai, 1985: 76–80). Khmer legends say that the area around Vat Phou was the birthplace of the Hindu god, Shiva (Nishimura, 2004a: 49). In particular, Phou Kao, the hill behind Vat Phou temple, with a gigantic longitudinal stone standing on top as a natural lingam (phallus symbol of Shiva), was worshipped by the Khmer and is still revered by the people of Champasak today. The Champasak area flourished as a mid-way trading base between northern Champa and southern Funan (Ishii and Sakrai, 1985: 76).[32] Archaeological research on the banks of the Mekong River and in the Champasak Plain surrounding the temple complex has revealed an extensive archaeological and cultural landscape, including the remains of two ancient urban settlements dating from the fifth to the twelfth centuries CE, tentatively identified as the sites of the ancient Khmer cities of Shestrapura[33] and Lingapura (Government of the Lao PDR, 1999: 12). In the process of Angkor being developed with the Siem Reap area as a centre, the political and economic centre moved from Vat Phou to Sambor Prei Kuk, and then to Siem Reap. As an ancestral land, Vat Phou was considered as a place of pilgrimage by generations of Angkor kings. After the fall of Angkor, Champasak went through a period as an independent state, then as part of the Lao kingdom of Lan Xang, then it was incorporated into the Thai state, then became an independent Champasak kingdom, then it became part of a French colony, and it finally became part of Laos (Nishimura, 2004b: 7). UNESCO's World Heritage Centre considers that the whole of the Vat Phou site represents a development ranging from the fifth to the fifteenth centuries CE, mainly associated with the Khmer Empire.[34]

Management framework

The area designated as the World Heritage Site covers approximately 400 km² (Nishimura, 2004d: 5), like Angkor. There are 52 villages within the site (Nishimura, 2004b: 9), with a population of approximately 50,000,[35] around half of the population in Angkor.

The main difference from Angkor is that the designated site is one solid area of the Champasak cultural landscape, taking into consideration the relationship between nature and humanity.[36] In particular, the Champasak Heritage Management Plan mentions 'the landscape of agriculture and settlement around the site and the land use patterns and agricultural engineering techniques developed by the site's ancient inhabitants which make the site a living as well as a historically significant cultural landscape' (Government of the Lao PDR, 1999: 170).

The zoning system reflects such a philosophy. It is organized hierarchically with additional protection given, and restrictions of various kinds – the reverse order of those in Angkor. Out of four zones, Zone 1 constitutes almost the entire area covered by the Management Plan and where local people live.[37] The restrictions imposed on them include the major felling of trees for field enlargement or any other purpose; public works such as irrigation, road construction, electrification or provision of other services; the introduction of buildings substantially higher than current practice (up to twelve metres) (ibid.: 169–99, 174)

Management mechanism: beyond Angkor

As in the case of Angkor, UNESCO, this time better prepared than in Cambodia, through its regional office in Bangkok took initiatives in preparation for the nomination of the Vat Phou site with the full participation of the local authorities and a capacity-building programme. The former cultural adviser in UNESCO Bangkok is also the person who prepared for the nomination of Angkor as a World Heritage Site. This reflects the lessons learnt in Cambodia, where insufficient preparation for the nomination amongst other things has led to confrontations at all levels, including that between UNESCO and the then representative of the Cambodian government for Angkor.

The Laotian government had for some time worked, together with the UNESCO office in Bangkok, with ethno-archaeological researchers in order to understand the history and archaeology of the site as well as to prepare the framework of site protection and management. In 1995 the National Inter-Ministerial Co-ordinating Committee for Vat Phou (NIMCC) was established, but has not yet been made an international body such as the ICC in Angkor. In Angkor, APSARA was created as a new body for the management and development of the site, which caused tensions and conflicts with existing authorities, in particular with the Angkor Conservation Office and its umbrella organization the Ministry of Culture and Fine Arts, with the provincial authorities, and later with the Cabinet. At the Vat Phou site, there is no APSARA, but the staff of Vat Phou Museum, which is the equivalent of the Angkor Conservation Office, has been in charge of conservation, but is rather under-employed. The Vat Phou Museum reports to the Champasak District Office of the Ministry of Information and Culture. There is no equivalent of the heritage police. The office that is directly responsible for management differs according to the scale of the matter. Consent is required from the District Committee for minor developments including the construction of individual houses and the alteration of buildings, from the Provincial Heritage Committee for government works and other major developments (except national irrigation and road schemes), or from the NIMCC for national irrigation and road schemes (ibid.: 176).

In addition, the local communities are involved in the management structure, as the Village Administrative Authorities are included in the 1997 Decree of the President of the Lao PDR on the Preservation of Cultural, Historical and Natural Heritage No. 03/PR (Articles 9 and 10). Furthermore, a Village Liaison Committee was established to liaise between the Site Manager and the Site Management and Training Centre (ibid.: 284). But even though the local communities were included in the management mechanism, the relatively independent authority given to the District Committee later turned out to be problematic, in a sense similar to Angkor, in terms of its being the immediate authority to take charge of the development of the site. This point will be discussed later.

Inhabitants and their use of the site

Most inhabitants of the Vat Phou site are rice farmers of Lao ethnicity and syncretists who believe in both indigenous spirits and Buddhism. Local people continue to worship Phou Kao and the Vat Phou temple complex, even though they are not the descendants of the original builders, nor Hindu.[38] They not only worship at temples containing Buddha statues, but also throughout the site because of powerful spirits dwelling there. In February they annually organize the Vat Phou Festival, with up to 10,000 visitors (ibid.: 232). The forest of the Champasak area is a hunting ground for birds as well as a place to collect firewood and other forest products for construction, food or handicrafts. The people there nonetheless believe that the forest is an abode of powerful spirits, so that their exploitation of the forest resources has been minimal.

Conservation, development and relocation of local inhabitants

Social changes and the conservation orientation of the local authorities at the site have jointly worked toward restricting local ways of life, leading to the ultimate relocation of substantial numbers of local inhabitants. Clay quarries and brick factories began to be built at the site in recent years in response to a growing demand for buildings made with more durable materials (ibid.: 44). This activity was later stopped in order to protect the site from the archaeological point of view. While the existing ponds for fish-farming were allowed to remain, no new ponds could be built.

In May 2002, a year after the Japanese government's Non-profit Cultural Assistance Programme promised to build a new drainage system, site office and site museum, more than 100 households of villagers of Ban Nongsa (approximately one-third) in front of the Vat Phou temple were removed to the area to the west by the Champasak District Office of the Ministry of Information and Culture. They include villagers who had been cultivating rice within the temple compounds. The official reasons cited for this drastic action included concerns about natural threats such as floods as well as human threats, including vandalism. The area was bulldozed and fenced with barbed wire, while the dislocated villagers were given land or money as compensation. The effort to protect the site has partially excluded the former residents, but this decision did not take into account their need to use a well located inside the site. Subsequently, the dislocated villagers and the local district office began a new type of 'cat and mouse' relationship, with the villagers cutting the wire in one section to enter their former residential area to obtain water supplies and the district office then replacing the barbed wire. This incident shows clearly that the villagers were dislocated forcefully, without prior consultation.[39]

Tourism development

Tourism development here has not yet occurred on a large scale due to the relative difficulty of access to the site, and the fact that the Vat Phou site normally requires half a day for visits. Most visitors stay in the towns of Pakse or Champasak, where guest houses are available, or even reside in another more distant area of the country or Thailand because improved road systems allow good access to the site. Before the inscription of the site on the World Heritage List, there were approximately 3,000 visitors a year; now there are over 10,000.

In 2000 the Japanese government funded the building of a bridge over the Mekong River to facilitate transport and traffic from Thailand and is planning to build a new road along the Mekong River down to the Vat Phou site, which will again mean removing several riverside villages. If this plan goes ahead, it is most likely that the number of tourists will increase. However, because these visitors will be taking day trips from Thailand, the economic benefit will have less impact on the local communities, who not only lack accommodation to offer but also have few saleable traditional souvenirs apart from bamboo baskets to steam sticky rice, commonly found in the country. Clearly, there is an urgent need to consider how best to protect the site and the ways of life of people as well as to develop a mechanism for the local communities to have fair shares of the benefits obtained from tourism development.

TOWARDS A COMMUNITY-BASED APPROACH TO THE MANAGEMENT OF HERITAGE SITES

The alarming situation concerning heritage sites with resident populations in the Asia–Pacific Region, in particular in the Mekong River region, led the International Centre for the Study of the Preservation and Restoration of Cultural Property (ICCROM) to establish a Living Heritage Sites Programme in 2002–2003. The first Strategy Meeting of the Living Heritage Sites Programme was held in September 2003, in close co-operation with the SEAMEO Projects in Regional Centre for Archaeology and Fine Arts (SPAFA) in Bangkok. In November 2005 a workshop on 'Living Heritage: Empowering Community' was held by ICCROM and SPAFA in Phrae, northern Thailand, with the participation of representatives from eight regional countries, together with three invited speakers from outside the region, including the author and conservators from India and New Zealand. A week-long workshop appeared fairly beneficial since most participants are members of national authorities responsible for managing heritage sites.

In Phrae, ICCROM and SPAFA developed a pilot project with community participation in heritage management. The project is impressive, adapting the human ordination tradition and applying it to teak trees of some age in order to protect them from logging, and using secondary school students to act as the chief guardians, promoters and guides of the historical heritage of Phrae, such as the former palaces of the Phrae king, which have recently been converted to museums.

At the workshop radical community archaeology was introduced by Sayan Praicharnjit, an archaeologist from Thammasat University, whose project in Nan Province is all-inclusive in the excavation of local kiln sites, where the local communities manage site museums. The kiln sites are not fenced. In his view, state-centralized and non-participative management alienated villagers and ordinary people from heritage sites, which caused them to disrespect cultural heritage, resulting in looting and the destruction of the sites. He explained that he had been able to initiate this project because the state had not yet started work at these sites; his project has received royal blessing. In particular, Princess Sirindhorn, also an archaeologist, presented an award to one of the site managers in 2005 for his ability and voluntary efforts in maintaining the ancient kiln site museum. In addition, the Thailand World Heritage Committee proposed this archaeological site to be included on the Tentative List of World Heritage (Praicharnjit, 2005).[40]

While regional archaeological staff may recognize the benefit and needs of community-based archaeology and conservation, some confessed that there was no way that they could demand this approach from the higher authorities. In some cases, the fact that ICCROM and SPAFA organized such a workshop may be influential, for certain governments are eager to show how they are willing to go along with 'international' trends and meet international standards. At least in Angkor, the Cambodian government is now well aware of its needs to balance the conservation of heritage and tourism development, as well as actively to protect local ways of life, because international support is vital for the survival of the government itself. The government created a section directly to deal with land use and development and local population in mid-2004, with the first Director-General of SPAFA, a Cambodian architect (returned from Canada to act as the Director of this unit), reorganizing the old Culture Unit. In November 2003 APSARA launched Phase II of its operation, i.e. Conservation and Sustainable Development. Since then APSARA has vigorously initiated services to local communities and organized education and training sessions for various groups of stakeholders (Khuon, 2005).

The direction in which the international agencies are heading concerning heritage, conservation and tourism is towards a community-based approach or an approach that recognizes not only the importance of preserving the monumental heritage, but also of the effective utilization of the heritage, taking into account the principle of 'sustainable change'. These agencies, however, must contend with questions such as: What heritage? Whose heritage? For whom is the site to be conserved, and by whom? How is the site to be used and managed? All of these questions are becoming essential issues in relation to World Heritage Sites.

CONCLUSION

The World Heritage programme has promoted new perspectives with which we are able to see our own heritage or discover new heritage values in our cultural and natural environments. It has certainly provided Southeast Asian countries with opportunities to realign their socio-political and economic priorities and reconsider their whole approach to heritage. Not surprisingly, therefore, the programme has become a significant political tool used by the states to promote their own national agenda, pride and international image. Southeast Asian governments are very concerned that they control their own sites in such a way as to maximize the revenue from them. Because of this, the governments (or their agents) often exclude local populations from a site, which has led to chief stakeholders contesting cultural and socio-economic resources, as we have seen in the cases of Angkor and Vat Phou.

While there is a legal framework and different interpretations of laws and guidelines, the law on paper is often ignored in some countries where people 'see' law more through the enactment of strongmen (cf. Asian Development Bank, 2000: 97–98). Local knowledge and practices are often disregarded as belonging to the so-called 'little tradition', whereas the 'built environment' represents a more glorious national 'great tradition' (cf. Redfield, 1956)

The manner in which heritage has traditionally been managed is, however, increasingly being questioned. It is no longer considered adequate to create open-air archaeology museums or conserve a built environment managed by experts and states for the gaze of outsiders alone; now the site has to be a 'living' one. The latter requires traditional communities living at the site to continue to follow some of their practices, as they themselves and their ways of life are regarded as integral parts of heritage. There is a growing concern to bring into balance conservation, tourism development and local ways of life as well as to promote active community participation in conservation and tourism development. In brief, the new challenge is the incorporation of sustainable change in heritage management. How much to conserve and how much change to allow requires dialogue and negotiations among all stakeholders.

Angkor has gone beyond the phase of conservation-centred management accompanied by the exclusion and marginalization of local communities to a new stage of sustainable development with a more inclusive approach. It certainly presents an iconic site for the whole region, giving us a model for negotiating tourism and conservation in relation to World Heritage Sites.

Alternatives are that local communities take initiatives in managing their own heritage, as seen in the example of the kiln sites at Nan in northwestern Thailand. When this trend becomes widespread and local management widely practised, it may be a time when the World Heritage programme becomes less significant. This scenario will certainly be a positive one in terms of the democratization of heritage management. Still, having international concerns and the presence of experts and visitors may also be beneficial in times of socio-political upheaval and natural disasters in the country.

In conclusion, World Heritage Sites have become the new meeting-grounds of not only hosts and guests, but also various experts who have diverse interests. The programme has begun to incorporate a more sensitive yet forceful approach towards protecting the socially vulnerable population: protection may now be included in one of the conditions for the nomination of 'living' World Heritage Sites. The programme also now calls for attention to be paid to the need to consider how best to utilize existing socio-economic resources, i.e. local knowledge, skills and local people's association with the sites, rather than just to depend on external expertise and resources. A positive appraisal of local value systems and resources in site management is likely to enhance the local sense of belonging, monumental conservation and the tourism experience.

NOTES

1   I am particularly grateful to Masao Nishimura for providing me with copies of his written papers as well as his verbal comments on the Vat Phou site, and also to Khun-Neay Khuon from APSARA for making available up-to-date information and legal documents on Angkor compiled in 2005. I would also like to thank UNESCO and ICCROM for their support and interest in this research.

2   The composition of sites is as follows: 2 sites in Cambodia, 5 sites in Thailand, 5 sites in Vietnam, 2 sites in the Lao PDR, 3 sites in Malaysia, 7 sites in Indonesia and 5 sites in the Philippines (http://whc.unesco.org/en/list) (see also Figure 1.1).

3   See http://whc.unesco.org/en/list.

4   World Heritage Sites with inhabitants in Southeast Asia include Angkor, Hoi An (Vietnam), Vigan and the Cordilleras (Philippines), Luang Prabang and Vat Phou (Laos) (Engelhardt, 1997: 2).

5   There are several other spellings used for the site, i.e. 'Wat Phou' and 'Vat Phu', but this spelling has been used by the French, UNESCO, and many other authors since the world heritage nomination (Nishimura, 2004a: 49). Wat or Vat means 'temple'.

6   See http://whc.unesco.org/en/list/481.

7   See UNESCO (1983) and Pressouyre/UNESCO (1996).

8   See Selwyn (1996: 18–28) on authenticity.

9   See http://whc.unesco.org/en/list/668.

10   See http://whc.unesco.org/exhibits/cultland/histerm.htm for the history and terminology of 'cultural landscapes'. In 1993 Tongariro National Park in New Zealand became the first property to be inscribed on the World Heritage List under the revised criteria describing cultural landscapes (cf. http://whc.unesco.org/sites/421. htm).

11   The criteria for nominating Angkor on the List are as follows: i) it represents a unique artistic achievement, a masterpiece of creative genius; ii) it has exerted great influence over a span of time and, iii) within a cultural area of the world, on developments in architecture, monumental arts and landscaping; iv) it bears a unique exceptional testimony to a civilization which has disappeared; and v) it is an outstanding example of an architectural ensemble which illustrates a significant stage in history (UNESCO, 1993: 22).

12   See http://whc.unesco.org/en/list/722.

13   See http://whc.unesco.org/en/list/722.

14   Of the Mon-Khmer language group of the Austro-asiatic language family.

15   Cf. Rooney, 1994: 28; Jacques and Freeman, 1997: 13.

16   Even though the French use the spelling of 'Angkor Vat' like 'Vat Phou', UNESCO and many other authors use the spelling 'Angkor Wat'.

17   See http://news.bbc.co.uk/2/hi/asia-pacific/3866683.stm.

18   He is now the vice-prime minister.

19   An excerpt of his speech at the Ta Nei meeting held on 20 July 2000, in which the author participated.

20   My emphasis. An excerpt of his speech at the Ta Nei meeting held on 20 July 2000.

21   They include honey, fish, birds, edible insects, wild potatoes, fruits, vines, bamboo, firewood, bees-wax, herbal medicine, rattan, tree bark to make joss-sticks, and leaves to wrap festive cakes.

22   E.g. a tug-of-war, singing matches, or throwing cotton-filled scarves between two groups.

23   Entrance fees are US$20, $40, and $60 for a one-day, three-day, and week-long pass respectively.

24   See Cambodia Times (March 10–16, 1996: 6) 'YTL Confident of Winning Siem Reap Project'.

25   In Cambodia karaoke establishments often involve prostitution.

26 One needs to pay high fees to obtain an official license.

27 Yeang (Dipterocarpus alatus) is also known as Chheu Teal. For more detail see Dy Phon (2000: 243).

28 Decision of the Royal Government of Cambodia, No. 70/SSR dated 16 September 2004, on the determination of standards for the utilization of land in Zones 1 and 2 of the Siem Reap/Angkor sites.

29 Order of the Royal Government of Cambodia, No. 02/BB dated 23 June 23 2004, on the cessation and eradication of anarchical activities in the Angkor Archaeological Park of Siem Reap Province.

30 See http://whc.unesco.org/en/list/481.

31 Of the Tai-Kadai language stock.

32 See http://whc.unesco.org/en/list/481.

33 See also http://www.littera.waseda.ac.jp/laos/iseki_english/kenkyuhan/con_kenkyuhan/wat01.html.

34 See http://whc.unesco.org/en/list/481.

35 This approximate figure was provided by Masao Nishimura.

36 The 'great works of art' criteria for the nomination of the site on the World Heritage List are as follows. Criterion iii) The Temple Complex of Vat Phou bears exceptional testimony to the cultures of Southeast Asia, and in particular to the Khmer Empire which dominated in the region in the 10th–14th centuries. Criterion iv) The Vat Phou complex is an outstanding example of the integration of a symbolic landscape of great spiritual significance to its natural surroundings. Criterion vi) Contrived to express the Hindu version of the relationship between nature and humanity, Vat Phou exhibits a remarkable complex of monuments and other structures expressing intense religious conviction and commitment (http://whc.unesco.org/en/list/481).

37 Zone 1: Champasak Heritage and Cultural Landscape Protection Zone – the entire area covered by the Management Plan (390 km^2); Zone 2: Sacred Environment and Conservation Zone (92 km^2); Zone 3: Archaeological Research Zone (21 km^2); Zone 4: Monument Management Zone (2.85 km^2) (Government of Lao PDR, 1999: 166-199).

38 See also Government of the Lao PDR (1999: 62) for more details.

39 This account was provided by Masao Nishimura who witnessed the process of removing the villagers in May 2002. See http://www.iccrom.org/eng/prog2004-05/08livingheritage/LivingHeritageReport_2003.pdf (p.14) or Shimotsuma et al., 2003: 14.

40 A Singaporean archaeologist, Lim Chen Sian, from the National University of Singapore, presented another case of an all-inclusive excavation project of a buried fort built in part by the British in Singapore in the late nineteenth century. The fort area had been reclaimed for development in the 1970s without archaeological records since Singapore has no mandatory archaeological survey prior to new constructions.

CHAPTER 7

National Identity and Heritage Tourism in Melaka[1]

Nigel Worden

MELAKA AND 'MALAYNESS'

Melaka, as the most important historical city in Malaysia, has been presented in Malaysian tourist literature as 'a compact living museum – filled with an intriguing mix of its inhabitants' (Tourism Malaysia, 1998), and as a must for the visitor who wants to learn something of the historical roots of the country. What makes Melaka particularly interesting as a case study is that its heritage is not only a product for the tourist market but it has also been a central symbol or element in the construction of a highly contested contemporary Malaysian identity. In the words of the plaque unveiled by the former Prime Minister Mahathir Mohamed in 1989, Melaka is *'bandaraya bersejarah Malaysia. Di sini semuanya bermula (...) lahirnya sebuah negara'* ('the historic city of Malaysia. Here is where it all began (...) the birth of a nation'). Those words relating to the origins of a nation and to the historical interconnection between Melaka and Malaysia continue to have resonance. They are enshrined in the official website of the state government of Melaka under the heading 'Visit Historic Melaka – Means Visit Malaysia', which describes the state as 'abundantly rich, not just in natural resources but also history and folklore. Melaka is where it all began' (www.melaka.gov.my, accessed in 1998 and again in December 2007).

Melaka provides a classic example of the ways in which heritage is constructed, contested, promoted and changed. Since the 1980s tourism has become the most vibrant sector of Melaka's economy, with a wide range

130

of luxury and budget hotels, a specially restored and preserved heritage site in the city centre and a range of sophisticated visitor services (see, for example, the websites of 'Tourism Melaka' [www.tourism-melaka.com, accessed in 2004 and again in October 2007] and 'Melaka Net' [www. melaka.net, accessed in 1999 and again in 2007]). Although the economic recession of 1997–1998 dampened some of the expansion projects aimed at the local and regional market, the city's relative proximity to Kuala Lumpur International Airport (KLIA) in Sepang District, officially opened on 27 June 1998, as well as to the road system which links it to the capital city and to Singapore, have helped it to recover its position as a viable and desirable destination for both the short-term foreign visitor and the domestic tourist.

In Malaysia, as in other parts of Southeast Asia, the state has played and continues to play a major role in tourism development and identity construction (Picard and Wood, 1997a). During the colonial era tourism in Malaysia focused primarily on European activities and in the early decades of independence most tourist activities were centred in Singapore, Kuala Lumpur and Penang (Pulau Pinang) (Stockwell, 1993). Significant state funding was only provided in the 1980s with the establishment of a Ministry of Tourism and Culture (MTC) on 20 May 1987 from a merger between the Culture Division of the Ministry of Culture, Youth and Sports and the Tourism Development Corporation of Malaysia. Since then state investment in tourism has increased substantially and there have been further organizational adjustments as the government's perceptions of the sector and its strategic importance in the national economy have changed. The MTC was reorganized and renamed the Ministry of Culture, Arts and Tourism on 22 October 1992. It was then broken up on 27 March 2004 to form two ministries: the Ministry of Tourism, with its agency the Malaysia Tourism Promotion Board (or Tourism Malaysia), and the Ministry of Culture, Arts and Heritage (www.motour.gov.my, accessed in 2005 and again in 2007). Interestingly the responsibility for heritage has been separated from that of tourism proper, but whilst the Ministry of Tourism has specific responsibilities to develop tourism as an industry, its sister ministry is charged with the task of preserving and developing Malaysian heritage as well as regulating, promoting and developing heritage tourism (www.heritage.gov.my, accessed in 2007).

Increasing government involvement in the sector was accompanied by the awareness that tourism could be harnessed to the state's broader project of promoting a distinctive 'Malay' cultural identity (Tan, 1991; King, 1993). Penang and Melaka in particular benefited from the increased focus on cultural, historical and heritage tourism rather than sun, beaches and recreation that climaxed in the successful 1990 'Visit Malaysia' campaign. Yet, unlike Penang, which was a colonial creation, Melaka presented a heritage rooted in a distinctively Malay past, expressing and symbolizing 'a golden age' of Malay commerce, political power and cultural expansion. It thus came to play a key role in the construction of Malay, and by extension Malaysian, national identity (see Kahn, 1997). As Cartier has argued 'Postcolonial state policies (...) produced interruptions in Melakan landscapes that symbolically uphold the ideology of the contemporary state at the expense of Melaka's global, cosmopolitan heritage' (2001: 194). The official symbols of the state also resonate with 'Malayness', Islam and a Malay-centred Malaysian nationhood. The state emblem comprises five Malay sacred daggers (*kris*) representing the five Melakan heroes: Hang Tuah, Hang Jebat, Hang Lekiu, Hang Lekir and Hang Kasturi; it also contains the crescent moon and star as symbols of Islam; and it depicts the Melaka tree with two mousedeers relating to the story of Parameswara, the founder of Melaka, who subsequently converted to become the first Muslim ruler of the state, Raja Iskandar Shah. The state flower is the kesidang worn by Melakan Malay women as a hair decoration. The state flag also incorporates the Islamic star and crescent using the colours of the Malaysian flag (www.melaka.gov.my, accessed in 1998 and again in 2007).

These preoccupations of course beg the question of what constituted the Malay 'nation'. In the 1980s the Malay-dominated Malaysian government had two goals in this regard. The first was to identify the historical Malay past with the territorial boundaries of modern Malaysia. This involved some deft remodelling. As late as the 1940s 'Malay' identity had been associated with linguistic, cultural and political structures that were much wider than the state of Malaysia which came into being in 1963. The failure of 'Greater Indonesia' (*Indonesia Raya*) in the 1940s and the 'Confrontation' (*Konfrontasi*) between Sukarno's Indonesia and Tunku Abdul Rahman's Malaysia from 1963 until 1966 meant that the Malaysian government had to promote a national heritage and an identity that excluded the wider 'Malay' world elsewhere in Southeast Asia and particularly in Indonesia.

Secondly, the construction of a Malay national heritage in the 1970s and 1980s was closely linked to the state's New Economic Policy that promoted the interests of those defined as 'indigenous' (*bumiputera*), primarily the ethnic Malays, over the other inhabitants of the country. In 1971 a state-sponsored conference on national culture had declared that 'national culture must be based on the indigenous culture of this region' (Crouch, 1996: 166; Said, 1996: 55). In this process the ethnic complexity of the region was reduced to a crude division between Malay, Chinese and Indian which in turn drew on colonial and Orientalist categorizations (Hirschman, 1986, 1987; Shamsul, 2001). The emphasis on Malay 'traditional' culture emphasized the antiquity and local specificity of the *bumiputera*: Malaysian culture in this sense became Malay culture (Kahn, 1992).[2] In this regard the promotion of Melaka's heritage represented much more than a tourist product. It was a critical part of the reconstruction and reinterpretation of Malaysia's history, which was matched by a similar process in educational texts and academic historical writing (Khoo, 1979).

This association of Melaka with Malayness was rooted in several factors. The fifteenth-century Sultanate came to be portrayed as the ancestral state of peninsular Malaysia, as distinct from the pre-colonial states that spanned the Straits of Melaka and with which in historical terms Melaka was intimately linked. It thus came to serve, much as Majapahit did for Indonesia, as a geographical and territorial forerunner of the modern Malaysian state and as a symbol of the essence of nationhood (Reid, 1979). Therefore, there are few references to the Sumatran roots of the port, for the Malaysian state has shown little interest in the Srivijayan past or in archaeological work that cannot be closely identified with a 'Malay' ethnicity (Andaya, 2001).

In addition to this geographical national identity, Melaka has also come to be upheld as the epitome of Malay values, which transcended its conquest by Europeans powers. In this image it was prosperous; it dominated the trade routes of the region; it was respected by outside powers, notably China and Siam; and, despite its culturally and ethnically diverse population, it was internally harmonious. Of particular significance was its political identity, represented by the concept of *kerajaan*, which is often incompletely translated as 'kingdom' but which implies much more about the authority of the ruler (*Raja*). Some Malaysian scholars have argued that the 'Malacca tradition' of kingship, law and authority survived the Portuguese conquest through the Johor–Riau empire and into the eighteenth century, and was by implication incorporated into the modern Malaysian nation-state (see, for example, Daud, 1987; for analysis see Pillay, 1977 and Milner, 2004: 248). As recent historians have shown, the British colonial power played no small part in encouraging a notion of 'Malay' ethnicity and culture for its own political purposes, by stressing the links to a Melakan past and especially to its monarchical tradition (Reid, 2001; Andaya, 2001). The glories of the Sultanate were further extolled in the nationalist (*bangsa*) histories of the 1920s and 1930s and by the Malay nationalist movement in the 1940s, despite some ambivalence about the competing claims of loyalty to the *Raja* on the one hand and *bangsa* on the other (Milner, 1994: 193–225, 273). As a result the Sultans of the Federated Malay States were won over to the version of Malay nationalism promoted by the United Malays National Organization (UMNO), especially when their role was assured in the post-colonial constitution (Milner, 1982; Omar, 1993). In contrast to neighbouring Indonesia where the monarchical and hierarchical traditions of pre-colonial Majapahit were a source of some embarrassment to the revolutionary nationalist movement, in Malaysia the Melakan feudal past was harnessed to a nationalism which was promoting the symbolic powers of the Sultans within the framework of *kerajaan*.

A further feature of Melakan 'tradition' which was used as a metaphor for the Malay nation was Islam. The increasing disparity of economic position among Malays in the 1970s and 1980s led to a greater stress on Islam as a means of forging Malay unity, not least by UMNO in order to pre-empt the claim of the opposition Parti Islam Se-Malaysia (PAS) that it represented the faithful. Increasingly Islam, like the Malay language, became a marker of the *bumiputera* (Brown, 1994: 248–256; Hamayotsu, 1999: 2–6). Yet for the Muslim religion to be a symbol of the nation it needed to be associated with a national history rather than with PAS's appeal to a wider Muslim loyalty which transcended national boundaries. Melaka's 'Malayness' therefore included an emphasis on its position as the first Islamic state of the Malay world.

MELAKA'S CULTURAL HERITAGE

The tourist experience of Melaka is conditioned by these factors, but the creation of Malay cultural heritage in a predominantly European, Chinese and multicultural settlement has required some skilful reordering of Melaka's history and heritage landscapes. The 'heritage core' of the town is defined by European buildings – the Dutch Stadthuys (1650) and Christ Church (1753), the remnants of the Portuguese fortress, A Famosa, St Paul's Church, built by the Portuguese as Our Lady of the Hill and turned into a burial ground by the Dutch and renamed St Paul's, and finally the British clubhouse (1912). However, this colonial environment has been reclaimed to some extent by a Malay heritage: the History and Ethnography Museum and the Literature Museum, displaying local traditions and writers, are housed in the Stadthuys and its precincts, and the Proclamation of Independence Memorial is located in the British clubhouse. The Malay Governor's Collections have been placed in Seri Melaka, the residence of the Dutch and then the British Governors. Not far from the Stadthuys is also the Melaka Islamic Museum which celebrates the history, principles and achievements of Islam in a traditional nineteenth-century wooden building which was the home of Melaka's first school of Islamic Studies and then the Melaka Islamic Council.

The absence of buildings and artefacts from the pre-colonial Malay era means that the indigenous past has been materially as well as metaphorically reconstructed. A replica of the Sultan's fifteenth-century wooden palace (*istana*) was opened by the Prime Minister in 1986 at the foot of St Paul's Hill, built on a smaller scale but based on near-contemporary descriptions and architectural speculation (Sherwin, 1981). The official website of the state government describes it as 'the only palace from Malacca's glorious past built with such detail and refinement' (www.melaka.gov.my). Although the original palace was on the hill summit and the houses of the lower-ranking nobility were erected on its slopes and at its foot, the presence of the colonial church, fortress and the Seri Melaka residence on the original site (www.virtualmuseummelaka.com, accessed in 2002 and again in 2003) meant that the replica had to be relocated (Hashim, 1992: 211). The palace replica is surrounded by the Historic City Memorial Garden in Islamic design, with a central walkway leading to the main entrance of the palace and containing a monument commemorating the declaration of Melaka as a historic city, topped by a golden replica of a Malay royal headdress, a symbol, according to the American Express-sponsored walking tour brochure (n.d.), of the Malaysian citizens' allegiance to the throne. It thus has an aura of authenticity and awe, lacking at other constructed heritage sites in Southeast Asia such as Jakarta's Taman Mini.

This striking palace building is a clear indicator of the type of heritage emphasis that is placed on Melaka's pre-colonial past. Inside is housed the Cultural Museum (*Muzium Budaya*) with replicas of the court and its ceremonial. The economic achievements of Melaka's pre-colonial past or the social complexity of its thalassocracy are overlaid by the emphasis on *kerajaan* ceremonial and courtly ritual, reflecting the emphasis of contemporary chronicles which show that 'a *Raja*'s work was expected to be concerned largely with ceremony and convention (...) "real issues" were not the business of a *Raja*' (Milner, 1982: 48–49). The displays are visually arresting, but even in the less dramatic storyboards and mini-tableaux of the History Museum, there is little attention given to the context of this world of courtly traditions. It is perhaps not surprising, and characteristic of heritage representation in many places, that the 'underside' of Melaka's pre-colonial past is missing. There is, of course, no mention of the dangers of attack in Melakan streets, of the rampant diseases, or of the slaves who formed a significant part of the town's labour force.

This emphasis on the *Raja* and the court is a direct product of the importance of the Melakan *kerajaan* political tradition to contemporary Malaysian identity. However, an indication of the ambivalence which a feudal past presents to the construction of the post-independent nation is revealed in the representations of the classic Malay story of Hang Tuah and Hang Jebat. In this legend, which is set during the Sultanate period, Hang Tuah obeys the orders of the *Raja* to kill his lifelong friend Hang Jebat, who has been accused of treason against the absolutist ruler. In the *Hikayat Hang Tuah*, it is Hang Tuah who is portrayed as the 'paragon of Malay chivalry' by following the command of his *Raja* despite the personal costs of killing his friend. But, in the course of the 1950s, Hang Jebat was re-defined as the righteous rebel who stood up for justice. This was 'a first foreshadowing of our present day generation' in the era of nationalism and anti-colonialism, although it fell short of an association with a popular Robin Hood-type figure who might become too closely linked to the ideals of Communist insurgents (Josselin de Jong, 1965; Harper, 1999: 285).[3] In modern Melaka Hang Tuah's mausoleum is preserved and both figures are memorialized in street names. Yet the issue of who to regard as hero is ambivalent. The *Son et Lumière* show, which tourists may view outside the palace in both Malay and English, remarking that 'Malay customs and culture would never condone Jebat's treachery', describes the conflict as a 'black day for Melaka' and a cause of division 'as has happened so often in our history', implying that the dispute was a cause of the Sultanate's ultimate downfall. However, a large display board in the *Muzium Budaya* was more ambivalent. With the title 'Clash of the Champions' it described the contest as one of differing ideologies. 'Hang Tuah stood for selfless service and blind faithfulness to the sovereign, no matter what the sacrifice. Hang Jebat advocated justice

(...) and was prepared to avenge [by] the most extreme methods – rebellion (...). The end of the duel is not important: what is important is the spirit and what one fights for in the encounter, and that still lives vividly unto this day.' In this account the virtue of loyalty to the *Raja* is not challenged, but the right to stand up for justice is also maintained. The board thus marks a delicate balancing act between the competing loyalties of the *kerajaan* and *bangsa* and deflects attention from their inconsistencies in an appeal to personal morality.

There is however no ambivalence in the representation of Islam. Tableaux at the History Museum represent the Sultanate as unambiguously Islamic, from the moment of the arrival of Sheikh Abdul Aziz and the instant conversion of Melaka's ruling prince, Parameswara. Melaka's intimate connection with Islam is also expressed and celebrated in the Melaka Islamic Museum, 'only a stone's throw away from the Dutch Square' and housed in a stately, three-storey building erected in the 1850s (www.melaka.gov.my). Although academic writing has stressed the somewhat ambivalent position of Islam in the Melaka Sultanate (see, for example, Wake, 1983), and indeed some nineteenth-century Islamic revivalist movements in Melaka attacked the 'impurities' of the *kerajaan* elite (Milner, 1994: 141–153), none of this is evident in the museum displays. There is no hint of unease with the courtly tradition, no suggestion that its roots or its values are anything other than purely Islamic. The association of the *kerajaan* with Islam and this in turn with the Malay *bangsa* is unambiguous. Islam is thus made indigenous and a tenet of local Malay identity, avoiding extremism without losing its purity. Given the challenge of the PAS populist Islamic opposition party in the late 1970s and 1980s, which stressed international Islamic unity and accused the UMNO-led government of betraying the true faith, this interpretation is not surprising (Jomo and Cheek, 1992).

The authority for these heritage representations of *kerajaan* and of Islam in Melaka comes from the *Malay Annals* (*Sejarah Melayu*), the masterpiece of classical Malay literature.[4] The historical accuracy of the *Annals* has been much contested, with some scholars dismissing them as an 'elaborate fiction' written after the Portuguese conquest, while others defend their status as a cultural rather than a historical document (Wake, 1983: 130; Cheah, 1988: 10; Johns, 1979: 46, 64). As Hashim has argued, the aim of the *Annals* was not to 'establish some form of reality or factual authenticity (...) [but] to try and sanctify the early Malacca rulers and the royal family' (1992). The *Annals* thus present an image of the glories of the Muslim court which resonated with the needs of the *kerajaan*. It is no coincidence that they were named as such by British scholars and knowledge of them was most widely disseminated at the time when the Melakan 'tradition' was being promoted by the colonial state (Shamsul, 2001: 363). They give both authority and authenticity to Melaka's current public history.

While many local visitors head for the *Istana*, most foreign tourist buses focus on central 'special space'. This is dominated by Dutch images, with the red pink Stadthuys and Reformed Church, and a monument of a windmill standing incongruously on the square between them. The Portuguese colonial past is less apparent, with the notable exception of the Porta de Santiago, the gateway to the former fortress. This reflects the destruction of earlier Portuguese constructions but is also explained by the financial and technical support given to the restoration of the heritage centre by the Dutch government, including the restoration of the Stadthuys (Vis, 1982).

The images of the Portuguese and the Dutch given in Melaka's museums are strikingly different. The Portuguese are cast in the role of colonial exploiters because they were responsible for the destruction of the Sultanate; the internal divisions and succession disputes that weakened late fifteenth-century Melaka are conveniently ignored. Thus in the Maritime Museum, housed in a reconstructed replica of the man-of-war, *Flor de la Mar*, along the riverside, a board announces that 'the Portuguese (...) never followed the accommodating policy of the Melaka Sultanate but instead followed the policy of crusaders by milking dry the wealth the trade brought'. By contrast the Dutch are portrayed neutrally, even approvingly. A Dutch East India Company (*Vereenigde Oost-Indische Compagnie*, VOC) chamber-room housed in the History Museum is faithfully restored without adverse commentary. Presumably the Dutch funding behind this restoration muted a post-colonial critique, but the depiction of the Portuguese as destroyers and exploiters means that their Dutch opponents can be portrayed in a more favourable light, which accords with historical Malay perceptions. Importantly in their rivalry with the Portuguese the Dutch allied themselves with the Malay ruler of Johor (Lewis, 1995: 14). Moreover, unlike the Portuguese, who are portrayed as fanatical Catholics, the VOC was little interested in conversion and was tolerant of Islamic practices. Their rule thus marked a much less dramatic break with the ideal vision of the Sultanate than did that of the Portuguese, and is represented accordingly.

There is very little representation of the British in the public history of Melaka. Indeed there is little in the current touristic promotion of Melaka which indicates a strong British presence. In the History Museum a single diorama represents the nineteenth century, citing the often-quoted description of the town in 1879 as 'very still, hot, tropical, sleepy and dreamy. Malacca looks a town "out of the running", utterly antiquated, mainly un-English, a veritable Sleepy Hollow' (Bird, 1883: 125). In part this reflects Melaka's decline in the late eighteenth and nineteenth centuries, when first British Penang and then Singapore predominated in the region. But the British are seen as having little to do with the Sultanate and that is what is of primary significance.

Domestic tourists and some foreign visitors also pay a visit to the Proclamation of Independence Monument, housed with supreme irony in the former British colonial Malacca Club building. It was in front of this building whereby in 1956, despite protests from Kuala Lumpur, Tunku Abdul Rahman chose Melaka as the place to announce Malaya's forthcoming independence. By this historic event the symbolism of Melaka's past was used as an identifier with the future of the new nation: Melaka literally gave birth to Malaya and the wider Malaysia, and 'visiting Melaka you visit Malaysia'.

The nature of Malaysian independence means that the representation of the nationalist movement at the Monument is rather different from that in many post-colonial countries. There is no demonized colonial oppressor, and though there is mention of the 'anti-colonial struggles' of the nineteenth century, such as the Naning War, little is said about the nature of twentieth-century colonial rule and nothing about the lifestyles of those who earlier inhabited the Clubhouse. Malaysian independence was not won through armed conflict against a colonial power and there are no memorials to glorious military engagements or revolutionary heroes of the kind depicted in nationalist museums throughout Indonesia. Rather independence is linked with the fifteenth-century Sultanate, depicted in the opening panels of the exhibition and so prominently represented in the reconstructed palace nearby. The opening statement reads, 'The sequence of history has its own peculiarities. Melaka, the first Malay state to fall under the Western powers, became the place for the declaration of the date of independence of the Federation of Malaya, 445 years later'. The process of the negotiated settlement of the 1950s is then recalled through a series of detailed information panels which emphasize the dignity and authority of the nationalist leaders in images resonant of the Sultanate itself. The Malay ruling élite which controlled the politics of independence is thus linked directly to the Melakan past, maintained in the interim by British recognition and utilization of *Raja* authority. Here the story of Melaka's role in the construction of the nation comes to a fitting climax.

This strong association of Melaka with Malayness inevitably meant that a non-Malay heritage, or more importantly the cosmopolitan character and history of this once great trading centre, was viewed as being of less significance by the constructors of the museums and sites of the city. Cartier has pointed out that 'In the context of making choices about how to represent national heritage, the state has relatively marginalized the histories of Chinese and Indian diasporic populations' (2001: 198). Yet at the same time much emphasis is placed in the tourist promotional literature on two categories of Melaka's population which are presented as unique.

The first comprises the hybrid population of *Peranakan*, or 'Straits Chinese' as they were called in the colonial era. There is a special *Baba Nyonya* Heritage Museum which is privately funded and located in a family house on Jalan Tun Tan Cheng Lock, while another house has been converted into the *Baba* House Hotel. The distinctive features of the *Baba Nyonya* heritage which are essential to their identity are precisely their highly Malayized character and their claims to a long period of settlement in Melaka (Tan, 1979: 96–97). This can include some manipulation of history in suggesting that all *Peranakan* originate from the intermarriage of Chinese and Malay in the seventeenth and eighteenth centuries and their adoption of Malay language and dress, although otherwise remaining distinct from the local population. In fact, a distinctive *Peranakan* identity only emerged in the mid-late nineteenth century in opposition to new Chinese immigrants who now form the large majority of Melaka's population (Clammer, 1979: 3–6). The *Peranakan* were thus localized, nationalized and Malayized and as such had a role to play in the heritage representations of Melaka which was denied to the Chinese majority.

The *Peranakan* house museums claim, in the words of the promotional literature, to take the visitor 'back to revisit the traditional lifestyles of the Babas'. Both the *Baba* House Hotel and the *Baba Nyonya* Heritage Museum are set out with the furnishings and possessions of a 'typical' late-nineteenth-century *Peranakan* family. Yet the families themselves are marked by their absence. The result is an exoticization of the *Peranakan*, and a freezing of their existence in a past time which bears little relation to the present. Indeed, the loss both of *Baba* economic prominence to later Chinese immigrants, and their favoured political status during the colonial period, means that in the post-independence era there has been an undermining of *Baba* identity accompanied by a sense of nostalgia for a lost past (Tan, 1979: 229).[5] In contrast to the official state museums representing the glories of the Sultanate which is resurrected in the new Malaysian *bangsa*, the *Peranakan* private houses appear as relics of an increasingly irrelevant past. Yet this past is an important one in heritage terms. Cartier indicates that 'On a world scale, Straits Chinese style architecture exists substantially only in Malaysia and Singapore, and to a lesser extent in Xiamen, China.' It is 'a distinctive regional style amalgamating façade treatments of western beaux-arts, neo-classical, and art deco architecture with traditional Chinese shophouse building structure' (2001: 207).

The heritage roots of the distinctively Malayized *Peranakan* are also reflected in the often-mentioned but apocryphal story of the marriage of the Ming Emperor's daughter Hang Li Po to the Melakan Sultan.[6] This event marks the union of Chinese and Malay as well as indicating the respect with which the Melakan Sultanate was regarded by China, the greatest power of the time. But of the history of the large majority of Chinese-speaking residents who are descended from nineteenth-century immigrants there is little trace in the museums and guidebooks, although visitors are surrounded by Chinese shops and dwellings. The only Chinese temple depicted in tourist literature is the seventeenth century Cheng Hoon Teng Temple, which is associated primarily with the *Peranakan*.

Neglect of this Chinese heritage has not been without controversy. In the 1980s plans by the Melaka state authorities to build on Bukit China, 42 hectares of prime hillside land in the city centre, was strongly contested by Chinese residents since it was used as a Chinese cemetery and held particular cultural significance as 'a natural symbol of the stake that the Malaysian Chinese community has in the country' (Kua, 1984; and see Cartier, 2001: 199–201). Seen as a direct assault on the Chinese cultural heritage, the episode led to heightened tensions and the plans were finally only shelved in 1985 after protests in the national Parliament and an international conservation campaign (Cartier, 1993, 2001). In one sense the Bukit China controversy marked an opposition to urban development and a movement for landscape preservation characteristic of many cities, but in Melaka the ethnic element of a Malay-led local state assault reflected the wider sense of the neglect of the Chinese heritage. In defending Bukit

China much was also made of its links with the remoter Melakan past, of its association with the Hang Li Po story, and of its role as a symbol of inter-racial relational significance in that era (Tan, 1984). Given the overwhelming dominance of the Sultanate era in the Melakan heritage, this made more tactical sense than a focus on the importance of the site to more recent Chinese immigrants or even as a solely 'Chinese' space.

Another non-Malay community which receives much focus in Melakan tourist activities is that of the *casados*, depicted as the descendants of Portuguese–Malay marriages in the sixteenth century who have maintained some of the traditions of their European origin, notably Catholicism, music, dance, and language which in its hybrid form is referred to as *kristang*. Dance displays are a major tourist attraction held at the *Medan Portugis* on the waterfront south of the city centre, which is represented as the traditional *casado* kampung.

As Sarkissian has demonstrated, by no means all *casados* are descended from the era of Portuguese occupation in the sixteenth century (1993, 1995–1996: 37–41). Moreover the concept of a distinct *casado* community and cultural tradition only emerged in the 1930s, and the dancing and musical traditions, which are anyway eclectic in their forms and roots, began as a response to the visit of the Portuguese Minister in Melaka in 1952 (Sarkissian, 2005: 154, 159). The *Medan Portugis* was built by the local state in 1984 and opened by Prime Minister Mahathir. The promotion of this exotic invented tradition was driven by the policy to promote cultural tourism, but its timing was significant in other ways. By the 1980s UMNO was increasingly dependent on non-Malay support, yet still needed to retain its policy of favouring the *bumiputera*. The Melakan Portuguese, while not defined as ethnically Malay, could nonetheless be represented as rooted in the Malay past. By 1995 they had been admitted to UMNO membership and were appealing for official *bumiputera* status on the grounds that 'the facts of history support the view that the Portuguese decedents [sic] are of Malay stock and culturally they are closer to the Malays than the Portuguese' (Fernandis, n.d.). The *casados*, like the *Peranakan*, were thus Malayized, but, as Sarkissian demonstrates, the 'image of smiling Portuguese dancers is (...) a romanticized ideal. In reality, residents are a heterogeneous mix combining at different historical moments Portuguese, Dutch, and British genes with (among others) those of Goanese and African sailors or local Chinese, Indian, and even Malay Catholic converts' (2005: 157–158). Nevertheless, young educated Melakan Eurasians have managed to make adept use of their hybrid identity 'as a means of creating a place for themselves in the modern Malaysian nation' (Sarkissian, 2005: 168).

By contrast the Chitties, who claim descent from Indian traders of the Sultanate era, have been unable to stake a claim to such status, and are often associated with later Indian immigrants of the nineteenth and twentieth centuries. Lacking both an invented tradition which could be adapted for tourism and also claims to *bumiputera* status, they are almost absent in Melakan heritage representations and are struggling to maintain a distinct identity (Mearns, 1995: 26–27, 178–179).

The heritage representations shown in Melaka are thus a product of the cultural policies and historical constructions of the 1970s and 1980s. They have not found universal acclaim. Melaka was rejected as a UNESCO World Heritage Site in the late 1980s on the grounds that too much of the original city centre had been destroyed, notably the original waterfront, which following reclamations had been used for office, retail, hotel and housing development and a sea-world amusement park (Cartier, 1996: 50–51; 2001: 201). Cartier puts it in stark terms: 'The reclamations destroyed the original Melaka harbour, the central site of Melaka's historic globalized economy, limiting Melaka's potential to advance an authentic tourism imaging strategy based on the historic port, and compromising Malaysia's application to the World Heritage Convention for Melaka town' (2001: 201). Subsequently these developments on the waterfront have shown no sign of slowing down and 'the state's "megadevelopment project" ethos marginalized the conservation of both cultural and natural heritage resources' (ibid.). Indeed the current state government's website, whilst recognizing the importance of the historic port's heritage and the tourism which it attracts, reinforces the drive to modernize and industrialize Melaka and dispel its image of 'a sleepy backwater' (ibid.).

Moreover a repeat attempt in the late 1990s met with UNESCO criticism that local communities, notably Chinese residents, were being neglected. Local conservationists in both Penang and Melaka realized that 'the cities will have to come to terms with the layered, multi-cultural occupation of their historic urban sites' (Nasution, 1998: n.p.) and complained that money 'has been mainly lavished on ill-researched museums and a sound and light show presenting a glossy version of the city's history (...) too little has been spent on restoration itself' (Nasution, 1998: 30). Despite this, Melaka was nonetheless finally granted World Heritage Site status on 7 July 2008.

Other important shifts have also taken place in Malaysia which render Melaka's heritage representations less appropriate to the cultural and ideological emphasis of the modern nation. In the 1990s the earlier cultural policy of *bumiputera* promotion became outdated with the emergence of a Malay middle class which made little identification with a feudal past but looked rather to inclusion in the modernizing world. Politically UMNO became increasingly dependent on the non-Malay vote. The result was a cultural policy shift marked by Mahathir's declaration in 1991 of the 'Vision 2020' by which Malaysia aimed to achieve full economic and industrialized development by the year 2020. In so doing the *Melayu Baru* (New Malay) was defined not by ethnicity but by urban middle class identity (Shamsul, 1999; Said, 1996: 64; Harper, 1999: 371–381). In the 1992 UMNO General Assembly, Mahathir called for 'a new culture which is relevant to the present business climate' and at the 1997 Assembly he declared that 'the Malay culture in this era is not the same with [sic] the Malay culture when we were fighting for independence and during the early post-independence period' (Case, 1995: 101; www.smpke.jpm.my/gn-data/ucapan.pm/1997/970905a. htm/clause 57). English, the language of the international economy, has increasingly replaced Malay. The symbols of *kerajaan* have been down-played and the constitutional role of the Sultans reduced, with Mahathir arguing in 1990 that Melaka's fall in 1511 had resulted from the *Raja's* self-indulgence and disunity with his people (Said, 1996: 53). Such moves led to tensions within UMNO and the symbols of language, *kerajaan* and Islam have certainly not been abandoned. But they were no longer the predominant defining features of *Melayu Baru* in the '2020' nation. Instead of an ethnic focus on *bangsa Melayu*, the emphasis was now on the national *bangsa Malaysia* in which 'the Chinese and Indians are no longer the outsiders' (Hooker, 2004: 161).

Modernization was now seen as the primary concern. In this context Melaka, the 'Historic City', needed to remould its image. A 1992 publication by the Melakan State government stressed that Melaka was 'historical in one sense, modern in another', and 'a growing industrial city and thriving holiday resort', part of what will become a 'fully industrialized' state by 2020 (Malaysia Mining Corporation Berhad, 1992: 129, 162–163; www.melaka. gov.my, 1998, revised 2007). Golf courses, leisure resorts and a 'Disney-type theme complex' were envisaged, designed to attract tourists, especially from Japan and Singapore, who would hopefully stay for longer in the town (Cartier, 1998; *Melaka Highlights*, 1997). In all of this, the earlier heritage concerns were down-played or even over-ridden. For instance plans in 1995 to reclaim more of the shoreline for commercial and leisure development cut off the *Medan Portugis* from the seafront, thus isolating the 'Portuguese Community' from 'the natural element that has become synonymous with their History and Heritage' (Singho, n.d.: 23; Hiebert, 1995). As Mahathir wrote in 1992, 'Melaka does not remain a mere historical curiosity (...) its potential as a centre for economic growth and investment is tremendous' (Malaysia Mining Corporation Berhad, 1992: 11).

The Southeast Asian economic downturn of the late 1990s led to a shelving of most of these schemes. Yet as national economic recovery takes place the focus on modernization has continued the down-grading of Melaka as a symbol of the Malaysian nation. Kuala Lumpur's Petronas Twin Towers are a more appropriate emblem of the economic drive of the *Melayu Baru*. As the Melakan local government itself recognized in its 1992 publication, 'Melaka is the ancient capital of the nation while Kuala Lumpur is the capital of modern Malaysia' (Malaysia Mining Corporation Berhad, 1992: 157). Stopover visitors at Kuala Lumpur's new international airport continue to spend a day in the town, but increasingly Melaka's heritage role is at odds with the modernizing images of the Malaysian nation in the twenty-first century. The Malaysian preoccupation with building 'the tallest, the biggest, the longest and the widest' at the expense of its cultural heritage has introduced an increasing tension in its tourism policies, and such heritage landscapes as Melaka and Penang have become the focus of struggles and debates about heritage, identity, urban land use, tourism and development among a host of political and non-governmental organizations (Goh, 1998: 171–172; 2001).

NOTES

1   The first version of this chapter was published as 'Where it all began: the representation of Malaysian heritage in Melaka', *International Journal of Heritage Studies* (2001), vol. 7, no. 3, pp.199–218. This current version was published in a special issue of *Indonesia and the Malay World* (2003), vol. 31, no. 89, pp. 31–41, edited by Michael Hitchcock and Victor T. King. We are grateful to the editors of Indonesia and the Malay World and Taylor and Francis for allowing us to reprint this revised and up-dated version. Nigel Worden has also given his permission for us to proceed with revision and re-publication. The research involving personal observations and interviews was conducted in Melaka between 1995 and 1999. The author has not continued his research there and felt that he would not be in a position to revise the paper, though he was willing for Victor T. King to undertake some editing and up-dating, given that the editors wished to include this incisive analysis of a very

important heritage site in Southeast Asia. The author also wishes to thank Khamis Abas, Josephine Chua, Rosli Haji Nor, John Tunbridge, Christopher Wake and Kerry Ward for their comments and assistance with the earlier versions of this chapter. The chapter was written before Melaka was inscribed (together with George Town) on the World Heritage List as one of the 'Historic Cities of the Straits of Malacca' on 7 July 2008.

2   This is in notable contrast to the use of heritage in Singapore where emphasis is placed on the multi-ethnic state and its historical roots (Yeoh and Kong, 1996; and see Can-Seng Ooi, Chapter 5 in this volume).

3   Hang Jebat became a hero of nationalism in the absence of clear proto-nationalist leaders akin to Indonesia's Diponegoro. The Communist insurgents fighting in the forests in the 1950s were antagonistic to UMNO's vision of an independent Malaya, and so were unsuitable as nationalist heroes in the anti-Communist Malayan state at that time.

4   The notion of Melaka as the centre of the Malay world stems directly from the *Annals* and these in turn are given high prominence in the Malay Literature displays in the Stadthuys, where they are represented as not only acting as the basis for the creation of a standard Malay language in the 1950s but also as extolling the social values of the Sultanate and 'a source of reflection and guidance for the life of young people in our time'.

5   From the late 1980s a series of conventions held by the Peranakan communities of Melaka, Penang and Singapore have encouraged a re-assertion of a distinctive heritage; for instance the theme of the eleventh Baba and Nyonya Conference held in Melaka in 1998 was 'The Baba and Nyonya in the eyes of the youth'.

6   For its academic debunking see Cartier, 1997: 574–575 and Wade, 1997: 49.

CHAPTER **8**

Interpreters of Space, Place and Cultural Practice

Processes of Change through Tourism, Conservation and Development in George Town, Penang, Malaysia

Gwynn Jenkins

INTRODUCTION

Few communities, particularly those placed within an historic urban port settlement, have avoided influences from outside the boundaries of their localized environment. Port settlements, by their very nature, are globalized settings in which the confluence of cultural influences has either strengthened each community's ethnic identity and distinctive cultural traits, and fused them into eclectic hybrid realities, or alternatively absorbed them, resulting in the loss of any sense of a distinct cultural identity. As Barth (1969: 10) notes, the manner in which such influences are addressed determines whether the communities lose or retain their cultural distinctiveness through which they perceive their sense of 'otherness'.

Cities, in which the daily activities of urban communities are framed, are experienced through the senses: they 'look, smell, sound and feel different; they have [a] different character or ambience' (Rapoport, 1984: 54). For the tourist and tour operators they have distinct and unique selling points and are promoted as such. It is this sense of 'otherness' that is attractive to the tourist. However, following increasing globalization, and with it the potential of cultural homogenization in the rapidly developing Asian region, the distinctions between communities are becoming blurred. Logan's edited book, *The Disappearing 'Asian' City* (2002) debates the loss of an Asian urban cultural identity and heritage, and explores the suggestion that a distinctive 'Asianness' is disappearing in favour of 'un-Asian' environments influenced by Western architecture and planning schools.

Urban development patterns across the region have concentrated on such needs as basic infrastructure in the form of roads, water supplies and the provision of 'better' housing for the poorer sectors of their society. More recently, development has seen the introduction or addition of malls and highways for the expanding middle class populations, even at the expense of satisfying basic urban needs. Maintaining and/or conserving the 'traditional' Asian urban form and its related community identity, however, has rarely featured in national development plans. In the main, the focus has been to create 'modern' environments rather than to follow existing patterns or to conserve the tangible built heritage, which is seen either to represent former repressive colonial powers or to project an image of backwardness.

As recognized by the Nara Seminar on Development and Integrity of Historic Cities, held in Japan in March 1999 under the auspices of UNESCO, historic cities face challenges from many sides. These comprise rapid urbanization, depopulation, the economic development of the expanding middle class coupled with social change, conservation of single monuments as opposed to holistic sites, the 'over-emphasis on catering for the demands of tourism', and the neglect of the inter-relationship between the historical core and its surroundings (UNESCO, 1999). All have played roles in the dynamics of change related to culture and identity. So too has the gradual development of a built-heritage conservation industry and with it the potential erosion of cultural sites through 'gentrification'.

As an historic island port settlement, and since 2008 (together with Melaka) a World Heritage Site, George Town's urban history has followed similar lines. Most recently, however, new developments and development proposals for the city have shown a marked change in the perception of the value of the old traditional environments and of the remaining communities within the original urban settlement. The need for a more defined tourism product has clearly played a role in this change, as have the continued efforts of the embattled 'heritage conservation' community. An illustration of this shifting emphasis is found in recent efforts to revitalize the city's first commercial district as a venue of social, economic and environmental renaissance. The intent is to revive the perceived grandeur and elegance of an area that was once the locus of the wealthy elite, as well as to provide for a new generation of educated rising middle-class consumers. However, given that the latter community is relatively small, attracting the tourist dollar is seen as key to the financial viability of this planned development. If it comes to fruition it may lead to the potential repopulation of the city, with a suburban shift targeted specifically at foreign populations.

THE EVOLUTION OF THE URBAN FORM, COMMUNITY, PLACE AND MEANING

Founded in 1786 by a British merchant, on behalf of the East India Company, George Town became a thriving trans-shipment hub for traders between India and China as well as for those trading within the region. The core communities were regularly inundated by influxes of new labour, which passed through on their way to the plantations and mines, pilgrims who departed Malaya from Penang to Mecca, or arrived for such notable religious festivals as Thaipusam or St Anne's, and merchants who came to develop their business empires across the region.

For over two hundred years, the city resonated with a vibrancy rich in multi-ethnic colour, sounds, tastes and smells. By the start of 2000, however, with the repeal of the 1966 Rent Control Act,[1] large areas of long-established neighbourhoods lost their tenant populations, taking with them community patterns that had evolved over the centuries. The patterns had created a sense of continuity, although this was greatly diminished by urban to suburban migrations following the Pacific War and the closure of the island port in 1969. Fragmentation and disturbance to the established landscape came with the creation of the Penang New Urban Centre in the 1980s, which introduced the American cultural icon of the office tower – KOMTAR [Kompleks Tun Abdul Razak] – and the shopping mall into a two-storey Asian environment (Jenkins and King, 2003) and was to herald rapid social and cultural change.

A description of the formation and layering of these urban communities and their perceptions of place and identity offers an insight into a living cultural heritage city, an almost invisible city that was the focus of community interpretation, which was then repackaged for tourist consumption by the government, and which was also the centre of developers' nostalgic dreams.

As Yeoh and Kong (1995: 21) observe in their analysis of Singapore's history, community and identity:

> In exploring the relationship between place and identity, we identify two interconnections: first, the place has its own identity – a character and personality that distinguishes it from other places; and second, that people identify with a place, feel a sense of belonging and attachments to it.

George Town's cultural map

For those who settled George Town, and brought with them the architectures, belief systems and cultural practices of their homelands, their economic rise and fall is reflected in the urban landscape, the architectural forms, the houses of worship, the proximity of different ethnic communities and the interconnectivity through markets and trade.

James Wathen, in 1811, describes the urban scene in his travel journal, the spirit of which remains today:

> Turning the eye southward, Georgetown and the harbour are seen. The various styles in the construction of habitations of this small town have a strange effect – the European house, the Hindoo [sic] bungalow, the Malay cottage, the Chinese dwelling and the Burman hut are mingled together with regularity and apparently without plan, the first settlers having each built his residence according to the customs of the country (cited in Clodd, 1948: 120).

From the initial settlement, mapped in 1798, the urban landscape spread outwards in waves of suburban migrations, absorbing and submerging cultural villages in its path. Each year, religious festivals continue to weave their way through the city streets and out into the suburbs, making visible the connecting paths between communities, and their historical links. In many parts of the early suburbs, religious buildings remain the only tangible connection with a former community as development pressures have shifted populations and destroyed their architectural identities.

Within the inner city, particularly the historic area tenuously protected by the Municipal Council's *1987 Draft Conservation Guidelines* (MPPP, 1987), and the perceived boundaries of a recently (July 2008) inscribed UNESCO World Heritage Site, the connection between community and architecture is less disturbed (Jenkins and King, 2003). The colonial administrative quarter to the north can be identified through predictable, neo-classical, Euro-Indian buildings (Figure 8.1). Perpendicular to this

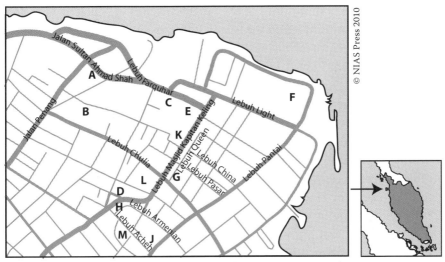

© NIAS Press 2010

A. Cheong Fatt Tze Mansion
B. Hainan Temple
C. Penang State Museum
D. Syed Alatas Mansion
E. St George's Church
F. Fort Cornwallis
G. Sri Mahamariamman Temple
H. Sun Yat Sen Mansion
J. Khoo Kongsi
K. Kuan Yin Teng
L. Masjid Kapitan Keling (Tamil)
M. Masjid Melayu Lebuh Acheh

Figure 8.1 Map of George Town

quarter, to the Northeast, the quayside remains lined with company *godowns,* or warehouses, many of which now lie empty, behind which arose the once thriving business district. As fortunes were amassed over the centuries, banking houses were established and by the turn of the twentieth century department stores arose, selling many kinds of imported household goods from Europe and Asia. Allied and Japanese bombing did much to set in motion the decline of this area, which later suffered the loss of its *raison d'être* following the relocation of its port.

Inland, behind the Northern administrative area and the north-eastern district lies a grid of streets little changed from that depicted on a 1798 map. These streets differ in architectural character from the administrative and banking districts' grand monuments to commerce. Here we can find rows of mainly two-storey Indian and Chinese shop-houses that line either side of the streets and are interspersed with places of worship and business serving the surrounding communities. At its heart lies Little India, which supports one of the longest surviving communities, that of the Muslim and Hindu Tamils, whose ancestors arrived as Sepoys on the East India Company ships. The area serves the Indian communities of the northern states of Malaysia as well as the suburban communities on the island. It was also the area preferred by law firms and their reciprocal businesses, stationers, tailors and wig-makers, until the Control of Rent Repeal, which coincided with the closure and relocation of the nearby High Court for renovation. A few have stoically remained in anticipation of the Court's return, and new lawyers' offices have opened, thus to some degree reversing the trend.

Before the Repeal, 32.7 per cent of the city's residential communities' working population was self-employed, and 86 per cent of them worked in their street of residence or close by (Jenkins, 1999: 7). A similar pattern could be found for employees, who made up 55 per cent of the workforce, 22 per cent of whom worked in their home street or close by. Thus, their participation in community interconnectivity was high (Jenkins, 1999). Typically, as lower income groups crowded into cheap, controlled rented housing, activities revolved around their own and their neighbours' places of worship. This is predominantly still the case as former residents return to conduct their prayers and interconnected commerce supports their needs. For example, the Muslim flower stalls make flower garlands for the Hindu community, and provide flowers and flower heads for both the Hindu and Chinese communities. A statue of Lord Murgah is adjacent to their stalls and is worshipped by both the Hindus and the Chinese.

As The Penang Global Ethic Project discovered, the urban landscape of the historic city and early suburbs is an interconnected web of cross-cultural reciprocal activities, with core areas dominated by particular ethnic groups, mostly sited around places of worship, and with ethnically and linguistically mixed communities between the cores. Despite the aftermath of the Control of Rent Repeal, this pattern still exists, but is challenged by the desire to provide the tourist with an 'authentic product', the re-colonization by outsiders with over-romanticized visions of city life amongst the 'locals', and an enthusiasm to repopulate depleted areas in line with modern lifestyles.

TRADITIONAL USERS AND PRODUCERS OF THE URBAN SPACE

Remaining within the historic core of George Town are the 'traditional' living-cultural-heritage communities. These multi-cultural, multi-ethnic users and producers interpret the historic environment through their daily cultural practices, and in doing so they have become the objects of the tourists' (and the tourism industry's), conservationists', suburbanites' and developers' 'gaze'. Just how they respond in terms of retaining, enhancing, evolving or losing their cultural identity is the focus of the investigation in this chapter. If we look briefly at the history of these urban communities and juxtapose them with the recent activities of the tourism, conservation and development industries, a vision of their future emerges.

Background

THE TOURISM INDUSTRY: MALAYSIA

Successful promotion of tourism over the last three decades has meant that by 2005 tourism was recognized as one of the main vehicles of Malaysia's economic development, contributing six per cent of Penang state's GDP (SERI, 2005a: volume 12, 18). In the 47 years from 1959 tourist arrivals have risen from 25,000 (Kadir Din, 1997: 104) to 16.6 million (New Straits Times, 31.1.05: cited in www.mocat.gov.my). Even in 2004, the year worldwide travel was curbed because of the region's SARS crisis, it is estimated that tourists spent M$6.49 billion on shopping in Malaysia, a 47 per cent increase on the previous year (News Straits Times, 24.1.05: cited in www.mocat.gov.my). Tourism Malaysia, the national tourism promotion agency, and the Shopping Malaysia Secretariat have prioritized the search for high-yield tourists, and as a result plan to increase the number of tourism promotion offices overseas to 70 (from approximately 30, May 2006), with a particular focus on West Asia and China (New Straits Times, 31.1.05: cited in www.mocat.gov.my). These overseas offices organize seminars, workshops and consumer fairs, often in collaboration with tour operators and international hotels.

The ministerial body in charge of the tourism portfolio in Malaysia changed from the Ministry of Trade and Industry's agency, the Tourist Development Corporation of Malaysia (TDC) to the Ministry of Culture, Arts and Tourism (MOCAT) in 1987 (Kadir Din, 1997: 104). In 1992, through Acts of Parliament, the TDC became the Malaysian Tourism Promotion Board, known as Tourism Malaysia, and was relieved of its development functions to concentrate on the promotion of Malaysia as a holiday destination for both domestic and international tourists (www.tourism.gov.my). In 2003 MOCAT separated into the Ministry of Tourism and the Ministry of Culture, Arts and Heritage.

Alongside the promotion of Malaysia overseas, the recent change from a six to a five-day working week for civil servants, and increases in disposable income through economic development, are enabling domestic tourism to play a larger role in tourism development nationwide. To support this, Tourism Malaysia, through its Domestic Promotion Division, has encouraged the concept of *Cuti-Cuti Malaysia,* Malaysian Holidays, organizing promotional tourism fairs and short-stay (typically three-day two-night) holiday packages around the country. Individual states offer a selection of holidays such as the Water Festival, Squid Catching, Food and Fruit, and Heritage packages. The website (www.tourism.gov.my) also updates the would-be tourist with a list of latest tourism products.

THE TOURISM INDUSTRY: PENANG ISLAND

On the northwestern coast of Malaysia lies the equatorial island of Penang with an estimated population of 678,000 people.[2] George Town lies on its northeastern tip. In simple terms the rest of the island is divided as follows: to the northwest is the beach hotel tourist belt, to the southeast the industrial area and international airport, and to the west the still idyllic rural farming and fishing communities centred on the small town of *Balik Pulau* ('Back of the Island'). Running through the centre, like a spine, are the Penang Hills, comprising a collection of hills covered in primary forest, which is also the location of a former hill station. The island's population is predominantly Chinese in the main urban areas, though there are many other communities throughout the island, such as indigenous Malays, Indian Hindus, Eurasians, Burmese and Thais, all identifiable through their historical places of worship, place names, remnants of their settlement patterns, foods and architecture. The tourism industry is presently promoting beach, eco-, heritage and cultural tourism, but when the Island's government first turned to the tourism industry as a means to recover from the relocation of its port from the island to the adjacent mainland in 1969, the focus was on the 'sun, sea and sand' holiday. Investment in this area coincided with the emergence of national interest in the industry in the early 1970s.

Penang Island is no stranger to an influx of peoples of different cultures and languages, although until tourism began to develop for long-haul travellers, along the northwest beach area, most early hotels were focused on George Town. The boom periods of the 1930s and 1940s saw the rise of small corner-site, city hotels, and an increase in brothels offering services to sailors, travelling salesmen and those unable to afford concubines. The city beach hotels became the playgrounds of the leisured middle classes of

Europe who drifted from the Sarkies brothers' hotels of Singapore, Penang and Rangoon – when such notables as Noel Coward and Somerset Maugham graced the lawns of Penang's Eastern and Oriental Hotel. By the 1960s, the 'hippy trail' western tourists began to arrive (Kadir Din, 1997: 117). The island also became the rest and recreation destination for the British and Australian forces and later the American forces during the Vietnam War. Backpackers now inhabit the hostels and hotels of the former hippies, benefiting from the hoteliers' introduction to scrambled eggs and baked beans on toast from their previous guests who preferred to stay amongst the hustle and bustle of active city life. Today, the business profile of Chulia Street, the main backpacker area of George Town, remains focused on the host community rather than the guests, who find themselves amongst coffee shops, a morning wet [fresh produce] market, brothels, Chinese medical halls, furniture shops, frame makers, rattan and bamboo blind makers, and hardware stalls as well as night food-hawker stalls. Tourism on Chulia Street is simply one of many businesses.

The responsibility for the promotion of Penang's tourism industry falls to the Penang Development Corporation (PDC), established in November 1969 (PDC, 1989). Its intention was to bring order to the chaos of high unemployment, overcrowding and racial disquiet through the development of the industrial zone for the manufacturing industry, housing, a new urban centre and the development of the tourism industry (Jenkins and King, 2003: 50).

International hotels created a tourist enclave set amongst the coconut-palm-fringed beaches of Batu Ferringhi, encouraged by a variety of tax allowances and other government incentives. The impact of mass tourism on the once idyllic *kampongs* was little understood, though the Consumers Association of Penang's critical analysis, *See the Third World While it Lasts*, identified that the problems of sky-rocketing land prices and costs of basic commodities as well as the pollution of the natural and cultural environments far outweighed the so-called benefit to the local community (Hong, 1985: 35). Peggy Teo further suggests that 'socio-spatial segregation is not uncommon especially where tourist enclaves exist' (2003b: 557), although her description of Batu Ferringhi's beach hotels reserving stretches of the beach only for their own tourists is a perception rather than a reality. The sense of 'exclusion' of locals as expressed in Teo's survey is more likely to have arisen from the dominance of venues specifically targeted at tourists' tastes and spending power, rather than the use of the beach. Even after the tsunami, which hit Penang's shores on 26 December 2004, the beaches remain a popular destination for the island's mainly lower-income population. Since 1995, the hotel belt has expanded to include estates of holiday homes, service apartments and a shopping mall as well as roadside restaurants and gift-shops, few of which serve the local community.

The Malaysian government's promotion of Malaysia My Second Home (MMSH), aimed at retired expatriates – which has incidentally offered an opening for a few Malaysians who once relinquished their citizenship for life in a foreign land, and have later returned under this scheme – has encouraged the formation of expatriate 'colonies' mainly in the beach areas. Penang attracts the highest number of applicants for MMSH in the country, with special appeal to the United Kingdom,[3] Indonesia, Hong Kong, Taiwan and Singapore (SERI, 2005a: 3).[4] Inevitably, the development boom has strained resources and the once pristine white sands and crystal blue sea are bygone memories. As one expatriate pragmatically explained; 'If the sea was blue, we couldn't afford to buy here – the prices would skyrocket.'

By 2004 'The Pearl of the Orient', as Penang Island was once promoted, appeared to have lost its lustre. Media campaigns such as *The Star Newspaper*'s 'Stand up for Penang' and *The New Straits Times*'s 'Let's Stop the Rot', brought to the attention of the nation the state of basic issues such as cleanliness, rubbish removal, traffic and lackadaisical enforcement efforts, as well as the dilapidated condition of many heritage buildings. It also exposed the poor maintenance of tourism products and the lack of new products to attract return visitors (SERI, 2004: 20). Despite the efforts to encourage a more civic-minded society, led by the then newly-appointed head of the Municipal Council,[5] and a visibly improved environment, other influences have taken their toll on the tourism appeal of the island.

During the development boom year in Penang of 1996, the estimated arrivals of tourists reached 3,444,148, comprising 44.2 per cent domestic and 55.8 per cent international visitors. After the Asian economic crisis of 1997, however, domestic arrivals shrank whilst international arrivals increased until by 2000, out of 3,780,000 arrivals, 34.2 per cent were domestic tourists and 65.8 per cent were international tourists (SERI, April 2002: 18). The following four years (2001 to 2004) for which annual statistics have been issued demonstrate the effects of external events, such as viral outbreaks, terrorist attacks, economic fluctuations and more recently the tsunami of the west coast of Sumatra, and subsequent earth tremors. The 11 September 2001 terrorist attacks in the USA coincided with a seven per cent drop in international arrivals, and a further three per cent following the Bali bombings in 2002 and 2005. The Iraq war, the SARS virus, the worldwide terrorist bombings and finally the tsunami resulted in the industry describing 2003–2004 as 'a dreadful year for the tourism industry – the worst of all economic sectors' (SERI, 2003: 23). The international market dived to a mere 38.3 per cent of the 3,030,000 arrivals, whilst the domestic market increased its share of the sector to a record 61.7 per cent (see Table 8.1 for the change in source markets between 2004 and 2005).

Table 8.1 Market mix of tourist arrivals, Penang: January–September 2004 and January–September 2005

	January–September 2004 (%)	*January–September 2005* (%) (↑ or ↓)
Malaysia (domestic)	55.4	61.0 (↑)
Middle East	6.1	6.8 (↑)
United Kingdom	6.5	3.9 (↓)
Singapore	4.7	3.9 (↓)
Japan	4.0	3.0 (↓)
Australia	3.7	2.9 (↓)
Indonesia	4.2	2.8 (↓)
Taiwan	1.3	2.2 (↑)
USA	1.4	1.9 (↑)
Mainland China	1.7	1.5 (↓)
Hong Kong	1.6	1.2 (↓)
South Korea	0.8	1.0 (↑)
Netherlands	1.4	1.0 (↓)
Others	5.4	5.3 (↓)
Total	**100.0**	**100.0**

Sources: PDC Consultancy Sdn Bhd (Jan–Jun 2004 data); SERI (Jul–Dec 2004 and Jan–Sept 2005 data); SERI 2005b: 19.

Promotional marketing directed towards the Middle East, Korea and Taiwan improved their contribution to overall international arrivals. Even though the overall figures of 2004 returned to those of 2000, with 3,520,000 arrivals, the tourist profile shows that domestic arrivals continued to dominate the sector, accounting for 56.6 per cent of all arrivals. Although the published statistics do not include the last quarter of the year, which is regularly dominated by European visitors, this trend of domestic tourism exceeding international tourism has become a regular feature since 2000.

The anticipated continuous downturn in international tourist arrivals to existing destinations has encouraged one of the first beach hotels of the 1970s to capitalize on the lull in post-tsunami business in order to upgrade into a six-star spa resort, catering for a smaller number of 'super rich tourists'. There are also rumours of others following suit or closing down altogether, though little is publicized for fear of damaging the industry.

Three major hotel chains, whose development proposals in the 1990s did much to disturb the heritage conservation groups, have changed direction, one to become service apartments, the others stalling altogether.[6] Similarly, the Eastern and Oriental Hotel's proposal of a 26-storey tower of service apartments, rising from above the ballroom, has yet to materialize, although by the end of 2007, as other mega projects were announced around the state, the subject once again began to appear in the local papers.

Contributing nearly half of Penang Island state's GDP each year, tourism and its related activities is a valuable revenue earner and employer (SERI, 2001: 25). Its survival therefore is crucial to the economic health of the state.

THE INTERPRETERS OF THE SITE

Penang Island, its beaches, tropical forests, hills and hill station, golf courses, durian orchards and *padi* fields together with the historic settlement of George Town, are packaged and marketed for tourist consumption by the various sectors of the tourism industry, each with its own interpretation and (re)presentation of the 'site'. This section looks into interpretations of Penang by its external promoters.

Promotion to 'far-off lands'

The thirty or so Tourism Malaysia offices world-wide are issued with travel manuals listing a selection of popular tours offered by independent tour and travel agents for each state. For Penang Island, these range from a nine-hour Penang-in-a-day marathon to dinner and a show at the Penang Cultural Centre (Tourism Malaysia, 2004). Both provide 'image bite' tourist packages, for those with little time, interest or courage to explore for themselves.

More accessible than the tourism office, as it reaches directly into the global homes of would-be-tourists, is the Internet. The Official Website of Tourism Penang www.tourismpenang.gov.my, sponsored by the Penang Tourism Action Council (PTAC),[7] is one such site. This has evolved into a well-written, well-informed site with regard to organized state events, traditional community festivals, heritage environments, local customs, and food. To its credit it is regularly up-dated as the almanac of cultural festivals unfold throughout the year, and offers well-guided accessibility to many aspects of the Island. It is edited and run by a group of web and graphic designers who are also enthusiasts for Penang's culture and heritage and who work away from the limelight of the more outspoken heritage conservation NGOs. Their agenda is simple: the fascinating history of multi-cultural Penang and its communities needs to be told, and told well. The 'interpreters' are not all from Penang. However, they are involved in continuous research and cross-cultural dialogue, thus they take responsibility for whatever they produce.[8]

There are other websites, written and produced by local cultural heritage enthusiasts, such as Penang Insights, Penang Talk, Penang Files, and a regional network site established by the former Honorary Secretary of the Penang Heritage Trust, Lestari Heritage Network.[9]

Promotion on the island

For a tourist visiting Penang Island by air, sea or land (train), access to information on arrival is surprisingly difficult. Government-produced information exists, but the connection between promoter and receiver is 'haphazard'.[10]

The Tourism Malaysia Information Centre at Penang International Airport[11] is located in an easy-to-miss position between baggage claim and customs on the domestic arrivals route out of the airport, and promotes other destinations in Malaysia. Two poorly positioned brochure racks stand half empty, close to the exit. These often carry promotional fliers of one tourism product, for example the Toy Museum. Its counterpart in Penang International Ferry Terminal is little better: again, it is focused on promoting the country, and although it does carry information on Penang, its opening hours relate to government office times rather than coinciding with tourist movement, for example ferry arrivals from Indonesia or Malaysia's Langkawi Island. There is no visible tourism promotion at the Butterworth Train Station, even though the trains come from Thailand and Singapore, including the designated luxury tourist train, the Eastern and Oriental Express.[12]

The Tourism Malaysia Office is on the 56th floor of the 65-storey KOMTAR tower, the pinnacle of the 1980s concept of modernity. The former State government's Penang Tourism Action Council (PTAC) office is also on the same floor; both are now Federal 'agencies'. Though the tower is not difficult to find without a map, the lift to either tourism office is.

At the bottom of the tower is the Penang Tourist Guides Association's (PTGA)[13] tourist information centre, which puts tourists and tours together. This was once ideally located in the central Mall on the main floor of KOMTAR, but was moved into an obscure location, difficult for tourists to find, and its original site is now a promotions desk for the events organization arm for state government festivals, for example the Chinese New Year Open House and Bon Oduri.

PTGA has 400 registered members but only a handful are regularly requested to conduct the heritage walking tours of Penang Heritage Trust tours.[14] The historical accuracy or focus of their talks can vary widely as research material is scattered or in private hands, and often inaccessible due to the language, script or calligraphy in which it is written. Most guides prefer the air-conditioned bus tours rather than risk exposure to the sun on walking/trishaw tours. As interest in heritage has grown, these few guides have regular commissions, causing resentment amongst other tour guides,[15] some of whom also see the self-guided tour brochures (see below) as competition.

Guides to self discoveries

Many inner city monuments have since the 1980s sported sponsored information signboards, which describe each site as individual entities rather than a holistic story of Penang's multi-ethnic, multi-cultural urban history. Two American Express trails around George Town, sponsored in the 1990s, defined the urban space and place in terms of connectivity. The subtlety of this was difficult to understand. Meanwhile, additional signboards appeared, but these tended to compete with the existing American Express information signboards, and provided similar materials and content.

Sponsorship from the Penang Tourism Action Council supported a brochure, *Penang Heritage Trails*, in which two self-guided *Historic George Town Trails* depicting the built heritage follow the original routes laid out by American Express. An addition was a new living-heritage trail of *Traditional Trades*, which drew on research work by Penang's school children, under the direction of Arts Ed (Arts Education Programs for Young People), and listed and produced pamphlets for the 'endangered trades' of the historic inner city in 2001.[16]

A further self-guided tour, which was introduced in March 2006, has taken guidance from The Penang Global Ethic Project (www.globalethicpenang. net) supported by, amongst others, the University of Science, Malaysia, the Konrad Adenauer Foundation, the Malaysian Interfaith Network, and Lestari Heritage Network.[17] This tour describes one of the oldest streets of George Town, Jalan Kapitan Kling, formerly Pitt Street, as an example of religious co-existence and cultural reciprocity. Pitt Street, which developed soon after the settlement was founded, runs roughly from North to South, stretching from St George's Church (1818) adjacent to the European administrative quarter on the North Shore, to the Acheen Street Mosque, founded in 1808. It joins the places of worship of the earliest communities, for between the Acheen Street Mosque and the church, the Chinese Kuan Yin Temple (est. 1802), the Hindu Sri Mahamariamman (est. 1833) and the Tamil Muslim Mosque of Kapitan Kling (est. 1801) can be found (see Figure 8.1 on p. 151). This tour brochure is the first one that connects heritage buildings with living inner-city communities and is well used by mainly local residents.

Whilst the Penang Tourism Action Council once promoted Penang to the world beyond its shores by sponsoring or providing interpretations of the Island through its web-site, its self-guided tours (for the more research-inclined tourist), and through staged events (for 'image-bite, culture-bite tourism'), it was also concerned with the demands for leisure and entertainments facilities of the rising local middle class. Recent changes in state government have subdued the Federal promotion of Penang, which is now seen politically as an 'opposition state'.

Together with the State Executive Counsellor for Tourism and the Municipal Council, the PTAC encouraged and staged cultural-interpretation events to enhance local and national cross-cultural understanding. In addition, it also supported the more traditional inner-city communities and promoted 'happening places' such as Upper Penang Road – a revived 'yuppie' enclave of restaurants and clubs opposite the Eastern and Oriental Hotel. None of this work was specifically directly undertaken for the benefit of tourism; it is yet to be seen if this promotion will be revived.

As the economic demographics of the island population change (as well as the political leadership), the challenges to the historic inner city communities may become more acute, particularly as they are now recognized for their tourism potential. Management must seek to strike an appropriate balance, and develop a good comprehension of the cultural needs of the users and producers of the urban landscape, which is the key to its success and sustainability.

CULTURAL RECONSTRUCTIONS, REPACKAGING FOR TOURISM AND DEVELOPMENT

In 1996, two years before UNESCO came to assess George Town's potential for Heritage City listing, there were no 'venues' in the inner city specifically for tourists other than a dilapidated Fort Cornwallis. The State Museum was closed and under renovation, neither the Islamic Museum nor the Sun Yat Sen Museum existed, and the Cheong Fatt Tze Mansion and Peranakan Museum were yet to be restored and opened to the public. The Khoo Kongsi was toying with the idea of a 'theme park attraction' within its temple and stage enclave, but nothing had been realized (Khoo and Jenkins, 2002: 220). At that time, Leong Yin Kean's Italianate villa was still a dilapidated low-end brothel and bike shop, not the elegant 'fine dining' restaurant it is today.

What the tourists experienced were the urban communities, their ways of life, their places of worship, festivals and commerce, and the streets in which they lived. Government-organized events took place on *Padang Kota*, the town field, or nearby streets, and very occasionally in the compound of the Khoo Kongsi. It was a time when city life was vibrant, the communities had possession of the buildings, the interstitial space was almost impenetrable, and houses for rent were unheard of.[18]

Eight years after the Control of Rent Repeal, the once bustling though slightly shabby city has large pockets of neglected, abandoned and derelict buildings and now many cleared sites. Streets, once alive with trading activity, are now discarded save for a few tenants who remain loath to move from an auspicious address. These are areas where tenant evictions took place in the expectations of profiteering either from rent increases or in the hope that a sympathetic council would allow redevelopment in preference to conservation. Around the periphery of the heritage core, a vast wall of newly constructed high-rise towers heralds the expanding economy. The vistas of the hills and the sea from the city have been eroded, yet these are critical to the geomancy of the buildings and the well-being of the people of the inner city.

Whilst on the one hand there is extreme dereliction and dilution of community life, on the other there have been great strides in creating awareness of the value of the inner city, in particular its architecture. As well as the tourist venues mentioned above, former colonial administrative buildings have undergone renovation. A few commercial outlets have restored their premises and 'gentrification' is slowly beginning to take place, led by a mixture of Penang and Caucasian heritage enthusiasts.

The Historic Enclave Action Plan 1997

In 1997 an Australian team of conservation professionals, who had already conducted dilapidation surveys on two historic buildings in Penang, were invited by the state government to prepare the Historic Enclave Action Plan. This plan encompassed two areas of potential tourism interest, Little India, and Lebuh Acheh, Lebuh Armenian Heritage Development Area.

The Australian Action Plan, funded by MOCAT, had little time to study the areas, the communities, and the existing use and meaning of space in any depth, though they were sensitive in attempting to dilute the state tourism industry's enthusiasm for commercial implants. Their staged proposal for the Historic Enclave Action Plan coincided with the 1997 Asian economic crisis and was not realized.

Little India

In the late 1990s, Little India became the focus of a commercial retail consultancy, which considered the area's potential as a new cultural-tourism product, managed along similar lines to a shopping mall, with attractive anchor tenancies and subsidized minor ones of traditional trades. The proposal reflected what already existed and had existed throughout Little India's history. The suburban shopping mall formula was a contrived and engineered product, whereas Little India's life has evolved over two centuries, according to supply and demand, and its survival following the Rent Repeal proves that this process is sustainable.

The retail-mall concept was abandoned in 2002, when the Municipal Council, recognizing Little India for its tourism potential, advertised a new proposal for a street enhancement or beautification project in the area. They were little prepared for the negative public response, but to their credit they requested a Cultural Impact Assessment[19] of their design proposal, a first of its kind.

The fascination of the area is not the architecture of unimposing early shophouses, with lime-washed walls, simple shutter openings and terracotta-tiled roofs, but the vibrancy that resonates from the mainly Tamil community, both Muslim and Hindu. Queen Street, for example, is the site of the Hindu Sri Mahamariamman Temple, but for one month of the year serves as the location of the Muslim Ramadan market. Market Street, at right angles to Queen Street (Figure 8.1, p. 151), links Little India to the quay, the *genius loci* of the area. Here the majority of the traders are Tamil Hindus, while at the western end of the street they are mostly Tamil Muslims. Trade follows a perpetual rhythm. The *ottu kedai* lean-to shops, attached to the sidewalls of shophouses, appear at first to be randomly placed and inconsistent in business hours. However, their trading patterns are synchronized with the path of the sun. Those shaded in the morning are open for morning business but close in the heat of the afternoon; those shaded by the afternoon sun then open their shutters for trade. As the heat of the day diminishes, these *ottu kedai* are joined by cycling hawkers who crowd around the crossroad corner sites, eager to catch trade from all four directions.

The trading profile there is evolving from spice and sundry shops, *tosai* and banana leaf restaurants, green grocers and mini markets (selling everything from false hair pieces and toe rings for personal adornment, to bottles of rose water or cows urine for use in daily prayer) to video, VCD and CD shops offering the latest Bollywood movies. These changes, however, are still supported by daily prayer rituals, which supplicate for a good day's trading. Early morning sees the streets in front of the shops swept and hosed down, a mixture of turmeric and sandalwood splashed on the pathway to the building, and a cube of camphor burnt. Women traditionally create a rice flower pattern, or *kolam*, which is intended to feed the birds and ants. At the close of business, in the evening, further camphor is burnt, a coconut is smashed on the pathway, and again the street is swept and hosed.

The adjustment of the street enhancement design considered these issues in order to meet the needs of the community. Little India is also the heart of many annual festivals, Muslim, Hindu and Chinese, both static and processional. The area for beautification was a grid of nine streets. The orchestration of this project, therefore, had the additional challenge of avoiding building work conflicting with religious festivals.

A further culturally sensitive area was the use of patterns within the imprinted concrete for the road improvement scheme. These patterns, a popular feature of road beautification in Penang, were negotiated with the dominant communities of the area in which they were placed, and subtly identify the Muslim or Hindu areas.

In a traditional urban environment, the relationship between building and street is holistic. The gutter-less roofs drain rainwater into an open drain along the front loggia walkway, known as 'the five-foot-way'. These open drains are considered unsightly and 'un-modern' but are unique to the historic environment. A compromise was reached with the various Chambers of Commerce in the area, and the semi-pedestrianized Market Street drains were covered whilst the eight side-street drains remained open, thus partly maintaining both the character and the holistic function of the early engineering in the area.

Despite the project running into many difficulties and its completion only being 'more-or-less' concluded by early 2004, the area has survived two years of disruption and is once again flourishing. The streetscape for pedestrian use has greatly improved, the vibrancy has been retained, and both people within the council departments and private individuals have gained from learning and working through these issues together.

In early 2006 further funding was given in order to complete other areas of the project. This work was designed and implemented by a team who did not analyse the former design. As a result, the philosophy and principles of the initial amended proposal have been ignored, obstructions have been placed in barrier-free zones and, in some cases, beneficial geomancy, both Chinese *feng shui* and Indian *Vaashtu Shastra*, has been impeded. This demonstrates how easily the fragile semiotics of a place and space can be lost through the lack of cultural connectivity in the interpreters.

Only a few buildings remain empty, too derelict for use, or incomplete due to illegal work. Overall, the physical area has improved with minimal loss of cultural integrity. For the tourist in search of cultural 'otherness', Little India is a clean, tidy, easy to negotiate, and culturally fascinating site.

Lebuh Acheh, Lebuh Armenian Heritage Enclave

The 'touristification', conservation and urban renewal of the second area within the Historic Enclave Action Plan of 1997, the Lebuh Acheh, Lebuh Armenian Heritage Enclave, has proved much more challenging than that of Little India. The promotion for this project began as early as 1989, and was endorsed by the Economic Planning Unit (EPU) in 1993.

This enclave lies to the south of Pitt Street (Figure 8.1), roughly between the Mesjid Kapitan Kling (Indian Tamil Muslim Mosque) and Mesjid Lebuh Acheh (Acheen Street Mosque – Arab Muslim), and is noted as the area of the five main Chinese Clan *Kongsi* Temples, built to support descendants of the Yap, Lim, Khoo, Cheah and Tan family clans. There is also an Indian Hindu community of bottle recyclers, the Chettiars, who live and work along Armenian Street.[20]

The area survey, carried out before a design proposal was put forward, noted that of the 293 existing shophouses, 50 per cent were residential, many with multiple occupancy. The proposal however retained only 13 residential properties, 17 'were to be encouraged to convert to specific tourist shops (...)' (Khoo and Jenkins, 2002: 214), the remainder were to be used for other commercial activities intended more for the local community and city, and a minimum of new in-fill development was considered.

Properties in the area were mostly tenanted, and owned by the five Chinese Kongsi Associations, the Chettiar community, or the *Majlis Agama Islam Penang* (MAIP) that was empowered to administer the Muslim endowment or *waqf* properties of the Mosque. Very few were privately owned, although one is the restored former base of Sun Yat Sen, now a museum.

When these proposals were made, the area was dilapidated, as controlled rents did not encourage owners to invest in repairs. The properties, however, were fully occupied and the street life of this multi-cultural, predominantly residential area was active. Tourists found much of interest; the Acheen Street Mosque, not then restored, was inviting and hospitable and its compound active with family life. The Muslim printing presses could be heard along Acheen Street, and the call to prayer reached to a population in excess of the 40 males required for a mosque *qariah* (Muslim parish).

The 24 houses in the Khoo Kongsi temple compound bustled with family life around the soon-to-be-restored opera stage and clan temple. Plans for the theme park entertainment had not begun and talk of evictions was unheard of. The traditional ways of life and festivals continued uninterrupted, as they had for decades.

In 2008, in contrast to the liveliness and cultural continuum of Little India, the Lebuh Acheh, Lebuh Armenian Enclave is an area of contrasts: dereliction and conservation, evictions and 'gentrification'. The *genius loci* of the space is oscillating from becoming a fusion of traditional and 'gentrified' lifestyles, a 'petrified' living-cultural-heritage theme park, or a playground for 'culture-vulture' yuppies, with art galleries and restaurants to suit their expensive tastes.

As the Khoo Kongsi stage and then the main Temple were restored, the community was evicted from the 24 houses which formed the enclave; many have been re-housed in neighbouring streets (Khoo and Jenkins, 2002: 219). The once living-cultural-heritage inner enclave, where tourists were free to wander and discover the magic for themselves, has become a product, packaged by the Kongsi trustees. The functions of the buildings hold little relevance, other than as revenue earners as entry into the enclave is now charged. The threatened theme park was never built, but recently eight houses have been renovated for commercial activities, though they have remained empty and unused since completion. Other than the ticket office, the remaining 16 houses are still in a dilapidated condition.

The communities of the *waqf* land fared little better. Those along Lebuh Acheh – Acheen Street – were re-housed in modern low-cost flats, far from their former community enclave. Their shophouses, built of different styles and ornamentation, were considered by those eager to develop the area as unsightly, symbolizing the non-development of the Muslim community, and a proposal to build a new apartment block on the land they occupied was agreed. The urban mosque compound is a unique example of mid-nineteenth-century architecture, its layout following the principles of the city of Medina (*Utusan Konsumer*, 2002: 11). Thus, the heritage lobby asked that conservation be considered. Their request was countered by an accusation that the conservationists wanted to hamper 'plans on *waqf* land for the benefit of the Muslims who are in desperate need of homes' (Sangeetha, 2001), forgetting that the tenants had been evicted by the administrators of the *waqf* land. Thus, whilst the communities have been evicted, the 'cultural melting pot' of this historic enclave is being reconstructed. The tourists and remaining communities have lost two enclaves of living-cultural-heritage.

In 1997 Joel Kahn examined the issues surroundings the conservation of two historic buildings within the site, the Syed Alatas Mansion and the Acheen Street Mosque itself, suggesting that 'uncoupled from the intimate relationship' with tourism in Penang, their conservation reflected a broader cultural process taking place amongst the educated middle-class Malays (Kahn, 1997: 104). But Kahn had also uncoupled the projects from the multi-ethnic, multi-cultural communities surrounding the sites, as well as those also involved in the wider issues of identity reconstructions taking place nationally. In hindsight, it would appear that as projects at the very start of the conservation movement, the mosque, the mansion and the Khoo

Kongsi became, and to some degree remain, synonymous with identity reconstructions in all sections of the Muslim and Chinese communities, both ethnic and economic.

A recent event which expresses the identity reconstructions of the Chinese Community took place over the Chinese New Year Holiday, the Year of the Dog – 2006. Since 2000, the Lebuh Armenian, Lebuh Acheen Street Enclave has played host to the Penang State Chinese New Year Open House. 4 February 2006 was a national event with rumoured appearances by the King, the Prime Minister and by the Minister of Culture, Arts and Heritage. The event was larger than previously, although only the Minister attended. Events were staged not only in the predominantly Chinese area of Armenian Street and the Yap, Khoo and Cheah Kongsis but in front of the Acheen Street Mosque, making the call for prayer inaudible. These were organized by the members of the Chinese Kongsis and other Chinese Associations, who mostly lived in the suburbs or new townships, and had little or no relationship with the space in which they were performing or with the street communities.

Hotel caterers set up their stalls of 'authentic' Penang street food, and tourists were bussed in from the beach and city hotels in order to experience a staged 'traditional' Chinese New Year event. Amongst all the side shows on calligraphy and traditional trades was a 'mock-up' display of the altar used by the Hokkien community during the birthday celebrations of the God of Heaven, *T'ien Kung*, 'the most solemn of all sacrificial offerings' (Wong, 1967: 51). This is a special altar reserved for this occasion and when used is raised above the ground on timber stools. A pair of full-length sugar canes is burnt at the end of the ceremony. They represent the sugar cane plantation in which the anti-Manchu people of Fukien Province hid to escape slaughter by their enemies.

In order to encourage inter-ethnic understanding of Malaysia's main cultural groups, events such as the Chinese New Year Open House are staged. However, the reinterpretation of the living heritage environment coupled with the ignorance of the value of the community and of the semiotics of the setting in which it was placed meant that the event could just as well have been presented in an exhibition hall. The real street culture was irrelevant to the 'cultural experience'.

In contrast, the following evening, when the amplified sounds had died away and the mountains of litter were cleared, the street returned to its community. In front of their houses were placed the stools, altars and sugar cane in preparation for the *T'ien Kung* celebration. As the altars were laden with roast pork, oranges, pineapples and folded red and gold 'hell's money', the families began their prayers to the God of Heaven.

Not far away, along the waterfront, the Hokkien jetty community fireworks and firecrackers could be heard. Known locally for their elaborate celebrations, the Chew jetty community attracts a large crowd of city dwellers, with the occasional street-wise tourist thrown in. For the local community, festivals such as these require no promotion as they are part of the rich almanac of events throughout the year. For the tourists, including many local suburban residents, however, these festivals are unpromoted and unknown until newspaper articles appear the following day.

These vibrant jetty communities are also under threat from development plans and their existence may soon be reduced to mere memories. Ironically, nostalgia for the recent past plays an increasing role in urban revitalization projects, as cultural reconstructions are no longer limited to 'staged' events.

CONCLUSION

In his paper presented at the 2003 workshop on Macao's application for inscription on to the UNESCO Heritage List, Herb Stovel looked back at the collective efforts to retain the heritage values of historic cities, and noted that it appeared 'that the battle is being slowly lost' (2003: 85). Even such notable urban sites as Vienna and Istanbul were being considered for removal from UNESCO's List for their failure to halt modern development and protect important heritage buildings and sites. Development pressures on historic cores are a global phenomenon.

> Even where historic centres survive, their values apparently intact, they often do so as oases surrounded by featureless and meaningless outlying areas serving more directly the needs of business, residents, and industry. Heritage becomes something set aside from community development instead of something at its core, and heritage advocates find themselves promoting retention of values and fabric irrelevant to the needs of most in society (Stovel, 2003: 94).

Looking back at the two case studies of the Historic Enclave Action Plan, we see two very different scenarios. Little India was a 'local' street enhancement project, designed and implemented by a local team, the engineered-shopping-mall management proposal from Kuala Lumpur having been ignored. Arguments, debates and dialogues could happen face-to-face with people known to the community, whose input was invaluable to its success. The Indian Chamber of Commerce represented all Indians, Muslim and Hindu, and the Liga Muslims represented all Muslims – Indian and Malay and others; the community interconnectedness, therefore, was well-established before the work began and was its strength during two years of disruption. Although there have been many changes, most reflect the changes to Malaysia's society in general, but the *genius loci* remains for both locals and tourists to enjoy.

The Lebuh Acheh, Lebuh Armenian Heritage Enclave (LALA) is a very different area. It has been mostly residential with distinctly separate communities, although interaction between these communities took place at the nearby market. Tourism, conservation and development plans have dislocated the communities and created openings for 'gentrification', whilst the few remaining residents are in danger of becoming the default actors of authenticity.

The rapid social changes affecting Penang's suburbs are felt by the Five Chinese Kongsis, which are now readjusting their *raison d'être* to attract young members; their monumental temple buildings are no longer serving their original purpose. International interest in LALA – from the initial German-supported proposal, the French-supported conservation project, the Syed Alatas Mansion, the Australian Action Plan, Heritage NGO and government interest, and finally Federal recognition and funding for the conservation of a few buildings – has taken the enclave out of the hands of the community and into a higher political realm. The state-organized tourist festival, intent on encouraging cross-cultural understanding, has also failed to see the local community as an asset. As Richard Engelhardt, UNESCO's Regional Advisor, in his public lecture in Penang, 1998, forewarned:

> (...) with the loss of its traditional caretakers, a site becomes an increased burden on the state or is left at the mercy of land speculators who have no long-term commitment to the site and therefore no interest in preserving the site for sustainable development' (1998: 5).

In spite of all this, there are pockets of interconnectivity and reciprocity amongst the remaining communities, and the true connection between people, culture, place, space and identity can be seen through the almanac of traditional festivals. How long this will last in the LALA enclave depends on the pressures on the remaining community. Little India, on the other hand, has created a sustainable formula through two centuries of continuity. If left to administer itself, it will probably remain for tourists and locals to enjoy for many years to come.

As Herb Stovel concludes in his Macao paper, 'development is the engine of an urban economy but heritage and identity will always be the soul of the city' (2003: 98). If the experience of lived cultures and communities is to be of any value to the tourist, the site is best interpreted by its users and producers, those for whom it carries a daily connection, rather than by organizers of 'image-bite, culture-bite' tourism packages. Tourism should simply be the way this 'soul' – the established connectivity between community, space, place and cultural practice – is viewed.

NOTES

1   By keeping property rentals at low levels, the 1966 Rent Control Act had helped to preserve a large number of George Town's historic buildings by disincentivising and thus discouraging landlords from upgrading or redeveloping their properties. The 2000 repeal of the Act has reversed this tendency, leaving many low-income tenants facing greatly increased accommodation costs, and thus either voluntary relocation or eviction, and making the properties much more attractive to investment and development.

2   The Penang Island State comprises a section of the adjacent mainland with a population of 790,000, and the island of Penang.

3   From a conversation with a British couple buying an apartment in Batu Ferringhi. Other expatriates living here under the Malaysia My Second Home programme confirm this view.

4   These also include expatriates retired from government service in Hong Kong.

5   After two years of his leadership, Penang's population are enjoying visible improvements. The public toilets are cleaner, small parks have appeared and old park areas have been tastefully re-landscaped.

6   Following the illegal demolition of the former Metropole Hotel, the developers began the construction of a high-rise hotel. The project stopped following the Asian economic crisis and re-emerged (Jenkins and King, 2003:119) as service apartments. The second hotel project stalled after the controversial demolition of seven heritage houses in 1998 (Lim, 1998). The international hotel intended for the site never emerged, and still today (2009) the site remains un-developed.

7   Penang Tourism Action Council was formerly a State Government Tourism promotion arm under the leadership of the State Executive Councillor for Tourism.

8   In March 2008, the incumbent coalition government was replaced by the opposition coalition. As a result the PTAC was taken into Federal 'custody', chaired by Penang's former State Executive Councillor for Tourism. The current 'opposition' Councillor appears no longer to refer to the PTAC, although the situation is far from clear.

9   These are all linked to the new site visitpenang.com (http://www.visitpenang.com/) – at the time of writing (August 2008) the site itself lacked basic information about cultural happenings and events, perhaps reflecting the rumoured cancellation of funds, which took place upon the change of government.

10   This is equally the case with arts and entertainment for the island in general, for there appears to be only fragmented promotion of events, causing many to be poorly attended.

11   The author travels through the airport at least twice a month.

12   Tuesday – after breakfast the train arrives at Butterworth, whence coaches take you across to George Town on the local ferry. At Weld Quay trishaws take you through many of George Town's interesting districts. Return to the Eastern and Oriental Express for lunch (www.orient-express.com/web/eoe/eoe_c2b2_malaysia).

13   The Penang Tour Guides Association was formed in 1991, and offered a one-month course in tour-guiding for M$500. Today, accredited private colleges intermittently offer a three month-long course for M$5,000 followed by a recognized examination under the Ministry of Tourism. For the heritage lectures, the colleges recruit active and well-known local heritage enthusiasts.

14   The same situation holds true when government officials require interpretations of the historic sites to visiting dignitaries.

15   This was taken from a conversation with the few heritage tour guides.

16   These guides are no longer easily available from PTAC, and the information they use is no longer current as the endangered traders have moved away as rents have risen.

17   Lestari Heritage Network, set up by the former honorary secretary of the Penang Heritage Trust, has taken over the role of the former NGO, AWPNUC, Asia and West Pacific Network for Urban Conservation.

18   Taken from the author's experience of trying to rent a shophouse in the inner city since 1995. This was only achieved in 1999.

19   The author, whilst employed by Laurence Loh Arkitek, Penang, undertook the research for the report.

20   The author lives next door to this community.

CHAPTER 9

Aspiring to the 'Tourist Gaze'
Selling the Past, Longing for the Future at the World Heritage Site of Hue, Vietnam

Mark Johnson

INTRODUCTION

The notion of the 'tourist gaze' (Urry, 1990; 1993) is a commonly repeated analytical framing device in the study of tourists and tourism. It has become a short-hand expression for the emergence of a detached and largely visual consumption of (other) people, places and cultures. It also signals the carefully ordered and orchestrated process of selective representations inherent in touristic encounters. As a way of deconstructing the notion of authenticity, interrogating the exoticizing and nostalgic imagination and elucidating the disciplinary regimes that engender particular ways of seeing, the concept of the tourist gaze has been extremely useful. However, the tourist gaze has also been criticized for assuming too much about the stability and coherence of dominant representations, privileging conformity and determinism over agency and ignoring the discrepant readings and divergent perspectives of different sets of social actors, their encounters with and ways of engaging in both the production and consumption of the variously staged authenticities of peoples, places and histories (e.g. Tilley, 1997; MacCannell, 2001; Perkins and Thorns, 2001).

The criticisms that might be made of the 'tourist gaze' in general are applicable to recent analysis of tourism in Vietnam in particular. Writing on tourism in Vietnam since the start of the renovation period in 1986 has emphasized the persistent power of foreign tourists' imaginings and representations, and in particular the way in which both the history of conflict and colonialism has been sanitized and presented in nostalgic and orientalizing ways (e.g. Biles, Lloyd and Logan, 1999; Kennedy and Williams, 2001; Alneng, 2002). My concern in this chapter is to complicate that story of tourism and the 'tourist gaze' in Vietnam. I do this by focusing not on tourists' readings and encounters, but on those who are on the front line of representing the official story and mediating the tourist gaze at the Complex of Hue Monuments, a World Heritage Site encompassing not only the old walled Citadel and Imperial City (some 5 km²) but also temples, pagodas and Royal Tombs that are distributed around the old capital city and along the Perfume River.

As I demonstrate, individuals working for the Hue Monuments Conservation Centre (HMCC) while reproducing dominant narratives of place, also articulate a critical and often ambivalent relationship both to the history and representation of the heritage site and to the tourists themselves. I focus in particular on two different sets of people working for the HMCC – researchers and tour guides. As heritage professionals in the HMCC, researchers identify with the official renovated view of Hue as a landmark of Vietnamese creativity and aesthetic achievement and a lasting legacy of the Nguyen emperors. However, they are also concerned with up-holding and preserving cultural authenticity against the perceived onslaught of tourists and the interference and mismanagement of state and party officials. Tour guides similarly reproduce and participate in selling the official version of Hue, but, as I demonstrate, subvert the story by drawing analogies between the perceived failures of both past and present regimes.

Moreover, researchers and tour guides articulate alternative ways of engaging with the past and imagining the future through their identifications with different groups of Vietnamese visitors. Vietnamese visitors are broadly categorized both by researchers and tour guides into two types: those who have a genuine interest in and appreciation for Hue's culture, history and heritage and those who do not. Researchers, while recognizing the importance of tourist revenue, bemoan the increasing presence of frivolous Vietnamese visitors, identified as Vietnam's *nouveaux riches*, who they perceive as diluting the meaning and authenticity of the site. Tour guides, by contrast, express a far more ambivalent and contradictory relationship to these different groups of tourists. On the one hand, those tourists who are deemed to have a genuine interest in culture and history validate tour guides' expressed commitment to their role as 'mentors' or 'interpreters' of the past (Cohen, 1985: cited in Dahles, 2001). On the other hand, tour guides express an affinity for and identify most closely with that group of tourists whose engagement with the Hue monuments is minimal, characterized by playfulness and leisurely detachment. It is precisely here that the notion of the tourist gaze, and, in particular, that aspect of the tourist gaze taken to mean the superficial and detached visual consumption of place, might be critically reworked and deployed. More specifically, I argue that the tour guides, in a context in which struggles over the meaning of the past and frustrations with the process of economic and social renovation in the present, long for and aspire to occupy the position of those who embody the 'tourist gaze'.

There are two points to be made by way of clarification at the outset. First, in aspiring to occupy the 'tourist gaze', tour guides are neither identifying with nor seeking to turn the tables on *foreign* tourists who are often construed as, to invoke Lacan (1977), having the gaze that defines the 'other'. On the contrary, both research staff and tour guides were largely unconcerned with foreign tourists, and talked far more about their fellow Vietnamese compatriots. I have argued elsewhere that the refusal to engage in and entertain at any length the narratives of foreign tourists is one way of 'limiting their [foreign tourists'] claims over the site, and its history: their presence in the present' (Johnson, 2001: 85).

Second, tour guides desire to escape from the ordinary, where to quote Urry (1990: 10), 'Everyday obligations are suspended [and] there is license (...) for non-serious behaviour.' However, the aspiration to the 'tourist gaze' does not, in this situation, arise from, nor is it premised on, the modern Western distinction between work and leisure as originally theorized. Nor is it, I think, a reflection of a more general global cosmopolitan gaze (Szerszynski and Urry, 2006), characterized by detachment from place and locality, a point that I shall return to in the conclusion. Rather, it arises out of the cultural contradictions people face and engage with in the context of both the recent history of anti-colonial struggle and nationalist conflict and the current social and economic changes engendered by market reforms taking place under the auspices of a bureaucratic and still largely authoritarian socialist state (Luong, 2003a). In this situation, identifying with those who embody the 'tourist gaze' seems to be one way to experience, at least vicariously, a certain freedom or break from the past, or more precisely from the constraints and burdens of the on-going ideological struggles in the present about the past. It is also a way for some individuals to articulate their aspirations for a more open, prosperous and forward-looking future. In this sense, I argue, it is not so much about transcending the ordinary work-a-day world, as it is about the hope and expectation of seeing that world transformed.[1]

BACKGROUND: RENOVATING HUE

The city of Hue, in central Vietnam, was formerly the royal capital of Vietnam and seat of the Nguyen dynasties until the abdication of the last emperor, Bao Dai, in 1945 to the Viet Minh.[2] Following Bao Dai's abdication, Hue continued to be both a geographically strategic and symbolically important site in the various colonial and post-colonial struggles and conflicts of the twentieth century, but its importance as a political and administrative centre of Vietnam was in terminal decline. Moreover, for a short period following reunification in 1975, it was largely ignored by the socialist state. More recently, however, Hue has literally and figuratively undergone restoration, an effect of both the broader processes of *doi moi* (renovation) initiated by the Vietnamese State in the mid-1980s, and the listings of the Hue Monuments (the Citadel, the Forbidden Purple City, royal tombs and surroundings) as a World Heritage Site by UNESCO in 1993.

The renovation and reconstruction of Hue has raised a number of historical and ideological problems, at least for the state and the ruling Vietnamese Communist Party (VCP). Hue is still seen to be tainted by association with a 'feudalist' past, and in particular with the still widely held view of the later emperors being the puppets of the French colonial regime (Long, 2003). Moreover, while the temporary taking of Hue during the 1968 Tet Offensive was of crucial symbolic importance during the American War, Hue is not as overtly part of the recurrent memorializations of the 'struggle for national liberation' that are found elsewhere in Vietnam. This may be partly explained both by the fact that prior to reunification Hue was politically aligned with South Vietnam and by the continuing controversy over the alleged massacre of civilians at Hue by retreating Viet Cong at the start of the American counter-offensive.

The potentially problematic nature of Hue's feudal history has been partially resolved through the 'depoliticized practices of heritage preservation and tourist promotion' (Long, 2003: 535) that at once construe Hue not as a site of historical interest, but rather as an 'architectural and artistic' place and as 'one of the culminations of Vietnamese creativity' (ibid.: 548). Similarly, as I have suggested elsewhere (Johnson, 2001), the effacing of the recent history of violent conflict in favour of an ahistorical and timeless aesthetic may be seen not only in official descriptions and constructions of Hue as being 'permeated by a unique and fascinating beauty in complete harmony with its environment' (UNESCO, 1995: 2; cited in Johnson, 2001: 80), but also, and more importantly, in the way in which discourses of restoration and preservation increasingly highlight not the destruction of war, but the effects of natural decay and deterioration. The narratives of decay and deterioration situate the meaning of the place outside the unruliness of historical narratives and events and locate it instead within an aesthetic ecology that links people and place together in essential ways.

The official scripting of the Hue Monuments in terms of aesthetics, however, is not simply about reconstructing a past that does not challenge dominant versions of revolutionary history. Rather it is also about creating and presenting a past in ideological keeping with the current process of renovation (*doi moi*) which, as Nguyen (2005) argues, is regarded as an extension of previous national salvation revolutions in 'peace time' (see also Tai, 2001). More specifically, Hue's renovation is an important part of recent attempts to define an enduring set of symbolic materials – both so-called 'tangible' and 'intangible' culture – that defines the best of Vietnamese national culture. This project of national self-definition is set against the uncertainties and contradictions of social and cultural change and the perceived encroachment of western culture seeping in as part of the 'open door' (*mo cua*) affected by market reforms and the internationalization of the economy: changes which are seen potentially to challenge the ideological control of state and Party.

There are two further points to be made with respect to the making of Hue as an 'artistic and architectural' site and the 'culmination of Vietnamese cultural creativity'. First, the emphasis on art and aesthetics is not simply an 'invented tradition' (Hobsbawm and Ranger, 1983). Art, literature and music were important both in the royal court during the Nguyen dynasty and among the educated colonial elites, and remained important at least for some intellectuals in both revolutionary and postcolonial times (see Bayly, 2004; Jamieson, 1993). Second, while a focus on aesthetics may be seen as an attempt to divert attention away from the more ostensibly problematic aspects of political history, it is important to recall that culture and aesthetics were very much part of the remit of state and Party control. Ninh (2002) outlines how, in revolutionary Vietnam, there were successive attempts to brush aside French bourgeois culture and Chinese feudal influences, both of which might be seen in Hue's courtly culture and built environment. This was accompanied by programmes of cultural rectification and the development of a state and Party aesthetic that emphasized, both literally and figuratively, the 'concrete and utilitarian' (ibid.: 171). Bayly's (2004: 323) work, however, further complicates this picture, exploring the place and role of cultural capital among Vietnamese intellectuals, particularly those who have travelled abroad as 'experts'. While cultural capital in the form of musical and artistic appreciation (drawing on both French and Vietnamese traditions) is a problematic marker of distinction in socialist Vietnam, it is also the means through which warm relationships are established with 'non-Vietnamese sharers of their cultivated tastes and pleasures in the wider socialist world'.

The key point, so far as Hue's renovation is concerned, is that whatever the view of Hue's artistic and architectural culture may have been previously, it is now officially promoted as one of the pre-eminent sites not just for the preservation of Vietnamese high culture in the past, but just as importantly for renewing national arts and culture in the present and the future. This does not mean it is no longer political. Quite the opposite, it is political in the sense that it is precisely this renovated view of Vietnamese national culture that is being actively pushed and funded by the state. Secondly, this renovated 'culture' is political in the broader sense that while it is undoubtedly one of the ways in which social distinctions are enacted and reproduced it is also an arena of contest and debate. What I explore in the remainder of the chapter are the ways in which two different sets of social actors (researchers and tour guides) engage in the construction and representation of the renovated view of Hue culture. As I demonstrate below, these different social actors identify in different degrees with what is now the dominant discourse. However, not only do they variously express ambivalence both about the way in which history and culture have been construed and are being represented, but they also articulate views that are at odds with and subvert these dominant representations.

WORKING BEHIND THE SCENES: RESEARCHERS AND TOUR GUIDES IN THE HUE MONUMENTS CONSERVATION CENTRE

Hue is the capital of Thua Thien-Hue province and is situated almost equidistant from Ho Chi Minh City (Saigon) and Hanoi, a seemingly straightforward statement of geography, which belies the various historical struggles that have variously made it, or at least attempted to make it, into a geographically significant social fact. The population of Hue city is approximately 300,000 while the population of the province as a whole is just over one million. There are four major industries in Hue city: beer production, cement and brick making, chemical and pesticide production, and textile manufacturing. Many people in Hue, however, commonly acknowledged and referred to tourism as the fifth and now leading 'industry': a reference to the fact that tourism has been pivotal to the recent economic growth of both the city and the province.

One of the most important components of the changing economic landscape in this particular locality is the Hue Monuments Complex that is overseen and managed by the HMCC. With well over a million visitors to the monuments each year and some 700 employees the HMCC has been instrumental in the growth of the local economy in general and the tourism industry and service sector in particular in this as yet still largely provincial city. The HMCC comprises a number of different departments and offices, among them the Office for Scientific Research and Tourist Guides. At the time of my research there were some 50 official tour guides and 15 research staff working in this office (the department size now stands at 100), with additional researchers and technical staff – archaeologists, architects and conservators – working in other departments and offices within the HMCC.

The rest of this chapter deals in more detail with the views of individual tour guides and researchers, but before proceeding with an account of this material, however, it is important to say something about the position of tour guides and researchers in the HMCC and their relation to each other.[3]

Tour guides occupy an ambivalent position in the institutional hierarchy of the HMCC. On the one hand, their educational background and training situates them above the majority of people who work either as security guards or as skilled and unskilled labourers maintaining and renovating the historic monuments. All of the tour guides I spoke to were either already university graduates or pursuing a course of study, and all had completed a special training programme for tour guides run by the HMCC (see below). On the other hand, tour guides are generally regarded, by senior administrative, technical and research staff in the HMCC, as only superficially knowledgeable about the imperial city and royal tomb complexes and with limited appreciation for or understanding of cultural authenticity, a view very much at odds with the way tour guides present and talk about themselves.

Technical and research staff *also* occupy an ambivalent position within the HMCC. While having greater status than tour guides and day-to-day control over many aspects of the work of conservation and restoration, they have very little authority and decision-making power in terms of the priorities accorded different kinds of projects. They distinguished themselves both from some of the more senior management and from tour guides not only on the basis of their higher educational qualifications – many having studied abroad for advanced degrees – but also in terms of their in-depth, studied and close-up appreciation of monuments, cultural heritage and history. Research and technical staff were regarded, and regard themselves, as doing serious research and conservation work, rather than what they perceived as run-of-the-mill tourist guiding. That is to say, in public discourse at least, individuals drew an important distinction between people working in the centre whose major, if not sole, preoccupation was said to be making money, and those who defined their work in terms of its intellectual, if not spiritual, rewards.

In fact, tour guides, while they are paid a lower monthly salary, are capable of earning more than many of the research and technical staff of the HMCC. The monthly wage of a tour guide was, at the time of research, reported to be about US$20 per calendar month. This was supplemented by a small expense allowance for travel, refreshments on the job and 'make-up' (for women). The monthly wage for senior research staff, at the time of my research, was reported to be around US$40. Research staff could also claim small expenses for travel and research. However, tour guides could earn up to the equivalent of a month's salary or more in a single day either through tips given by tourists who they take around the sites or through unofficial work as tour guides for private tour companies outside the HMCC. Nevertheless, precisely because of the perceived lower status of tour guiding, it was impossible for professional researchers to take on, or be seen to take on, the work of an interpreter and tour guide, though they might earn more money for it. This does not mean to say, however, that research staff did not wish they earned more money, or that they did not complain about their lack of it. Nor was it only that they could not publicly be seen to be too preoccupied with the monetary side of the job. Rather, as with the tour guides/interpreters from whom they sought to distance themselves, they expressed a complicated relationship between money and culture, a distinction that variously informs the ways in which these two sets of social actors talk about the past and the future.

WORKING FOR LOVE, NOT MONEY: OBSERVATIONS OF SENIOR STAFF AND RESEARCHERS IN THE HMCC

Most of my contact and interaction with research and technical staff in the HMCC were with the following three individuals: Van and Anh, two senior staff, and a more junior colleague Huy.[4] Van had completed a Masters course in conservation at Cornell University and Anh had completed advanced postgraduate level training in Japan, while Huy, who had only recently been promoted from his position as a tour guide, was hoping to be selected to train abroad in the near future. Throughout each of my research visits to Hue, they were exceedingly gracious with their time, and, among other things, helped to arrange interviews with a number of tour guides.

Anh is a man of great energy and enthusiasm for his work as an archaeologist and conservator. Within the first fifteen minutes of meeting me, he had pulled out his maps and given me a clear and concise overview of the archaeology of the region as he knew it. He then took me on the first of several tours of the Imperial City and tomb complexes. There are two things in particular that I want to highlight here that emerged from our conversations and walks together. First, while the tour guides that I accompanied on my initial tours of the Imperial City and tombs directed my gaze towards grand views and vistas, and presented general historical overviews, Anh's view was directed at the detail. He pointed out the workmanship involved in a single piece of joinery, discussed the variety of ceramic materials and glazes used and specified the kind of tools and techniques employed by the original craftsmen. In what could have been taken directly from UNESCO guidelines, he told me that restoration work should be done using methods and materials as near as possible to the original, and was proud of being thorough in this regard. While dedicated to careful restoration, Anh was not in favour of reconstruction, and opposed the rebuilding of the main palace in the Imperial City, though he understood that there was some pressure on the HMCC to do so by officials who thought it would attract greater visitor numbers. Also, he told me that prior to *doi moi*, he had lived and worked in Hanoi, where, he said, 'all I did was read books' without the chance to do any 'real' research. He recounted how, since the policy of *doi moi*, the government had a change of heart with respect to giving money to researchers actually to do research on various sites around Vietnam. That is why he decided to come and live in Hue. In Hanoi, he said, there were too many officials, 'just officials doing official business, no one does any work'. He said they had in the past tried to get other archaeologists from Hanoi involved in the work in Hue, but he said, 'They only come as tourists and then go back home.' 'Archaeologists are the most important here in Hue,' he said on more than one occasion. 'More and more tourists keep coming, want to know what's this, what was here? Archaeologists must do the research to be able to give them the answers.'

Overall, Anh was generally impatient with anything that got in the way of serious scientific research and conservation work: work that he deemed was necessary both to ensure that the site was authentically restored and to provide valid and accurate information for visitors. He generally regarded bureaucrats and officials with disdain and viewed them at best as grudgingly supporting serious research, and at worst as prone to distorting the historical record and only really being interested in what would be most likely to attract the tourist. These were opinions that seemed to be shared by the other researchers, as was Anh's comment that 'Even if you're poor, as long as you are rich in possibilities for doing research then that's good.' As Huy, a former tour guide/interpreter, now a member of the research staff told me, 'We do our work for love, not because of money.' Though I did not get to know Huy as well as Anh and Van, he most especially seemed to regard his work as a researcher at the HMCC not just as having intellectual rewards, but more fundamentally as having the character of a guardian of Vietnamese national culture. He was also particularly disparaging of what he described as Vietnam's *nouveaux riches* who, he maintained, simply came to the Hue monuments to flaunt their riches and have pictures taken of themselves. Huy was the most disparaging of tourists' and by extension tour guides' superficial knowledge, though perhaps the latter was in part because he had only recently moved from being a tour guide to being a full-time researcher himself.

In contrast to Anh's extroverted and energetic personality, and Huy's more strident nationalistic sentiments, Van was quiet and reflective, though he was no less personable because of this, and of the three it was Van I got to know best. Van was often highly critical of the current situation in Vietnam, and of the official running of things in Hue in particular, more so than either Anh or Huy. Much of his work during the times I visited was spent in the laborious process of translating and preparing information placards for individual buildings and other points of interest around the monument complex. The information placards had to be translated from Vietnamese to English and back again, Van told me, so that the head historian and researcher (who was ultimately answerable to the official from the Ministry of Culture in Hanoi) could ensure there was no slippage in meaning during the translation to English from Vietnamese. Van regarded this process as a waste of his time and an unnecessary intrusion of bureaucrats who, he suggested, actually knew very little about the site and only followed whatever the approved party line was at that particular moment. He too was concerned with 'authenticity' and understood his work to be more than a money-making enterprise. However, he was, for a variety of reasons, much less enthusiastic about it than Anh, as is demonstrated in the following edited extract from field notes of one of several extended conversations we had together.[5]

Sitting by the Perfume River drinking iced coffee at the end of the working day I related to Van some of the things I had seen and heard in Hue, including my encounters with tour guides, and my previous night's experience listening to 'traditional' songs on the Perfume River, and so on.

Van then began telling me something about his perspective on tourism in Hue. He started by saying that he thought that culture and money were two different things. He asked me what I had thought about the musicians and singers whom I had heard on the boat the night before. I said that I had found their music very beautiful and enjoyable. Van said I had probably enjoyed them because I was a tourist and it was my first experience of them. He thought their singing and songs had no soul in them because they were doing it simply for money. He asked me how much I had paid to go on the boat trip, and I told him five dollars. He told me they would go out on the river twice every night. 'Night after night. They sing the same songs. How could they be sung with genuine feeling and emotion?' But he said it was good that tourism was helping to renew an interest in the traditional arts.

Tourism, Van told me, was now Hue's number one industry, but local people did not know how to deliver it. He suggested that tourism in the West was more like a science, but that this was far from the case in Hue. People in Hue, he explained, were really impoverished, not very advanced or developed. The general lack of quality education was one of the reasons why tourism was not properly managed in Hue. When I suggested that new training schemes in various aspects of tourism had been or were being initiated, he said they were mainly directed at training hotel staff. Van said that the real problem was that most of the directors of tourist companies and other organizations were not appointed because of their educational qualifications or knowledge but because they were either former generals or because of their connections with ranking party officials.

Another problem, he said, was the very low wages which even educated individuals received. He was paid only $40 per month. He told me that even the tour guides fared better than he did, since they could earn extra money through tips and by working as paid interpreters and guides on the side through local tour companies. He had in the past sometimes taken work as an interpreter and tour guide. He often thought about going to work in Ho Chi Minh City, where he could be paid $200–300 per month. Hue was just a small unimportant province with little work, and to find good work required strong connections. Even the factory where his wife worked was closed a few years ago due to corruption, he said. He was now supporting himself, his wife and two daughters, including the eldest, aged 14, on his small salary. 'It's very difficult,' he concluded.

As the above comments suggest, Van has a complicated relationship with and ambivalent views on heritage and tourism. On the one hand, he is, despite his criticisms, in many respects singing from the same hymn sheet as the official renovated view of Hue both as a centre of Vietnamese art and culture and as an important drawing card for tourist dollars and development. On the other hand, as with Huy and Anh, he also views the increasing commoditization of culture for tourists as a threat to its authenticity and positions himself as someone who is able to judge and know the difference between that which is real and that which is simply a pale and soulless imitation. I was clearly regarded, moreover, presumably because of my status as a university researcher, as someone who should have been able to appreciate the difference but was apparently unable to because of my limited touristic knowledge and experience, a view I would hardly dispute especially so far as the music and songs were concerned. However, even more so than either Anh or Huy, he was particularly critical of the failure of state and Party officials either to appreciate fully the distinction between money and culture or to manage the relationship between them and effectively capitalize on culture. He attributed this failure both to a lack of education and training, and to the placement of unqualified individuals in leadership positions. The consequences of this failure were seen not only in the perceived diminution of cultural authenticity but also in the general impoverishment and lack of development in Hue, which his own poorly remunerated situation was seen to exemplify.

In their own way, each of the individuals I have described above assert their superior knowledge and ability to discern between appropriate and inappropriate forms of renovation and between authentic and inauthentic cultural and artistic expression. In this they clearly reproduce forms of cultural distinction articulated by other Vietnamese intellectuals (Bayly, 2004) and claims to authenticity redolent of international heritage discourses codified by UNESCO (on the latter see Holtorf, 2001; Holtorf and Schadla-Hall, 1999).[6] Underlying the above claims was the distinction drawn between money and culture, a distinction which in Bourdieu's (1984) terms might be seen as making a virtue out of necessity, reaffirming and enhancing their own cultural capital through their claims to suffer impoverishment for a nobler cause. This is also articulated in their critical if somewhat contradictory view of tourism as, on the one hand, leading to a dilution of authenticity, and, on the other hand, as not being sufficiently well developed or extensive enough. In certain respects, their worries about the dilution of cultural authenticity are in part attributed to tourists themselves, and in particular to those Vietnamese tourists characterized as the *nouveaux riches* who are clearly talked about in ways that are suggestive of the 'tourist gaze' described by Urry (1990), as I discuss further below. However, they also clearly feel that this need not be the case. Rather, the three indicated that the real culprits are the officials and bureaucrats who not only sought to maintain control over the history of the site, but also pandered to the superficial tourist gaze, rather than supporting work that encourages better informed and more engaged tourists, that is, those who asked real questions and deserved real, scientifically validated answers and genuine cultural experiences.

INTERPRETING HUE: THE GUIDES' VIEW OF HISTORY

Having explored some of the views of research staff in the HMCC, I turn now to tour guides, whose relationship to culture and heritage is no less ambivalent and contradictory, but who also adopt a somewhat different approach and articulate a different set of ideas with respect to tourists and tourism. The difference between them is not, as research and technical staff would have it, because tour guides are primarily interested in money rather than in cultivating a genuine understanding of and appreciation for Hue's culture and history. It is true that many of them overtly expressed an interest in earning money, but it is far too simple to describe them as being simply ill-informed and uninterested in culture or heritage. Rather, as I discuss below, the distinctions tour guides draw between money and culture is caught up in a much broader and potentially more radical series of oppositions that reflect different ways of evaluating the past and articulating aspirations for the future. To begin with, however, it is important to provide some more general background about tour guides and their work for the HMCC and the way in which they variously interpret and engage with the monuments and history.

Most tour guides have had at least some university education, and some were graduates, usually in history or in a foreign language, mainly French or English. They attend a six-month training course at the beginning of their employment, and at its completion they are required to sit for an examination. If candidates are considered to have 'low ability' they are expected to return to study on their own until they are considered proficient enough. In the course of this training it is clear that they are expected to master a fairly rigid script to present to tourists at each of the monuments.

During the first few days of the initial period of my research, I hired two tour guides from one of the local private companies working outside of the HMCC, in order to gain some sense of how the monuments were presented to foreign tourists. Unbeknownst to me at the time, the guides that accompanied me that day (one in the morning, one in the afternoon) were actually employees of the HMCC, who were picking up a bit of extra income working for the private firm. I paid the firm US$22 out of which my guides were given $16 to share between them, a considerable addition to their normal salary of $20 per month. At each site we visited that day I was taken along what was obviously a well-rehearsed route, led to particular vantage points and given a set, generally well-polished description of the place. The landscape they recounted for me as we walked around the imperial city and tombs was one inhabited by former emperors, mandarins and concubines, of palace intrigues and lavish feasts, of cultivated arts and the poetic harmony of place organized according to the principles of *feng shui* and aligned in accordance with the instruction of royal geomancers.

My initial experience of these guided tours of the Hue Monuments was largely in keeping with the pre-processed and sanitized presentations of culture and history that characterize many tourism and heritage sites, whether in Vietnam or elsewhere (e.g. Urry, 1990; Kennedy and Williams, 2001). Crucially, however, it did not take long or much encouragement on my part before the guides moved beyond these officially scripted presentations. As Dahles (2001: 173) similarly notes of tour guides in Yogyakarta, the attempt at policing and enforcing a dominant discourse is often 'more conspicuous in its efforts than in its effect', and is continually undermined by tour guides who 'sprinkle their narratives with subversive elements'.

Thus, for example, on our motorcycle ride back from Khai Dinh's tomb, I asked one of my tour guides, Tuan, whether or not and to what extent the official view of the Nguyen emperors had changed in recent times. Prior to 1980, he replied, all the Nguyen emperors were viewed as collaborators with the colonial French, whereas now the history that he read in books identifies both positive and negative aspects of each in terms of what they did for Vietnam. He went on to tell me about his history professor, who was doing much research into the emperors, and about his inability previously to do this research properly, because of 'the uneducated soldiers who ran the government'. Whereas previously (meaning in the intervening period between reunification and changes brought about by the policy of renovation) his history teacher was restricted in his studies, now, according to Tuan, he was once again able to do his research.

It is clear that like the research staff of the HMCC, Tuan was aware of the shifting interpretive frameworks within which historical knowledge was produced. Nor was he alone among the tour guides in openly talking about the way in which the historical view of the emperors had changed. One might suggest that, like the more senior researchers in the HMCC, it is precisely because they have had first hand experience of overt ideological control over history that they are all the more cognizant of the contested nature of historical narratives. Further, contrary to the view of tour guides held by senior researchers, both Tuan and Phu (the other tour guide on that first day) said that even after they had completed their tour guiding course they continued to do research and reading on their own. While we were at the Museum of Antiquities, for example, Phu purchased a book for himself on the nationalist scholar and writer Phan Boi Chau, telling me that he took every opportunity to buy books on any relevant subjects, though, like Tuan, he expressed a frustration over the lack of learning resources available to him. The research centre of the HMCC does have books and other resources that are available for consultation on site, but these are limited as is the range of literature available for purchase. Although both Phu and Tuan's representation of themselves as being serious and diligent students of Hue history and culture may have simply been for my benefit, to make an impression on me as a reliable and informed tour guide and interpreter, subsequent interviews and conversations with other tour guides suggest otherwise.

Lam is a young woman in her mid-20s and had been a guide for five years. Lam had studied to be a teacher, but decided the day-in and day-out of working with children wasn't something she wanted to do, so she decided to try being a tourist guide. She said that some people bring their own guides with them, but people who really wanted to know more about Hue, would use 'local' guides. I asked Lam if she liked being a guide. She said she liked the fact that they were given responsibility for checking up on the monuments, keeping inventories of artifacts in particular buildings, and reporting when things needed repair. She often felt tired (at the end of a long day talking and walking around with tourists) but happy when tourists asked questions and were interested in what she had to say.

In fact, Lam drew a distinction, echoing that of research staff, between two different kinds of tourists, those who listened and were interested in what she said and those who were not bothered, whom she identified in terms of 'Northern' and 'Southern' Vietnamese respectively. She said, 'Some people don't pay attention. I think it is impolite. When this happens and they are only interested in [taking] pictures, don't listen, I don't feel satisfied with my work.' However, she also said that the most enjoyable part of her job was just meeting and talking to people informally, and it was most often the case that those who were least interested in the site were also the most friendly (see discussion further below).

While Lam commented on the fact that some tourists were more interested in taking pictures than in listening to her accounts of the emperors, another tour guide, Hien, recounted an incident in which she was involved in a dispute with a tourist over the interpretation of history. She said that once when she was working at Khai Dinh's tomb, a Vietnamese tourist (whom she identified as being a 'Northerner') said, 'This was a very bad king. He was just a figure-head. He did nothing to protect the people. Spending people's money to build this tomb.'

MJ: 'What was your reply?'

Hien: 'He couldn't do anything. Previously three kings had fought against the French and all failed. The situation Khai Dinh was in was not better but worse. He was receiving a salary from the French.'

Apparently they got into a big argument, but Hien was not able to continue with it, because they had finished their time at Khai Dinh's tomb and left to see another one. Hien said she appreciated his viewpoint, but thought he was still stuck with past (revolutionary) ways of thinking. Usually, Hien said, tourists just asked her questions about the emperors' everyday lives, where they slept, what they ate, etc. If she was not able to answer all of their questions, sometimes she would go back to the office at the HMCC and ask other people or try and do some research on her own. Sometimes she sent letters to the people with what she had found out. Like Lam, she reported a sense of satisfaction in her job when she was with tourists who expressed an interest in the sites, even those who held strong opinions and different viewpoints from her own.

Like Tuan and Phu, then, Lam and Hien appear to invest a great deal of themselves in their work, and express a genuine interest and sense of responsibility for the monuments and history, with which they see themselves as having been entrusted, though they lack the credentials and cultural capital that distinguishes, and informs the distinctions of, research staff in the HMCC. It is also clear, from what Hien and others said, that they embrace the new orthodoxy that views the Nguyen emperors as having, in Tuan's words, both good and bad points, but who had overall left an important legacy in the monuments, or as another tour guide put it, 'They did some things wrong, but they left something wonderful.' However, like the research staff members I spoke to, while they accept and articulate the official renovated story of the Nguyen emperors, they do so in a reflective way. Indeed, their involvement with and particular knowledge of Hue culture and history have also become a personal resource for making sense of and critically commenting on their own lives and experience. This was certainly the case with Tuan, who, as the following extract from my field notes exemplifies, was very adept at creatively turning the past into a running commentary on the present:

Tuan lives at home with his father (his mother, he told me, died some time ago now). He originally tried studying medicine but failed the examination on two occasions and decided he would try something else. Earlier in the day, I had asked Tuan about his father's occupation. He told me that he was formerly a university lecturer in English, but that after reunification he had been retrained as a high school teacher. As we were talking more of the story emerged. His father had, according to Tuan, for a period of three months been conscripted by the ARVN (Army of the Republic of Vietnam), although he said he never actually saw any combat duty, but just worked as a clerk. However, after reunification, because of this, he was blacklisted and was not allowed to be a university professor.

Tuan said that he would like to find work in a government office as a civil servant, but that because of his father's record, it would be difficult. For now he was content to work for the HMCC in the hope that if he worked hard, he might eventually be promoted to a more senior position. He said that he had been to several places, took and passed their examinations, but that because he did not have the right connections, the job would be given to someone else. He said, look at the government officials in Hanoi, it used to be former soldiers who had fought for their country, but now it was just being filled up by their sons who had done nothing. Tuan went on to compare it to the old feudal systems of the Nguyen dynasties with mandarins seeking favours from the emperor and mandarins being solicited by others lower than themselves.

Tuan went on to ask me if I had been told about the emperor's concubines. He said that in order to place their daughters as concubines of the king, their fathers would approach the eunuchs working in the palace. Similarly if concubines wanted to sleep with the emperor, they would have to approach eunuchs to get them to whisper a word in the emperor's ear. With so many concubines, he said, sometimes they would wait six years before even ever seeing the emperor. Again he compared this to currying favours with company directors and party officials.

He then went on to tell me that concubines had to study court etiquette for six months before they even went into the imperial city. Then he said something to the effect that 'I had to study two years, plus six months, before they let me approach foreigners.' To which I replied, 'That must make foreign tourists the new emperors', and we laughed, not a little nervously, together.

As is evident from the above, tour guides' involvement in and engagements with culture and history are not simply naïve or superficial reproductions of the new orthodoxy. What is particularly striking is the way in which Tuan's personal frustration over the perceived inequities and corruption he and his father have encountered in present-day Vietnam are read and interpreted as akin to practices of a previous regime commonly characterized in revolutionary discourse as 'feudal'. Nor was Tuan alone in this, as other tour guides drew similar connections and analogies between the two. The significance of this is that while the Nguyen emperors have to some extent been freed through their official rehabilitation from their association with the excesses of the more distant past, they have become burdened with the perceived failures and difficulties of the present. To put it otherwise, the two are in some respects blurred together in the present. Hence while tour guides are genuinely interested in and committed to Hue culture and heritage, as I suggest below, they also identify with a very different way of viewing and engaging with the Hue monuments: one that is seen to represent different kinds of possibilities and aspirations for living in both the present and the future.

BETWEEN THE NORTH AND THE SOUTH: ENCOUNTERS
WITH AND IMAGININGS OF VIETNAMESE TOURISTS

In the preceding section I suggested that tour guides articulated a sense of job satisfaction, particularly in dealing with tourists whom they perceived to be genuinely interested in Hue culture and history in general and in what they had to say in particular. As I demonstrate, it is here we encounter most clearly the contradictory and seemingly paradoxical relationship of tour guides to Hue culture and history, for while they routinely said they gained job satisfaction working with interested tourists, most of the guides that I spoke to also said that they preferred that group of tourists who demonstrated the least interest in the place, would enjoy taking pictures and would rather chat informally with the guides than listen to tour guide accounts of the monuments.

As noted above, tour guides undergo a six-month period of training, though this may extend to a longer period if they are unsuccessful in passing the initial examination. The first part of the training course consists of lectures given by specialists and scholars about history, historical monuments, Vietnamese culture and Hue city in particular. The specialists and scholars include researchers in the HMCC and from universities and official institutes in Hanoi. The second part of the course is learning about being a tour guide and the role of the interpreter. That is to say, there is a sense in which learning the score was seen not simply in terms of the accounts of the past they were meant to rehearse, but also in terms of the audience they were playing to. As Phuong, the head of interpreter training, put it in terms of tour guides gaining official recognition: they are tested both on 'what they say' and 'how they say it'. Phuong told me that in the classes guides learned about 'psychology': that is, how to behave with each kind of visitor, according both to their nationality and the particular knowledge of each group. The most important thing tour guides had to learn was what kind of people the visitors were and what their tastes were.

I asked if they could give me an example of what exactly they meant by this. Phuong laughed when I asked her this. The example she gave was of Vietnamese visitors from different parts of the country:

> Vietnamese visitors from the North thirst for knowledge. They want to learn a lot, so the tour guide must be knowledgeable and be able to answer all their questions. Vietnamese from the South [laughing] just come to see the buildings and take pictures.

Was it really true, this difference between north and south? I asked. She said there were in fact two different kinds of people from the North:

> People from the countryside – these people want to learn, everything is strange for them because they have less chance, less opportunity. They are eager to listen. Hanoi people have a long history and culture, longer than Hue. They have a basic knowledge of culture and history already, so it's easier for them to learn more. They ask lots of questions and compare it to their own history and historical knowledge. They respect this place, particularly the appearance of the monuments that are still intact – they respect it.

She said that there were not as many tourists from the central part of Vietnam as from the North and South. The tourists from the central part of Vietnam she suggested usually just listened attentively but didn't ask questions or speak out.

> Tourists from the South, they have the money. Some tour guides prefer them, because the pay is more and you don't have to talk so much. They are not so interested in history and culture, but are more interested in having their pictures taken. Also it's easier to talk to them. People from the North are profound, also people from the central part. The South is different; they speak out what they think. [Laughing, appears embarrassed] For me, I don't like people from the North. They don't say what they think.

There were a number of things I found surprising in this and other similar conversations. The first was the significance attached to the perceived differences between Vietnamese visitors from the North and the South. Distinctions were, of course, also made between different sorts of foreign visitors according to their nationality. Phuong, for example, told me that she thought Americans and Europeans really wanted to learn about culture and traditions, whereas the Taiwanese were 'not so interested in learning', they too just wanted to have a look and take pictures. Similarly when I asked Lam (see above) about how she would characterize different groups of foreign tourists, she said they were interested, but very few of them had a good understanding of Vietnamese history. The French, she said, were the ones who 'wanted to understand more'. She thought that the French came to see their colonial influence on Vietnam and be reminded about their past as well.

However, in my conversations with both Phuong and Lam, as well as with other tour guides, as with the research staff, it was the differences between Vietnamese from different parts of the country which they tended to elaborate on rather than differences between foreign tourists, as the following quotes from other tour guides suggest:

> Northern people always go in groups, they like the scenery and are interested in history and always need a tourist guide. They want to know more about culture and history than Southern people. Southern people go with the group, but each person buys their own ticket. They just want to take photos.

Commenting on their differing perceptions of the various tombs, another tour guide said,

> Northerners think Minh Mang's tomb is very beautiful. Southerners think Minh Mang's tomb is very old and dull with not much to see. Southerners prefer Khai Dinh's tomb, it's not as old and more colourful.

There are two things I wish to draw out from the above. First, on a more general point, as suggested at the outset, studies of tourists and tourism tend to privilege the experiences, views and impacts of foreign tourists, particularly in non-Western settings. Tour guides' concern with and distinctions between different sorts of Vietnamese visitors is a useful reminder that in-country tourism may be as much if not more significant in certain respects than foreign visitors in places such as Hue. Or, as one tour guide put it, we don't think about foreign tourists – a 'foreigner is a foreigner'.[7] Indeed, in terms of overall visitor numbers, Vietnamese nationals still represent the majority of visitors at the Hue Monuments Complex.[8]

Secondly, given the repeated attribution of greater cultural knowledge and historical interest to visitors from Northern Vietnam, and given that tour guides, like the research staff in the HMCC, said they liked it when tourists were attentive and interested, one might have anticipated that tour guides preferred tourists from the North. However, while respecting the devotion and perceived cultural and historical depth of the Northerners – with which a certain affinity is certainly expressed – it became clear to me over the course of my research that many tour guides preferred the Southerners. As Phuong's embarrassed laughter (above) suggests, however, there was also, for some, a certain awkwardness in actually coming out and saying so directly, even if only because it might have been seen to contradict other statements they made and confirm the prejudices of other HMCC staff who suggested that tour guides were not really interested in or engaged in an authentic way with culture and history, but only money.

In fact, tour guides' preferences for Southerners over Northerners in part had to do with the tips they were paid. As noted at the outset, it is the tips paid to tour guides, rather than their monthly salary, that potentially offers the greatest economic rewards. Often identified as being from 'Saigon' (though some of the guides also referred to Ho Chi Minh City, the official post re-unification name for Saigon), Southerners were regarded by the tour guides as not just having more money to spend than people from other parts of Vietnam, but also as being more generous, if not downright frivolous, with their money.

However, the preference for Southerners is not based simply upon their perceived larger and more generous wallets. Rather, I would suggest that money condenses and registers a much broader range of qualities and characteristics that tour guides identify with in their perceptions and constructions of Southerners. Tour guides felt that visitors from the South were more sociable and were, as Phuong and Lam indicated, both easier to talk to and fun to chat informally with. Tour guides repeatedly mentioned the easy-going, fun-loving character of visitors from the South. Thus, for example, on one of many walks around the Imperial City, we stopped in the former palace of military mandarins. The palace was being renovated and was temporarily housing a photographer's booth where tourists could pay to dress up in royal costumes and have their pictures taken. As we walked through the palace, a group of Vietnamese visitors was standing around watching and laughing while two of them were dressed up in the costume of the empress and queen mother and had their pictures taken. Phu, the tour guide who I was with at the time, told me they were from Saigon. When I asked him how he knew this, he said he could tell because of their accents, their general demeanor and their dress. Visitors from the North, he suggested, were far too respectful to dress up in such a silly manner. Other tourist guides repeated similar comments. For example, one tour guide told me that Northerners dressed more conservatively, with women wearing long dresses, while Southerners, she suggested, wore 'modern' styles and more comfortable clothing, including 'mini-skirts'.

At another level, however, tour guides are also reproducing a wider set of perceived contrasts that I frequently heard from a variety of people living in Hue between Ho Chi Minh City/Saigon and Hanoi, including members of the research and technical staff. Ho Chi Minh City is associated not just with greater economic prosperity but also with greater opportunities for individuals to pursue and develop their careers. Hanoi is associated with state bureaucracy, party officials and the necessity of having connections and affiliations with important people. As one tour guide put it, 'Go to Ho Chi Minh City, it is open and competitive, getting a job is based on compatibility not connections.' Or as another put it, 'People go to the South for economics. People go to the North for study or travelling. Only a few go to the North to live. The South is more open – it is easier to earn a living.' Whilst I frequently heard young people in particular talk about the possibility of migrating to Ho Chi Minh City to find work, rarely did I hear anyone talk about moving to Hanoi. My concern here is not with whether or not or to what extent their views of Northerners and Southerners or their characterizations of Ho Chi Minh City and Hanoi are accurate. Rather, I am interested in what these attributions mean to the tour guides and what they are saying through the no doubt overdrawn contrasts they make between them.

On the one hand, Northerners appear to affirm for tour guides their own sense of attachment to and pride in Hue as heritage interpreters. Tour guides spoke with appreciation about the respect accorded themselves and the monuments by Northern tourists. Moreover, while Northerners might hold outdated views about the Nguyen emperors, their willingness to express alternative opinions and challenge tour guides' stories was generally deemed to be a positive rather than a negative characteristic and further evidence of their genuine engagement with the place. Tour guides in this respect clearly find some points of identification with Northern tourists. That is to say, while tour guides embrace the officially renovated view of Hue as a site of cultural and aesthetic achievement, they are also aware of the political context within which this interpretive shift has occurred and, as I have demonstrated, are able to deploy the otherwise downplayed aspects of this 'feudal' past – the bureaucracy, corruption and patronage of the royal court – in order to critically comment on the present.

On the other hand, whereas the researchers in HMCC only ever expressed the utmost disdain for the stereotypical frivolous Southern tourists (which they may or may not have any actual experience of themselves), tour guides had, or at least articulated, a more complex relationship with them. Tour guides also said they thought that Southerners were superficial: certainly they did not affirm their role as site interpreters and serious students of history in the way that Northerners did. It was, paradoxically, precisely this superficial and frivolous quality that tour guides seemed to identify with. As I suggested at the outset, the characteristics attributed to Southerners clearly fit those kind of tourists and that extreme form of the tourist gaze Urry (1993: 184) defined as the 'spectatorial', i.e. a 'communal activity', comprising a 'series of brief encounters' and 'glancing and collecting different signs'. Tour guides, like the research staff, continually made reference to the fact that what Southerners were really interested in was taking pictures, or more precisely having their pictures taken at the site. They also talked about the leisurely gait and self-confident demeanour of Southerners, their general sociability and their flamboyant style, the Vietnamese equivalents of the Congolese *sapeur* described by Friedman (1994), for whom visiting the site was both about seeing and being seen.

Far from construing these tourists, their gaze and their gait simply in a negative way, Southerners appeared to offer tour guides an alternative and vicarious experience of the site as a different kind of place altogether from the one they normally experienced, one that was not completely determined by the on-going struggles over the meaning of the past in the present. However, this was also about articulating contrasting futures and as I suggested at the outset was as much about transformation as it was about transcendence and escape. Similar to the distinctions drawn between Ho Chi Minh City and Hanoi, Southerners were seen as exemplifying the possibilities of a more open and affluent society, while Northerners were seen as exemplifying the persistence of a closed and austere, if more intellectually orientated, society. Not surprisingly, most of the tour guides conveyed a greater sense of affinity for and identification with Southerners. Nevertheless, for most of the guides this was not simply conceived of as a straightforward exchange of one set of promises for another. Rather, I would argue that the contrasts that tour guides drew between Southerners and Northerners was one way to articulate and make sense of the contradictions they faced and of their own ambivalent feelings towards the transformations currently on-going in present day Vietnam. In other words, while the apparently free and easy gaze of Southern tourists provided both a welcome relief from their ordinary situation and held out the possibility of a more hopeful future, it was also one which in certain respects was seen to be fundamentally at odds with their genuine engagements with and appreciation for their own culture and history.

SUMMARY AND CONCLUSIONS: NOSTALGIC LONGINGS AND THE 'TOURIST GAZE'

In this chapter I have sought to complicate those analyses of tourism in Vietnam that have emphasized how culture and history have been carefully packaged and presented in ways that gloss over more difficult and contentious aspects of the past, consolidate the official view of Vietnamese national identity and pander to the prejudices and orientalizing gaze of foreign tourists. More specifically I have demonstrated how those involved in the making and presentation of heritage in Hue reproduce, contest and reshape the renovated view of Hue's history and culture, and critically deploy the past to comment on their present situation. I have also shown how encounters with and constructions of local Vietnamese visitors offer alternative vantage points and competing views of both the past and the future.

On the one hand, researchers and experts in the Hue Monuments Conservation Centre most clearly and overtly identify with what has now become the official view of Hue as a testament of Vietnamese cultural creativity and a key to a renewed sense of national identity. However, they lament the previous neglect of the monuments and see the state and Party as having finally caught up with what they knew all along: that Hue's culture and heritage is an important national resource that should be subject to proper investigation and preservation. They also articulate two related concerns. The first is that tourism tends to dilute the authenticity of the site and the arts associated with it. In doing so, they distinguish themselves on the basis of their ability to discriminate between the real and 'soulful' and that which is simply unconvincing performance and reconstruction intended to generate the most money from undiscriminating tourists. Secondly, they feel that their work as well-qualified scientists and guardians of culture is often undermined and not satisfactorily appreciated or remunerated.

In sum, researchers in the HMCC might be seen in Bourdieu's terms (1984) as the dominated fraction of the dominant class – high in cultural capital, but with little economic or decision-making power. They consciously distinguish themselves both from what they regard to be the crass materialism of the *nouveaux riches* and from bureaucratic and party functionaries who are said to be selling out cultural authenticity for a quick buck. They also see the latter as trying to maintain too close a control over the meaning of the site. However, while highly critical of the inadequacies of the state and Party, whom they see as compromising the heritage of the past, they ultimately have the most invested in the official renovated view of Hue propagated by state and Party. That is to say their critical views of heritage management do not fundamentally challenge the reconstructions of Hue as a site of artistic and aesthetic achievement. Rather, they see themselves as struggling to conserve and preserve this past against the ravages of time, the ideological whims and inefficient management of the state and the potential onslaught of uninterested and ill-informed tourists.

On the other hand, tour guides also identify with, and clearly reproduce and represent the official view of Hue culture in their daily encounters with tourists. As with the research staff they generally take their work as site interpreters very seriously, and defend that position which views the monuments as an important and lasting cultural achievement that ought to be respected and appreciated in its own right. They do not overtly challenge the revised view of the Nguyen emperors as 'having done some things wrong, but left something wonderful'. However, they subvert this in more subtle ways as they draw on the past to comment on their own lives in the present. They do this in particular by drawing analogies between the present-day situations they face and the situations of other subalterns in previous feudal regimes. Drawing an analogy between the inadequacies and inequities of the past and the present not only means that the past is seen to be compromised by the perceived failures of the present, but also involves highlighting precisely those aspects of the past that the official renovated view of Hue is now seeking to downplay, if not forget about altogether.

In sum, tour guides, while respecting and attentive to culture and history, see it as inextricably linked to and bound up with their frustration over the present state of affairs and more specifically the lack of opportunities and constraints that are said to characterize their lives. This informs the contrasts they draw and the contradictory identifications they make between those Vietnamese tourists who are said to be attentive, respectful and engaged with the monuments and their history (i.e. those identified as Northerners) and those who express little interest in the monuments and are simply there to have a good day out and have their pictures taken (i.e. those identified as Southerners). The former are associated with cultural and historical depth, but also with hardship, struggle and corrupt bureaucracies.

The latter are associated with cultural and historical shallowness, but also with an open, forward-looking and optimistic future: contradictions which Nguyen (2003) has elsewhere characterized as the tug Vietnamese young people in particular feel between a 'still' and 'moving' society and their attempts to negotiate between them.

Finally, I want to return here to the suggestion that it is precisely in respect of tour guides' identifications with those tourists characterized as being most superficial that the notion of the tourist gaze might itself be usefully renovated. Specifically, while the notion of the tourist gaze construes the putatively visual consumption and artificial engagements of tourists with people, place and culture as being by and large a negative social feature and consequence of late modernity and global capitalism, what the above ethnography suggests is that, in this context and for this particular set of social actors at least, the tourist gaze is in fact something to aspire to. That is to say, here is a situation where the heritage landscape, despite, or rather because of, attempts to sanitize and de-politicize it, far from being a source of nostalgia for a lost past, is far too real and immanently part of the continuing struggles and frustrations of the present. By contrast, I suggest that the gaze from afar that seemingly breezes over and transcends this landscape provides a much needed and vicariously experienced escape from the ever-present past and articulates a longing for an as yet to be realized future.

Indeed, the situation I describe above is a useful reminder and corrective to the tendency of Western social theorists and anthropologists to universalize their own views of and worries about the world (see also Friedman, 2002). Thus, for example, Szerszynski and Urry (2006) have recently argued that there is a global cosmopolitanism emerging that entails a wholesale change in people's vantage point in which 'humans increasingly inhabit their world only at a distance' (2006: 113). Such sweeping generalizations are inevitably accompanied both by anxieties about our being 'fated to become mere visitors in our own worlds' (ibid.: 128), and by nostalgic longings for a future past where we might recapture something of the more embedded and less alienated lives of our pre-modern forbears (Ingold, 2000: chapter 12; cited in Szerszynski and Urry, 2006: 122). From the vantage point of the prosaic worlds of researchers and tour guides in Hue, who daily negotiate the complexities of state and Party bureaucracy, poor wages and their own ambivalent and at times contradictory views of the past, the future and the place they are living in here and now, the luxury and conceit of such longings does, quite literally, seem a world away.

NOTES

1   I am grateful to the British Academy South-East Asia Committee and the University of Hull Research Support Fund for supporting the research on which this chapter is based. The chapter has benefited from the comments and suggestions of Kenny Archibald, Vassos Argyrou, James Carrier, Suzanne Clisby, Victor King and An Phuong Nguyen. Huong Bui provided help with some Vietnamese translation.

2   Hue was originally the royal seat for the first Nguyen dynasty that controlled large parts of what is now South Vietnam from the mid sixteenth century until 1777. This was followed by the short-lived Tay Son dynasty (1788–1802) that incorporated both the Nguyen state in the South and the Le dynasty in the North. However, Nguyen Phuc Anh, one of the grandsons of the last king of the former Nguyen dynasty, re-established control in the South, and with the help of foreign assistance overthrew the Tay Son, installed himself in Hue as ruler over a unified Vietnam and declared himself the emperor Gia Long in 1802. Thus began the second Nguyen dynasty that ruled over a unified Vietnam until the abdication of Bao Dai. A detailed account of the rise of Nguyen Phuc Anh is provided in Wook, 2004.

3   Ethnographic research in Hue was conducted during on two short periods of fieldwork, the first in June–July 1997, the second in January–February 1999. The material I present is drawn from unstructured interviews and informal conversations with individual tour guides and research staff over the course of my two research visits. These conversations took place in a variety of settings and contexts including extensive walks and tours around most of the major monuments, shared meals together and long cups of coffee, beer and fresh lemonade, sitting beside the Perfume River.

4   All individuals are referred to by pseudonyms.

5   Except where otherwise indicated, the field notes I present in this chapter are generally paraphrased accounts based on my recollections compiled immediately after the actual events and conversations took place. Depending on the situation I sometimes took brief notes and where I am quoting verbatim from notes taken at the time of the conversation, these are indicated by quotation marks.

6   In a recent article on 'the limits of authenticity', Vann (2006) has argued that it is mistaken in the Vietnamese context to conflate two sets of ideas that are bound up in Western discourses of authenticity, namely originality versus imitation and real versus fake (Handler, 2000: cited in Vann, 2006: 294). In Vietnam, she contends, at least with respect to consumer goods, the key distinction is between goods that are 'real', i.e. goods that approximate what they purport to be, and those which are 'fake', i.e. goods that do not in any way thus approximate. The question of originality, by contrast, she suggests is at best a secondary concern and the question is more about the quality of the goods produced, with 'model' goods providing the measure of quality against which other 'mimic' goods are measured. Her point is that it is inappropriate and misleading to apply Western notions of authenticity, particularly as they are encoded within international law on intellectual property rights. Whether

or not Vann's arguments are valid in this context is beyond the scope of this chapter. Having said that, I would suggest that notions of uniqueness and originality are salient in the context of discourses about Vietnamese culture, though they are no doubt informed and reinforced by Western-derived discourses of authenticity purveyed by international bodies such as UNESCO. Nevertheless, there are obviously different and competing views of 'authenticity' at play here that warrant further work and exploration.

7   As an aside, I should note that, with the exception of tourists from Hong Kong and Taiwan (who were seen as being most like Southerners), most foreigners were regarded by tour guides as generally mean-spirited, a view repeated by many of the vendors who sold drinks and post cards at the entrance of some of the tomb complexes.

8   In 1999, the number of foreign visitors was 246,745 whilst Vietnamese visitors totalled 653,339. By 2005, these numbers were 552,943 and 768,083 respectively. Source: HMCC official website, www.hueheritage.org.vn.

CHAPTER **10**

Vietnam's Heritage Attractions in Transition

Wantanee Suntikul, Richard Butler and
David Airey

INTRODUCTION: HERITAGE ATTRACTIONS

Tourism is a multi-dimensional, multi-faceted phenomenon covering many different types of activities and, as such, is difficult to define conclusively (Cooper et al., 1999: 8). Tourists travel to different destinations with different motivations. According to McIntosh et al. (1995: 41), cultural attractions such as historical places, monuments, architecture, people and art are important motivations to travel. McCannell (1976: 41) defines a tourist attraction as 'an empirical relationship between a tourist, a sight and a marker (a piece of information about a sight)'.

Many types of attractions fall into the heritage tourism sector, which accounts for a considerable portion of tourism in developed countries (Garrod and Fyall, 2000: 683). It has been noted that tourism to heritage attractions can play a role in their gaining wider public and official acknowledgement of their status as cultural heritage sites (Stoessel, 1997: 82). In the context of tourism, the term 'heritage' has been used in connection with both cultural and natural aspects of a destination (Herbert, 1989). For Boniface, culture is a necessary component of a heritage attraction (1999: vii). In the 1990s the word 'heritage' became ubiquitous as a buzzword used by various destinations in their promotion of tourism (Palmer, 1999: 315). Heritage tourism is a flexible term, which has been applied to travel to any destination with an element of historical significance, and has thus been widely defined (Richter, 1999: 108), a situation which can often give rise to confusion and the faulty categorization of tourists (Poria, Butler and Airey, 2003).

Pretes (2003: 139) expounds on the presence of nationalistic discourses on tourism sites, which both protect and display physical manifestations of a nation's history. Such sites become carriers of messages from those in power to tourists, and aid in the formation of a shared national identity (Johnson, 1995) and, by extension, a personal identity for individual people within the nation as well as an image by which outsiders perceive the nation (Palmer, 1999: 317). Hall and Jenkins (1995: 44) have remarked that those with the power to preserve and designate sites as heritage attractions are in a position selectively to edit and present the past in a way that prioritizes their own values and interpretation of history, and that visitors to such sites often accept this history as fact rather than as a contested representation. The aspects or sites of heritage that are shown to tourists, and the way in which they are presented, is of course the prerogative of the exhibitor, and heritage sites and their presentation will tend to prioritize events, and readings of events, that favour those currently in power in the country. Consequently, access to heritage attractions will vary according to the social and political context in which the attractions exist and how likely the history evoked by the attraction is to depict those in power in a positive light (Richter, 1999: 121).

It would be illusory to proclaim that there is a single 'meaning' for any given heritage attraction, and there cannot be said to be one single 'correct' narrative associated with a heritage attraction; most presentations show only one version of many. The expectations and cultural backgrounds of domestic tourists also differ from those of international tourists, and different types of tourists will perceive and consume heritage attractions differently. There is no consensus among anthropologists on questions of authenticity in the presentation of cultural heritage, even on such basic issues as whether 'authenticity exists in tourism and whether this matters' (Shackley, 1994: 396). Sofield and Li (1998: 386) have noted the flexibility of the idea of authenticity in the context of tourism development, citing China as an example. Heritage attractions will have different meanings for different types of visitors and even for different individuals (Cheung, 1999: 570–588). Foreign tourists may be impressed by a heritage attraction, but the experience, in most cases, will be unlikely to cause feelings of personal identification (Timothy, 1997: 752). Only in those cases where tourists have sought out specific sites because of a personal connection to what they feel is their own heritage are they likely to feel personally involved with the site (Poria, Butler and Airey, 2004)

HERITAGE AND TOURISM IN VIETNAM

In 1986, the Congress of Vietnam introduced an economic program called *doi moi* (Renovation), which could be compared to Gorbachev's contemporaneous *glasnost* campaign. The new policy called for measures which included the decentralization of the planning system, a decrease in the number of government ministries and bureaucracies and, perhaps most importantly for the development of tourism, the establishment of a 'socialist market economy'. *Doi moi* has succeeded remarkably in moving the country from a stagnant, centrally-planned Soviet-style economy with macroeconomic instability to a mixed market-oriented economy (Kokko, 1998: 2). Parallel with this economic shift, Vietnam has been rediscovered by tourists from around the world. In 2006, over 3.5 million foreign visitors arrived in Vietnam (www.vietnamtourism.com), as compared to just over 54,000 in 1986 (Theuns, 1997: 306).

Although Vietnam is still benefiting from the 'novelty effect' as a relatively new travel destination for international travellers, this advantage is by its nature short-term. Operators in the Vietnamese tourism industry strive to capitalize on the characteristics of Vietnam that make it unique, especially those aspects that distinguish it from other nearby destination countries in East and Southeast Asia. Vietnam's history and culture, the American/Vietnam War and the country's unique natural heritage are among the generally-recognized 'assets' of Vietnam as a destination. Two areas – people and culture, and ecotourism – are being prioritized by both state and private stakeholders as areas for development (Cooper, 1997: 60; VNAT/UNDP/UNWTO, 2001: 23).

The 1999 Tourism Ordinance puts the responsibility for identifying and administering tourism attractions in Vietnam with the provincial and municipal People's Committees, with the exception of 'national resorts', which are defined and controlled by the Prime Minister (VNAT/UNDP/UNWTO, 2001: 164).

HERITAGE ATTRACTIONS IN VIETNAM

There are over 2,500 historical sites in Vietnam, as identified by the Ministry of Culture. Some of these are of regional or even international importance. Listing as a UNESCO World Heritage Site is possibly the most outstanding designation for a cultural attraction, as it indicates that such a site is of unique and global cultural significance. Vietnam has five such sites (see Table 1.1): the citadel and mausoleums of Hue, listed in 1993; Ha Long Bay, listed in 1994; the port of Hoi An and the ruins at My Son, both listed in 1999; and Phong Nha–Ke Bang National Park, listed in 2003.

In a survey of likely international travellers conducted in Singapore in 1996 addressing 'opportunities of tourism in Vietnam', 78 per cent of the surveyed travellers believed that Vietnam should make better use of its historical culture and heritage to attract travellers (Tran Kiem Luu and Mai Kim Dinh, 1997: 50–54). In a parallel survey of travel agents, also in Singapore in 1996, 82 per cent cited heritage as a major factor in modern-day Vietnam's attractiveness. Vietnam possesses a unique mixture of different types of 'heritage' sites, appealing to different groups of visitors. These include sites representing traditional Sino–Vietnamese culture and the romantic relics of French colonialism as well as less conventional types of attractions capitalizing on the controversial trend of 'war tourism' and the chance to experience one of the world's last surviving communist societies.

Kim has commented that 'it is often said that Vietnam's heritage consists of its struggle against foreign aggressions for the last two thousand years' (Kim, 1997: 314). Logan has commented on the irony of Vietnam being marketed as an 'untouched' destination when Western powers have left their stamp on the country repeatedly through colonialism, war and communism. French colonial architecture, Sino–Vietnamese relics and Soviet-influenced structures are key factors that distinguish Vietnamese cityscapes from those of any other Southeast Asian nation and thus are assets peculiar to the country's tourism image (Logan, 1998b).

Ashworth and Larkham (1994: 16) note that 'heritage is a contemporary commodity purposefully created to satisfy contemporary consumption'. Marketing is seen as a way of 'repackaging' a destination to appeal to the broadest possible market or to specific markets (Apostolakis, 2003: 806). The marketing of heritage as a tourism commodity raises important issues regarding a country's relationship with its history. In Vietnam, displaying heritage necessitates maintaining reminders of bitter wars and colonial occupation. Henderson has noted that '(h)eritage attractions in Vietnam and more widely remain a highly political issue and the influence of government policy cannot be ignored, with recent history being used to promote a message of unity and solidarity, directed as much at the resident population as visitors' (2000: 276).

War-related sites are particularly problematic in this respect, involving issues of how a country or society honours its fallen combatants and commemorates victory or confronts defeat, especially in cases where some of the visitors to the attraction may be citizens of the erstwhile enemy state or group (Henderson, 2000). War veterans travelling to former battlegrounds make up a growing niche of 'personal heritage tourism' (Smith, 1996: 247–264). In Vietnam's case, this involves US veterans of the American/Vietnam War. Plans to build an 'American War Crimes Museum' on the site of the former American Consulate at Danang, the point of US troops' first landing in Vietnam in 1965, were scrapped to avoid a diplomatic contretemps, although such a museum was built at a different site (VNAT, 1997: 311–313). A similarly titled museum in Ho Chi Minh City was renamed the War Remnants Museum in 1993 (http://en.wikipedia.org/wiki/War_Remnants_Museum_(Ho_Chi_Minh_City)).

There is a growing realization of the significance of heritage sites in symbolically representing a group, community or nation and in historical or political memorializing. However, there are a number of groups or communities with a claim to representation in any site, further complicating the issue (Richter, 1999: 109–114). To this, one could add that there are also a variety of different groups patronizing any attraction, with different interests and backgrounds and to each of whom the site must 'speak' differently (see also Mark Johnson's chapter in this book). Problems of authenticity, pertinent to all heritage tourism, are especially crucial in the development of these types of attractions. An important function of heritage sites is to aid visitors in the interpretation of history. The choice of which sites are promoted and the manner in which they are presented determine the image of a country that is perceived by visitors, and by natives as well.

The necessity to protect sites from over-development and vandalism also arises with an increase in tourism. The preservation and use of Vietnam's cultural heritage are the responsibility of the national and provincial Ministries of Culture and Information. Increasingly, however, initiatives for preservation and reconstruction of historic structures are formulated, planned and financed at the local level by the communities in which the structures are situated (VNAT/UNDP/UNWTO, 2001: 122).

Wars, the elements, lack of money and misguided restoration attempts have all ravaged Vietnam's heritage sites, and the surge of construction associated with the current phase of rapid economic development also puts historical buildings and environments at risk. The first laws providing for the protection of historical cultural artefacts in Vietnam were issued directly after the 1945 revolution, and legislation has continued to be articulated since then (ibid.). Article 46 of Vietnam's 1980 Constitution states that 'Historical and cultural relics, public works of art and sites of scenic or other significance shall be restored and protected' (Government of Vietnam, 1995: 106). Article 34 of the 1992 Constitution elaborates: 'The state and society seek to preserve and develop the national cultural heritage; they take good care of preservation and museum work; they look after the repair and maintenance of, and seek to obtain the best effects from, historical vestiges, revolutionary relics, items of the national heritage, artistic works, and places with beautiful scenery' (ibid.: 166). A 'Cultural Heritage Law' that came into effect on 1 January 2002 broadened the understanding of protected heritage to include 'expressions of folklore' such as lifestyle, customs, traditional medicines and other practices (VNAT/UNDP/UNWTO, 2001: 122).

The rest of this chapter consists of a description and analysis of specific prominent heritage attractions in Vietnam. Different themes in the discourse on the relation between attractions and heritage are exemplified in the various sites that are discussed. The intention of this discussion is to demonstrate how the issues of heritage tourism mentioned above manifest themselves in specific empirical instances at specific attractions in Vietnam. The demonstration starts with an overview of developments in Hanoi's Ancient Quarter, which introduces themes and issues of general relevance in heritage tourism there. These issues are then explored in greater depth in case studies of two important heritage attractions in the city: the Hoa Lo Prison Museum and the Ho Chi Minh Mausoleum. The first-named author carried out field studies at these two attractions, with the intention of determining how Vietnam's open door policy has affected them.

A desire to understand the causes and effects of change in heritage attractions was a primary motivation for the research. Both of the attractions chosen for analysis have undergone changes during *doi moi*, whether in terms of function, physical qualities or profile of visitors, and they are both embedded in a shifting societal and cultural context, bringing about changes in the significance and role of the attractions. These tangible and intangible changes both reflect and influence changes in the attitude of both the government and tourists towards these attractions, as will be discussed in the sections that follow. Data and insights for these two case studies were gathered from interviews and observations on-site in the course of several visits, supported by research of secondary sources including government documents.

THE ANCIENT QUARTER

Hanoi was the capital of the Vietnamese state from around 1010 CE until 1802, when the Nguyen dynasty relocated the capital to Hue. During the French colonial era Hanoi was restored as the chief administrative centre of the Indochinese Union in 1887. When Vietnam was divided in 1954, Hanoi became the capital of the Democratic Republic of Vietnam. Hanoi's environment and architecture were influenced by the Chinese and Vietnamese cultures during the feudal past, the French during the colonial era and the Soviet Union after the Vietnam War. The mixture of different cultures and architectural styles make Hanoi a unique and picturesque city. According to Logan (1995: 328), the urban environment in Hanoi is identified as one of the great heritage townscapes in Asia. In the past, Hanoi was divided into three sections: the Ancient Quarter or 'Area of 36 Commercial Streets' north of Hoan Kiem Lake, the Western Quarter south of Hoan Kiem Lake and the Citadel or Ba Dinh Quarter south of West Lake.

The Ancient Quarter was historically and still is the primary commercial area of Hanoi, with small shop-houses, markets and pagodas along small and narrow streets. The dominant residential building typology is known as the tube house, being no more than two to four metres wide, but as deep as 150 metres (Vu, 1999). Most of the residential and commercial buildings in the area were built after the 1870s (Logan, 1995: 329).

The romantically scenic, human-scaled streetscapes of the Ancient Quarter, its exotic atmosphere and the opportunities it offers visitors to experience a relatively intact vestige of a bygone era have made this sector of Hanoi one of the city's prime tourism attractions. With the increased tourist traffic to Hanoi in parallel with Vietnam's increasing accessibility to foreign travellers, tourism is becoming an important economic, political and social force that is playing a determining role in the re-development of the Ancient Quarter. Since the beginning of the open door policy in 1986, Vietnam's economy has become increasingly market-oriented. A growth in profit-driven, tourism-related enterprises is one consequence of this economic shift. In recent years, many of the buildings of the Ancient Quarter have been converted from their original uses into hotels, cafes, shops and other uses catering to the tourist trade.

The pressure of market forces is also being felt in the property market of the Ancient Quarter. Because it is much more expensive to restore a historical building properly than to demolish it and replace it, and because the historical buildings of the Ancient Quarter are low-rise and small-scale, making relatively 'inefficient' use of the site, real estate economics do not bode favourably for the retention of these structures. Developers are often required to re-house inhabitants displaced by their developments, adding to their expenses and increasing the need to maximize profitability from their projects by building higher and at a greater residential density. Demand for land for lucrative tourism development purposes has certainly contributed to the upward spiral of property prices as well. Soaring demand for hotel space is cited as one important factor in driving up land values in the Ancient Quarter. In 2001, lot prices on the main commercial streets of the Ancient Quarter reached US$10,000 to US$11,400 per square metre, an increase of three to four times over a period of just six years (Tu, 2001). To date, much of the redevelopment in the area has consisted of property owners capitalizing on tourism by replacing the two-storey tube houses with four- or five-storey hotels or other tourism-related constructions, often using funds obtained from less-than-legal means such as hoarding, smuggling or black-market trading (Logan, 1996: 79).

Calls for the preservation and restoration of the constructed urban heritage of the Ancient Quarter in the face of market forces are being raised by both international and domestic interest groups. In 1993, the Ancient Quarter became the first part of Hanoi for which heritage protection regulations were enacted (Logan, 1996: 86). The tourism industry's stakes in the debate surrounding the relative merits of development or preservation for the Ancient Quarter are far from simple. While the preservation and restoration of the old urban fabric would seem to be a matter of utmost importance for the continued viability of the Ancient Quarter as a tourism attraction, the very success of tourism is contributing to an economic environment in which the future of these old buildings and streets is endangered. In addition, the continued qualitative and quantitative growth of tourism requires development of a scale and character that can be at odds with the fragile and small-scale character of the historic streetscape. Some measures, such as the banning of motorized traffic from many of the area's main thoroughfares, the planned re-instatement of a tram line and the creation of a pedestrian zone, are explicitly aimed at increasing the attractiveness of the area to tourists (*Bangkok Post*, 2001; Vu, 1999; Bich, 2000). However, as of the author's last visit to the area in 2006, the planned tram line had not yet been constructed.

The wish of those capitalizing on the Ancient Quarter's allure to tourists to see the Ancient Quarter extracted and 'frozen in time' as an exotic spectacle for tourist consumption rather than being allowed to evolve and modernize as an integral and living part of the city has been criticized as an example of what Said has termed 'orientalism': the Western practice of substituting a stereotyped representation of foreign cultures for a true interaction with them on equal terms (1987). Behind the historic façades of those buildings that have not been adapted to tourism-related uses such as travel agents, guesthouses, souvenir shops and Internet cafes, however, the lived reality of the residents of the Ancient Quarter is compromised by the physical constraints and bad state of repair of the old houses, with many families with as many as seven members sharing fewer than ten square metres of living space (Bich, 2003), with fifty per cent of the households having to share a latrine with another household, and twenty per cent of houses lacking a kitchen (Vu, 1999). A relocation programme is being undertaken to alleviate this overcrowding, expected to reduce the population of the old quarter from 100,000 in 2003 to 60,000 by 2010 by moving inhabitants to new housing in suburbs (Vu, 1999; Ngoc, 2000).

Any truly sustainable future for the Ancient Quarter can only be formulated by careful and integrated strategic planning involving private and government participation, and must strive for a 'win-win-win' situation in which the viability of the Ancient Quarter as an intact social context, an attractive tourism destination and an economically viable property market is maintained. Government guidelines for the development of the Ancient Quarter state, 'It is not necessary to keep all the buildings intact. The top priority is to preserve the style and soul of old architectures while at the same time improving living standards in par with those of a modern city' (Circular 72, May 26 1994; quoted in Vu, 1999). This case study provides an illustration of the extent to which heritage tourism relies on a careful balance of these factors and the role it plays in helping achieve this balance. UNESCO began its 'Hanoi Project' for the preservation of the city's historic city sectors in 1990, specifically citing the economic importance of maintaining these sectors' attractiveness as tourism sites and encouraging the publication of books and videos on urban and architectural history for tourists, highlighting the importance of historical preservation (Logan, 1995: 332–333). This is an acknowledgement and an example of the role that can be played by tourism in providing both the justification and the economic support for historical preservation, while also providing a channel for the dissemination of information about the importance of preserving heritage.

THE HOA LO PRISON MUSEUM

According to Logan (2005), in a Confucian society, such as Vietnam before French colonization, it was not common practice to incarcerate offenders because it was believed that punishment was best left to the family and village. The French introduced the practice of placing offenders in houses rented from Vietnamese, which was costly and ineffective. Therefore, a prison was one of the first projects the French undertook in Hanoi in the late 1890s and early 1900s, along with a cathedral and a *Palais de Justice* (Supreme Court) (Interview A, 2004).

Hoa Lo Prison was established in 1896 on the site of Phu Khanh, a craft village, which at the time was regarded as a Hanoi suburb (ibid.). Originally built for 450 prisoners, the population of the prison increased to more than 2,000 by 1953 (display board in Hoa Lo Prison Museum). The early prisoners called the prison *Hoa Lo,* which figuratively means 'Hell's Hole' (Logan, 2005), in contrast to the official innocuous name of *Maison Central.* The Hoa Lo Prison has a long and significant history. Under French colonial rule a large number of Vietnamese nationalists, communists and peasant fighters were imprisoned there, including some of the country's greatest future leaders, according to the historian Pham Tu (Stewart, 1997). Among these were Le Duan, a General Secretary of the Vietnam Communist Party 1960–1969, Nguyen Van Linh, General Secretary in 1986, Do Muoi, General Secretary 1991–1997 and former Foreign Minister Nguyen Co Thach (*Japan Economic Newswire,* 1994).

During the Second World War, under Japanese occupation, some French officials were imprisoned at Hoa Lo (Interview A, 2004). In 1954, Vietnam divided into a capitalist South and a communist North. During the ensuing war between North Vietnam and America between 1964 and 1975, Hoa Lo was used to detain American pilots whose aircraft had been shot down over Hanoi. The total number of American prisoners in Hoa Lo during the war is unclear. According to the Japan Economic Newswire, the prison accommodated more than 700 American prisoners, but Lander cites a figure of only 300 (Lander, 2000). Hoa Lo continued to function as a prison after the communist victory until 1993, housing mainly Vietnamese criminals (ibid.).

During the 'open door' policy of market economy growth in Vietnam, the city of Hanoi expanded and its population increased. Hoa Lo, once a suburb, gradually became part of the city centre. In 1993, the Hanoi authorities, seeing this as an inappropriate location for a prison, decided to construct a new jail on the city outskirts and abandon the physically degraded prison at Hoa Lo. A debate ensued as to whether to keep all or part of the old prison as a memorial or to make the whole site available for economic development purposes (Lander, 2000).

In 1993, the government approved a US$60 million project for a 22-storey luxury service apartment and office complex on the site of Hoa Lo Prison. The project is a joint venture between Burton Engineering, a Singaporean company, and the state-owned Hanoi Civil Construction Company (Stanley, 1994). According to the former Director of the Hoa Lo Prison Museum, the Hanoi authority originally wanted to preserve only the gate (entrance) of the prison, whereas the joint-venture requested the whole area for development. However, both of these variants were met with very vocal protest from former inmates of the Hoa Lo Prison, who wanted to preserve it as a memorial site to their struggle for independence (Interview A, 2004). Demands also came from the general public, both foreigners and Vietnamese, who were curious about Hoa Lo Prison and wanted it to be made publicly accessible. A compromise was made, whereby the joint venture project obtained 8,000 square yards of the prison site, with the remaining 3,000 square yards to be preserved and set aside as a museum (Stanley, 1994). The developers were also required to contribute US$1.5 million to the rebuilding of the prison at its new location outside the city (*Japan Economic Newswire*, 1993). Also in 1993, control of Hoa Lo Prison was transferred from the Department of Police to the Department of Culture within the Ministry of Culture, reflecting the change of the use of the building (Interview A, 2004).

The years from 1994 to 1997 were a transitional period for Hoa Lo, with land being cleared for the joint venture project, and with the maintenance and organization of the museum displays. Some problems arose during the construction of a new tower, including damage done to the foundation of the prison which cost the joint venture VND1 billion (about US$67,000) to repair and reinforce. The total cost of the restoration of Hoa Lo Prison was about VND11 billion (US$733,000) (Interview A, 2004). It was declared a national historical monument in 1997.

Because of the many different powers and purposes it has served throughout its chequered and brutal history, the symbolic associations of the Hoa Lo Prison are various, complex and often contradictory. Accordingly, the types of tourists who come to visit and the reasons for their visits are diverse. For the Vietnamese, the site is a tangible reminder of their country's long struggle for independence and of the injustices suffered at the hands of the French colonizers. Overseas Vietnamese (*viet kieu*) and those from the South of the country, however, may have more conflicting feelings about the history and sentiments represented by the site (Logan, 2002). An ever-increasing number of Americans and French, for whom the prison also represents a painful part of their national heritage, are visiting each year. The prison is even a site of religious tourism in the form of monks who come at public events to pray for the dead (Interview A, 2004).

From the point of view of the Vietnamese government, which provides all funding for the museum, the prison serves as a site to reinforce patriotic and nationalistic feelings amongst the Vietnamese who visit. Given the future revolutionary leaders who were imprisoned there for anti-colonial activity in the 1930s, the prison can be called one of the birthplaces of revolutionary education in Vietnam (Logan, 2005). Exhibits in some of the prison's former cells and torture chambers illustrate and describe the brutal practices and implements of the French captors in graphic detail, including a prominently displayed guillotine. The exhibition of these artefacts and the telling of these stories within the very walls in which the events occurred rather than in the sterile and abstracted environment of a new museum adds to the visceral effect of the exhibits.

Aside from attracting Vietnamese visitors, the museum is also a site on the standard tourism circuit of Hanoi for overseas tourists. The prison museum's employees are specifically trained to deal with these visitors. Staff members are required to have a university education, and must speak either English or French well. English courses have been given to the museum staff on site since 1998 (Interview A, 2004).

According to a former Director of the Hoa Lo Prison Museum, positive sentiment for the preservation of the prison as a memorial was expressed by those who had fought on both sides of the American/Vietnam conflict, with both American and Vietnamese veterans seeing the site as an important tangible reminder of their experiences during that war. However, many Americans visiting the site, especially those who experienced the prison first-hand as prisoners of war, have expressed outrage at the way in which the 'Hanoi Hilton' phase of the prison's history is depicted in the museum's displays. The room concerning the imprisonment of American POWs is brightly lit and open, in comparison to the other rooms in the prison, those rooms presenting French atrocities against the Vietnamese being particularly dark. In exhibited photos, American prisoners are shown attending Mass, receiving letters from home, meeting journalists and eating a banquet. An accompanying plaque reads: '(t)hough having committed untold crimes on our people, but [sic] American pilots suffered no revenge once they were captured and detained', and claims that all POWs were handled in a manner complying with international law (Lake, 2001).

This version of this era in the prison's life is at stark odds with the vision of humiliation and unbearable conditions that have entered the American cultural consciousness, based on the reports of former prisoners, among the most famous of which is US Senator and recent presidential candidate John McCain. Senator McCain tells of hellish conditions in the prison, his experience of beatings and solitary confinement and his two suicide attempts. On a visit to the prison museum in 2000, he expressed incredulity at the official representation offered by the exhibits with the cynical comment 'that's entertainment' (Lander, 2000).

This characterization of the treatment of American prisoners was staunchly denied by Vietnam Foreign Ministry spokeswoman Phan Thuy Thanh (BBC, 2000), indicating the depth of the rift that must still be overcome between two sides with mutually antagonistic views, not just concerning the manner in which historical events should be represented, but also concerning whether certain historical events actually ever happened. The Hoa Lo Prison is a relic site, meaning that it is intended to preserve the site exactly as it used to be. The management of the prison museum sees their institution as exhibiting historical 'reality' without embellishment, even to the extent of eschewing the selling of souvenirs or the hanging of promotional posters (Interview A, 2004). As is always the case with a site with such a long and eventful history, authenticity of representation is a topic that is open to interpretation. No presentation can ever do equal justice to all historical facets of the place, so any exhibit involves an editing of historical facts which will inevitably have the effect of prioritizing a certain historical narrative above others.

Of course the version of the American/Vietnam War that is presented at the Hoa Lo Prison Museum is aligned with the didactic task of the site and it could be argued that the communications concerning war-related sites will usually prioritize the version of the truth that best serves the exhibitor's agenda. However, the visits paid by Senator McCain and other less-famous American war veterans as well as non-veterans show that this is a site whose heritage significance resonates with people beyond the borders of Vietnam. As Vietnam continues to attract increasing numbers of foreign travellers, those in charge must acknowledge that the Vietnamese national heritage is also a part of the global historical heritage. To represent this shared heritage in a way that is fair and true to the various histories of a site, and that gives an equal voice to all the narratives involved without resorting to a sterilized inoffensive 'middle ground', is the true challenge of such sensitive sites.

THE HO CHI MINH MAUSOLEUM

The Mausoleum of Vietnam's national hero Ho Chi Minh is a national heritage site of extraordinary importance which is also of particular interest to many types of foreign visitors to Vietnam. It is a site of high symbolic content and many foreign dignitaries visit the Mausoleum as a sign of respect for or solidarity with their Vietnamese hosts.

Construction of the Ho Chi Minh Mausoleum began on 2 September 1973 and the structure was opened on 29 August 1975. It is located on Ba Dinh Square in Hanoi, at the site where Ho Chi Minh proclaimed Vietnam's independence on 2 September 1945. The inspiration for building a monument in Hanoi as the final resting place of Ho Chi Minh came from Lenin's Mausoleum in Moscow, which also served as the architectural model for the structure. This was against the will of the revered leader himself, who had wished to be cremated and three urns containing his ashes placed at locations in northern, central and southern Vietnam (Vladimir, 1996).

The Mausoleum is the most politically symbolic site for Vietnam. For nationals it is a patriotic site of unequalled importance and a point of national pride. Every province of Vietnam contributes financially to its upkeep and every year each province sends a tree to be planted at the site (Interview B, 2004).

According to the Chief of the Ho Chi Minh Mausoleum, the administration of the Mausoleum is at the level of a Ministry. Besides the central task of guardianship over Ho Chi Minh's body, the management is responsible for the technical maintenance of the facility, the organization of ceremonies for important visitors to the Mausoleum and maintaining security in the area. The current Chief served in the Vietnamese army before studying in Russia and Bulgaria, attaining a doctorate in military studies.

Ten thousand people come to the attraction on a normal weekday, with fifteen to twenty thousand a day on weekends. Traffic can become even heavier. In September 2003, an average of 31,000 people a day came to view Ho Chi Minh. About one quarter to one third of visitors are foreigners. The number of foreign visitors has increased during *doi moi*, as has the number of domestic visitors. Before *doi moi*, most international visitors were diplomatic or government guests. Today most are sightseers. In an interview, the Chief of the Mausoleum distinguished between two concepts of attractions in Vietnam: commercial sites which are money-earning and spiritual sites which serve ideological, rather than economic, purposes. The Mausoleum falls unequivocally into the latter category. No admission fee is charged, although non-compulsory leaflets are on sale. Private enterprise is not allowed in or around the Mausoleum. The management has established a self-financing visitor service unit that sells souvenirs, film, water and other goods to tourists (Interview B, 2004).

The running and maintenance of the tomb is an extremely expensive undertaking, especially for a developing nation. Much of the original cost of the monument was funded by the Soviet Union. The special embalming of the body is estimated to have cost between US$300,000 and US$500,000 and the equipment for maintaining the body in a preserved state cost upwards of US$5 million at the time. As with many deceased communist leaders in the decades before and since, Ho Chi Minh's body was embalmed by Soviet specialists. The process was carried out during the war with the United States in a cave outside Hanoi to avoid bombardment (Vladimir, 1996).

A special military unit is responsible for the Mausoleum's security, consisting of white-uniformed guards and the personnel of the 595th Technical Detachment, who man the air conditioning and other machinery. This machinery has not been replaced since the building opened and requires constant fixing and attention. It is nonetheless considered a great honour to work at the Mausoleum, and the building boasts a team of highly adept technicians even though the wages paid them are lower than they could earn elsewhere.

South Korean President Kim Dae-Jung's first visit to the Ho Chi Minh Mausoleum in 1998, when he laid a wreath at Ho Chi Minh's tomb, was perceived as a significant gesture of reconciliation between his country and Vietnam. On a visit to Vietnam two years earlier, the previous South Korean President Kim Young-Sam had refused to make an official visit to the monument on the grounds that Ho Chi Minh was a communist and an aggressor against South Korea's ally the United States (*Korea Times*, 1998). This shows that the political significance of the Mausoleum and the political subtext of an official visit paid to it by a guest head of state is multifaceted and changes according to the political climate of the time and the agenda of the visitor.

Russian President Vladimir Putin visited the Ho Chi Minh Mausoleum in March 2001, despite the dissolution of the once-close political ties between his country and Vietnam (ITAR–TASS News Agency, 2001). The Prime Minister of Japan, Junichiro Koizumi, paid his respects at the tomb in April 2002, although Ho Chi Minh had led the Vietnamese struggle against Japanese occupation during the Second World War (Deutsche Press-Agentur, 2002). The visits of these world leaders could be seen as symbolic of a reconciliation or confirmation of solidarity between two nations that also signals Vietnam's increasing integration into the global 'family of nations' after the lifting of the US-imposed embargo in 1994.

Before a state visit to Vietnam by US President Bill Clinton in November 2000, there was much discussion regarding whether he should pay a visit to the Mausoleum. Ho Chi Minh was perceived as an enemy of the United States, raising the question of whether a US President paying his respects at the tomb would be interpreted as a sign of respect to the host country or disrespect to his own country. The issue was further complicated by the fact that Bill Clinton had avoided military duty during the American/Vietnam War. In a 30 September 2000 broadcast, Voice of America Radio implied that a Vietnamese government announcement that the Mausoleum would be closed for two months from 8 October for maintenance was intended to save the President embarrassment, although the Vietnamese military newspaper *Quan Doi Nhan Dan* rebuked this claim, saying that closure for maintenance was a scheduled yearly event that requires the interruption of access for normal visitors but does not affect important guests (*Japan Economic Newswire*, 2000).

Since the beginning of *doi moi*, the Ho Chi Minh Mausoleum has functioned as a sightseeing attraction in addition to being an ideological monument, and the management of the attraction is adapting its role to this once unaccustomed but now growing class of visitors. Foreign language proficiency was not seen as a useful skill for Mausoleum personnel before *doi moi*, but now it is being perceived as necessary (Interview B, 2004). All guards at the building are given lessons in English to better serve as interpreters for foreign visitors of the meaning of the site (Vladimir, 1996). Even after having declared that the Mausoleum is a spiritual site, the Director justifies the ban on private enterprise near the monument not in terms of maintaining respect for Ho Chi Minh, but rather in terms of avoiding annoyance for tourists through too many vendors and lack of price control. Yet he also states that it is the goal of the attraction to attract more visitors who come to pay their respects to Ho Chi Minh rather than sightseeing tourists, claiming that UNESCO's call for celebration of the centenary of Ho Chi Minh's birth in 1990 signalled that Vietnam's national hero had become an international hero and that the Mausoleum would thus gain in significance as a spiritual attraction for foreigners as well as Vietnamese.

While the Mausoleum remains a patriotic landmark for the Vietnamese, *doi moi* has brought an influx of tourists for whom the Mausoleum holds a quite different fascination as a sightseeing attraction. This group of tourists' relation with the Mausoleum is different from the accustomed crowds of domestic pilgrims, bringing the pressure of commercialization, which is being kept at bay by the government, whether to preserve the sanctity of the site or to avoid annoyance to tourists (Interview B, 2004). Measures such as the learning of English by guards and the provision of goods for sale to tourists indicate that international sightseers are not seen as a mere anomaly or fringe group, but rather as an emerging market sector. Vietnam's place in global politics and global markets continues to be signalled by the visits of foreign heads of state and ambassadors to the Mausoleum. However, even with the current amicable trade and political relations with the United

States and the Western world, the figure of Ho Chi Minh himself remains a controversial spectre of Vietnam's past, as exemplified by President Clinton's avoidance of the Mausoleum on his state visit to Hanoi.

CONCLUSION

Vietnam is in a state of transition. The political and economic structure of the country is being remodelled from within by the reforms of the *doi moi* programme, while the 'open door' policy is opening the country up increasingly to influences from without, including foreign capital, foreign investors and foreign tourists, bringing with them both opportunities and expectations. The heritage of a country plays an especially important role in the midst of a period of transition, serving as a cultural 'anchor' – a reminder of what remains constant amidst the whirlwind of change. For domestic tourists, Vietnam's heritage sites provide a tangible experience of identification with their county's proud past that can provide a sense of orientation when looking into the exciting but uncertain future. However, as a developing country, Vietnam is concerned with projecting a vision of a modernizing and progressive society to its own people and to visitors from abroad. The conflicts between the equally important themes of memory of the past and optimism for the future, as played out in the physical and economic context of Vietnam, can be observed clearly in the three case studies presented in this chapter.

Tourism can play a defining role in the fate of heritage sites. While spurring development of an area, tourism will also suffer if over-development threatens to compromise the very qualities or attractions that lured visitors in the first place. Heritage tourism can aid in conservation, and encourage the restoration of historical sites and areas by tying economic gain to the degree of preservation of the qualities of the physical artefacts that bind a place to its history. The intelligent and considered development of heritage tourism can support forms of urban and regional development that achieve a balance between concerns for heritage preservation and economic development initiatives. A counterexample for this can be observed in Singapore, where the wholesale demolition of complete historical quarters of the city in the 1970s in the name of modernization has robbed the city of significant parts of its built heritage of colonial and ethnic architecture – a mistake the city is currently trying to remedy by rebuilding some of these areas in imitation historical styles (Peleggi, 1996: 444). Both Singaporeans and tourists responding to a 1995 survey recognized the city-state's few remaining colonial relics, and not its modern structures, as the primary attractions for tourists. Whilst respondents to the survey bemoaned the highly commercial nature of many conservation projects, this very commercialization is seen as necessary to make such projects economically viable (Teo and Huang, 1995: 610). This conflict evokes the case of the Hanoi Ancient Quarter discussed in this chapter.

The attractions discussed here are sites where visitors, increasingly foreign, come into contact with representations of Vietnamese culture and history, which thus present opportunities for the interpretation and the promulgation of a national image to outsiders. The learning of English by the staff at many attractions is one sign of accommodating international tourists so as to allow for better dissemination and exchange of information to aid in the interpretation of attractions.

A 1988 Vietnam government management report declared confidently, 'In the future, even if she handles several hundred thousand or a few million visitors a year, Vietnam can hardly become a hotbed for social ills as she is a socialist state always capable of drastic control measures' (quoted in Elliott, 1997: 235). Developments in the meantime have caused a much less confident and more protectionist stance regarding tourism, as indicated by the 1996 'social evils' campaign, which in part strove to isolate the Vietnamese people from the potential contaminating effects of too much contact with foreign tourists. The new laws and regulations discussed in the case studies above have shown the ways in which the government balances this apprehension with a desire to reap the potential benefits of the tourism trade.

The experiences of the sites investigated in this chapter in mediating between different interests involved in heritage tourism – domestic and foreign, the past and the future, economics and ideology, individual and collective – can be seen as a microcosm of the current situation facing Vietnam as a country and as a tourism destination.

CHAPTER 11

Handicraft Heritage and Development in Hai Duong, Vietnam[1]

Michael Hitchcock, Nguyen Thi Thu Huong and Simone Wesner

INTRODUCTION

Handicrafts are broadly conceived of as items, often portable, that are made with manual and artistic skill. They may simply be made to satisfy immediate needs, the material culture of existence, but are often further developed as trade goods and exchange commodities. Some, however, may be imbued with a kind of cultural significance and may be symbolically perceived as markers of gender, age, ethnic and national identities, whereas others have become an integral part of the observance of certain beliefs, notably religious ones.

As acceptance of the notion of heritage spreads, these culturally significant artefacts are usually the first to be recognized as signifiers of heritage, but over time the concept may be more widely applied to the more mundane material culture, not least when industrialization starts to occur and handicrafts become less commonplace. Once handicrafts become heritage they are also often pressed into the service of another industry, tourism, in which they have long played an integral part as souvenirs, tangible reminders of journeys, relationships, events and above all memories. Tourism may provide an additional market for the makers of handicrafts, but the transition may not necessarily be an easy one and some capacity building may be required to help crafts people exploit these opportunities.

Some aid agencies have recognized that they have a role to play in this respect and thus this chapter concerns an intervention that was funded by the European Commission between 2002 and 2004 as part of the Asia Urbs programme. The overall scheme was designed to link municipalities in Asia and Europe and this particular project aimed to help develop the economic and heritage potential of the city of Hai Duong in Vietnam. It focused on building the management capacity of the municipal staff in developing tourism and regeneration activities, particularly with regard to handicrafts. The project involved three municipalities (Hai Duong, Hackney Borough Council and Limerick Corporation), one NGO (An Viet Foundation), two regeneration/development agencies (Shannon Development and Renaisi) and one university (London Metropolitan University). The action was designed to build sustainable links between the municipalities in order to share best practice and enhance long-lasting business and cultural links.

Hai Duong has a population of approximately 150,000 and is the capital of the province bearing the same name. It is situated at the crossroads of long-established routes running north–south and east–west, and is located on Highway 5 between the capital, Hanoi, and northern Vietnam's coastal city, Haiphong. Interestingly, all three cities of this delta region have names associated with water: Hanoi means 'inside the river', Hai Duong means 'sea sun' and Hai Phong means 'sea defence'. Hai Duong is one of five cities surrounding the capital that have been included in a centrally co-ordinated development initiative. The city is an important administrative centre and is the seat of both provincial and municipal government. Surrounded by fertile land the city is also a major food and animal products processing centre, and is home to a wide variety of small and medium-sized industries involved in handicraft manufacture.

In addition to international visits involving local government officers and representatives of businesses, the project also delivered a series of workshops on practical subjects such as marketing, craft design, web-site design, costing and pricing. Heritage trails were mapped out and a small book entitled *Traditional Handicraft Villages of Hai Duong* was written for the project by the archaeologist, Tang Ba Hoanh. Written in Vietnamese and translated into English (Tang, 2004), the book was designed to be accessible and was aimed at day-trippers, especially cyclists, from Hanoi. Other project outputs included a CD as well as web-sites to market handicrafts and disseminate information on the programme. The information on which this chapter is based was collected during the course of action research on the project, in which all three authors were involved.

In order to support the project the first-named author undertook a series of studies to map out the city and province's craft centres. The methods were essentially ethnographic, but instead of long-term field-work this study utilized a hybrid approach known as Participatory Rural Appraisal that has been adapted for use in development studies, and more recently tourism studies (Hampton, 1998: 645). This research might also be characterized as pre-field-work because it involves visits lasting several weeks as opposed to participant observation conducted over a much longer period (Michaud, 1995: 682). This approach was swift and inexpensive since it involved only one researcher working with well-informed local people, in this case officials working for the Municipality of Hai Duong. A variety of qualitative techniques was used to gather information, including spontaneous questioning in Vietnamese with the help of an interpreter along with semi-structured informal interviews and more detailed repeat interviews with key informants.

Prior to this study the researcher had made two short visits to Hai Duong, the first when travelling as a guide lecturer on a tour bus from Haiphong to Hanoi, and the second while attending a conference in the Vietnamese capital. The project later was especially fortunate to have the help of Tang Ba Hoanh, an archaeologist and a leading authority on Vietnamese handicrafts, as well as a former Director of Hai Duong Museum. In compiling his book for the project, Tang Ba Hoanh surveyed thirty-two different trades and craft villages, including horn-carving, mat-making, embroidery, furniture-making, jewellery-making and pottery. He also described the evolution of crafts under the different Vietnamese dynasties, foreign occupations and wars, showing the linkages with contemporary craft production.

HANDICRAFTS AS SOUVENIRS

The transformation of traditional handicrafts into souvenir arts in the lesser-developed world is a vexed issue because of the following conundrum: tourism undoubtedly brings developmental benefits, but also brings about cultural adaptations that can lead to deleterious cultural erosion. There is an apparent contradiction between the need to earn income on the one hand and the desire to protect the dignity and integrity of cultural heritage on the other. These two positions need not necessarily be polar opposites and one might regard them as part of a continuum in which a balance is struck between economic realities and cultural integrity. It may, however, be difficult to strike equilibrium in especially poor places where stark choices have to be made with regard to people's livelihoods. Even in such cases the development of handicrafts may be worth pursuing since they potentially have a number of other developmental benefits aside from economic growth. Crippen, for example, has noted that the production of handicrafts has a value in raising self-esteem among rural women in India; and in Chiang Mai, Thailand, a weaving career may provide an alternative to employment in sex tourism (2000: 274). The production of souvenirs may be regarded as an important lifeline in the societies that produce them, but to the people who purchase them they may mean something entirely different.

Souvenirs are often regarded as trivial and ephemeral, though they may be counted among the most valued items purchased during a vacation (Littrel, 1990: 229). Items bought on holiday are often more than mementos of the times and places of the travel experience, and may be associated with a generalized image of a particular culture, or even a specific town or village, especially if associated with a renowned ancient culture or heritage. Sometimes tourists become specialist collectors and experts, thereby creating a demand for publications and niche tours devoted to handicrafts.

The transformation of local handicraft product that is often produced to satisfy demand within a given society to a souvenir designed to satisfy an external market is not necessarily demand-led but often supply-led. This transformation may simply arise out of necessity since changes in local buying patterns, often occurring when a preference for cheaply made industrial goods undermines local craft production, threaten the livelihoods of artisans (Popelka and Littrell, 1991: 393). Given that the developing world's share of receipts from the tourism sector may be as high as twenty-six per cent (Sinclair and Tsegaye, 1990: 496) this is clearly not a market to be ignored and thus tourists often become the new customers for tenacious crafts people. As producers adapt to these new markets, they may find that their goods eventually find their way into boutiques and become generalized export commodities, a process that is often helped by designers familiar with the ways of international fashion. Sometimes these designers are supported by aid agencies and charities, though governments in the developing world may also be active in providing finance and other inducements to support the development of 'designer crafts'.

The move from local handicraft to souvenir production often involves changes in the social relations of production, particularly with regard to the use of standardized components and semi-mass-production methods. An attendant feature of productive change is the introduction of new materials leading to a kind of 'mix and match' approach to the creation of souvenirs (Bunn, 2000: 167). Such changes may boost output, but are often accompanied by a reduction in skill, as is the case with the Hmong of North Thailand, who make crossbows of questionable quality for tourists. In this context quality seems not to be an issue, since the bows are cheap and will rarely be fired; output may be raised, but because so many shops sell the same product, the individual maker has to operate on slim profit margins (Cooper, 1984). Teague (2000), however, takes a different view concerning Nepal, where there is a long established souvenir craft industry which grew out of the even older pilgrim trade. He maintains that, although producers specialize in order to speed up production, all the craftspeople possess a range of skills; generalist skills have not been discarded in favour of specialization.

The transformation to souvenir production does not necessarily lead to the introduction of newer methods at the expense of older ones; production methods can remain virtually unchanged whereas the products themselves may undergo extensive diversification (Cohen, 1993a: 2). The reason for this is not readily apparent, but it could be linked to the way crafts are often presented within the context of tourism. Tourists often show interest in the way unfamiliar crafts are produced, and appreciate access to 'backstage' areas where 'traditional' skills are on display, even if such places are what Cohen has called 'false backs' in the sense of being deliberately contrived (Cohen, 1988: 372).

Traditional techniques may also be quite cost effective since they may use readily available materials and can have low overheads, an important point to consider in an industry like tourism, which is often seasonal. In such cases it is the skills of the maker and retailer that add value, but unless the product has a high market value, the margins may be minimal. Tourists moreover may be unwilling to pay high prices for quality products with which they are unfamiliar and of which they are unable to discern the true value. In many respects the use of the term 'souvenir' is inadequate to describe what has become an international craft market, often dependent on the trade and transport facilities provided by tourism. Handicrafts of the kind found in shops and roadside stalls in Southeast Asia are, for example, readily available in shops and markets in Europe and North America. The Internet increasingly plays a role in stimulating demand, raising consciousness and avoiding export bottlenecks, and provides a wide range of services for crafts people while enhancing customized production (Grieco, 2000).

Handicrafts sold in these contexts, though often derived from traditional art forms, are often miniaturized or modified to attract the eye of purchasers and to suit the needs of long-distance, especially airborne, travellers; lightweight materials are often substituted for heavier traditional ones. There is, however, a counter trend in what Cohen refers to as 'gigantism' in which ordinary-sized functional items (e.g. combs, spoons, knives), which might otherwise be insufficiently attractive in their normal state to spark the interest of potential customers, are enlarged (Cohen, 1993a: 5). There are, however, problems associated with adapting traditional goods and developing new ones for customers such as tourists since producers may well understand the needs and preferences of their own societies, but cannot invariably apply these criteria to customers from other cultures (Graburn, 1982, 1976).

A widespread concern with the use of handicrafts in tourism and international trade is product recognition, since many traditional goods are simply too plain to arouse the interest of tourists. Surface decoration may be added to please the customer and add provenance, as well as raise the value added. This kind of approach occurs in Peru where the producers of pots for tourists sign up market vessels, but leave cheaper versions un-signed (Bankes, 2000: 217). Craftsmen and women who are unable to access markets directly often produce a product that is given a finish by another group that has greater access to the needs of customers. Sometimes these 'finishers' are members of the urban majority population (Cohen, 1993a: 2), as is the case with certain craft shops in Hanoi selling products made by upland minorities.

Souvenirs are symbols of the tourist's travels, tangible proof of where he or she has been, and it is perhaps not surprising that a popular concern is whether or not they are authentic. Tourists often place emphasis on the hand-made when considering the question of authenticity, particularly with regard to quality and the time invested in its manufacture (Littrel, Anderson and Brown, 1993: 205). Such purchases not only reawaken memories of the special people encountered on a holiday, but may also stand as generalized symbols of the developing world. In the case of one of Littrel's respondents a souvenir was not so much prized for its authenticity, but because of its association with the artisan as a representative of the poorer people of the world (1990: 238). The appeal of many tourist arts often resides in a definable ethnicity, an expression of the perceived cultural difference between the tourist and the person living in the tourist destination (Graburn, 1987: 396). Furthermore, as Adams has argued with regard to the Toraja of Indonesia, artistic forms are often sites for the articulation of various ethnic and regional relationships, with tourism providing the vehicle to express them (Adams, 1998a).

Tourists often eschew evidence of encounters with modernity, but producers often latch on to this and make their objects more 'authentically' old fashioned, according to codes that can be recognized by the visitors. Such products are often sold as antiques and, indeed, 'antiquing' has become a style of manufacture (Causey, 2003: 150; Cohen, 1993a: 3). For example, the darkening of freshly carved and light coloured timbers to give them the patina of antiquity using a range of cheap products, including boot polish, has long been practised in Bali. The resuscitation of ancient crafts, particularly around important heritage sites, is also a feature of souvenir production, though today's artisans need not necessarily have any historical connection with the ancient culture whose prototypes they copy.

For the tourist the authenticity of the artifact is often linked to the perceived authenticity of the experience, and the purchase of a souvenir often represents the only interaction between the tourist and the host community beyond the confines of the hospitality industry (Evans, 2000). The vendor with whom the tourist interacts is, moreover, often assumed to have a close cultural link to the items being sold, though this is not necessarily the case. Handicrafts are shipped along the hub and spoke distribution systems of market economies and may move between quite different producers and retailers. Goods drawn from the length and breadth of Indonesia may, for example, be purchased in Bali, often without much information about whence they came (Forshee, 2001: 165). In some cases production may also be delegated to a client group, such as the Zapotec/Mixtec who work in the style of the Dineh (Navaho), and sometimes certain ethnic groups become so closely connected with a particularly successful product that others cash in on their reputation (Evans, 2000: 132). Cheap Sumba textiles, for example, that are widely sold in Indonesian tourist resorts often have little to do with the island of that name since they originate in factories in Java. A common occurrence is the packaging of souvenirs with other attributes of identity in a way that closely resembles the way heritage is presented in the West (Gabriel, 1994: 148).

Another quite common occurrence has been the growth in the market for what might be called 'solidarity souvenirs' that are sold cheaply to promote various causes, including development. The tourist does not necessarily have high expectations of such products and may not even like them: their quality is secondary; it is the message that counts. Some of the most striking solidarity souvenirs can be found in Mexico, and they first appeared during the Chiapas insurgency of the mid 1990s. They comprised dolls wearing Indian dress, masks and bandoliers, though it remained unclear whether the profits went to *Zapatista* causes. The popularity of Ghanaian Kente cloths may also be partly understood in terms of solidarity, as they have been adopted by Black Americans as generalized symbols of African pride and affinity (Grieco, 2000). Similar notions have been reported among Jewish tourists visiting Israel, who often come with a set of expectations reflecting individual concerns about identity (Shenhav-Keller, 1995: 152). The way they respond to souvenirs is partly dependent on their reaction to specific symbolic codes; these tourists do not necessarily buy items as evidence of travel, but as an element of their construction of identity (ibid.: 149).

Another important consideration is Graburn's contention that goods destined for tourists may be characterized as 'outwardly' directed, in contrast to those that are 'inwardly' directed and are retained for traditional purposes (1974: 4–5). But in some contexts, especially where there is a long experience of international trade, it may be difficult to distinguish between an 'outwardly directed' product and a 'traditional' artifact. Nevertheless, some common genres can be identified in souvenir products, such as idyllic landscapes and picturesque representations of indigenous peoples, and by working within these widely accepted genres the makers of handicrafts adopt a set of symbols that are assumed to be meaningful to tourists. The holistic system of signs that is often a feature of 'inwardly' directed goods is often usually modified or changed entirely in 'outwardly' directed products.

HANDICRAFTS AND TOURISM IN VIETNAM

Vietnam has a long established tradition of handicraft production, not only to satisfy local needs but also for export. Access to waterways helped to boost trade since handicrafts such as ceramics that can easily be damaged on road journeys could be safely shipped out to sea. Investigations of shipwrecks along Vietnam's coast have yielded insights into this seaborne trade, notably the popularity of Chu Dau wares. Under French rule Vietnam was administered as part of Indo–China and during this period the French provided a showcase for Vietnamese products at the Colonial Exhibition in Paris (1931) and elsewhere. A nascent tourism industry was established under colonial rule, but the numbers of visitors were limited and in any case were often not strictly international since many tourists were French officials and businessmen taking leave within the country.

The growth of the Vietnamese tourism industry was severely disrupted by the struggle for independence against the French and the American/ Vietnam War, and thus Vietnam is a relative newcomer to international tourism. By 2000 Vietnam was attracting 2.1 million international tourists and had approximately 11.2 million domestic tourists. The World Tourism Organization had predicted a long-term global expansion rate of 4–5 per cent per annum in the early part of the present century, but like elsewhere the industry in Vietnam was affected by the events of 11 September 2001, though tourism rapidly recovered. According to Le Dang Doanh, a senior economist at the Ministry of Planning and Investment, tourism arrivals rose to four million in 2006 and were expected to double to eight million by 2010.

Vietnamese crafts also feature significantly in the tourist experience and this has been accompanied by a strong rise in export growth. Handicraft exports have risen from a value of US$200 million in 1997 to US$350 million in 2000, and though this is encouraging, there is still scope to improve the variety and design of goods sold to tourists and overseas importers. An important draw is Vietnam's cultural heritage, including both tangible elements (for example the cities of Saigon, Hue and Hanoi) and intangible ones (for example performing arts, festivals). The Ministry of Culture and Information and counterparts in provincial governments are the public bodies responsible for the protection and utilization of Vietnam's heritage, and the government has recently formulated a five-year development plan for heritage. This includes the preservation of the historical built environment and support for historical, art and ethnographic museums. The Ford Foundation has made a highly significant contribution to this effort by funding training in arts management. The Vietnamese government recognizes the need to involve local communities in providing services and developing enterprises associated with tourism and would like to develop public awareness programmes to inform local people about how they can benefit from tourism.

HANDICRAFT HERITAGE IN HAI DUONG

Such has been the scale of industrial development running alongside the main highway that travellers being whisked through on coaches and minibuses bound for Hanoi might be forgiven for wondering if Hai Duong actually had any heritage. Despite initial appearances the city and the surrounding area have a very long history of settlement and are located in the Red River Delta, one of the heartlands of Vietnamese civilization. In particular the province is home to many ancient ceramic kilns, notably the site of Chu Dau, which dates from the fourteenth century and was most active in the fifteenth and sixteenth centuries, before its decline in the seventeenth century (Tang, 1993: 16).

Hai Duong lies along two important tourism corridors, but it was difficult to gauge the numbers of visitors passing through since until recently these statistics were not collected. At the time of the project the city was already on the domestic tourism map in terms of day trips, particularly at weekends and on public holidays, and an estimated 1,000 to 2,000 visitors passed through annually on Highway 5. In terms of signage there was little to indicate that the city had anything special to offer, and entries in guidebooks remained brief. Vietnam had only recently become aware of the complex management skills needed to develop heritage tourism. By 2007 the picture began to change markedly with the province's Department of Commerce and Tourism forecasting a 29.2 per cent increase in visitor arrivals, bringing the annual total up to 1.5 million, 85,000 of whom were foreign nationals (www.footprintsvietnam.com).

The area surrounding Hai Duong is a rich source of China Clay (Kaolin) and the city was originally a major ceramic and porcelain-producing centre, from which products were exported to China and elsewhere in Southeast Asia from the sixteenth century onwards. Excavations for new housing often reveal evidence of early commercial activities, including the sites of kilns. Access to sea and river transport, vital for the safe shipment of porcelain, enhanced Hai Duong's desirability as a craft centre, and investigations of shipwrecks have revealed Hai Duong export wares. The Red River Delta is also suitable for intensive wet rice cultivation and there are important connections between agriculture and handicraft production. This was partly because craft production could be fitted in around farming activities, thereby helping to diversify the economy and provide additional sources of revenue. The countryside and coast also provided the craft producers with a source of raw materials such as wood, sea grass and bamboo. Villages involved in handicraft production tended to specialize, and in some cases these specialities were established many centuries ago. Master craftsmen who are named historical figures founded some settlements, and villagers continue to venerate them at ancestral shrines in village community halls.

The design repertoire of the city and province was strikingly influenced by China, and to a certain extent Hai Duong is not only a repository of Vietnamese craft knowledge, but Chinese as well. Following the long-established custom of master carpenters, they depict the four professions that make up Chinese-influenced societies: teaching, trading, farming and blacksmithing. Wood-block printing was established in the fifteenth century, and the city later became a centre for carpentry, embroidery, jewellery, horn-carving, embroidery, silversmithing, stone-carving, mat-making, wine production, lychee and pastry products. The city's products thus tend to be typical of mainstream Vietnamese commercial activities and, unlike the crafts produced by the country's numerous minority peoples, do not serve as ethnic and cultural markers. In addition, the goods produced by minorities, though requiring high levels of skill, tend to be associated with non-professional artisans and are characterized by what may be called domestic modes of production. In contrast, Hai Duong's products, which are commonly made with semi-industrial processes and production lines, cannot readily be linked to the assertion of identity. There remains, however, a strong sense of heritage and identification with the region's history as a major craft-producing centre, and there is considerable local interest in both conserving local skills and adapting them to take advantage of new commercial opportunities.

There is considerable pride in the region's ceramic heritage and there are plans to develop a special gallery at Hai Duong Museum. A Saigon-based company, Hapro, is investing in a revival of the Chu Dau style. The company secured a large industrial site close to the modern village of Chu Dau and began manufacturing in 2002. The company brought in a professional artist from Hai Duong who began by instructing 60 young villagers in drawing and printing. Around 200 workers were trained in a variety of skills, including firing, moulding and shaping, in Hai Duong and

Chu Dau. In Hai Duong there are about twenty workers who are skilled enough to carry out all the processes. Given the worldwide interest in Asian ceramics, the combination of the museum collection and a local ceramic revival would have considerable value in niche tourism. An interpretation centre dealing with the Chu Dau excavations was established in the factory in anticipation of tourists visiting the factory. The company makes a wide variety of modern designed products but has also experimented with the more traditional designs associated with the Chu Dau archaeological site. These are sold locally in the factory, but are also sold at outlets frequented by tourists in Hanoi and elsewhere. The company has also experimented with producing very high quality Chu Dau replicas and seems confident that there is a market for them.

Handicrafts are made for export markets including China, Korea, Japan and France, and the customers usually have precise ideas about what designs and materials should be used. Sometimes the foreign buyer supplies all the materials as well, as is the case with Japanese greetings cards made in Hai Duong, and thus it is only the craft skills of the Vietnamese that are used. Handicrafts are also made for the tourist market that are either sold on roadside stalls to passing tourists, or are sold to shops frequented by tourists in major destination centres such as Hanoi. Chinese tourists comprise an especially important market and this is reflected in the design and genre of goods. With regard to woodcarving, for example, there tends to be a predominance of dragons, chopsticks, tortoises, galloping horses, crabs and heavenly generals. Other products that appear to have a wider tourist market in mind include recognisable tourist genres such as embroidered scenes of the Vietnamese countryside. In other words the goods are profoundly outwardly directed in Graburn's sense, especially towards the Chinese market. Western tourists tend to be comparatively less attracted by these products and often opt for practical items such as salad forks, though it tends to be Westerners who buy over-sized ordinary goods. The fact that tourists are simply seen as yet another potential market renders the term 'souvenir' inadequate and it appears that the use of 'commodity' is more appropriate.

Among many tourists in Vietnam, especially Western ones, there is a somewhat ill-defined market for solidarity products or at least goods that would appear to reduce the cultural gap between visitors and the Vietnamese. The cone-shaped hats worn by rice farmers and the green pith helmets formerly worn by soldiers and officials are popular with visitors while they are in Vietnam, but do not seem to be worn much when the tourist returns home. Some of these products are mildly political, suggesting sympathy for Vietnam's struggles with the French and Americans, such as badges, tee-shirts and other paraphernalia adorned with images of Ho Chi Minh, but again it seems doubtful that they would receive much use after the end of the holiday. Within Hai Duong itself there is, however, a company that has turned the solidarity issue into a thriving charity and business through training child victims of the on-going ravages of Agent Orange in horn-carving. This concern is not especially well presented to tourists, but has become widely known among the growing expatriate community in Hanoi.

Hai Duong handicraft producers are intensely commercially driven and while there is talk about the importance of its handicraft heritage among both officials and workshop owners, they are in reality prepared to try and make anything, providing that it sells. There is also an underlying enthusiasm for fashion, and one of the most popular gifts for project partners from Europe to bring were the latest copies of fashion magazines such as *Vogue*. Once handed over these magazines would be examined in great detail and might serve as the basis for experiments with product development. The producers also liked to have practical examples of craft products that were commercially viable, especially if they could pull them apart to see how they were made. They evinced a pride in being able to copy almost anything to a very high standard and any discussion about intellectual property rights provoked amusement. When a foreign-born factory manager, for example, complained about the disregard for copyright in Vietnam at a conference on handicrafts organized by the International Labour Organization (ILO) in Hanoi, he was greeted with laughter. In fact, so highly esteemed is the ability to copy precisely, the art of replication might be considered to be part of the craft heritage of Hai Duong.

It was often hard to pin down what this strong sense of handicraft heritage actually meant in the commercially-oriented context of Hai Duong, but it would be wrong to disregard it. The Vietnamese term for heritage, *tài sản thừa ké*, conveys the sense of utilizing one's inheritance, but a direct translation does not capture what it means for the Vietnamese. In fact there would appear to be division between what one might call the hardware of handicraft production – that is the products themselves – and the software – the skill and knowledge of the makers. Many of the skills that were used in these modern situations were based on traditional ones, and it was clear that a sense of heritage also included a sense of pride in being able to adapt to and profit from the contemporary economy. There was also considerable respect for craftsmen and women who were able to make both traditional and contemporary products, and sometimes this high regard was couched in academic terms in translations from Vietnamese to English. It was not unusual for the British and Irish participants in the Hai Duong project to be introduced to 'professors' of various craft skills, especially when these leading exponents were simultaneously makers and teachers.

This veneration of skill and industriousness seems to be widespread in Vietnamese culture and may be linked to an on-going reverence for Confucian culture. Confucius famously revered people who created things, such as craftsmen and farmers, and disdained those who simply bought and sold as mere merchants who did not produce anything. There is a widespread pride in the ability of the Vietnamese to turn natural products into something useful, and there are numerous aphorisms to support this outlook. Some of these sayings contain a sense of struggle, which is perhaps not surprising in a country that has experienced so much strife in recent history. It is often said, for example, that a Vietnamese is never without a weapon since he or she has only to reach into the forest to grab a piece of bamboo that can be turned with one cut into a spear. There are also lots of children's sayings that emphasize the virtues of industriousness.

CONCLUSIONS

The debates that appear on the literature on handicraft and tourism can be usefully applied to the situation in Hai Duong, not least because of the centrality of handicrafts to the region's development. There would appear to be more attention to quality than has been noted among the Hmong of Thailand, and traditional skills are not dispensed with in order to serve tourist and export markets. A 'backstage' area has appeared near to the Chu Dau site, but it is not a 'false back' since it is a genuine factory area. Gigantism and the use of tourist genres such as landscape designs have appeared in Hai Duong, and there have been attempts to produce replicas of antiquities. The latter often were of low quality initially but over time there have been attempts to boost quality. Authenticity is not really an issue since copying is seen as quite normal and there is little interest in the issue of copyright. Various kinds of solidarity products have appeared and production is largely outwardly directed towards tourism and export markets. Despite an intensely commercial approach there remains a profound sense of heritage that tends to be vested in the producers' skills and knowledge rather than the finished product. Heritage in this context is perceived more in spiritual than material terms.

NOTE

1   The authors very gratefully acknowledge the European Commission's Asia Urbs programme and the People's Committee of Hai Duong, the London Borough of Hackney and Limerick Corporation for their contribution to the programme. The authors would also like to thank Tang Ba Hoanh for his work on the traditional handicraft villages and his contribution to the programme.

CHAPTER 12

Tourism and Natural Heritage Management in Vietnam and Thailand

Michael J. G. Parnwell

INTRODUCTION

'Nous avons mangé la mer' (after Condominas, 1957).

The voracious appetite of modern development threatens to leave future generations with a cupboard bare of natural resources and an environment damaged beyond repair. Tourism is just as hungry to consume and able to despoil as most other forms of economic activity. Visitors from metropolitan and industrial centres venture far afield in search of unspoiled, wild, spectacular or shrinking landscapes and natural places, often oblivious to the transformative impact their visitation has on the places and scenery they covet and ostensibly cherish. As such places become fewer in number and more limited in extent, and as tourism further expands, spatially and socially, unlocked by affluence and mobility, the pressure intensifies and the impact magnifies. Paradoxically, as natural areas are, in consequence, afforded greater protection from the pernicious and avaricious effects of modern development they become more attractive and marketable as tourist destinations, but simultaneously more vulnerable to degradation. Touristic potential enhances conservation value, and tourist spending helps finance conservation efforts, but the combination of preservation and scarcity intensifies attractiveness and must-visitness. Without very careful management, or perhaps a fundamental change in the ethos of recreation, the world's natural heritage is in danger of being appreciated to death (Papayannis and Howard, 2007: 300).

This chapter examines the management of the physical environment, natural resources and landscape against a back-drop of strong tourism demand and (inescapably intertwined) the pressures of modern development, set within a framework of 'natural heritage' conservation. It uses the broadly comparable examples of Ha Long Bay in northern Vietnam and Phang Nga Bay in southern Thailand to contrast the management of 'exceptional' natural heritage within the framework of UNESCO's world heritage programme, with its global profile and associated political and instrumental leverage, compared with the management of marginally less spectacular but nonetheless vitally important natural areas using more local policy devices. The chapter assesses the relative merits of natural heritage 'spectacularization' from a conservation point of view, and also highlights the challenges of natural resource management and sustainable tourism development in multi-use, multi-stakeholder and multi-responsibility settings. The discussion points to the need for an integrated and holistic approach to environmental management for natural heritage conservation, where tourism is viewed not in isolation but as part of an organic set of pressures. Both case studies suggest steady movement towards integrated coastal zone management, and reveal a degree of coalescence in the strategies and policies of Thailand and Vietnam which reflects more generalized changes in the world of conservation and sustainable development.

NATURAL HERITAGE

Defined as the phenomena of the physical world, 'nature' is the physical system that supports human life. Nature thus has intrinsic value. But its value to humankind is also a cultural construct. We have an aesthetic appreciation of nature; it is something that is cherished, enjoyed, consumed; it can be tamed, enhanced, destroyed, protected and rebuilt. Landscapes *are* not, they become; they are what we make of them. But who decides what is good and what is bad, what form of nature is best, what mode of behaviour towards nature is or is not appropriate? Who are the drivers of interest, and what are the determinants of value? Are values universal, or universalizing, or universalizable? Or are they layered and scalar; variable and differential; perhaps hegemonic and imposed? Can we find grounds for consensus on the human treatment of the natural environment, given multiple and competing needs, wants and perspectives? Can we expect that local, or even national, attitudes towards nature in Southeast Asia will be identical to those that prevail elsewhere in the world? Janet Cochrane (1993: 318–319), for instance, suggests that Southeast Asians perceive nature and wilderness areas differently from many Westerners (see also Bruun and Kalland, 1995). Several national parks in the region were formerly game reserves during the period of colonial rule, thus establishing an ethos of utilization rather than preservation. In the Malay world the word *'taman'* that is used to describe 'park' in National Park equates more to a controlled 'garden' than to a natural 'wilderness' (Cochrane, 1993: 319). For Thailand, Stephen Sparkes (1995: 71) describes a polarized dichotomy of village *versus* forest and culture *versus* nature: 'all of nature (...) is subordinate to culture in the form of Buddhist ideology' (ibid.: 83).

'Natural heritage' is also a cultural construct (Sundin, 2005) and a discursive creation (Lowenthal, 2005). Notwithstanding the intrinsic importance of nature, the notion of 'heritage' is one that centres on human interests, needs, preferences and identity, with a clear past-present-future logic. It is consistent with the current environmentalist concern to 'save' resources and functioning ecosystems – our physical and discursive inheritance from the past – for the use, benefit and appreciation of future generations – their heritage (World Commission on Environment and Development, 1987). Of importance here are the modalities of saving, set against the politics of sustainability. Where do people fit into natural heritage? Are landscapes, physical structures and nature itself to be preserved in a pristine state or monolithic form, fossilized and museumized, protected from human influence, impact or even presence? Is this possible given the developmental status quo? Can human needs, wants and wishes be accommodated within a framework of natural heritage conservation? Who decides on the appropriate balance between preservation and mobilization? Whose claims on natural heritage carry the greatest legitimacy? Does heritage 'belong' to the world, the nation or the locality? Such questions concerning natural heritage are identical to those of nature conservation more generally, and are constantly being reworked without ever adequately being resolved.

An associated question is whether natural heritage should be preserved for its intrinsic qualities or as a means towards satisfying immediate and future human needs and desires? Put simply, should natural heritage, as a social and cultural construct, fulfil a social and cultural purpose? Is this a point of departure from nature conservation *per se*? Heritage belongs to 'us', so 'we' should decide what to do with it. But the temptation is often too great. We preserve something because it is important to us, but because it is there we cannot resist the occasional nibble, and gradually a veritable feast. Should natural heritage thus be viewed as responsibility or opportunity? (Papayannis and Howard, 2007: 302).

While all forms of nature are important because of their intrinsic value, not all natural places and ecosystems have the same worth or significance as 'heritage'. Thus clear choices have to be made as to which is more deserving of or should be prioritized for preservation attention. Who decides, and perhaps more importantly who has the power to decide or influence decisions? (Jha, 2005: 983). Generally speaking, the more dramatic in scale or spectacle a site may be, the more extensive may be the spread of awareness and conservation concern, and thus the more powerful the preservation agenda. This is an inevitable consequence of a global predilection for the spectacular and distinctive, as manifest in the list of the 'World's Greatest Natural Areas' that was compiled by the International Union for the Conservation of Nature (IUCN) World Commission for Protected Areas in 1982 ahead of the Third World Parks Congress in Bali, and from which many of the current natural World Heritage Sites were drawn (Ishwaran, 2004: 47); or in the current New Seven Natural Wonders of the World exercise (see below). But is a small clump of trees on a hillside not as important as a natural area to someone whose livelihood depends on the resources it yields, or whose ancestral heritage it contains, when set against a monolithic landscape such as the Grand Canyon? Or is a coral reef any less important to a local fisher whose livelihood depends on the resources it nurtures and yields than to the SCUBA diver who would see the fisher's destructive practices as a threat to this colourful ecosystem and to his/her recreation interests? A delicate balancing act is thus clearly required to juggle the needs of development and conservation, the interests of the global and the local, and the rights of the present and the future (Olwig, 2005; Bianchi, 2002).

Who has responsibility for natural heritage stewardship? Since 1972, with the promulgation of the Convention on Protection of the World Cultural and Natural Heritage, UNESCO (and the IUCN, which has been a very important partner body for natural heritage) has positioned itself as the principal international institution for framing the notion of 'heritage' and protecting the world's 'sites of outstanding universal value' (UNESCO,

2004: 5) from the ravages of development and change (Ishwaran, 2004). This multilateral organization uses its institutional power and profile, together with astute international diplomacy, to raise global awareness and to leverage international compliance with a common set of conservation principles and modalities. The pride and prestige that accrue to countries and localities from having national treasures inscribed as World Heritage Sites, and the potential humiliation of losing such a tag once inscribed (e.g. being inscribed on the List of World Heritage in Danger, as in the case of the Rice Terraces of the Philippine Cordilleras: see Table 1.1, which lists all of Southeast Asia's UNESCO natural and cultural World Heritage Sites), is used as a powerful device for raising awareness of the importance of heritage preservation at all levels of society and government (Kuijper, 2003: 269). Awareness is an essential pre-requisite for effective action, and status can be a subtle means to lever awareness and commitment. The sense that a local property is of global significance is an influential first step in encouraging compliance with core conservation objectives and nurturing a caring custodianship.

UNESCO's 174 natural heritage sites incorporate more than 500 of the world's formally protected areas, but these account for just nine per cent of all the world's protected areas (Ishwaran, 2004: 46), and of course many important natural habitats and physical features still have no formal protection status. This clearly means that UNESCO has been and has to be selective in the sites that it can award world heritage status to. On the one hand, this has naturally and understandably meant a strategy of 'spectacularization', meaning that urgent priority is generally afforded the most dramatic, breathtaking and spectacular natural sites because of a mandate to protect locations that are of 'universal value' (Milne, 2005: 16). But this leaves important questions, which this chapter seeks to engage, about how less spectacular or globally distinctive natural heritage is being protected? Who looks after the small when attention is focused on the grand? Does conservation more generally operate in the interests of all forms of natural heritage? At what point, if at all, do the two processes – conservation and heritagization – coincide and coalesce? These are questions that the following discussion seeks to engage.

The acquisition of world natural heritage status can be a double-edged sword. Whilst it has the potential to initiate, facilitate and promote regulatory change which can benefit a wider ecology than that contained within a specific site, it can also serve as a magnet to potentially quite destructive forces. There is a potentially huge return to be enjoyed from gaining World Heritage Site status, not just in terms of international prestige but also economic reward. The standing and profile that formal inscription as a UNESCO World Heritage Site affords a location serves as 'a marker of authenticity and quality for international tourists' (Bianchi, 2002: 82). Touristic potential makes previously valueless things valuable (Porter and Salazar, 2005: 363), and thus the touristic potential of heritage designation may be as strong a motivation for nomination as heritage preservation (Bianchi, 2002: 82). Heritage tourism has become a very important component of the overall tourism industry (Porter and Salazar, 2005: 362), and ecotourism has provided very strong motivation and momentum for natural heritage conservation (UNESCO, 2004: 15). But heritage tourism is a razor-sharp double-edged sword (Jha, 2005: 981; Porter and Salazar, 2005: 362; Kuijper, 2003: 269). Balancing heritage conservation and resource mobilization for tourism is a challenging juggling act, as we have seen earlier. Heritage tourism has immense potential to motivate heritage conservation, and also huge capacity to finance conservation measures (Lowenthal, 2005: 84; Papayannis and Howard, 2007: 299), but tourism can equally be a damaging or even destructive force.

Heritage tourism thus provides a useful marker for wider conservation–development debates and dilemmas. The following discussion will examine how conservation–development tensions are being worked out both within and outwith the UNESCO world natural heritage framework. The chapter explores the broadly comparable cases of Ha Long Bay in Vietnam and Phang Nga Bay in Thailand, both sites of spectacular drowned karst landscapes and both experiencing mounting development pressures from divergent sources (especially tourism), but only the former enjoying UNESCO World Heritage Site status. The following sections look at these countries' respective approaches to natural heritage protection, set necessarily within the wider sphere of coastal resource management. The discussion identifies interesting but subtle variations in approach which can in part be explained by the presence or absence of the UNESCO framework, and in part by differences in regulatory context. Irrespective of this, the investigation reveals a growing degree of convergence in strategy which can be attributed to more generalized changes in conservation practice worldwide.

NATURAL HERITAGE MANAGEMENT IN VIETNAM: HA LONG BAY

Ha Long Bay is the finest example of a drowned karst (limestone) landscape in Asia, for which it has been afforded World Heritage status.[1] The spectacular landscape feature of Ha Long Bay is the limestone islands and islets that protrude, with dramatic sheer cliffs, out of the sea: *fenglin* (isolated towers) and *fencong* (clusters of conical peaks) (see Figure 12.1).

Figure 12.1: Typical Ha Long Bay landscape

The Bay extends over 1533 km^2 containing 1969 islands and islets, although the World Heritage Site itself covers just 434 km^2 with 775 islands (Nguyen, 2001: 51) (Figure 12.2 opposite). Some of these contain dramatic caves and grottoes, and terrestrial lakes. The Bay area is also important for its marine and terrestrial biological diversity, with some 1000 fish species and other important flora and fauna, including seven unique species, and natural habitats such as coral and mangrove (IUCN, 1992; Nguyen, 2001). The area also contains archaeological sites which suggest the Bay area as a locus of early Vietnamese civilizations and cultures (e.g. Hoa Binh and Ha Long). The Bay has historically been an important site on the ancient trade routes between China, Japan and Southeast Asia. Present-day settlement in the World Heritage Site includes four traditional fishing communities residing in floating houses and boats.

The Bay thus offers a diversity of features and, for both domestic and international tourists, attractions.[2] Its attractiveness, distinctiveness but also its vulnerability to developmental pressures have been formally recognized since the early 1960s, when the Ministry of Culture declared Ha Long Bay a Historical and Cultural Relict and Natural Scenic Spot in 1961, and a National Protection Area in 1962 (IUCN, 1992). The Bay was inscribed as a World Heritage Site in 1994 for its 'outstanding landscape and

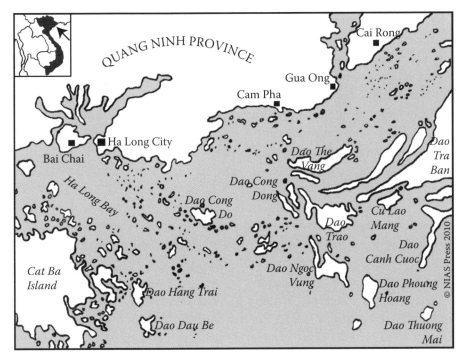

Figure 12.2: Ha Long Bay, Vietnam

aesthetic characteristics', and additionally in 2000 for the site's scientific and geological values. The Socialist Republic of Vietnam became a signatory to the World Heritage Convention in 1987 (UNESCO, 2004: 37), a year after the country signalled a significant shift in domestic and international policy following the *doi moi* reforms of 1986.[3] Ensuing developments in Ha Long Bay represent a microcosm of some of the progress and tensions that Vietnam has experienced since the introduction of *doi moi*. On the one hand, the partial liberalization and the growing internationalization of the economy have provided many more opportunities and imperatives for economic expansion and growth, not least in the field of tourism, which has been one of the country's strongest performing sectors over the last two decades.[4] More than seventy per cent of leisure and tourism destinations in Vietnam are located in coastal areas which account for some eighty per cent of total tourist numbers (Sekhar, 2005: 817). The high density of tourists concentrated in only a few coastal locations puts extreme stress on the natural environment in these areas, requiring deft environmental management. But the regulatory role of the state has been weakened by the *doi moi* reforms relative to the influence and logic of the market. Rapid economic development has heralded an escalating environmental crisis, which the government has struggled to manage, particularly at the local level: 'Vietnam is seen as a "conflicted environmental state", in which local environmental departments (...) are largely passive, ineffectual and argumentative, lack technical expertise and carry limited weight in internal governmental debates' (Konstadakopulos, 2008: 52; see also Lask and Herold, 2004). But paradoxically, Vietnam's greater openness to the outside world has increased its exposure to international values, standards, protocols and modalities with regard to environmental protection. The reshuffling of the regulatory pack has been particularly in evidence in Ha Long Bay over the last two decades.

The touristic value of Ha Long Bay has increasingly been recognized and mobilized during the post-*doi moi* push for development. Numbers of visitors were initially quite modest. Even as recently as 1995, a year after the Bay's official inscription on the World Heritage list, only some 200,000 people were visiting the Bay as tourists (i.e. obtaining official permits to visit the area). By 2003 this figure had reached 1.3 million, and 1.5 million in 2006, by which time just over half the visitors to the Bay were Vietnamese domestic tourists (www.halong.org.vn). Visitor numbers are expected to double, to three million, by 2010, fuelled by a significant increase in tourists from mainland China, by which time Quang Ninh Province (where Ha Long Bay is the main tourism destination) will have become Vietnam's principal tourism focus (www.halong.org.vn/details.asp?lan=en&id=567).

With such a rapid growth in visitor numbers has come intensifying pressure on Ha Long Bay as a tourist attraction, either creating greater stresses at the sites that are already visited by tourists or increasing pressure for more sites to be opened up to accommodate growing tourist numbers, thereby expanding the industry's ecological footprint. The principal value of the Bay to tourists is its aesthetic quality and the human experience of a wide and natural landscape. Thus large numbers of craft bobbing about the Bay, taking tourists to and from the sites and attractions, and increasingly participating in *in situ* activities such as kayaking, significantly transforms the aesthetic value of the site. World Heritage Site status has simply added to the attraction and the intensity of these pressures.

However, it is not just the expansion of tourism in the post-*doi moi* era that has intensified the pressures facing Ha Long Bay. The reform period has seen a significant intensification of development activities in and around the Bay, which not only have degraded the physical environment and thus threatened this globally distinctive site, but which also directly impinge on tourism. Ha Long Bay adjoins one of Vietnam's principal coal-mining areas, which provides employment to some 71,000 people (Nguyen, Nierynck, Tran and Hens, no date; Galla, 2005: 103). Coal-mining is a state-owned sector that often lies at or beyond the extent of the state's regulatory reach, and as such has a poor environmental record, with waste from coal extraction finding its way into the Bay. Quang Ninh Province (QNP) also forms part of the important Hanoi–Haiphong–Quang Ninh development corridor, which is a strategic focus for future intensive development as part of Vietnam's industrialization drive. The Master Plan for the Socio-Economic Development of QNP (1996–2010) aims to transform the province into a core centre of industry, trade, services and tourism (Galla, 2005: 104; Nguyen, Nierynck, Tran and Hens, no date). To facilitate this, a deep-sea port is being constructed at Cai Lan, adjoining Ha Long City, which threatens to intensify transportation use of the Bay, with large ships skirting the Bay's dramatic karst islands and increasing the risk of accidents, spills and other forms of pollution (UNESCO, 2003). The formal municipal waste management organization in Ha Long City, where most tourists are accommodated and itself a rapidly growing urban centre, can only cope with around fifty per cent of the 45,000m^3 of waste that the city generates each year (Nguyen, Nierynck, Tran and Hens, no date).

Important mangrove ecosystems have been cleared to accommodate the infrastructure required for modern development, or to make way for fish and prawn farms that have been booming along with Vietnam's open economy and which are a significant source of pollution in the Bay, together with nitrates and phosphates from agriculture (ibid.). Fish catches in Ha Long Bay dropped by fifty per cent from 1987–1992 (IUCN, 1992), in part because of damage to and destruction of coral ecosystems (an important breeding and nursery environment for young fish) through sedimentation, pollution and inappropriate fishing practices. Thus a host of developmental and environmental pressures congregates in and around Ha Long Bay.

Whilst developmental pressures have intensified markedly over the last decade or so, there has also been a growing awareness of the need to protect the country's natural resources, including aesthetic, physical, cultural and recreational resources for tourists, and a growing raft of environmental protection measures has accordingly been introduced. World Heritage inscription may be seen as an important catalyst for this conservation-focused trend. UNESCO has leveraged much more serious compliance with international standards of environmental management, and Vietnam's greater openness and exposure to the 'outside world' has allowed much greater involvement of international agencies and actors in Vietnam's domestic regulatory affairs (Sekhar, 2005: 819). These in turn have influenced domestic policy and practice (ibid.: 818). There is provision in the 1992 Constitution for heritage conservation, and in 2001 a Law on Cultural Heritage was promulgated, modelled significantly on the operational guidelines of the World Heritage Convention (UNESCO, 2004: 38).

An important motivation for the national heritage conservation effort, however, has been to mobilize and promote tourism development (UNESCO, 2004: 48). But tourism represents a threat as well as an opportunity, something that was recognized by the World Heritage Committee in 2001 as UNESCO sought to build a tourism programme that would encourage partnerships with the tourism industry that could help promote linkages between sustainable tourism and heritage conservation (Pedersen, 2005: 60). But the promotion of sustainable development requires rationalizing and accommodating the needs and interests of a diverse array of stakeholders, each with their own sense of rights, legitimacy, responsibility and paramountcy. It is a highly complex juggling act. The following discussion will look at how Vietnam has risen to the challenge of natural heritage management for sustainable development.

Vietnam applied for World Heritage Site status for Ha Long Bay in 1992, but the initial application was refused. It was deemed that domestic legislative provision was inadequate to guarantee protection of the Ha Long Bay site according to UNESCO's strict requirements for custodianship of natural heritage of global importance. No sufficient management plan for the Bay's protection and preservation was in place, there was inadequate data about the Bay's ecosystem, the resources it contained and the pressures it faced, and there was not even proper demarcation of the proposed property (UNESCO, 1992: 90–92). The legislative basis for protection, together with enforcement capacity, had to be strengthened. There was also a clear need for a tourism management plan, given that the Bay was already an important tourist attraction. Rejection by UNESCO led to the institution of systematic environmental management, the introduction of protective legislation at both the national and provincial level, and a steady improvement in tourism management within and around the Bay (IUCN, 1994; UNESCO, 2004) as the government set out to establish its case for renomination (formally granted in 1994). The resultant natural heritage preservation framework both set in train, and reflected, a process of enhanced environmental management in Vietnam that continues to the present day. An Environmental Protection Law was introduced in 1993, followed by a Cultural Heritage Law in 2001 (Galla, 2002: 72). Various decrees that are relevant to Ha Long Bay have also been introduced for the management of marine resources, control of shipping traffic, control of environmental pollution, regulation of socio-economic development, etc (UNESCO, 2004). A five-year Development Plan for Ha Long Bay was introduced in 1998, and a fifteen year Tourism Plan is currently in operation (1995–2010) (ibid.). The management of both development and conservation in Ha Long Bay is guided by a Master Plan which runs from 2000–2020 (Galla, 2001: 137).

At the heart of heritage management in Ha Long Bay has been an evolving integrated approach to coastal zone management which reflects the multiple and complex challenges that the Bay faces and the need to engage these holistically (Sekhar, 2005: 819; Galla, 2002: 72–74). As such, tourism cannot be isolated from all other processes and pressures. An integrated approach to natural heritage management is a considerable logistical as well as political challenge, not least for a transitional country and communist state such as Vietnam where the approach confronts the prevailing culture of development administration, which is quite hierarchically structured and where operational territory is quite vigorously protected. It requires the simultaneous involvement of different stakeholders from the national through to the local levels in both planning and implementation. Although considerable progress has been made in this regard in the context of Ha Long Bay, there is as yet no integrated planning framework at the national level (Sekhar, 2005: 817). Vietnam has a fairly rigid administrative hierarchy, with power concentrated at the central and provincial levels, and with districts and communes largely responding to initiatives handed down from above (ibid.). There is also an underlying tension between the increasingly environment-oriented approach that is promoted by central government and the development-needs priorities that are frequently expressed at the local level (ibid.: 823). There is an extensive legal framework, but this is not applied in a coordinated and coherent way. There also tends to be a lack of coordination between different local agencies, which have conflicting agendas and goals, constituting a significant hurdle for an integrated approach to environmental management. Efforts have been made to strengthen community involvement in development planning, such as the Regulation on Democratization at the Commune Level, which was introduced in 1998 (ibid.: 822).

The experience of the Ha Long Bay Management Department in developing a cross-cutting, multi-agency approach to natural heritage management is increasingly viewed as a model for more general application in Vietnam, aided by various external assistance projects. A Vietnamese Environmental Protection Agency was created in 1993, and environmental protection and marine environmental protection laws were introduced in 1994 around the time that Ha Long Bay was awarded World Heritage Site status. A ten-year National Strategy for Environmental Protection (2000–2010) provides further guidance for integrated environmental management, and much of this was written by external experts (World Bank, 2006).

There is growing interest in approaches to coastal resource management – relevant to the context of Ha Long Bay – that cut across sectors and which involve multiple sets of stakeholders, linked to commune structures. With the assistance of the IUCN, the government is developing a network of 15 Marine Protected Areas, and is promoting an integrated coastal management framework for action at the national and local levels (IUCN, 2007: 22). A national marine pollution control programme that cuts across the jurisdictions of several ministries and departments was introduced in 2001 (Sekhar, 2005: 817). Bi-lateral assistance from the Netherlands (2000–2003) has introduced pilot projects aimed at introducing Integrated Coastal Zone Management (ICZM) to Vietnam. A division for ICZM has been established within the Ministry of Natural Resources and Environment (ibid.: 818), although activities are still dominated by national and provincial departments, with minimal devolution of planning and decision-making responsibility to the commune level.

An integrated and co-ordinated approach to natural heritage management in Ha Long Bay is facilitated by a Master Plan on Conservation and Promotion of Values of Ha Long Bay (2002–2010) and a Cultural

Heritage Law (Nguyen, Nierynck, Tran and Hens, no date). An integrated approach is essential given the multiple challenges and pressures that the Ha Long Bay World Heritage Site faces. The creation of the Ha Long Bay Management Department in 1995 was an important and at the time ground-breaking first step towards integrated management, creating a single agency that crossed traditionally sharp lines of demarcation between various departments and ministries, and which now has co-ordinating authority over several agencies (Galla, 2001: 140).

Ha Long Bay runs a Heritage Management Centre, and visitor fees were introduced in 1997 as a means of raising revenue to support conservation and management activities. The Bay's management achieved financial self-sufficiency in 2001 (UNESCO, 2004). Nonetheless, there are other important functions that cannot adequately be supported by visitor-derived revenue, including scientific research and large capital infrastructure projects which are necessary for enhancing tourism and other forms of development management and impact mitigation. Scientific research tends to take place as part of bilateral assistance packages, or through link-ups with the international academic community.

The emerging holistic approach to heritage management has led to the introduction of several measures to deal with some of the more important threats to the Bay's aesthetic and physical integrity. Sewerage, drainage, water treatment and water quality monitoring projects have been introduced for Ha Long City and Cam Pha, and stricter legislation has been passed to prevent ships from discharging waste or cleaning their tanks in the Bay and the Buffer Zone. The Hong Gai coal port was closed down and subsequently redeveloped for tourism and commercial development. The construction of the Bai Chai bridge, linking Bai Chai with Ha Long City, has also helped significantly to reduce the volume of commercial shipping and transport/ ferry traffic using the Bay, which historically has been a source of pollution (ibid.). There is enhanced monitoring of development activities and the health of key habitats such as mangrove and coral, and more marine and oceanographic research taking place through the Institute of Oceanography in Haiphong (ibid.). The impact of tourism is managed by restricting access to and rotating the use of caves and grottoes and other core attractions. More innovative developments include the use of fishing communities, whose livelihoods derive from the Bay, to patrol Ha Long Bay and report any transgressions of regulations, and they are also paid to collect garbage found floating in the Bay. Greater attention is also now given to education and awareness-raising (e.g. through TV documentaries) among the local population, the Vietnamese more generally and also international visitors to Ha Long Bay World Heritage Site.

The final step in the holistic and integrated approach to natural heritage management is the Ha Long Bay Ecomuseum Project. The ecomuseum concept evolved from the 'new museology' of the 1970s and 1980s (Elliott, 2006) which saw a shift in thinking about the relationship between people and museums. The aim was to move away from the museum as an elite institution to one that fundamentally involves, integrates and is owned by the community within which it is placed and which it seeks to represent (Davis, 2004: 94). The Ha Long Bay Ecomuseum seeks to provide an innovative means of addressing a variety of local management challenges, such as resource conflicts, the impacts of tourism and the limited contribution that tourism makes to the local economy (Worts, 2006). Initiated in 2002, the Ecomuseum seeks to promote a holistic approach to tourism development and conservation management by viewing the entire Bay as a living museum with all elements constantly in a process of interaction (Galla, 2001: 138), and drawing all stakeholders together in a participatory programme (Worts, 2006). The promotion of public participation has been quite a challenge in a country where civil society is at an embryonic stage of development (Lask and Herold, 2004: 399).

The Ecomuseum will include an interpretive Hub which would be tourists' first point of contact with Ha Long Bay, providing a rich educational experience (derived from extensive local research and data gathering) through a Discovery Centre designed to help raise visitors' awareness of the diversity but also the fragility of the natural and cultural treasures that the Bay offers and contains (Galla, 2002). Suitably informed, tourists can choose from a menu of touristic experiences centred on core interpretive themes which, in theory, are carefully controlled and managed by the Ha Long Bay Management Department via the Hub, offering the visitor an improved and more meaningful experience, whilst also encouraging appropriate forms of tourist behaviour (such as with regard to littering, trampling vegetation, damage to cave stalagmites, nature and landscape appreciation). Local communities (fishing, floating villages, boat-builders) are not only promoted as an integral part of the tourism experience (a back-drop, but with an emphasis on authenticity), but in the process intensive efforts are made to ensure that they benefit directly from tourism in terms of livelihood (e.g. through crafts production and sale via the

Hub), employment and self-identity. Traditional skills and knowledge are preserved not as a museum reconstruction for the benefit of visitors, but as a functioning local commercial operation that brings economic benefits from cultural tourism to local communities (Worts, 2006).

The holistic approach to environmental management in Ha Long Bay is characterized by the Cua Van Floating Cultural Centre, which forms the first operational part of the Ecomuseum project. The Centre enables fishing communities to participate in the preservation and management of both cultural and natural resources whilst facilitating their socio-economic development (Nguyen, Nierynck, Tran and Hens, no date). Education is a core theme of the Ecomuseum concept, with particular emphasis placed on raising local awareness of conservation issues, especially among women and local children, the latter being seen as essential for the future prioritization of conservation and for energizing local support (UNESCO, 2003: 49). Galla (2001: 142) suggests that many local people are oblivious to the global importance of their natural heritage resource, and as such are also indifferent to the various planning controls that have been introduced by the national and provincial governments. The Ecomuseum is also intended to help resolve conflicts over resource use and access by explaining the different sides of the development-conservation conundrum. An Eco Boat, funded by the international NGO Fauna and Flora International, is also used as a floating classroom for both local people and foreign visitors for education purposes.

Another objective of the Ecomuseum is to find ways of encouraging tourists to stay longer (and thus spend more locally) and explore more deeply than just the superficial elements of the karst landscape. Resource flows to and through the Ecomuseum will provide the financial means of supporting infrastructural projects which are intended to mitigate the impacts of increasing tourist numbers. Training is also provided to enhance the quality of staff, especially managers who are charged with balancing development and conservation.

NATURAL HERITAGE MANAGEMENT IN THAILAND: PHANG NGA BAY

Phang Nga Bay is quite similar to Ha Long Bay in terms of the characteristics of the natural landscape and the range and intensity of developmental pressures that have been brought to bear on this dramatic natural site. But

Phang Nga Bay lacks the regulatory leverage of world heritage status, and instead has to rely on a more generic policy and management environment for protection. Thailand has also been exposed to the developmental pressures of the free market and as an important and relatively more mature tourist destination for much longer than Vietnam. Has the lack of protection for Phang Nga Bay as a natural heritage site of global importance resulted in a weaker regulatory environment than has increasingly been evident in Ha Long Bay?

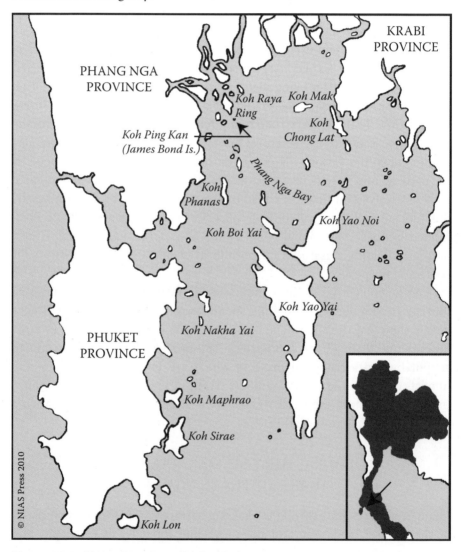

Figure 12.3: Phang Nga Bay, Thailand

Phang Nga Bay also contains a drowned marine karst landscape, and although its spatial extent, some 3,000 km^2, is greater than Ha Long Bay, the smaller number of islets and limestone towers, forty-two, tend to class it as less 'spectacular' than Ha Long Bay, and as such of lesser global significance, even though it has in the past been mooted as a possible World Heritage Site (Nickerson-Tietze, 2000: 66) (Figure 12.3). However, the point we discussed earlier is that although it lacks the spectacular or flagship credentials of Ha Long Bay, it nonetheless represents an important piece of 'natural heritage', and its intrinsic ecological value is no less significant because of its lower global status. Phang Nga Bay is one of the biologically most productive bays in the Andaman Sea (ibid.). The mangrove forests that surround the Bay's coastal edges are amongst the most extensive and diverse in Thailand, with some 28 mangrove species recorded. Some of the islands contain important stands of limestone scrub forest and evergreen forest, and also intertidal forested wetlands. In addition to a diversity of marine (82 fish species) and bird species (the Bay alone has 88 bird species, including the globally threatened Malaysian Plover and the Asian Dowitcher), the Phang Nga Bay Marine National Park is home to some 206 animal species, including the White-Handed Gibbon, the Serow, the Dusky Langur, the Crab-Eating Macaque and the Smooth-Coated Otter. Marine mammals include the Dugong, which is also a threatened species, and the Black Finless Porpoise (www.ramsar.org/profile/profiles_ thailand.htm). More than half of Thailand's 153 km^2 of coral reefs are located in the Andaman Sea, and Phang Nga Bay contains some of the most spectacular coral reef ecosystems off Thailand's west coast, making it both a significant attraction for tourists but also a vital ecosystem that supports the livelihoods of the Bay's 13,000 small-scale fishers living in 114 coastal fishing communities (Nickerson-Tietze, 2000: 66).

Whereas Ha Long Bay is a tourist attraction in its own right, Phang Nga Bay principally functions as the playground for one of Thailand's largest tourism destinations, Phuket, which is only some 20–30 km from the Bay.[5] Whilst this means that Phang Nga Bay has been spared much of the infrastructural development that is commonly associated with tourism, its proximity to this tourism hot-spot creates an important set of management challenges. Many tourists visit Phang Nga Bay on day trips from Phuket and another growing tourism destination, Krabi. Boat trips and individual sea canoes take tourists into and close up to the landscape, into the caves, and into the spectacular '*hong*' or collapsed cave systems. A traditional Muslim stilted fishing village on Koh Phan Yee, established by Javanese migrants two centuries ago, is also a core attraction to tourists – so much so that it is now a quaint souvenir mall, food centre and tourism stop-over more than a functioning fishing village. There are two larger inhabited islands in the Bay, Koh Yao Yai and Koh Yao Noi, both of which have resorts and accommodation for tourists, although they are relatively tranquil in comparison with Phuket. Tourism activities in the Bay include kayaking, boating, caving, rock climbing, camping and trekking (for a fuller discussion of some of the impacts of tourism in Phang Nga Bay, see Kontogeorgopoulos, 2004a, 2004b, 2005). It was also an area that was quite significantly affected by the Boxing Day Tsunami in 2004, the recovery efforts from which provide an important back-drop to the present discussion.

Phang Nga Bay is similar to Ha Long Bay in that it has been experiencing increasing developmental stresses from a number of sources which are exerting a great deal of pressure on the aesthetic landscape and the Bay's natural resources, both of which constitute important components of Thailand's 'natural heritage'. Thailand has experienced four decades of economic boom, set within a regime of relatively unrestricted access to natural resources and habitats, and characterized by weak enforcement and widespread evasion of regulatory frameworks, leading to over-exploitation of natural resources, habitat degradation and growing social conflicts over resource access (Henocque and Sanchai, 2006: 4). A lack of regulation of common-property resources set against the increasing capitalization and technification of fishing effort in Thailand has led to overfishing in the Bay[6] and conflict between small- and large-scale fishing operations (small-scale fishers account for eighty per cent of the sector but land just five per cent of total production) (World Bank, 2006: 9). Phang Nga Bay accounted for seventeen per cent of Thailand's total fisheries production in 1992, but the Bay's fishing communities have the lowest per capita income of Thailand's small-scale fisheries sector (Nickerson-Tietze, 2000: 66–67). The problem has been compounded by the use of destructive fishing gear (especially 'push nets') and practices, such as dynamite and cyanide fishing, and the use of chemicals on coral reefs to catch fish for the thriving ornamental fish market.

The degradation of the Bay's coral reef ecosystems, both as a consequence of human activity and compounded by the 2004 Boxing Day tsunami, is a serious issue with implications both for the tourism sector and for livelihoods more generally. Eighty-three per cent of the coral reefs in the

Andaman Sea were classified as being in 'fair', 'bad' or 'very bad' condition in 1998, and all are at risk of continued degradation (World Bank, 2006: 6). Roughly twenty per cent of the coral reefs of Phang Nga Bay were severely damaged by the 2004 tsunami, and a further twenty per cent suffered a moderate impact (Thamasak, Makamas and Rattika, 2006: 565; Brown, 2005: 373). The principal human sources of coral decline are sedimentation and wastewater pollution (especially from poorly regulated shrimp farms and cage mariculture), coral bleaching (resulting from climate change, and accelerated by the El Niño event in 1998), and poorly regulated tourism (anchor and diver damage, garbage, collection of natural products like shells, jetty construction) (Thamasak, Makamas and Rattika, 2006: 563).

Mangroves, which are another of the Bay's vitally important natural habitats, have experienced even more dramatic decline over the last three decades. Mangroves are an important breeding and nurturing environment for the Bay's marine life, and additionally provide vital protection to the coast from periodic severe weather events and natural calamities (like the cyclone that hit Burma on 3 May 2008, and the tsunami of 2004), and from erosion more generally. Degradation of the mangrove ecosystem is also indicative of a wider environmental malaise. Nationally, mangrove cover declined by half between 1975 and 1993 (World Bank, 2006: 5), principally as a consequence of a rapid increase in shrimp-farming, but also widespread coastal infrastructural development (see below). Phang Nga is one of three sites in Thailand that has experienced the most significant loss of mangrove habitat, from 3,108 km^2 to 1,674 km^2 over the same period (ibid.). Sea grass, which is an important natural habitat for fish, turtles, lobsters and the threatened Dugong, has also experienced a steady decline as a consequence of the continued use of illegal push nets by fishers, of shrimp farming discharges, and of urban, industrial, agricultural and residential pollution (ibid.: 6; Hines, Kanjana, Duffus and Dearden 2005). Sea turtle populations in Phang Nga Bay have declined by ninety per cent since the early 1990s as a consequence of overfishing, of habitat destruction, and of the capture and the collection of turtle eggs, even though this has coincided with increased protection legislation: enforcement remains quite weak (ibid.: 7).

Considerable environmental pressures have been experienced within Thailand's coastal zone as a consequence of tourism and of modern development more generally. In 2004, eighty-four per cent of the country's eleven million international visitors congregated in just five coastal provinces: Phuket/Phang Nga Bay, Krabi, Surat Thani, Songkhla and Chon

Buri (World Bank, 2006: 18). Demographic expansion in the coastal zones has been much faster than the national average as economic activity and human settlement has intensified along the coasts, leading to increased demand for scarce freshwater resources, and a rapid increase in pollution. Coastal areas account for more than fifty per cent of the country's total pollution, even though only a quarter of the population is found here. Coasts receive eighty-seven per cent of total industrial pollution (ibid.: 17). The sustainability of many forms of coastal development, not least tourism, is threatened by the short-termist, growth-oriented attitude that has long prevailed in the country. There is an urgent need for intervention on behalf of the natural environment, and most particularly – as with Ha Long Bay – an integrated approach that treats environmental pressures and threats holistically:

> A new approach to management, including new regulations, economic instruments, and active enforcement is needed to lessen the current pressures on the marine and coastal resources (...) the linkages between the various resources and pressures calls for an integrated, participatory approach that looks at the coastal area as a whole and effectively strengthens and integrates the efforts of local and national government agencies, institutions and stakeholders (ibid.: 23).

A number of responses have been made to the challenges of rapid economic development and environmental transformation in and around Phang Nga Bay, all of which have significance both for the development of tourism and the protection of natural heritage. A Marine Policy and Restoration Committee was established in 1996, and the 1997 Thai Constitution established the Normative Principle for Ocean Governance which makes specific provision for the management, preservation and balanced exploitation of the marine environment. This constituted a major breakthrough by mainstreaming coastal zone management in Thailand, and in line with the general tenor of the Constitution emphasized the decentralization of resource administration and management to local communities (Nittharatana, Cherdchinda and Siriwan, 2007). The Ninth Economic and Social Development Plan (2002–2006) had a focus on marine resource conservation, and Thailand's National Marine Policy was overhauled in 2003 to allow the incorporation of a framework for integrated and holistic management. To facilitate coastal management and natural heritage conservation, Thailand has twenty-six Marine Protected Areas, seventeen of which are in the Andaman Sea (World Bank, 2006: 30). The Phang Nga Bay Marine National Park was established in 1981 and covers an area of some 400 km². The Bay was also declared a protected Ramsar Site[7] of international ecological importance in August 2002. MPAs and MNPs are an important device for protecting valuable coastal ecosystems such as coral and mangrove: thirty per cent of Thailand's coral and mangroves are located within MNPs (ibid.). Nonetheless, 'the major emphasis of marine park management is to support the tourism economy rather than focusing on conservation and regulation enforcement' (Nittharatana, Cherdchinda and Siriwan, 2007).

Whilst legislative provision for coastal environmental protection in Thailand is steadily improving on paper, weaknesses still remain in actual practice, not least in moving towards the integrated framework which provides the only realistic means of protecting natural heritage. Several agencies have an administrative stake in coastal management, such as the Office of Natural Resources and Environmental Policy and Planning, the Department of National Parks, Wildlife and Plant Conservation, the Pollution Control Department, the Department of Water Resources, the Royal Forestry Department and the Department of Marine and Coastal Resources (DMCR) (World Bank, 2006: 36). Competing agendas, departmental rivalry and territoriality, and overlapping regulations hinder the development and implementation of an integrated approach to coastal zone management. Phang Nga Bay lacks a single body with the power to leverage co-operation and integration as was the case with the World Heritage framework in Ha Long Bay. There is little co-ordination of activities by national agencies, provincial governments, non-governmental organizations and the private sector in coastal management.

Since the early 2000s the coastal management agenda has started to shift towards an integrated and holistic approach, similar in both timing and character to the transformation that was identified in the case of Ha Long Bay. This suggests that, although UNESCO's World Heritage framework is undoubtedly influential in affording protection to key natural heritage sites, the conservation world is itself changing, and in the process is building a regulatory environment that appears increasingly conducive to natural heritage preservation and more sustainable forms of tourism development. The DMCR with assistance from the Asian Development Bank and the IUCN has developed a legal framework to promote an integrated approach, framed within the Marine and Coastal Resources

Management Act – Area-Function Participation Approach (World Bank, 2006: 27–28). Phang Nga Bay provided the test ground for a pilot multi-agency partnership in management of coastal resources involving key stakeholders (local communities, government departments [especially the Department of Fisheries], local NGOs, universities and international agencies [principally the UNFAO within the aegis of its Bay of Bengal Programme]). This is the first project of its kind in Thailand (Nickerson-Tietze, 2000: 65), and uses education for raising environmental awareness, enforcement using community patrolling and monitoring, and economic incentives to encourage compliance with existing legislation. The aim is to build a Bay-wide management and environmental governance regime (ibid.: 68), similar to that being promoted by the Management Department in Ha Long Bay.

Also of significance is the CHARM [Coastal Habitats and Resource Management] Project, introduced in 2002 by the Department of Fisheries with financial and technical support from the European Commission. The Project adopts another of the currently in-vogue modalities for integrated coastal protection: co-management. This is a multi-actor approach which gets all stakeholders working together around a common agenda, each (e.g. public sector, business, NGOs, communities, international agencies) contributing and specializing in what they each do best in the field of environmental management. The CHARM Project is also being tested in Phang Nga Bay (Henocque and Sanchai, 2006: 4).

Changes in the overall direction and character of coastal environmental management have been reflected in intensifying efforts to rehabilitate degraded coastal habitats, in the process restoring important natural heritage to a better state of health. DMCR introduced a Mangrove Management Plan (2004–2008) aimed at restoring some 1,152 km^2 of degraded mangrove forest (World Bank, 2006: 5). Phang Nga Bay is an important focus of this programme, with mangrove rehabilitation taking place in thirty-five villages which adjoin the Bay, especially the island-based Koh Yao Yai and Koh Yao Noi communities (see below) (ibid.: 11).

The coral reefs have also been the focus of increased conservation and rehabilitation attention, not least since the 2004 tsunami (see below). Coral restoration in the Andaman Sea commenced in 1994 in degraded coral reefs adjoining the Phuket resorts, involving the Marine Ecology Unit within the Phuket Marine Biological Center, which is under the auspices of the Department of Fisheries[8] (Thamasak, Makamas and Rattika, 2006:

567). Coral reef protection is also a responsibility of the Royal Thai Navy. Increasingly attention is now given to non-regulatory forms of protection, such as public awareness-raising through education (ibid.: 572). Over fifty per cent of Thailand's coral reefs are now under some form of formal legal protection, and various governmental and non-governmental organizations are involved in coral reef monitoring. For instance, Reef-Watch has been active in promoting safe snorkeling and SCUBA activities among tourists, and increasingly involves tourists and local communities in the monitoring and observation of coral reef ecological conditions. In July 2005 a group of twenty villagers from Koh Yao Noi in Phang Nga Bay formed their own Coral Reef Conservation Club (www.reefwatch.com). This was later provided with funding support from the CHARM Project.

The same community group also formed an Eco-Tourism Club whereby the accumulated knowledge of the coral reef ecosystem could be shared with responsible tourists who wanted to snorkel and dive on the reefs. The Club won the Tourism Authority of Thailand's Fourth Tourism Industry Contest in the 'Tourism Promotion and Development' category. In January 2003 the islanders' tourism programme, in partnership with the NGO Responsible Ecological Social Tours Project (REST), won the Destination Stewardship Award within the World Legacy Awards, jointly sponsored by Conservation International and the National Geographic Traveler magazine. This shows how local communities, sometimes in partnership with NGOs, are developing the power, agency and sophistication to take control of resource management and environmental rehabilitation at the local level and are getting formal recognition for their work.

This 'bottom-up' approach to natural heritage management now provides the cornerstone of coastal management strategy in Thailand (World Bank, 2006: 36), and was strongly emphasized in reconstruction efforts following the Boxing Day tsunami in 2004, which had a devastating impact on Phang Nga Bay. National and international agencies have sought to turn the tsunami crisis into an opportunity to make a fresh start on coastal resource management and rehabilitation, not least in the field of tourism. Much greater emphasis has been given to community-based management and stewardship of natural resources and natural areas in the post-tsunami period. Efforts have been made to ensure that the same mistakes from the past, which were having severe impacts on the aesthetic and physical environment of Phang Nga Bay, would not be repeated. The 2005 Notification on Environmentally Protected Areas and Measures in

Tsunami Affected Areas (principally Ranong, Phang Nga, Krabi, Phuket, Trang and Surin) sought to: control the use of beachfronts by permitting only activities that promote marine safety and beach security; control actions that cause pollution and negative impacts on natural resources and the environment; control the construction of buildings and other infrastructure to prevent further landscape deterioration; promote actions to enhance environmental quality; and to strengthen local communities to be self-reliant in restoring and overseeing natural resources and the environment (Nittharatana, Cherdchinda and Siriwan, 2007). Tourism was nonetheless an important part of the strategy to lead post-tsunami economic recovery, and in some instances there was a tension between these two objectives. For instance, in the Surin Islands Marine National Park in Phang Nga Province pressure was put on the Park authorities to open up previously off-limits Strict Nature Reserve Zones for diving and snorkeling because of damage to coral elsewhere in the reserve, both in 1998 after a severe El Niño event and after the 2004 tsunami, thereby extending the ecological footprint of tourism for the sake of economic expediency (Suchai et al., 2004; Suchai et al., 2006; Suchai et al., 2007: 409).

CONCLUSION

The drowned karst landscapes of Ha Long Bay, Vietnam and Phang Nga Bay, Thailand provide interesting case studies of some of the tensions and challenges faced by planners in trying to protect 'natural heritage' from the simultaneous ravages of tourism and other forms of development. This loosely comparative study has identified in both sites a similar array of pressures that are associated with generic dynamics of change occurring under modern liberal capitalist development, and also, despite striking differences in political and planning contexts, a degree of convergence in policy response in the form of holistic and integrated coastal management.

But the case studies can not be considered typical of all forms of natural heritage and associated conservation efforts. The attraction and value of the two sites, and hence the motivation to protect them for the benefit of present and future generations, lies in their spectacular physical structure. Few of the tourism activities that presently take place in these two bays are likely to have a significant impact on their basic physical character. Tourists don't do much climbing or walking or camping or collecting on the towers and islets. There is no extraction of limestone or other transformative activities that would gradually wear the features away. Water quality, biotic health and species density, and to some extent habitat intactness, are not the principal driving forces behind conservation efforts, at least from the point of view of heritage tourism. Only the density and intensity of visitor presence, which grates against their popular image as wild natural landscapes, can be said to be threatening the aesthetic appeal of the sites, and thus the future sustainability of tourism – although the 'tourism iceberg' principle (see Parnwell, 2009: 30–31: 238) suggests that there are many more potential tourists in the wings to take the place of those who turn their noses up at a repeat visit to Ha Long Bay or Phang Nga Bay because of the damage that tourism is perceived to be causing.

Most of the other officially designated natural heritage sites in Southeast Asia (see Table 1.1 on p. 8) have been nominated as much for their intrinsic as their aesthetic value. Indonesia's four UNESCO natural heritage sites, for instance, are all national parks (NP) containing a variety of ecosystems and associated wildlife. Ujong Kolon NP is of geological interest for its volcanic landscape and of scientific interest as the habitat, *inter alia*, of the threatened Javan rhinoceros; the Lorentz NP contains a huge diversity of habitats and ecosystems, from snowcap to tropical forest to tropical marine environments, lying at the interface of two major continental plates; and the Sumatra rainforest heritage site contains three NPs and several endangered animal and plant species. Only Komodo NP might be argued to be protected because of the 'spectacular' and unique 'Komodo dragons' that it contains, which Borchers (2009: 272) identifies as the best-known (and in many instances the only-known) attraction of a park that in fact contains diverse and distinctive marine and terrestrial habitats. Likewise, Gunung Mulu NP in Malaysia and Phong Nha–Ke Bang NP in Vietnam, as with Ha Long Bay and Phang Nga Bay both karst landscapes, are protected principally because of their spectacular and extensive cave systems. But elsewhere in the region (Table 1.1), habitats have been afforded World Heritage Site natural heritage status more because of their intrinsic than their aesthetic terrestrial or marine value.

When considering both aesthetic and intrinsic value, however, we must again return to the question – framed at the beginning of this chapter – as to whose values are pre-eminent in the determination of 'value'. Without systematic research one can only speculate about this, but it seems reasonable to suggest, without in any way meaning to be patronizing, that local people, whose horizons, because of high levels of local economic deprivation in these coastal areas, are more typically focused on the day-to-day struggle for livelihood and sustenance, and have little time to admire aesthetically and explore leisurely their physical surroundings in the way that visitors from far and near can and wish to do. These landscapes represent and contain resources that local people use and need, but which non-local people also covet or crave, and wish to control and conserve. Historically, the balance of power has been such that local people have remained poor when surrounded by rich resources, governments have wielded far too weak and ineffective a regulatory stick, and the various segments of the tourism industry have transformed and consumed nature, resources, landscapes, peoples and cultures with impunity and an apparent lack of accountability. But the case studies suggest that this situation is beginning to change. The holistic and integrated approach to natural heritage management which is increasingly favoured, both within the framework of UNESCO heritage protection and within the context of coastal zone management, recognizes and seeks to prioritize local communities, not only as deserving citizens who should share in the sustainable utilization of marine ecosystems but also as potential stewards and custodians of natural areas and the world's natural heritage. Democratization and participation are the new buzzwords of international development (Leal, 2007), and where given genuine political space to flourish, as in the concept of the 'ecomuseum' and in recent forms of community-centred tourism management, may provide an important pillar in natural heritage protection which recognizes and responds to the needs and rights of a range of stakeholders, not just a high-spending and high-brow elite.

NOTES

1   As of 17 March 2008, Ha Long Bay also topped the voting for the New Seven Wonders of Nature, a web-based exercise organized by the New7Wonders Foundation based in Switzerland (www.new7wonders.com/nature/en/liveranking, accessed on 17 March 2008). Phang Nga Bay, which is also featured in this chapter, ranked 47 in the same exercise on this date.

2   Indeed, as early as 1950 Ha Long Bay was listed as one of 'Les Merveilles Du Monde: Les Prodiges De La Nature, Les Créations De L'homme' (Laporte, 1950).

3   The 6th National Congress of the Communist Party of Vietnam in December 1986 approved an economic renovation policy aimed at stimulating the national economy by adopting market principles and reducing the involvement and intervention of the state in business. Foreign and domestic investment was encouraged, private

ownership was permitted, trade regimes were liberalised and the economy oriented much more towards the global market.

4   Numbers of foreign visitors to Vietnam increased from 250,000 in 1990 (27 per cent of whom were overseas Vietnamese), to 400,000 in 1992, 1,781,754 in 1999, 2,330,050 in 2001, 2,927,876 in 2004 and 3,583,486 in 2006 (www.vietnamtourism.com, various). Domestic tourists increased dramatically, e.g. from 2.7 million in 1993 to 9 million in 1999 (Sekhar, 2005: 817). There may be in the region of 25 million tourists in Vietnam (domestic and foreign) by 2010 (Sekhar, 2005: 817).

5   Incidentally, both Phang Nga Bay (The Man with the Golden Gun, 1974; Tomorrow Never Dies, 1997; The Beach, 2000) and Ha Long Bay (Indochine, 1991) have provided the back-drop for blockbuster films which have increased their 'must-see' attraction to international and domestic tourists, including 'James Bond Island' (Ko Tapu) in Phang Nga Bay.

6   Average fish catch per hour of fishing effort by trawlers in Phang Nga Bay in 1969 was 250 kg/hr, with 49 per cent of the catch being the target species, and 51 per cent by-catch (or 'trash fish'). By 1987 average catch was just 38 kg/hr, with 67 per cent by-catch, and a high proportion of juveniles making up the catch, thus pointing to continued longer-term decline (Ruangrai, Pongpat and Penporn, 1997: 5).

7   Site number 1185. The Ramsar Convention on Wetlands is an international framework for national action and international cooperation for the conservation of wetlands.

8   This has now been reorganized as the Marine and Coastal Biology and Ecology Unit of the Phuket Marine Biological Center within the Department of Marine and Coastal Resources.

CHAPTER 13

Heritage Futures

Michael Hitchcock, Victor T. King and
Michael J. G. Parnwell

With the exception of Thailand, all the countries of Southeast Asia are former colonies. On independence, and in the process of trying to distance themselves from the former colonial powers, the political elites of these countries constructed narratives of their origins in which heritage played a major part. That these narratives should often be concerned with nation-building and expressions of national consciousness, often derived simply from the expressions and desires of officialdom, is not surprising given the relative newness of most of the region's nation-states. Importantly they drew on the discoveries of archaeology and both pre-history and classical history in reconstructing and, some might argue, 'inventing' ancient traditions and golden ages when powerful kingdoms and sultanates held sway over the territories and populations which were subsequently incorporated into colonial empires. What is significant is that in creating these national heritages these new nations faced a number of problems, not least because the *raison d'être* of cultural heritage was often couched in ideas that were originally European, whether derived from the Enlightenment, as in the case of Indonesian attempts to find virtue in the people, following Herder, the German political philosopher, or following communism, in the case of Vietnam. Taiwan may be an exceptional case, but even the way part of its heritage, namely that of its indigenous minorities, as shown by Yoshimura and Wall in Chapter 3, is understood owes something to colonial intervention.

The fact that outside forces helped to shape perceptions of heritage, beyond those which were beginning to emerge in several Southeast Asian states in the early twentieth century, is augmented by the fact that UNESCO's protocols, notably the World Heritage Convention of 1972, have served as a basis for heritage policy throughout the region over the last three decades or so, though Taiwan, which was not one of the United Nations states parties in the Convention, again remains an exception. Given this external influence it is perhaps not surprising that what initially came to be seen as heritage was often human-made and either monumental or spectacular, testimony to the prowess and endurance of the cultures that created these edifices. But of course it is not this straightforward, since even in these monumental structures evidence of external forces can still be detected. At the Purple Palace in Hue, examples of both Chinese (Vietnam's ancient overlord) and French influences can be detected (see Chapter 9). Even the great Indonesian edifice of Borobudur, simultaneously a World Heritage Site and national monument, bears witness to Indian influence, though the relationship was not colonial, and European, in the sense that it was the interest shown in it by Western antiquarians that led to its excavation.

The fact that Western antiquarians showed great interest in the material evidence of ancient civilizations illustrates another important cultural difference between Western and Southeast Asian conceptions of heritage. In Western conceptions it is the material evidence that is the measure of what is or is not authentic, and great effort is invested in discovering and preserving what is deemed to be original and either charting or rectifying what has happened to it over time. This is in complete contrast to the prevailing attitude in Southeast Asia, possibly because preservation of organic materials such as wood and fibres was always difficult in a humid, tropical environment. Influenced by the NARA Document (1994) from Japan, Southeast Asian academics often use a computer analogue, in which the material culture is regarded as hardware and the human ability as software, so it is reasonable to argue that both are esteemed in Southeast Asia. This debate was raised in the NARA Document on Authenticity that arose out of a meeting held in Nara, Japan (1–6 November 1994) at the invitation of the Japanese government's Agency for Cultural Affairs. The Agency organized the conference in co-operation with UNESCO, ICCROM and ICOMOS. According to its authors the ensuing Document was drafted in the spirit of the Charter of Venice of 1964, and was intended to extend the scope of cultural heritage in an expanded world. In particular the Document asserts that:

All cultures and societies are rooted in the particular forms and means of tangible and intangible expression which constitute their heritage, and these should be respected. (http://www.international.icomos.org/naradoc_eng.htm)

There would appear to be considerable empathy with the Nara Document on Authenticity among those charged with conserving heritage in Southeast Asia, but whether or not governments in the region have formally adopted it as policy remains an important research question.

Another area of concern regarding the prevalence of Western-derived concepts of heritage in Southeast Asia pertains to the management of heritage sites. In certain cases, some principles of effective management from the West have been adapted successfully to a Southeast Asian setting. But with regard to the large-scale and internationally renowned heritage attractions of the region, especially those designated as World Heritage Sites, there is growing concern about the applicability of Western-derived concepts, not least within the current context of an upsurge in intra-Asian tourism.

The case of Angkor (...) indicates how global heritage tourism today continues to base policies around a Western-centric network of organizations and technologies (Winter, 2007: 41)

As Winter has argued, policies designed for tourism management derived from European models have proved inadequate to cope with the explosion in facilities aimed at the Northeast and Southeast Asian markets (Winter, 2007).

Clearly Western concepts of heritage tourism management have been transmitted to the region via international organisations like UNESCO, but what remains unclear is how precisely they have been adapted to local conditions and implemented in very varied cultural, political and historical circumstances. While several of the chapters in this volume have begun to address this issue (see, for example, Chapters 6 to 9 and Chapter 12), it is a research question that as yet remains unanswered, as no comparative framework would appear yet to have been formulated to assess the effectiveness and contextual relevance of heritage management cross-regionally and internationally, or across different forms and scales of cultural and natural, and tangible and intangible, heritage. It is possible that in the process of adaptation to local contexts, of the incorporation of local norms and priorities into heritage management, some models of good practice, especially with regard to coping with the impact of intra-Asian and domestic tourism, might have emerged. Research is needed to identify best practices, and to both collate and disseminate it cross-regionally. There is a pressing need for such kinds of enquiry because of the pace of change in Asia, the threat to heritage and the partial if not total obsolescence of Western-derived models.

In our view, another area that would merit further research is how official expressions of heritage in Southeast Asia that are often partly based on imported Western notions frequently sit uneasily with the ethnographic realities of the region. A common theme in the anthropological and sociological literature on Southeast Asia is the deeply felt sense of connectedness that the region's peoples have with the territories in which they reside, which in some countries is associated with the veneration of ancestors. Whatever the world religion that these people profess, be it Buddhism, Hinduism, Islam or Christianity, or if the follow animistic practises, there is a strong sense of belonging to and continuity with the generations that came before, leaving one to conclude that the belief in ancestors is an aspect of the underlying traditions of the region that have not really been accommodated and incorporated within the domain of either international tourism or heritage promotion. Certainly there is a significant amount of domestic tourism, with people returning to their villages of origin to mark important festivals, though the statistics on how much of this takes place are hard to find. With some notable exceptions it is not this aspect of heritage that is presented to foreign tourists, perhaps because it is so personal to the communities concerned and small in scale.

Given the ubiquity of and solidarity with this belief in ancestors, one is left wondering how much the major edifices valued by officialdom as monumental heritage mean to ordinary people throughout the region, not least when local communities are often excluded from such forms of heritage either in the interests of preservation or of tourism, or both. What would be interesting to ascertain is whether an ordinary Vietnamese, for example, feels equally strongly about the imperial palace in Hue as about the graves or shrines of his/her ancestors, or whether there is a strong emotional separation between that which belongs to the family and immediate community and that which is the preserve of the state or the international community.

A complicating factor is that the official terms used to describe heritage in the languages of the Southeast Asian nations do not necessarily or strictly mean heritage as people in the West tend to see it, even though dictionaries may offer 'heritage' as a translation. Take for example the Indonesian term for heritage, *warisan*, which is derived from *waris* meaning heir, an Arabic loanword, and which actually means 'inheritance'. 'World Heritage' is translated as *Warisan Dunia*, literally the 'inheritance of the world', and it remains unclear how local populations understand such terms and the extent to which they convey the notion that locals may be excluded. In at least one documented example, that of the temple complex of Besakih in Bali, many local opponents to its nomination to be a World Heritage Site objected on the grounds that the term 'heritage' implied that it was no longer used when in reality it was the island's most important Hindu edifice, the mother temple, and was actively used in the everyday and on-going ritual life of the Balinese (Hitchcock and I Nyoman Darma Putra, 2007: 105).

A related concern is the position of religion within the states of Southeast Asia, since so much of what is presented to tourists as heritage is religious or at least has a religious dimension. One problem with tangible heritage, especially major edifices, is that it has a fixed location, though the social and cultural environmental around it can change so that there is a disconnection between the structure and its local community. For example, the Chams of what is now Vietnam built shrines to venerate Hindu deities, but the peoples who live around these structures today usually do not subscribe to that belief system, though some of the towers have been adapted to Buddhist worship. Likewise in Indonesia the Buddhist religion's largest monument, Borobudur, is surrounded by a predominantly Muslim population, and despite the fact that both religions are officially recognised by the state as having equal value there have in the past been local attempts to desecrate this renowned monument. Sometimes the state itself is perceived to be the problem, even when its official position is that it upholds the value of religion. There have been cases of widespread resistance when the state has been perceived, rightly or wrongly, as interfering with something that is precious to the community. The temple complex of Besakih is again a good example: the Hindu Balinese rejected an attempt to turn the temple complex into a World Heritage Site fearing that its management would be taken out of the hands of the island's religious community.

In the Besakih case local resistance worked, but generally speaking conservation and preservation efforts in Southeast Asia have led to local people being excluded from the land they occupied and resources they utilized prior to their heritage, and its conservation, being designated as a national and global concern (see Chapter 6). However, more recently there has been a move to nurture 'living heritage sites' in which communities can maintain their livelihoods whilst providing a back-drop of human interest and cultural context to the refurbished monuments of cultural heritage, although usually within fairly strictly controlled parameters. Whilst the international heritage conservation community, especially in the case of UNESCO, is advocating openness and community participation as a means of spreading the benefits of heritage tourism to local communities, implementation of effective action at the local level is often hampered by prevailing political and personal power structures (see Chapter 6).

There are often strong underlying tensions between the visions of the authorities who are usually committed to new developments in the interests of urban renewal and economic regeneration, including the expansion of tourism, and the communities and advocates of sympathetic heritage preservation who promote a vision of living cultural heritage that facilitates continuity (see e.g. Chapter 8). The communities that comprise living heritage, moreover, provide a resource, or at least a back-drop, that might be regarded as more authentic than enactors or interpreters for both domestic and international tourism.

Another problem with state-led initiatives in Southeast Asia is that they tend to adopt a primordial view of ethnicity and traditional culture, and use these as a means of communicating narratives of nation-building, nationalism and national conscious-raising, often portraying inter-ethnic relations in a bland and uncontroversial manner. Ethnicity is often presented to the tourist in an idealized manner that has little bearing on either modern twenty-first-century reality or historical accuracy. Despite the slow progress in accommodating local peoples in development and heritage conservation initiatives, some positive signs, albeit limited in extent, can be found within the region, such as the living heritage community at Angkor (see Chapter 6, this volume).

Another arena in which one encounters discordance between the state and local communities, and problems about agency and competing discourses, is in the way heritage is actually presented to tourists. As Mark Johnson has shown in this volume (see Chapter 9), tour guides in Hue have daily to negotiate the obfuscations of the state and party bureaucracy, and their own ambivalent and sometimes contradictory perceptions of the past, their place in the present, and what the future may bring. It is not only tour guides who are involved in these processes but also conservators and researchers in the employ of the state charged with the making and re-presentation of Vietnam's heritage for the 'tourist gaze' (Urry, 1990). The outcome is often a carefully ordered and orchestrated process of selective representation with the rough edges of historical reality smoothed over for tourist consumption.

A common and perhaps curious feature of the presentation of cultural heritage in the region, whether through museums operating as 'contact zones' between tourists and local identity constructions, or through guides, guidebooks and other tourist-oriented media, is the persistence of the exotic, sometimes an aesthetic exotic. Often this exotic identity is directed away from the mainstream and projected on to minorities, who in turn strategize not only to gain the economic benefits of tourist visitation but also to score political points vis-à-vis the majority society, which often amounts to little more than demanding more respect. An attendant phenomenon is what might be called self-Orientalization (or strategic essentialism – Spivak, 1987), to reverse Said's famous observation (1979), in which the representatives of majorities or dominant elites and the tourism authorities, in efforts to authenticate their cultural heritage, describe themselves as 'truly Asian' or 'essentially Asian', usually with recourse to stereotypes, as the chapter by Ooi has shown (see Chapter 5).

The presentation of heritage as a tourism commodity also raises important questions concerning a country's relationship with its history, which in the case of Vietnam and Indonesia involves reminders of bitter pre-independence struggles and colonial domination. Given that an important function of heritage sites is to engage visitors in the interpretation of history, then questions of authenticity and accuracy become crucial unless one is not partaking in serious education but its more lighthearted and often less reliable companion – 'edutainment'. In fact, it is often the recourse to didactics that stretches the limits of authenticity as governments strive to drive home the horrors of pre-independence struggles. One wonders whether there is not already a bit of audience fatigue or even scepticism among domestic tourists, especially in countries where greater openness prevails today than before, and where there has been a dramatic increase in access to other sources of information. It is suggested that well-travelled tourists become inured to such official versions of oppression, though studies of what visitors to Southeast Asian nations actually think about the heritage of these countries are very rare. Local tourism authorities are in any case usually more interested in travel and hospitality quality than reactions to heritage, despite the economic importance of this aspect of tourism.

The tensions between planners, business interests and local communities can also be readily detected in the arena of natural heritage, as those charged with conserving the natural environment grapple with the need to support economic growth while protecting 'natural heritage' from the simultaneous ravages of tourism and other forms of development. Tourism in some cases, such as Ha Long Bay, might be regarded as being less destructive than other kinds of economic activity, since tourists do not yet stray far from accessible zones and do not yet partake of those activities that have had a significant impact on natural heritage in Europe (see Chapter 12 by Parnwell). There is, however, no reason to suppose that such activities (such as walking, climbing, collecting) might not increase in popularity in the future among large numbers of tourists in Southeast Asia as recreation fashions spread and change. Currently the issue that appears to be the most pressing is the density and intensity of visitor presence, which threatens the popular appeal and image of these sites as wild natural landscapes.

Aesthetics is an important issue because it would appear that many of the officially designated natural heritage sites in Southeast Asia have been nominated as much for their intrinsic as their aesthetic value. But as the chapter by Parnwell has asked, whose perspectives are pre-eminent in the determination of value? Are the dominant values those of Western visitors still steeped in the Romantic re-evaluation of landscape that occurred two centuries ago, or do such concerns emanate from officials who have absorbed Western perspectives through their education and their own enquiries, or even a combination of both? What would be interesting to discover is whether there is an underlying aesthetic rooted in Southeast Asian traditions that is also exerting an influence. Certainly there are examples of aesthetic responses to the environment in the region, whether it be in the silk paintings of Vietnam that often feature Ha Long Bay or the batik patterns of Java. Without systematic research it is not possible to determine precisely the extent to which indigenous aesthetic conceptions of the environment have had an influence on heritage.

From what we have already proposed and from what has been examined in several of the chapters in this book, it is clear that the concept of heritage is a contested and ambiguous one. Not only has it been formulated and deployed to serve various purposes for various constituencies, but the meanings and understandings of heritage also vary across cultures. It is our view that the major heritage sites of Southeast Asia, particularly those designated by UNESCO, many of which have grown to become very significant tourist attractions with all the attendant commercial and other pressures, would benefit from wide-ranging comparative research. These sites are not only objects, assets or resources, which are given a positive value as heritage by international and national conservation agencies and governments, but some of them have been and are used by political elites in nation-building projects as symbols or icons of the nation. What is more, as objects of the 'tourist gaze' they are evaluated and given meaning by domestic and international tourists (both Asian and Western) and they are promoted by government-sponsored and private tourist agencies which create and present particular images of these sites. Finally, they are often part of living cultural landscapes because local communities either live in or in close proximity to the sites and they in turn attach values to them.

These different and often contested and conflicting images and perceptions of heritage require investigation, as do the different ways in which sites are used and the various pressures which are brought to bear upon them. Because these sites differ considerably in their characteristics and because different governments and agencies have decided to manage them in different ways (though within the overall policies of UNESCO and other international organizations), it is important both in the academic study of heritage tourism and in the consideration of the dimension of policies and management that we need to evaluate and compare the different experiences of sites across Southeast Asia. Black and Wall (2001), for example, have provided a useful but rare, albeit relatively cursory, comparative examination of three UNESCO World Heritage Sites in Southeast Asia. What is needed now are much more ambitious, wide-ranging examinations of several sites, both cultural and natural, across those countries of Southeast Asia in which there is UNESCO-designated heritage (the Philippines, Vietnam, Laos, Cambodia, Thailand, Malaysia, and Indonesia), which begin to build upon some of the discussions and findings in this book. Very recently the three editors of this volume together with Dr Janet Cochrane have secured a British Academy-funded research grant to undertake a cross-regional comparative project on heritage management in several UNESCO sites. A further challenging research need, which has been alluded to earlier in this Conclusion and is touched on in some of the chapters in this volume, is to take the concept of 'heritage' beyond the spectacular and exceptional parameters used by UNESCO into more locally, culturally, ephemerally and ethereally framed notions, images, forms and needs.

Bibliography

Adams, Kathleen M. (1993a) 'Club dead, not Club Med: staging death in contemporary Tana Toraja (Indonesia)'. *Southeast Asian Journal of Social Science*, vol. 21, no. 2, pp. 62–72.

—— (1993b) 'Theologians, tourists and thieves: the Torajan effigy of the dead in modernizing Indonesia'. *The Kyoto Journal*, vol. 22, pp. 38–45.

—— (1995) 'Making-up the Toraja? the appropriation of tourism, anthropology and museums for politics in upland Sulawesi, Indonesia'. *Ethnology*, vol. 34, no. 4, pp. 143–153.

—— (1997a) 'Ethnic tourism and the re-negotiation of tradition in Tana Toraja (Sulawesi, Indonesia)'. *Ethnology*, vol. 37, no. 3, pp. 309–320.

—— (1997b) 'Nationalizing the local and localizing the nation: ceremonials, monumental displays and national memory-making in upland Sulawesi, Indonesia'. *Museum Anthropology*, vol. 21, no. 1, pp. 113–130.

—— (1997c) 'Touting touristic "primadonas": tourism, ethnicity, and national integration in Sulawesi, Indonesia'. In Michel Picard and Robert Wood (eds), *Tourism, Ethnicity and the State in Asian and Pacific Societies*. Honolulu: University of Hawai'i Press, pp. 155–80.

—— (1998a) 'More than an ethnic marker: Toraja art as identity negotiator'. *American Ethnologist*, vol. 25, no. 3, pp. 327–351.

—— (1998b) 'Domestic tourism and nation-building in South Sulawesi'. *Indonesia and the Malay World*, vol. 26, no. 75, pp. 77–97.

—— (2003) 'The politics of heritage in Tana Toraja, Indonesia: interplaying the local and the global'. In Michael Hitchcock and Victor T. King (eds), *Indonesia and the Malay World* (special issue on 'tourism and heritage in South-East Asia'), vol. 31, no. 89, pp. 91–107.

—— (2004) 'Locating global legacies in Tana Toraja, Indonesia'. In David Harrison and Michael Hitchcock (eds), *Current Issues in Tourism* (special issue on 'the politics of world heritage: negotiating tourism and conservation'), vol. 7, nos 4–5, pp. 433–435.

—— (2006) *Art as Politics: Re-crafting Identities, Tourism and Power in Tana Toraja, Indonesia*, (Southeast Asian Politics, Meaning and Memory Series). Honolulu: University of Hawai'i Press.

Adams, V. (1996) *Tigers of the Snow and Other Virtual Sherpas*. Princeton: Princeton University Press.

Adorno, T. and M. Horkheimer (1972) 'The culture industry: enlightenment as mass deception'. In S. During (ed.), *The Cultural Studies Reader*. London: Routledge, pp. 29–43.

Aitchison, C. (2000) 'Poststructural feminist theories of representing others: a response to the "crisis" in leisure studies' discourse'. *Leisure Studies*, vol. 19, pp. 127–144.

—— (2001) *Theorizing Other Discourses of Tourism, Gender and Culture*. London: Sage.

Albet-Mas, A. and J. Nogue-Font (1998) 'Voices from the margins: gendered images of "otherness" in colonial Morocco'. *Gender Place & Culture: A Journal of Feminist Geography*, vol. 5, no. 3, pp. 229–240.

Allerton, C. (2003) 'Authentic housing, authentic culture? tranforming a village into a "tourist site" in Manggarai, eastern Indonesia'. *Indonesia and the Malay World*, vol. 31, no. 89, pp. 119–128.

Allio, F. (1998) 'The Austronesian peoples of Taiwan: building a political platform for themselves'. *China Perspectives*, vol. 18, pp. 52–60.

Alneng, Victor. (2002) '"What the fuck is a Vietnam?": touristic phantasms and the popcolonization of (the) Vietnam (war)'. *Critique of Anthropology*, vol. 22, no. 4, pp. 461–489.

American Express (no date) *Into the Heart of Old Melaka: jejak warisan/heritage trail*. Melaka: Malacca State Development Corporation.

Amstutz, G. (1997) *Interpreting Amida: History and Orientalism in the Study of Pure Land Buddhism*. Albany: State University of New York Press.

Andaya, L.Y. (2001) 'The search for the "origins" of Melayu'. *Journal of Southeast Asian Studies*, vol. 32, no. 3, pp. 315–330.

Anderson, Benedict (1973) 'Notes on contemporary Indonesian political communication'. *Indonesia*, vol. 16, pp. 39–80.

—— (1983) *Imagined Communities: Reflections on the Origin and Spread of Nationalism*. London: Verso.

—— (1991) *Imagined Communities: Reflections on the Origin and Spread of Nationalism*. London: Verso (revised edition).

Ang Ien (2001) 'Desperately guarding borders: media globalization, "cultural imperialism" and the rise of Asia'. In Yao Souchou (ed), *House of Glass: Culture, Modernity, and the State in Southeast Asia*. Singapore: Institute of Southeast Asian Studies, pp. 27–45.

Apostolakis, A. (2003) 'The convergence process in heritage tourism'. *Annals of Tourism Research*, vol. 3, no. 4, pp. 795–812.

Appadurai, A. (1990) 'Disjuncture and difference in the global cultural economy'. In M. Featherstone (ed.), *Global Culture: Nationalism, Globalisation and Modernity.* London: Sage, pp. 295–310.

Arrigo, L.G., C. Huang and C. Chung (2002) 'A minority within a minority: cultural survival on Taiwan's Orchid Island'. *Cultural Survival Quarterly*, Summer, pp. 56–61.

ASEAN (Association of Southeast Asian Nations) (2000) *ASEAN Declaration on Cultural Heritage*, 25 July [Available at http://www.aseansec.org, last accessed on 31 July 2005].

Ash, Timothy Garton (1989) 'Does central Europe exist'. In Timothy Garton Ash, *The Uses of Adversity: Essays on the Fate of Central Europe.* New York: Random House, pp. 179–213.

Ashcroft, B., G. Griffiths and H. Tiffin (2000) *Post-Colonial Studies: The Key Concepts.* London: Routledge.

Ashworth, G. and P. Larkham (eds) (1994) *Building a New Europe: Tourism, Culture and Identity in the New Europe.* Routledge: London.

Asian Civilizations Museum (2007a) 'About ACM', *ACM's homepage* [available at http://www.acm.org.sg/themuseum/aboutacm.asp, last accessed on 21 February 2007].

—— (2007b) 'China – gallery 6', *ACM's homepage* [available at http://www.acm.org.sg/themuseum/galleries4.asp, last accessed on 21 February 2007].

Asian Development Bank (ADB) (2000) *Cambodia: Enhancing Governance for Sustainable Development.* Manila: ADB.

Askew, Marc (1996) 'The rise of *Moradok* and the decline of the *Yarn*: heritage and cultural construction in urban Thailand'. *Sojourn. Journal of Social Issues in Southeast Asia*, vol. 11, pp. 183–210.

Autorité pour la Protection du Site et l'Aménagement de la Région d'Angkor (APSARA) (1998) *Angkor: A Manual for the Past, Present and Future (2nd edition).* Phnom Penh: APSARA.

—— (2000) *APSARA Authority Activity Report for the Period June–December 2000 for ICC TC*, December 2000. Phnom Penh: APSARA.

—— (2005) *Legal Framework Related to the Management of Cultural Protected Zones 1 and 2 of Siem Reap/Angkor Region.* Siem Reap: APSARA.

Balfour, F. (1999) 'Vietnam hotels'. *Agence France Press*, 28 February 1999.

Bangkok Post (2001) 'Car banned'. In Brief, 19 July 2001.

Bankes, G. (2000) 'Ceramic arts of Peru and Ecuador: echoes of prehispanic past and influences of the tourist present'. In M. Hitchcock and K. Teague (eds), *Souvenirs: The Material Culture of Tourism.* Aldershot: Ashgate, pp. 209–222.

Barth, Fredrik (1969) 'Introduction'. In Fredrik Barth (ed.) *Ethnic Groups and Boundaries: The Social Organisation of Difference.* Bergen and Oslo: Univerities Forlaget and London: George Allen and Unwin, pp. 9–38.

Bayly, Susan (2004) 'Vietnamese intellectuals in revolutionary and postcolonial times'. *Critique of Anthropology*, vol. 24, no. 3, pp. 320–344.

BBC (2000) 'Spokeswoman calls visiting US Senator's remarks "untrue"'. *BBC Summary of World Broadcasts*, 1 May 2000.

Ben-Amos, Paula (1977) 'Pidgin languages and tourist arts'. *Studies in Visual Communication*, vol. 4, no. 2, pp. 128–139.

Benjamin, G. (1976) 'The cultural logic of Singapore's "multiculturalism"'. In J.H. Ong, C.K. Tong and E.S. Tan (eds), *Understanding Singapore Society*. Singapore: Times Academic Press, pp. 67–85.

Bhabha, Homi K. (ed.) (1994) *Location of Culture*. New York: Routledge.

Bianchi, Raoul V. (2002) 'The contested landscapes of world heritage on a tourist island: the case of Garajonay National Park, La Gomera'. *International Journal of Heritage Studies*, vol. 8, no. 2, pp. 81–97.

Bianchi, Raoul V. and Priscilla Boniface (2002) 'Editorial: the politics of world heritage'. *International Journal of Heritage Studies*, vol. 8, no. 2, pp. 79–80.

Bich, Ngoc (2000) 'Motorized traffic ban around evocative lake'. *The Vietnam Investment Review*, 11 September 2000.

—— (2003) 'From the Old Quarter to new'. *The Vietnam Investment Review*, 11 August 2003.

Bigalke, Terence (1981) *A Social History of 'Tana Toraja' 1870–1965*. Unpublished Ph.D. thesis, Cornell University.

Biles, Annabel, Kate Lloyd and William Logan (1999) 'Romancing Vietnam: the formation and function of tourist images of Vietnam'. In Jill Forshee (ed.), *Converging Interests: Traders, Travelers and Tourists in Southeast Asia*. Berkeley: University of California Press, pp. 207–234.

Bird, I. (1883) *The Golden Chersonese and the Way Thither*. London: John Murray.

Black, Heather and Geoffrey Wall (2001) 'Global-local inter-relationships in UNESCO world heritage sites'. In Peggy Teo, T.C. Chang and K.C. Ho (eds), *Interconnected Worlds: Tourism in Southeast Asia*. Oxford: Elsevier Science, Pergamon, pp. 121–136.

Boissevain, J. (1996) 'Ritual, tourism and cultural commoditization in Malta: culture by the pound?'. In T. Selwyn (ed.), *The Tourist Image: Myths and Myth Making in Tourism*. Chichester: Wiley, pp. 105–120.

Boniface, Priscilla (1999) *Managing Quality Cultural Tourism*. Routledge: New York.

Boniface, Priscilla and Peter J. Fowler (1993) *Heritage and Tourism in 'the Global Village'*. London and New York: Routledge.

Borchers, Henning (2009) 'Dragon tourism revisited: the sustainability of tourism development in Komodo National Park'. In Michael Hitchcock, Victor T. King and Michael J.G. Parnwell (eds) (2009) *Tourism in Southeast Asia: Challenges and New Directions*. Copenhagen: NIAS Press and Honolulu: University of Hawai'i Press, pp. 270–285.

Bourdieu, Pierre (1984) *Distinction: A Social Critique of the Judgement of Taste*. Translated by Richard Nice. Cambridge, Mass.: Harvard University Press.

Bradford, Malcolm and Ean Lee (eds) (2004) *Tourism and Cultural Heritage in Southeast Asia*. Bangkok: SEAMEO–SPAFA, Occasional Paper series.

Brown, Barbara E. (2005) 'The fate of coral reefs in the Andaman Sea, eastern Indian Ocean following the Sumatran earthquake and tsunami, 26 December 2004'. *The Geographical Journal*, vol. 171, no. 4, pp. 372–374.

Brown, D. (1994) *The State and Ethnic Politics in Southeast Asia*. London and New York: Routledge.

Bruner, Edward (1996) 'Tourism in the Balinese borderzone'. In S. Lavie and T. Swedenburg (eds), *Displacement, Diaspora, and Geographies of Identity*. Durham, N.C.: Duke University Press, pp. 157–179.

—— (2001) 'The Maasai and the lion king: authenticity, nationalism and globalization in African tourism'. *American Ethnologist*, vol. 28, no. 4, pp. 881–902.

Bruun, Ole and Arne Kalland (eds) (1995) *Asian Perceptions of Nature: A Critical Approach*. Richmond: Curzon Press, NIAS Studies in Asian Topics, Number 18.

Bunn, S. (2000) 'Stealing souls for souvenirs: or why tourists want the "real thing"'. In M. Hitchcock and K. Teague (eds), *Souvenirs: The Material Culture of Tourism*. Aldershot: Ashgate, pp. 166–193

Burke III, E. (1998) 'Orientalism and world history: representing Middle Eastern nationalism and Islamism in the twentieth century'. *Theory and Society*, vol. 27, no. 4, pp. 489–507.

Burns, Peter M. (2004) 'Tourism planning: a third way?'. *Annals of Tourism Research*, vol. 31, no. 1, pp. 24–43.

—— (2006) 'Social identities and the cultural politics of tourism'. In Peter M. Burns and M. Novelli (eds), *Tourism and Social Identities: Global Frameworks and Local Realities*. Amsterdam: Elsevier, pp. 13–24.

Butler, R.W. (1980) 'The concept of a tourist area cycle of evolution: implications for management of resources'. *Canadian Geographer*, vol. 24, pp. 5–12.

Cambodia Times (1996) 'YTL confident of winning Siem Reap project'. *Cambodia Times*, 10–16 March 1996, p. 6.

Canclini, Néstor García (2001) *Consumers and Citizens: Globalization and Multicultural Conflicts*. Minneapolis: University of Minnesota Press.

Carsten, Janet and S. Hugh-Jones (eds) (1995) *About the House: Levi-Strauss and Beyond*. Cambridge: Cambridge University Press.

Cartier, Carolyn (1993) 'Creating historic open space in Melaka'. *Geographical Review*, vol. 83, no. 4, pp. 359–373.

—— (1996) 'Conserving the built environment and generating heritage tourism in Peninsular Malaysia'. *Tourism Recreation Research*, vol. 21, no 1, pp. 45–53.

—— (1997) 'The dead, place/space, and social activism: constructing the nationscape in historic Melaka'. *Environment and Planning D: Society and Space*, vol. 15, no. 5, pp. 555–586.

—— (1998) 'Megadevelopments in Malaysia: from heritage landscapes to "leisurescapes" in Melaka's tourism sector'. *Singapore Journal of Tropical Geography*, vol. 19, no. 2, pp. 151–176.

—— (2001) 'Imaging Melaka's global heritage'. In P. Teo, T.C. Chang and K.C. Ho (eds), *Interconnected Worlds: Tourism in Southeast Asia*. Oxford: Elsevier Science, Pergamon, pp. 193–212.

Case, W. (1995) 'Malaysia: aspects and audiences of legitimacy'. In M. Alagappa (ed), *Political Legitimacy in Southeast Asia*. Stanford: Stanford University Press, pp. 69–107.

Cauquelin, J. (2004) *The Aborigines of Taiwan: The Puyuma: From Headhunting to the Modern World*. London and New York: Routledge.

Causey, Andrew (1999) 'Making a man *malu*: western tourists and Toba Bataks in the souvenir marketplace'. In Jill Forshee, Christina Fink and Sandra Cate (eds), *Converging Interests: Traders, Travelers, and Tourists in Southeast Asia*. Berkeley: University of California at Berkeley, Center for Southeast Asian Studies, Monograph No. 36, pp. 279–291.

—— (2003) *Hard Bargaining in Sumatra: Western Travelers and Toba Bataks in the Marketplace of Souvenirs*. Honolulu: University of Hawai'i Press.

Chang, T.C. (1997) 'From "instant Asia" to "multi-faceted jewel": urban imaging strategies and tourism development in Singapore'. *Urban Geography*, vol. 18, no. 6, pp. 542–562.

—— (2000) 'Renaissance revisited: Singapore as a "global city for the arts"'. *International Journal of Urban and Regional Research*, vol. 24, no. 4, pp. 818–831.

Chang, T.C. and W.K. Lee (2003) 'Renaissance city Singapore: a study of arts spaces'. *Area*, vol. 35, no. 2, pp. 128–141.

Chang, T.C. and P. Teo (2001) 'From rhetoric to reality: cultural heritage and tourism in Singapore'. In L. Low and D.M. Johnston (eds), *Singapore Inc.: Public Policy Options in the Third Millennium*. Singapore: Asia Pacific Press, pp. 273–303.

Cheah Boon Kheng (1988) 'The erosion of ideological hegemony and royal power and the rise of postwar malay nationalism, 1945–1946'. *Journal of Southeast Asian Studies*, vol. 19, no. 1, pp. 1–26.

Cheng, R.L. (1994) 'Language unification in Taiwan: present and future'. In M.A. Rubinstein (ed.), *The Other Taiwan: 1945 to the Present*. Armonk: East Gate Books, pp. 357–391.

Cheung, S. (1999) 'The meaning of a heritage trail in Hong Kong'. *Annals of Tourism Research*, vol. 22, no. 3, pp. 570–588.

Chibnik, Michael (2003) *Crafting Tradition: The Making and Marketing of Oaxacan Wood Carvings*. Austin: University of Texas Press.

Chua, A. (2003) *World on Fire: How Exporting Free Market Democracy Breeds Ethnic Hatred and Global Instability*. New York: Doubleday.

Chua, B.H. (1995) *Communitarian Ideology and Democracy in Singapore*. London: Routledge.

Clammer, John R. (1979) *The Ambiguity of Identity: Ethnicity Maintenance and Change among the Straits Chinese Community of Malaysia and Singapore*. Singapore: Institute of Southeast Asian Studies, Occasional Paper 54.

Clarke, Alan (2000) 'The power to define: meanings and values in cultural tourism'. In Mike Robinson, Philip Long, Nigel Evans, Richard Sharpley and John Swarbrooke (eds), *Expressions of Culture, Identity and Meaning in Tourism*. Sunderland: Centre for Travel and Tourism in association with Business Education Publishers Ltd, pp. 23–36.

Clarke, J. J. (1997) *Oriental Enlightenment: The Encounter Between Asian and Western Thought*. London: Routledge.

Clifford, J. (1997) *Routes: Travel and Translation in the Late Twentieth Century*. London: Harvard University Press.

Clodd, H.P. (1948) *Malaya's First British Pioneer: The Life of Francis Light*. London: Luzac and Company.

Cochrane, Janet (1993) 'Tourism and conservation in Indonesia and Malaysia'. In Michael Hitchcock, Victor T. King and Michael J.G. Parnwell (eds), *Tourism in South-East Asia*. London: Routledge, pp. 317–336.

Cohen, Erik (1983) 'The dynamics of commercialized arts: the Meo and Yeo of northern Thailand'. *Journal of the National Research Council of Thailand*, vol. 15, no. 1, pp. 1–34.

—— (1985) 'The tourist guide: the origins, structure and dynamics of a role'. *Annals of Tourism Research*, vol. 12, no. 1, pp. 5–29.

—— (1988) 'Authenticity and commoditisation in tourism'. *Annals of Tourism Research*, vol. 15, pp. 371–386.

—— (1993a) 'Introduction: investigating tourist arts'. *Annals of Tourism Research*, vol. 20, pp. 1–8.

—— (1993b) 'The study of touristic images of native people: mitigating the stereotype of a stereotype'. In D. Pearce and R. Butler (eds), *Tourism Research: Critiques and Challenges*. London: Routledge, pp. 36–69.

—— (1993c) 'The heterogeneization of a tourist art'. *Annals of Tourism Research*, vol. 20, no. 1, pp. 138–163.

—— (1996) 'A phenomenology of tourist experiences'. In Yiorgos Apostolopoulos, Stella Leivadi and Andrew Yiannakis (eds), *The Sociology of Tourism: Theoretical and Empirical Investigations*. London and New York: Routledge, pp. 90–111.

—— (2000) *The Commercialized Crafts of Thailand: Hill Tribes and Lowland Villages*. Honolulu: University of Hawai'i Press.

Condominas, Georges (1957) *Nous avons mangé le forêt de la Pierre-Génie Gôo: Chronique de Sar Luk, village mnong gar*. Paris: Mercure de France.

Cooke, S. and F. McLean (2002) 'Our common inheritance: narratives of self and other in the Museum of Scotland'. In P.C. Harvey, R. Jones, N. McInroy, and C. Milligan (eds), *Celtic Geographies: Old Culture, New Times*. London: Routledge, pp. 109–122.

Cooper, Chris, Stephen Wanhill, John Fletcher, David Gilbert and Alan Fyall (1999)

Tourism Principles and Practice. Longman: New York.

Cooper, M. (1997) 'Tourism planning and education in Vietnam: a profile, 1995–2010'. *Pacific Tourism Review,* vol. 1, pp. 57–63.

Cooper, R. (1984) *Resource Scarcity and the Hmong Response: Patterns of Settlement and Economy.* Singapore: Singapore University Press.

Copper, J. F. (ed.) (2003) *Taiwan: National-State or Province?* Boulder: Westview Press.

Crang, M. (1998) *Cultural Geography.* New York: Routledge.

Crick, Malcolm (1996) 'Representations of international tourism in the social sciences: sun, sex, sights, savings and servility'. In Yiorgos Apostolopoulos, Stella Leivadi and Andrew Yiannakis (eds), *The Sociology of Tourism: Theoretical and Empirical Investigations.* London and New York: Routledge, pp. 15–50.

Crippen, K. (2000) 'The threads that tie textiles to tourism'. In M. Hitchcock and Wiendu Nuryanti (eds), *Building on Batik: The Globalization of a Craft Community.* Aldershot: Ashgate, pp. 271–284.

Crouch, H. (1996) *Government and Society in Malaysia.* St. Leonards, NSW: Allen and Unwin.

Crystal, Eric (1994) 'Rape of the ancestors: discovery, display and destruction of the ancestral statuary of Tana Toraja'. In Paul Michael Taylor (ed.), *Fragile Traditions: Indonesian Art in Jeopardy.* Honolulu: University of Hawai'i Press, pp. 29–41.

Dahles, Heidi (2001) *Tourism, Heritage and National Culture in Java.* Richmond, Surrey: Curzon Press.

Daud, H. (1987) 'Konsep Raja dan Kerajaan daripada perspektif historiografi Melayu'. *Akademika,* vol. 31, pp. 3–14.

Davis, Peter (2004) 'Ecomuseums and the democratisation of Japanese museology'. *International Journal of Heritage Studies,* vol. 10, no. 1, pp. 93–110.

Deutsche Press-Agentur (2002) 'Koizumi visits Ho Chi Minh mausoleum, meets Vietnamese president'. *Deutsche Press-Agentur,* 28 April 2002.

Directorat Perlindungan dan Pembinaan Peninggalan Sejarah dan Purbakala (1993) *Undang-Undang Republik Indonesia No. 5, Tahun 1992, Tentang Benda Cagar Budaya.* Jakarta.

Dirlik, A. (1996) 'Chinese history and the question of orientalism'. *History and Theory,* vol. 35, no. 4, pp. 96–118.

Dy Phon, P. (2000) *Dictionary of Plants Used in Cambodia.* Phnom Penh: Imprimerie Olympic.

Echtner, C.M. and P. Prasad (2003) 'The context of third world tourism marketing'. *Annals of Tourism Research,* vol. 30, no. 3, pp. 660–682.

ERC–CI (Economic Review Committee – Services Subcommittee Workgroup on Creative Industries) (2002) *Creative Industries Development Strategy: Propelling Singapore's Creative Economy.* Singapore: Economic Review Committee.

Elliott, J. (1997) *Tourism: Politics and Public Sector Management*. Routledge: London.

Elliott, Sarah (2006) 'Targets for the arrows of fate: ecomuseology as a rescue mechanisms in response to the threatened cultural landscapes of Southeast Turkey'. Paper presented at the Forum UNESCO University and Heritage 10th International Seminar 'Cultural Landscapes in the 21st Century', Newcastle upon Tyne, 11–16 April 2005.

Engelhart, Richard (1997) 'Heritage for the future: the challenges of preserving the historic environment in the rapidly modernizing urban centres of Asia'. Keynote speech, 7th Regional Seminar on Conservation of Asian Cultural Heritage, *The World Cultural Heritage in Asian Countries – Sustainable Development and Conservation*. Tokyo, 15–18 October 1997.

—— (1998) 'Can Penang become a World Heritage Site? The Role of Public-Private Partnership in the Conservation of Living Heritage'. Public lecture, Penang, 9 February 1998.

—— (2007) 'Protecting indigenous cultures within a tourism environment: a rights based approach empowering local stakeholders'. Talk delivered at the University of Hawai'i at Manoa School of Travel Management, 27 February 2007.

Erb, Maribeth (1998) 'Tourism space in Manggarai, Western Flores, Indonesia: the house as a contested place'. *Singapore Journal of Tropical Geography*, vol. 19, no. 2, pp. 177–192.

—— (1999) *The Manggaraians: A Guide to Traditional Lifestyles*. Singapore: Times Editions.

—— (2000) 'Understanding tourists: interpretations from Indonesia'. *Annals of Tourism Research*, vol. 27, no. 3, pp. 709–736.

Eriksen, T.H. (1991) 'The cultural contexts of ethnic differences'. *Man*, vol. 26, no. 1, pp. 127–144.

Errington, F. and D. Gewertz (1989) 'Tourism and anthropology in a post-modern world'. *Oceania*, vol. 60, pp. 37–54.

Errington, Shelly (1994) 'What became of authentic primitive art?'. *Cultural Anthropology*, vol. 9, pp. 201–226.

—— (1998) *The Death of Authentic Primitive Art and Other Tales of Progress*. Berkeley: University of California Press.

Evans, G. (2000) 'Contempoprary crafts as souvenirs, artifacts and functional goods and their role in local economic diversification and cultural development'. In M. Hitchcock and K. Teague (eds), *Souvenirs: The Material Culture of Tourism*. Aldershot: Ashgate, pp. 127–147.

Ewing, K.P. (1990) 'The Illusion of Wholeness: Culture, Self and the Experience of Inconsistency'. *Ethos*, vol. 18, pp. 251–278.

Fan Yew Teng (1984) 'Bukit Cina should be preserved as it is. Press conference statement, 19 August 1984'. In Fan Yew Teng, *If we Love this Country...* Kuala Lumpur: Egret Publications, p. 128.

Fernandis, G. (no date) 'Some historical aspects of the Portuguese in Malacca: terms of reference in determining the *bumiputera* status of the Portuguese decedents [sic] of Malacca'. In G. Fernandis (ed.), *Save our Portuguese Heritage Conference 1995*, Melacca, Malaysia. Melaka: privately published.

Forshee, Jill (1999) 'Introduction: converging interests: traders, travelers and tourists in Southeast Asia'. In Jill Forshee, Christina Fink and Sandra Cate (eds), *Converging Interests: Traders, Travelers, and Tourists in Southeast Asia*. Berkeley: University of California, Center for Southeast Asian Studies, Monograph No. 26, pp. 1–19.

—— (2001) *Between the Folds: Stories of Cloth, Lives, and Travels from Sumba*. Honolulu: University of Hawai'i Press.

—— (2002) 'Tracing troubled times: objects of value and narratives of loss from Sumba and Timor Islands'. *Indonesia*, no. 74, pp. 65–77.

Forshee, Jill, Christina Fink and Sandra Cate (eds) (1999) *Converging Interests: Traders, Travelers, and Tourists in Southeast Asia*. Berkeley: University of California, Center for Southeast Asian Studies, Monograph No. 26.

Foucault, M. (1972) *The Archaeology of Knowledge*. London: Routledge.

Fox, James (1987) 'The house as a type of social organization on the island of Roti, Indonesia'. In C. Macdonald and members of IECASE (eds), *De La Hutte au Palais: Societes 'A Maison' en Asie du Sud-Est Insulaire*. Paris: CNRS, pp. 215–224.

—— (ed.) (1993) *Inside Austronesian Houses: Perspectives on Domestic Designs for Living*. Canberra: Comparative Austronesian Project, Research School of Pacific Studies, Australian National University.

Friedman, Jonathan (1994) 'The political economy of elegance: an African cult of beauty'. In Jonathan Friedman (ed.), *Consumption and Identity*. London: Harwood Academic Press, pp. 167–187.

—— (2002) 'From roots to routes: tropes and trippers'. *Anthropological Theory*, vol. 2, no. 1, pp. 21–36.

Gabriel, J. (1994) *Racism, Culture, Markets*. London and New York: Routledge.

Galla, Amareswar (2001) 'Heritage and tourism in sustainable development: Ha Long Bay case study'. *Cultural Heritage, Man and Tourism (Supplement)*, Report of the Asia–Europe Seminar, Hanoi, 5–7 November 2001, Asia–Europe Foundation, pp. 135–146.

—— (2002) 'Culture and heritage in development: Ha Long ecomuseum, a case study from Vietnam'. *Humanities Research*, vol. IX, no. 1, pp. 63–76.

—— (ed) (2002) *Protection of Cultural Heritage in Southeast Asia*. Paris and Canberra: Asia Pacific Organisation of the International Council of Museums.

—— (2005) 'Cultural diversity in ecomuseum development in Vietnam'. *Museum International*, no. 227, vol. 57, no. 1, pp. 101–109.

Garrod, B. And A. Fyall (2000) 'Managing heritage tourism'. *Annals of Tourism Research*, vol. 27, no. 3, pp. 682–708.

Geertz, C. (1963) *Old Societies and New States: The Quest for Modernity in Asia*. Glencoe: Free Press.

Gellner, E. (1983) *Nations and Nationalism*. Ithaca: Cornell University Press.

Glover, Ian C. (2003) 'National and political uses of archaeology in South-East Asia'. In Michael Hitchcock and Victor T. King (eds) *Indonesia and the Malay World*, special issue on 'Tourism and heritage in South-East Asia', vol. 31, pp. 16–30.

Goh Beng Lan (1998) 'Modern dreams: an enquiry into power, cityscape transformation and cultural difference in contemporary Malaysia'. In Joel S. Kahn (ed), *Southeast Asian Identities: Culture and the Politics of Representation in Indonesia, Malaysia, Singapore and Thailand*. Singapore and London: Institute of Southeast Asian Studies, pp. 168–202.

—— (2001) 'Rethinking urbanism in Malaysia: power, space and identity'. In Maznah Mohamad and Wong Soak Koon (eds), *Risking Malaysia: Culture, Politics and Identity*. Bangi: Penerbit Universiti Kebangsaan Malaysia, pp. 159–178.

Goldberg, A. (1983) 'Identity and experience in Haitian voodoo shows'. *Annals of Tourism Research*, vol. 10, pp. 479–495.

Gombay, N. (2005) 'Shifting identities in a shifting world: food, place, community and the politics of scale in an Inuit settlement'. *Environment and Planning D: Society and Space*, vol. 23, pp. 415–433.

Government of the Lao PDR (1999) *Champasak Heritage Management Plan, Parts I, II and III*. Vientiane: Government of the Lao PDR.

Government of Vietnam (1995) *The Constitutions of Vietnam*. Government of Vietnam.

Graburn, Nelson H.H. (ed.) (1976) *Ethnic and Tourist Arts: Cultural Expressions from the Fourth World*. Berkeley: University of California Press.

—— (1982) 'The dynamics of change in tourist arts'. *Cultural Survival Quarterly*, vol. 6, no. 4, pp. 7–11.

—— (1987) 'The evolution of tourist arts'. *Annals of Tourism Research*, vol. 11, no. 3, pp. 393–420.

Gregson, N., U. Kothari, J. Cream, C. Dwyer, S. Holloway and A. Maddrell (1997) *Feminist Geographies: Explorations in Diversity and Difference*. London: Addison Wesley Longman.

Grieco, M. (2000) 'Kente connections: the role of the internet in developing an economic base for Ghana'. In M. Hitchcock and K. Teague (eds), *Souvenirs: The Material Culture of Tourism*. Aldershot: Ashgate, pp. 246–253.

Gunn, C. (1972) *Vacationscape: Designing Tourist Regions*. Austin: University of Texas.

Hamayotsu, K. (1999) 'Reformist Islam, Mahathir and the making of Malaysian nationalism'. Paper presented to the Second International Malaysian Studies Conference, Kuala Lumpur, 2–4 August 1999.

Hall, C. Michael (2001) 'Tourism and political relationships in Southeast Asia'. In Peggy Teo, T.C. Chang and K.C. Ho (eds), *Interconnected Worlds: Tourism in Southeast Asia*. Oxford: Elsevier Science, Pergamon, pp. 13–26.

Hall, C. Michael and John Michael Jenkins (1995) *Tourism and Public Policy*. Routledge: London.

Hamid, H. (2001) 'Toraja village named a world heritage site'. *The Jakarta Post*, 29 April 2001. http://coldfusion.indonesianheritage.com/site-office/newsletter/info.cfm?id=236, downloaded 29 August 2001.

Hampton, M. (1998) 'Backpacker tourism and economic development'. *Annals of Tourism Research*, vol. 25, no. 30, pp. 639–660.

Han Mui Ling (2003) 'From travelogues to guidebooks: imagining colonial Singapore, 1819–1940'. *Sojourn. Journal of Social Issues in Southeast Asia*, vol. 18, pp. 257–278.

Handler, Richard (2000) 'Anthropology of authenticity'. In N.J. Smelser and P.B. Bates (eds), *International Encyclopaedia of the Social and Behavioural Sciences*. Oxford: Pergamon, pp. 963–967.

Harper, T. (1999) *The End of Empire and the Making of Malaya*. Cambridge: Cambridge University Press.

Harrison, David (2001) 'Tourism and less developed countries: key issues'. In David Harrison (ed.), *Tourism and the Less Developed World: Issues and Case Studies*. Wallingford: CAB International.

—— (2004) 'Introduction: contested narratives in the domain of world heritage'. In David Harrison and Michael Hitchcock (eds), *Current Issues in Tourism*, special issue on 'the politics of world heritage: negotiating tourism and conservation', vol. 7, nos. 4–5, pp. 281–290.

Harrison, David and Michael Hitchcock (eds) (2004) *The Politics of World Heritage: Negotiating Tourism and Conservation*. Special issue of Current Issues in Tourism, vol. 7, pp. 281–466, and re-issued in 2005. Clevedon: Channel View Publications.

Harrison, H. (2003) 'Clothing and power on the periphery of empire: the costumes of the indigenous people of Taiwan'. *Positions*, vol. 11, no. 2, pp. 331–360.

Hashim, M.Y. (1992) *The Malay Sultanate of Malacca*. Kuala Lumpur: Dewan Bahasa dan Pustaka.

Hefner, R.W. (1994) 'Reimagined community: a social history of Muslim education in Pasuruan, East Java'. In C.F. Keyes, L. Kendall and H. Hardacre (eds), *Asian Visions of Authority: Religion and the Modern States of East and Southeast Asia*. Honolulu: University of Hawai'i Press, pp. 75–95.

Hein, L. and E.H. Hammond (1995) 'Homing in on Asia: identity in contemporary Japan'. *Bulletin of Concerned Asian Scholars*, vol. 27, no. 3, pp. 3–17.

Henderson, J. (2000) 'War as a tourist attraction: the case of Vietnam'. *International Journal of Tourism Research*, vol. 2, pp. 269–280.

—— (2003) 'Ethnic heritage as a tourist attraction: the Peranakans of Singapore'. *International Journal of Heritage Studies*, vol. 9, pp. 27–44.

Hendry, J. (2000) *The Orient Strikes Back*. Oxford: Berg.

Henocque, Yves and Sanchai Tandavanitj (2006) 'Measuring the progress and outcomes of integrated coastal and ocean management: the CHARM [Coastal Habitats and

Resources Management] Project case study in Southern Thailand'. Report to the Intergovernmental Oceanographic Commission, May 2006.

Herbert, David T. (1989) 'Leisure trends and the heritage market'. In D.T. Herbert, R.C. Prentice and C.J. Thomas (eds), *Heritage Sites: Strategies for Marketing and Development*. Avebury: Ashgate, pp. 12–14.

Herzfeld, Michael (1993) *A Place in History: Social and Monumental Time in a Cretan Town*. Princeton: Princeton University Press.

Hiebert, M. (1995) 'A sea change'. *Far Eastern Economic Review*, vol. 158, no. 32, 10 August 1995, pp. 50–51.

Hill, M. (2000) '"Asian values" as reverse Orientalism: Singapore'. *Asia Pacific Viewpoint*, vol. 41, no. 2, pp. 177–190.

Hines, Ellen, Kanjana Adulyanukosol, Dave Duffus and Philip Dearden (2005) 'Community perspectives and conservation needs for Dugongs (*Dugong dugon*) along the Andaman coast of Thailand'. *Environmental Management*, vol. 36, no. 5, pp. 654–664.

Hirschman, C. (1986) 'The making of race in colonial Malaya: political economy and racial ideology'. *Sociological Forum*, vol. 1, no. 2, pp. 330–316.

—— (1987) 'The meaning and measurement of ethnicity in Malaysia: an analysis of census classifications'. *Journal of Asian Studies*, vol. 46, no. 3, pp. 555–582.

Hitchcock, Michael (1998) 'Tourism, Taman Mini and national identity'. *Indonesia and the Malay World*, vol. 26, no. 74 (June), pp. 124–135.

—— (2000) 'Introduction'. In Michael Hitchcock and Ken Teague (eds), *Souvenirs: The Material Culture of Tourism*. Aldershot: Ashgate, Voices in Development Management Series, pp. 1–17.

—— (2003) 'Taiwan's ambiguous Southeast Asian heritage'. *Indonesia and the Malay World*, vol. 31, no. 89, pp. 69–79.

—— (2004) 'Afterword'. In David Harrison and Michael Hitchcock (eds), *Current Issues in Tourism*, special issue on 'The politics of world heritage: negotiating tourism and conservation', vol. 7, nos. 4 and 5, pp. 461–466.

Hitchcock, Michael and I Nyoman Darma Putra (2007) *Tourism, Development and Terrorism in Bali*. Aldershot: Ashgate.

Hitchcock, Michael and Victor T. King (eds) (2003a) 'Tourism and heritage in South-East Asia', special issue of *Indonesia and the Malay World*, vol. 31, no. 89.

—— (2003b) 'Discourses with the past: tourism and heritage in South-East Asia'. 'Tourism and heritage in South-East Asia', special issue of *Indonesia and the Malay World*, vol. 31, no. 89, pp. 3–15.

—— (2003) 'Concluding remarks'. 'Tourism and heritage in South-East Asia', special issue of *Indonesia and the Malay World*, vol. 31, no. 89, pp. 161–164.

—— (2005) 'Afterword'. In David Harrison and Michael Hitchcock (eds), *The Politics of World Heritage: Negotiating Tourism and Conservation*. Clevedon: Channel View Publications.

Hitchcock, Michael, Victor T. King and Michael J.G. Parnwell (eds) (1993a) *Tourism in South-East Asia.* London: Routledge.

—— (eds) (1993b) 'Tourism in South-East Asia: introduction'. In Michael Hitchcock, Victor T. King and Michael J.G. Parnwell (eds) *Tourism in South-East Asia.* London: Routledge, pp. 1–31.

—— (eds) (2009) *Tourism in South-East Asia: Challenges and New Directions.* Copenhagen: NIAS Press and Honolulu: University of Hawai'i Press.

Hitchcock, Michael, N. Stanley and K.C. Siu (1997) 'The Southeast Asian "living museum" and its antecedents'. In S. Abram, V.L. MacLeod and J. Waldren (eds), *Tourism and Tourists: Identifying with People and Places.* Oxford: Berg, pp. 197–222.

Hitchcock, Michael and Ken Teague (2000) *Souvenirs: The Material Culture of Tourism.* Ashgate: Aldershot and Burlington, USA.

Hobsbawm, E. and T. Ranger (eds) (1983) *The Invention of Tradition.* Cambridge: Cambridge University Press.

Hofheinz, R. and K.E. Calder (1982) *The Eastasia Edge.* New York: Basic Books.

Holdiman, T. (1985) 'Indonesian adventure: rituals and culture in Tanah Toraja'. *Sunset,* (May), pp. 80–81.

Holloway, L. and P. Hubbard (2001) *People and Place: The Extraordinary Geographies of Everyday Life.* Harlow: Prentice Hall.

Holloway S.L., S.P. Rice and G. Valentine (eds) (2003) *Key Concepts in Geography.* London: Sage.

Holtorf, Cornelius (2001) 'Is the past a non-renewable resource?'. In R. Layton, P. Stone and J. Thomas (eds), *Destruction and Conservation of Cultural Property.* London: Routledge, pp. 286–297.

Holtorf, Cornelius and T. Schadla-Hall (1999) 'Age as artefact: on archaeological authenticity'. *European Journal of Archaeology,* vol. 2, pp. 229–247.

Hong, Evelyne (1985) *See the Third World While it Lasts.* Penang: Consumer Association Penang.

Hooker, Virginia M. (2004) 'Reconfiguring Malay and Islam in contemporary Malaysia'. In Timothy P. Barnard (ed.), *Contesting Malayness: Malay Identity Across Boundaries.* Singapore: Singapore University Press, pp. 149–167.

Hsieh Shih-Chung (1994) 'Tourism, formulation of cultural tradition and ethnicity: a study of the Daiyan Identity of the Wulai Atayal'. In S. Harrell and Huang Chun-chieh (eds), *Cultural Change in Postwar Taiwan.* Boulder: Westview Press, pp. 184–201.

Hubbard, P., R. Kitchin, B. Bartley and D. Fuller (eds) (2002) *Thinking Geographically.* London: Continuum.

Hudson, K. (1987) *Museums of Influence.* London: Cambridge University Press.

Hughes, Howard L. (2000) 'The elusive cultural tourist'. In Mike Robinson, Philip Long, Nigel Evans, Richard Sharpley and John Swarbrooke (eds), *Expressions of Culture,*

Identity and Meaning in Tourism. Sunderland: Centre for Travel and Tourism in association with Business Education Publishers Ltd, pp. 111–122.

Hung, H.F. (2003) 'Orientalist knowledge and social theories: China and European conceptions of east–west differences from 1600–1900'. *Sociological Theory*, vol. 21, no. 3, pp. 254–280.

I Nyoman Darma Putra and Michael Hitchcock (2005) 'Pura Besakih: a world heritage site contested'. *Indonesia and the Malay World*, vol. 33, no. 96, pp. 225–237.

ICC (International Co-ordinating Committee for the Safeguarding and Development of Historic Site of Angkor) (2001) *Eleventh Technical Committee.* Phnom Penh: ICC.

—— (2004) *Eleventh Plenary Session.* Phnom Penh: ICC.

Ingold, Tim (2000) *The Perception of the Environment: Essays in Livelihood, Dwelling and Skill.* London: Routledge.

Ishii, Yoneo and Sakurai Yumio (1985) *Formation of South-East Asian World* (in Japanese). Tokyo: Kodansha.

Ishwaran, Natarajan (2004) 'International conservation diplomacy and the World Heritage Convention'. *Journal of International Wildlife Law and Policy*, vol. 7, pp. 43–56.

ITAR–TASS News Agency (2001) 'Putin completes Vietnamese visit'. *ITAR–TASS News Agency*, 2 March 2001.

IUCN (International Union for the Conservation of Nature) (1992) *World Heritage Nomination: IUCN summary: 671 Ha Long Bay.* January 1992.

—— (1994) *World Heritage Renomination – IUCN Technical Evaluation: Ha Long Bay (Vietnam).*

—— (2007) *IUCN Viet Nam Strategic Framework 2007–2010: Finding the Balance in a Changing World.* World Conservation Union, Viet Nam Country Office.

Jacobsen, J.K.S. (2000) 'Anti-tourist attitudes: Mediterranean charter tourism'. *Annals of Tourism Research*, vol. 27, no. 2, pp. 284–300.

Jacques, Claude and Michael Freeman (1997) *Angkor: Cities and Temples.* London: Thames and Hudson.

Jahoda, G. (1999) *Images of Savages: Ancient Roots of Modern Prejudice in Western Culture.* London and New York: Routledge.

Jamieson, Neil (1993) *Understanding Vietnam.* Berkeley: University of California Press.

Japan Economic Newswire (1993) 'Vietnam's "Hanoi Hilton" jail to make way for hotel'. *Japan Economic Newswire*, 9 November 1993.

—— (1994) '"Hanoi Hilton" readied for Demolition'. *Japan Economic Newswire*, 29 November 1994.

—— (2000) 'Vietnamese, US media at war over Clinton's protocol'. *Japan Economic Newswire*, 7 October 2000.

Jenkins, C.L. (1997) 'Impacts of the development of international tourism in the Asian region'. In F.M. Go and C.L. Jenkins (eds), *Tourism and Economic Development in Asia and Australasia*. London: Cassell, pp. 48–64.

Jenkins, Gwynn (1999) 'Social and Physical Survey on Muntri Street and Love Lane, George Town'. Unpublished report for the Control of Rent Repeal Sub-committee, Penang.

Jenkins, Gwynn and Victor T. King (2003) 'Heritage and development in a Malaysian city: George Town under threat'. In Michael Hitchcock and Victor T. King (eds) *Indonesia and the Malay World*, special issue 'Tourism and heritage in South-East Asia', vol. 31, pp. 44–57.

Jeyifo, B. (2000) 'On Mazrui's "Black Orientalism": a cautionary critique'. *Black Scholar*, vol. 30, no. 1, pp. 19–22.

Jha, Sachida (2005) 'Can natural world heritage sites promote development and social harmony?'. *Biodiversity and Conservation*, vol. 14, pp. 981–991.

Johns, A.H. (1979) 'The turning image: myth and reality in Malay perceptions of the past'. In A. Reid and D. Marr (eds), *Perceptions of the Past in Southeast Asia*. Singapore: Heinemann Educational, pp. 43–67.

Johnson, Mark (2001) 'Renovating Hue (Vietnam): authenticating destruction, reconstructing authenticity'. In R. Layton, P. Stone and J. Thomas (eds), *Destruction and Conservation of Cultural Property*. London: Routledge, pp. 75–92.

Johnson, N. (1995) 'Cast in stone: monuments, geography and nationalism'. *Environment and Planning D: Society and Space*, vol. 31, no. 1, pp. 51–65.

Jomo, K.S. and A. Cheek (1992) 'Malaysia's Islamic movements'. In J. Kahn and F. Loh Kok Wah (eds), *Fragmented Vision: Culture and Politics in Contemporary Malaysia*. Honolulu: University of Hawai'i Press, pp. 79–106.

Josselin de Jong, P.E. de (1965) 'The rise and decline of a national hero'. *Journal of the Malaysian Branch of the Royal Asiatic Society*, vol. 38, no. 2, pp. 140–155.

Kadir H. Din (1997) 'Tourism and cultural development in Malaysia: issues for a new agenda'. In Shinhi Yamashita, Kadir H. Din and J.S. Eades (eds), *Tourism and Cultural Development in East Asia and Oceania*. Bangi: Penerbit UKM Malaysia, pp. 104–118.

Kagami, Haruya (2000) *Seisakubunka no Jinruigaku: Semegiau Indoneshia Kokka to Bali Chiiki Jumin* (in Japanese) *(Anthropology of Policy Culture: Indonesian State and Balinese in Competition)*. Kyoto: Sekaishisosha.

Kahani-Hopkins, V. and N. Hopkins (2002) '"Representing" British muslims: the strategic dimension to identity construction'. *Ethnic and Racial Studies*, vol. 25, no. 2, pp. 288–309.

Kahn, H. and T. Pepper (1979) *The Japanese Challenge*. New York: Thomas Y. Crowell.

Kahn, Joel S. (1992) 'Class, ethnicity and diversity: some remarks on Malay culture in Malaysia'. In J.S. Kahn and F. Loh Kok Wah (eds), *Fragmented Vision: Culture and Politics in Contemporary Malaysia*. Honolulu: University of Hawai'i Press, pp. 158–178.

—— (1997) 'Culturalizing Malaysia: globalism, tourism, heritage, and the city in Georgetown'. In Michel Picard and Robert E. Wood (eds), *Tourism, Ethnicity and the State in Asian and Pacific Societies*. Honolulu: University of Hawai'i Press, pp. 99–127.

Heritage Tourism in Southeast Asia

—— (1998) 'Southeast Asian identities: introduction'. In Joel S. Kahn (ed.), *Southeast Asian Identities: Culture and the Politics of Representation in Indonesia, Malaysia, Singapore, and Thailand.* Singapore and London: Institute of Southeast Asian Studies, pp. 1–27.

Kalakota, Ravi and Whinstone, Andrew, B. (1997) *Electronic Commerce: A Manager's Guide.* Reading, Mass.: Addison-Wesley.

Keesing, Roger (1989) 'Creating the past: custom and identity in the contemporary Pacific'. *The Contemporary Pacific,* vol. 1, nos. 1–2, pp. 16–35.

Kennedy, Laurel and Mary Williams (2001) 'The past without the pain'. In Hue-Tam Ho Tai (ed.), *The Country of Memory: Remaking the Past in Late Socialist Vietnam.* Berkeley: University of California Press, pp. 135–163.

Khoo Kay Kim (1979) 'Recent Malay historiography'. *Journal of Southeast Asian Studies,* vol. 10, no. 2, pp. 247–261.

Khoo Salma and Gwynn Jenkins (2002) 'George Town Pulau Pinang Malaysia: development strategies and community realities'. In William S. Logan (ed.), *The Disappearing 'Asian' City: Protecting Asia's Urban Heritage in a Globalizing World.* New York: Oxford University Press, pp. 208–228.

Khuon, Khun-Neay (2005) 'Angkor: a living world heritage site'. Power-point presented at the ICCROM/SPAFA workshop on 'living heritage: empowering community'. Phrae, Thailand, 21–25 November 2005.

Kim, S. (1997) 'Prospects for the Vietnam tourism industry'. *Proceedings of the International Conference on Sustainable Tourism Development in Vietnam,* Hue 1997, pp. 311–327.

King, Victor T. (1993) 'Tourism and culture in Malaysia'. In Michael Hitchcock, Victor T. King and Michael J.G. Parnwell (eds), *Tourism in South-East Asia.* London: Routledge, pp. 99–116.

Kingdom of Cambodia (1999) *Declaration No. 281/99 Sor. Chor* (list of bans on the practices of local villagers). Kingdom of Cambodia, Ministry of Interior, General Department of the National Police, Special Commissary for Heritage Protection.

Kis-Jovak, J., H. Nooy-Palm, R. Scheefold and U. Schultz-Dornburg (1988) *Banua Toraja: Changing Patterns in Architecture and Symbolism among the Sa'dan Toraja, Sulawesi, Indonesia.* Amsterdam: Royal Tropical Institute.

Klein, Naomi (2000) *No Logo.* London: Flamingo.

Kling, Zainal (1997) *'Adat:* collective self-image'. In Michael Hitchcock and Victor T. King (eds), *Images of Malay-Indonesian Identity.* Kuala Lumpur: Oxford University Press, pp. 45–52.

Kokko, A. (1998) 'Vietnam: ready for Doi Moi II?'. Stockholm School of Economics: SSE/EFI Working Paper Series in Economics and Finance, No. 286.

Konstadakopulos, Dimitrios (2008) 'Environmental and resource degradation associated with small-scale enterprise clusters in the Red River Delta of northern Vietnam'. *Geographical Research,* vol. 46, no. 1, pp. 51–61.

Kontogeorgopoulos, Nick (2004a) 'Ecotourism and mass tourism in south Thailand: spatial interdependence, structural connections and staged authenticity'. *GeoJournal,* vol. 61, pp. 1–11.

—— (2004b) 'Conventional tourism and ecotourism in Phuket, Thailand: conflicting paradigms or symbiotic partners?'. *Journal of Ecotourism*, vol. 3, no. 2, pp. 87–108.

—— (2005) 'Community-based ecotourism in Phuket and Ao Phangnga, Thailand: partial victories and bittersweet remedies'. *Journal of Sustainable Tourism*, vol. 13, no. 1, pp. 4–23.

Korea Times (1998) 'Kim to pay tribute to Ho Chi Minh's mausoleum'. *Korea Times*, 15 December 1998.

Kua Kia Soong (1984) 'Bukit Cina belongs to the people'. *The Star*, 22 December 1984 [reprinted in Kua Kia Soong (1990) *Malaysian Political Myths*. Kuala Lumpur: Selangor Chinese Assembly Hall, p. 129].

Kuijper, Maarten W.M. (2003) 'Marine and coastal environmental awareness building within the context of UNESCO's activities in Asia and the Pacific'. *Marine Pollution Bulletin*, vol. 47, pp. 265–272.

Kumar, K. (1992) 'The 1989 revolutions and the idea of Europe'. *Political Studies*, vol. XL, pp. 439–461.

Lacan, Jacques (1977) *Écrits: A Selection* (translated by Alan Sheridan). London: Tavistock.

Lake, E. (2001) 'Letter from Vietnam: the Hanoi Hilton'. *United Press International*, 27 July.

Lam, P.E. and K.Y.L. Tan (eds) (1999) *Lee's Lieutenants: Singapore's Old Guard*. St. Leonard's, NSW: Allen and Unwin.

Lander, M. (2000) 'McCain, in Vietnam, finds the past isn't really past'. *The New York Times*, 27 April.

Laporte, Michel (1950) *Les 7 Merveilles du monde*. Paris: Flammarion.

Lask, Tomke and Stefan Herold (2004) 'An observation station for culture and tourism in Vietnam: a forum for world heritage and public participation'. In David Harrison and Michael Hitchcock (eds), *Current Issues in Tourism*, special issue on 'The Politics of World Heritage: Negotiating Tourism and Conservation', vol. 7, pp. 399–411.

Leal, Pablo Alejandro (2007) 'Participation: the ascendency of a buzzword in the neo-liberal era'. *Development in Practice*, vol. 17, no. 4, pp. 539–548.

Lee Weng Choy (2001) 'Mcnationalism in Singapore'. In Yao Souchou (ed.), *House of Glass: Culture, Modernity, and the State in Southeast Asia*. Singapore: Institute of Southeast Asian Studies, pp. 95–116.

Leong, W.T. (1997) 'Commodifying ethnicity: state and ethnic tourism in Singapore'. In M. Picard and R.E. Wood (eds), *Tourism, Ethnicity and the State in Asian and Pacific Societies*. Honolulu: University of Hawai'i Press, pp. 71–98.

Lévi-Strauss, Claude (1983) *The Way of the Masks*. London: Jonathan Cape.

—— (1987) *Anthropology and Myth: Lectures 1951–1982*. Oxford: Blackwell.

Lewis, D. (1995) *Jan Compagnie in the Straits of Malacca, 1641–1795*. Athens, Ohio: Ohio University Center for International Studies, Southeast Asia Monograph Series, 96.

Lewis, R. (1996) *Gendering Orientalism: Race, Femininity and Representation*. London: Routledge.

Liao, Hsin-Tien (2002) *Colonialism, Post-colonialism and Local Identity in Colonial Taiwanese Landscape Painting (1908–1945)*. Unpublished Ph.D. thesis, University of Central England.

Lin, A.C.J. and J.F. Keating (eds) (2005) *Island in the Stream: A Quick Case Study of Taiwan's Complex History*. Taipei: SMC Publishing Inc.

Linnekin, Jocelyn (1990) 'The politics of culture in the Pacific'. In J. Linnekin and L. Poyer (ed.), *Cultural Identity and Ethnicity in the Pacific*. Honolulu: University of Hawai'i Press, pp. 149–173.

—— (1991) 'Cultural invention and the dilemma of authenticity'. *American Anthropologist*, vol. 93, pp. 446–449.

Littrell, M.A. (1990), 'Symbolic significance of textile crafts for tourists'. *Annals of Tourism Research*, vol. 12, pp. 228–245.

Littrell, M.A., L.F. Anderson and P.J. Brown (1993) 'What makes a craft souvenir authentic?'. *Annals of Tourism Research*, vol. 12, pp. 228–245.

Logan, William (1995) 'Heritage planning in post-Doi Moi Hanoi: the national and international contributions'. *Journal of the American Planning Association*, vol. 61, pp. 328–343.

—— (1996) 'Protecting historical Hanoi in a context of heritage contestation'. *International Journal of Heritage Studies*, vol. 2, pp. 76–92.

—— (1998a) 'Hanoi after the bombs: post-war reconstruction of a Vietnamese city'. In S. Barakat, J. Calame and E. Charlesworth (eds), *Urban Triumph or Urban Disaster? Dilemmas of Contemporary Post-War Reconstruction*. York: University of York Press, pp. 23–37.

—— (1998b) 'Sustainable culture heritage tourism in Vietnam cities: the case of Hanoi'. *The Journal of Viet Nam Studies*, vol. 1, pp. 32–40.

—— (2002) 'Introduction'. In William S. Logan (ed.), *The Disappearing 'Asian' City: Protecting Asia's Urban Heritage in a Globalizing World*. New York: Oxford University Press, pp. xii–xxi.

—— (2005) 'Hoa Lo: a Vietnamese approach to conserving places of pain and injustice'. In N. Garnham and K. Jeffery (eds), *Culture, Place and Identity*, Dublin: University College Press, pp. 152–160.

Long, Colin (2002) 'A history of urban planning policy and heritage protection in Vientiane, Laos'. *International Development Planning Review*, vol. 22, pp. 127–144.

—— (2003) 'Feudalism in the service of the revolution: reclaiming heritage in Hue'. *Critical Asian Studies*, vol. 35, no. 4, pp. 535–558.

Long, Colin and Jonathan Sweet (2006) 'Globalization, nationalism and world heritage: interpreting Luang Prabang'. *Southeast Asia Research*, vol. 14, pp. 445–469.

Lowenthal, David (2005) 'Natural and cultural heritage'. *International Journal of Heritage Studies*, vol. 11, no. 1, pp. 81–92.

Luong, Hy V. (ed.) (2003) *Postwar Vietnam: Dynamics of a Transforming Society*. Singapore: Institute of Southeast Asian Studies.

MacCannell, Dean (1976) *The Tourist: A New Theory of the Leisure Class*. New York: Schocken.

—— (1992) *Empty Meeting Grounds: The Tourist Papers*. London: Routledge.

—— (2001) 'Tourist agency'. *Tourist Studies*, vol. 1, no. 1, pp. 23–37.

Malaysia Mining Corporation Berhad (1992) *Melaka: The Historic City of Malaysia*. Kuala Lumpur: Malaysia Mining Corporation Berhad.

Mann, Susan (1997) 'The history of Chinese women before the age of orientalism'. *Journal of Women's History*, vol. 8, no. 4, pp. 163–176.

Manthorpe, J. (2005) *Forbidden Nation: The history of Taiwan*. New York: Palgrave Macmillan.

Marcus, George E. and Fred R. Myers (eds) (1995) *The Traffic in Culture: Refiguring Art and Anthropology*. Berkeley: University of California Press.

Martinez, D. (1996) 'The tourist as deity: ancient continuities in modern Japan'. In T. Selwyn (ed.), *The Tourist Image: Myths and Myth Making in Tourism*. Chichester: Wiley, pp. 163–178.

Mathews, H.G. (1975) 'International tourism and political science research'. *Annals of Tourism Research*, vol. 2, no. 4, pp. 195–203.

Mazrui, A.A. (2000) 'Black orientalism? further reflections on "Wonders of the African World"'. *Black Scholar*, vol. 30, no. 1, pp. 15–18.

McIntosh, R.W., C.R. Goeldner and J.R.B. Ritchie (1995) *Tourism: Principles, Practices, Philosophies*. New York: Wiley (seventh edition).

McLean, F. and S. Cooke (2003) 'Constructing the identity of a nation: the tourist gaze at the Museum of Scotland'. *Tourism, Culture and Communication*, vol. 4, pp. 153–162.

Mearns, D.J. (1995) *Shiva's Other Children: Religion and Social Identity amongst Overseas Indians*. New Delhi: Sage.

Meethan, Kevin (2000) 'Tourism: towards a global cultural economy?'. In Mike Robinson, Philip Long, Nigel Evans, Richard Sharpley and John Swarbrooke (eds), *Expressions of Culture, Identity and Meaning in Tourism*. Sunderland: Centre for Travel and Tourism in association with Business Education Publishers Ltd., pp. 195–213.

Melaka Highlights (1997) 'A developed state by 2010'. *Melaka Highlights*, vol. 13, January-April 1997.

Michaud, Jean (1995) 'Questions about fieldwork methodology'. *Annals of Tourism Research*, vol. 22, pp. 681–687.

Michaud, Jean and Michel Picard (eds) (2001) *Tourisme et Sociétés Locales en Asie Orientale, Anthropologie et Sociétés*. Quebec: Université Laval, special issue 25.

Milne, Robert C. (2005) 'World heritage and World Parks Congress perspectives, 1962–2003'. In United Nations Foundation, *World Heritage Reports 16*. World Heritage at the Vth IUCN World Parks Congress, Durban, 8–17 September 2003, Washington: United Nations Foundation, pp. 15–22.

Milner, Anthony (1982) *Kerajaan: Malay Political Culture on the Eve of Colonial Rule.* Tucson: University of Arizona Press.

—— (1994) *The Invention of Politics in Colonial Malaya.* Cambridge: Cambridge University Press.

—— (2004) 'Afterword: a history of Malay ethnicity'. In Timothy P. Barnard (ed.), *Contesting Malayness: Malay Identity Across Boundaries.* Singapore: Singapore University Press, 241–257.

Moon, O. (1997) 'Tourism and cultural development: Japanese and Korean contexts'. In S. Yamashita, Kadir H. Din and J.S. Eades (eds), *Tourism and Cultural Development in Asia and Oceania.* Bangi: Penerbit Universiti Kebangsaan Malaysia, pp. 178–193.

Morgan, N. and A. Pritchard (1998) *Tourism Promotion and Power: Creating Images, Creating Identities.* New York: John Wiley and Sons.

Morrell, Elizabeth (2000) 'Ethnicity, art, and politics away from the Indonesian centre'. *Sojourn. Journal of Social Issues in Southeast Asia,* vol. 15, pp. 255–272.

MPPP (1987) *Draft Design Guidelines for Conservation Areas in the Inner City Area of George Town.* Penang: MPPP, No. 3A/87, URS.

Munsterhjelm, M. (2002) 'The first nations of Taiwan: a special report on Taiwan's indigenous peoples'. *Cultural Survival Quarterly,* Summer, pp. 53–55.

Nasution, K.S. (1997) 'The soul of cities'. *Far Eastern Economic Review,* 21 August 1997, p. 30.

—— (1998) 'The challenge of living in heritage cities in Asia'. *Urban Age,* August 1998.

Nederveen Pieterse, Jan (1993) 'Globalization as hybridization'. Working Paper No. 152, The Hague: Institute of Social Studies.

—— (2003) *Globalization and Culture: Global Mélange.* Lanham Md.: Rowman and Littlefield.

Ness, Sally Ann (2003) *Where Asia Smiles: An Ethnography of Philippine Tourism.* Philadelphia: University of Pennsylvania Press.

Newby, P.T. (1994) 'Tourism: support or threat to heritage?'. In G. Ashworth and P. Larkham (eds), *Building a New Heritage: Tourism, Culture and Identity in the New Europe.* London: Routledge, pp. 206–228.

Newman, A. and F. McLean (2004) 'Presumption, policy and practice: the use of museums and galleries as agents of social inclusion in Great Britain'. *International Journal of Cultural Policy,* vol. 10, no. 2, pp. 167–181.

Ngoc Anh (2000) 'Thousand to be cleared out of City Old Quarter'. *The Vietnam Investment Review,* 28 August.

Nguyen Dinh Duong, Eddy Nierynck, Tran Van Y and Luc Hens (no date) 'Land use changes and GIS-database development for strategic environmental assessment in Ha Long Bay, Quang Ninh Province, Vietnam (www.vub.ac.be/MEKO/Vietnam/EU/Duong1.html).

Nguyen Van Tuan (2001) 'Management of the Karst Area of Ha Long Bay World Heritage Site, Viet Nam'. Proceedings of the Asia–Pacific Forum on Karst Ecosystems and World

Heritage, Gunung Mulu National Park World Heritage Area, Sarawak, Malaysia, 26–30 May 2001, pp. 51–54.

Nguyen, Phuong An (2003) *Between 'Still Society' and 'Moving Society': Life Choices and Value Orientations of Hanoi University Graduates in Post-Reform Vietnam.* Unpublished Ph.D. Thesis, University of Hull.

—— (2005) 'Youth and the state in contemporary Vietnam'. Working Paper Series in Contemporary Asian Studies, Lund University.

Nickerson-Tietze, Donna J. (2000) 'Community-based management for sustainable fisheries resources in Phang-Nga Bay, Thailand'. *Coastal Management*, vol. 28, pp. 65–74.

Ninh, Kim N.B. (2002) *A World Transformed: The Politics of Culture in Revolutionary Vietnam, 1945–65.* Ann Arbor: University of Michigan Press.

Nishimura, Masao (2003) 'Cultural heritage studies and a trial of enhancing (local cultures) in Wat Phou area, Laos'. *Collection of Reports II of Research Center for Enhancing Local Cultures in Asia, Year 2003* (in Japanese). Tokyo: Research Center for Enhancing Local Cultures in Asia, Waseda University, pp. 104–112.

—— (2004a) 'Representing "Vat Phou": an ethnographic account of the nomination process of Vat Phou and adjunct archaeological sites to the world heritage list'. *Waseda Daigaku Daigakuin Bungaku Kenkyuka Kiyo*, vol. 3, no. 40, pp. 49–63.

—— (2004b) 'The purpose and the theoretical background of the anthropological studies in Vat Phou area'. *Waseda University School of Letters, Arts and Sciences' Annual Journal of Cultural Anthropology* (in Japanese), vol. 1, pp. 5–13.

—— (2004c) 'Cultural landscape and memory'. *Waseda University School of Letters, Arts and Sciences' Annual Journal of Cultural Anthropology* (in Japanese), vol. 1, pp. 21–30.

—— (2004d) 'Contested views on the world heritage management. A case study of the Champasak world heritage, Lao PDR'. Power Point presentation at the 10th International Conference of the European Association of Southeast Asian Archaeologists (EurASEAA), London, 14–17 September 2004.

—— (2005) 'The impact of world heritage nomination on local communities, and possible strategy for the use of local knowledge and technology'. Power Point presentation at the international conference on 'Cross-Cultural Perspectives on Museums and Communities', Bangkok, 29 September 2005.

Nittharatana Paphavasit, Cherdchinda Chotiyaputta and Siriwan Siriboon (2007) 'Pre- and post-tsunami coastal planning and land-use policies and issues in Thailand'. FAO, Regional Office for Asia and the Pacific, Proceedings of the Workshop on 'Coastal Area Planning and Management in Asian Tsunami Affected Countries', Bangkok, 27–29 September 2006.

Nooy-Palm, C.H.M. (1979) *The Sa'dan Toraja: A Study of their Social Life and Religion, Volume 1.* The Hague: Martinus Nijhoff.

—— (1986) *The Sa'dan Toraja: A Study of their Social Life and Religion, Volume 2: Rituals of the East and West.* Dordrecht, Holland and Cinnaminson, USA: Foris.

Oakes, Tim (1999) 'Bathing in the far village: globalization, transnational capital, and the cultural politics of modernity in China'. *Positions: East Asia Cultures Critique*, vol. 7, no. 2, pp. 307–342.

O'Doherty, B. (1986) *Inside the White Cube*. Los Angeles: University of California Press.

Okamura, K. and Y. Zhang (1968) *Taiwan's Savage Clothes 1*. Taipei: Yushudou.

Olwig, Kenneth R. (2005) 'Introduction: the nature of cultural heritage, and the culture of natural heritage – northern perspectives on a contested patrimony'. *International Journal of Heritage Studies*, vol. 11, no. 1, pp. 3–7.

Omar, A. (1993) *Bangsa Malayu: Malay Concepts of Democracy and Community, 1945–1950*. Kuala Lumpur: Oxford University Press.

Ooi Can-Seng (2002a) 'Contrasting Strategies – Tourism in Denmark and Singapore', *Annals of Tourism Research* 29(3): 689–706.

—— (2002b) *Cultural Tourism and Tourism Cultures: The Business of Mediating Experiences in Copenhagen and Singapore*. Copenhagen: Copenhagen Business School Press.

—— (2003) 'Identities, museums and tourism in Singapore: think regionally, act locally'. *Indonesia and the Malay World*, vol. 31, no. 89, pp. 81–90.

—— (2004) 'Brand Singapore: the hub of new Asia'. In N. Morgan, A. Pritchard and R. Pride (eds), *Destination Branding: Creating the Unique Destination Proposition*. London: Elsevier Butterworth Heinemann, pp. 242–262.

—— (2005) 'State-civil society relations and tourism: Singaporeanizing tourists, tourist-ifying Singapore'. *SOJOURN: Journal of Social Issues in Southeast Asia*, vol. 20, no. 2, pp. 249–272.

Ooi Can-Seng, T.P. Kristensen and Z.L.Pedersen (2004) 'Re-imag(in)ing place: from Czechoslovakia to the Czech Republic and Slovakia'. *Tourism*, vol. 52, no. 2, pp. 151–163.

Palar, Job (2006) 'Toraja mamali, kurre sumanga [longing for Toraja, thank you]'. http://jobpalar.multiply.com/journal/item/5, (Accessed 1 March 2008).

Palmer, Catherine (1999) 'Tourism and the symbols of identity'. *Tourism Management*, vol. 20, no. 3, pp. 313–321.

Panitia Mangrara (1990) *Upacara Rambu Tuka' Mangrara Tongkonan Layuk Ke'te' Kesu'*. Unpublished paper.

Papayannis, Thymio and Peter Howard (2007) 'Editorial: nature as heritage'. *International Journal of Heritage Studies*, vol. 13, nos. 4–5, 298–307.

Parnwell, Michael J.G. (2009) 'A political ecology of sustainable tourism in Southeast Asia'. In Michael Hitchcock, Victor T. King and Michael J.G. Parnwell (eds) (2009), *Tourism in Southeast Asia: Challenges and New Directions*. Copenhagen: NIAS Press and Honolulu: University of Hawai'i Press, pp. 236–253.

Pedersen, Art (2005) 'World heritage and tourism'. In United Nations Foundation, *World Heritage Reports 16*. World Heritage at the Vth IUCN World Parks Congress, Durban, 8–17 September 2003, Washington: United Nations Foundation, pp. 60–64.

Peleggi, M. (1996) 'National heritage and global tourism in Thailand'. *Annals of Tourism Research*, vol. 23, no. 2, pp. 432–448.

Pemberton, John (1994) *On the Subject of 'Java'*. Ithaca: Cornell University Press.

Penang Development Corporation (1989) *Looking Back, Looking Ahead: 20 years of Progress*. Penang: Penang Development Corporation.

Pereira, A. (1997) 'The revitalization of Eurasian identity in Singapore'. *Southeast Asian Journal of Social Science*, vol. 25, no. 2, pp. 7–24.

Perkins, Harvey and David Thorns (2001) 'Gazing or performing: reflections on Urry's tourist gaze in the context of contemporary experience in the Antipodes'. *International Sociology*, vol. 16, no. 2, pp. 185–204.

Phillips, Ruth and Christopher B. Steiner (1999) *Unpacking Culture: Art and Commodity in Colonial and Postcolonial Worlds*. Berkeley: University of California Press.

Philo, C. and G. Kearns (1993) 'Culture, history, capital: a critical introduction to the selling of places'. In G. Kearns and C. Philo (eds), *Selling Places: The City as Cultural Capital, Past and Present*. Oxford: Pergamon Press, pp. 1–32.

Picard, Michel (1995) 'Cultural heritage and tourist capital: cultural tourism in Bali'. In M.F. Lanfant, J.B. Allcock and E.M. Brunner (eds), *International Tourism: Identity and Change*. London: Sage, pp. 44–66.

—— (1996) *Bali: Cultural Tourism and Touristic Culture* (translated by Diana Darling). Singapore: Archipelago Press.

—— (1997) 'Cultural tourism, nation-building and regional culture: the making of a Balinese identity'. In Michel Picard and Robert E. Wood (eds), *Tourism, Ethnicity, and the State in Asian and Pacific Societies*. Honolulu: University of Hawai'i Press, pp. 181–214.

—— (2003) 'Touristification and Balinization in a time of *reformasi*'. In Michael Hitchcock and Victor T. King (eds), *Indonesia and the Malay World*, special issue on 'Tourism and Heritage in South-East Asia', vol. 31, pp. 108–118.

Picard, Michel and Robert E. Wood (eds) (1997a) *Tourism, Ethnicity, and the State in Asian and Pacific Societies*. Honolulu: University of Hawai'i Press.

—— (1997b) 'Preface'. In Michel Picard and Robert E. Wood (eds), *Tourism, Ethnicity, and the State in Asian and Pacific Societies*. Honolulu: University of Hawai'i Press, pp. vii–xi.

Pillay, C. (1977) 'Some dominant concepts and dissenting ideas on Malay rule and Malay society from the Malacca to the colonial and Merdeka periods'. Unpublished Ph.D. thesis, Department of Malay Studies, National University of Singapore.

Popelka, C.A. and M.A. Littrell (1991) 'Influence of tourism on handicraft evolution'. *Annals of Tourism Research*, vol. 18, no. 3, pp. 392–413.

Poria, Y., R.W. Butler and D. Airey (2003) 'The core of heritage tourism: distinguishing heritage tourists from tourists in heritage places'. *Annals of Tourism Research*, vol. 30, no. 1, pp. 238–254.

—— (2004) 'Links between tourists, heritage and reasons for visiting heritage sites'. *Journal of Travel Research*, vol. 43, no. 1, pp. 19–28.

Porter, Benjamin W. and Noel S. Salazaar (2005) 'Heritage tourism, conflict and the public interest: an introduction'. *International Journal of Heritage Studies*, vol. 11, no. 5, pp. 361–370.

Pottier, Johan (2003) 'Negotiating local knowledge'. In Johan Pottier, Alan Bickers and Paul Sillitoe (eds), *Negotiating Local Knowledge: Power and Identity in Development*. London and Sterling, Va.: Pluto Press.

Praicharnjit, Sayan (2005) 'Community archaeology: participative action research and community development program toward an enhancement of the ability of local communities on cultural resource management, pilot practice in Thailand'. Paper presented at the ICCROM/SPAFA workshop on 'Living Heritage: Empowering Community', Phrae, Thailand, 21–25 November 2005.

Prasch, T.J. (1996) 'Orientalism's other, other orientalisms: women in the scheme of empire'. *Journal of Women's History*, vol. 7, no. 4, pp. 174–188.

Prentice, R. (2004) 'Tourist familiarity and imagery'. *Annals of Tourism Research*, vol. 31, no. 4, pp. 923–945.

Prentice, R. and V. Andersen (2000) 'Evoking Ireland: modeling tourism propensity'. *Annals of Tourism Research*, vol. 27, no. 2, pp. 490–516.

Pressouyre, Léon/UNESCO (1996) *The World Heritage Convention, Twenty Years Later.* Paris: UNESCO.

Pretes, M. (2003) 'Tourism and nationalism'. *Annals of Tourism Research*, vol. 30, no.1, pp. 125–142.

Pritchard, A. and N. Morgan (2000) 'Constructing tourism landscapes: gender, sexuality and space'. *Tourism Geographies*, vol. 2, no. 2, pp. 115–139.

Rahil Ismail, Ooi Giok Ling and Brian J. Shaw (2006) 'Heritage, politics and identity in Southeast Asia: an introduction'. *Geojournal*, vol. 66, pp. 161–163.

Rapoport, Amos (1984) 'Culture and urban order'. In John Agnew, John Mercer and David Sopher (eds), *The City in Cultural Context*. Boston: Allen and Unwin, pp. 50–75.

Raz, Aviad E. (1999) *Riding the Black Ship: Japan and Tokyo Disneyland*. Cambridge, Mass.: Harvard University Asia Center.

Reef-World (no date) 'Reef monitoring, Koh Yao Noi (Phang Nga)' (www.reef-world.org/past_projects/pp_10.htm).

Reid, Anthony (1979) 'The nationalist quest for an Indonesian past'. In Anthony Reid and D. Marr (eds), *Perceptions of the Past in Southeast Asia*. Singapore: Heinemann Educational, pp. 281–298.

—— (1988) *Southeast Asia in the Age of Commerce 1450–1680. Volume One: The Lands Below the Winds.* New Haven: Yale University Press.

—— (1993) 'Introduction: a time and a place'. In Anthony Reid (ed.), *Southeast Asia in the Early Modern Era: Trade, Power and Belief.* Ithaca: Cornell University Press, pp. 1–19.

—— (1994) 'Early Southeast Asian categorization of Europeans'. In Stuart B. Schwartz (ed.), *Implicit Understandings: Observing, Reporting, and Reflecting on the Encounter between Europeans and Other Peoples in the Early Modern Era*. Cambridge: Cambridge University Press, pp. 268–294.

—— (2001) 'Understanding Melayu (Malay) as a source of diverse modern identities'. *Journal of Southeast Asian Studies*, vol. 32, no. 3, pp. 295–313.

Rex, J. (1986) *Race and Ethnicity*. Milton Keynes: Open University Press.

Reyes, Giovanni B. (2005) 'Ifugao rice terraces: a delicate world heritage site [unofficial translation from Japanese]'. *Japanese Original Landscapes – Rice Terraces (Journal of Japanese Rice Terrace Association)*, vol. 6, pp. 48–50.

Richter, Linda K. (1989) *The Politics of Tourism in Asia*. Honolulu: University of Hawai'i Press.

—— (1996) 'The Philippines: the politicization of tourism'. In Yiorgos Apostolopoulos, Stella Leivadi and Andrew Yiannakis (eds), *The Sociology of Tourism: Theoretical and Empirical Investigations*. London and New York: Routledge, pp. 233–262.

—— (1999) 'The politics of heritage tourism development: emerging issues for the new millennium'. In Douglas G. Pearce and Richard W. Butler (eds), *Contemporary Issues in Tourism Development*. London and New York in association with the International Academy for the Study of Tourism: Routledge, pp. 108–126.

Robertson, Roland (1994) *Globalization: Social Theory and Global Culture*, 3rd edition. London: Sage.

—— (1995) 'Glocalization: time-space and homogeneity-heterogeneity'. In Mike Featherstone, Scott M. Lash and Roland Robertson (eds), *Global Modernities*. London: Sage Publications, pp. 25–44.

Rojek, Chris and John Urry (eds) (1997) *Touring Cultures: Transformations of Travel and Theory*. London: Routledge.

Rooney, Dawn F. (1994) *Angkor: An Introduction to the Temples*. Hong Kong: The Guidebook Company.

Ruangrai Tokrisna, Pongpat Boonchuwong and Penporn Janekarnkij (1997) 'A review on fisheries and coastal community-based management regime in Thailand'. Working Paper 32, International Center for Living Aquatic Resources Management, Manila (www.co-management.org/download.pongpat.pdf).

Rudolph, J. (1998) *Reconstructing Identities: A Social History of the Babas in Singapore*. Aldershot: Ashgate.

Sabapathy, T.K. (1996) *Modernity and Beyond: Themes in Southeast Asia*. Singapore: National Heritage Board.

Said, Edward (1979) *Orientalism*. New York: Vintage Books.

—— (1987) *Orientalism*. Harmondsworth: Penguin Books Ltd.

—— (1993) *Culture and Imperialism*. New York: Alfred Knopf.

Said, M.I. (1996) 'Malay nationalism and national identity'. In M.I. Said and Z. Emby (eds), *Malaysia: Critical Perspectives*, Petaling Jaya: Persatuan Sains Sosial Malaysia, pp. 34–73.

Sangeetha A. (2001) *'Draw up guidelines to develop heritage sites'. The Sun*, Malaysia: Northern Edition, 12 March 2001.

Sarkissian, Margaret (1993) 'Music, identity and the impact of tourism in the Portuguese settlement, Melaka'. Unpublished Ph.D. thesis, University of Illinois at Urbana-Champaign.

—— (1995–1996) '"Sinhalese Girl" meets "Aunty Annie": competing expressions of ethnic identity in the Portuguese settlement, Melaka, Malaysia'. *Asian Music*, vol. 27, no. 1, pp. 37–62.

—— (2005) 'Being Portuguese in Malacca: the politics of folk culture in Malaysia'. *Etnográfica*, vol. 9, pp. 149–170.

Saunders, Kim Jane (2004) 'Creating and recreating heritage in Singapore'. In David Harrison and Michael Hitchcock (eds), *Current Issues in Tourism*, special issue on 'The Politics of World Heritage: Negotiating Tourism and Conservation', vol. 7, pp. 440–448.

Schermerhorn, R.A. (1974) 'Ethnicity in the perspective of the sociology of knowledge'. *Ethnicity*, vol. 1, no. 1, pp. 1–14.

Schuerkens, Ulrike (2003) 'The sociological and anthropological study of globalization and localization'. *Current Sociology*, vol 51, nos. 3–4, monograph 1(2), pp. 209–222.

Sekhar, Nagothu Udaya (2005) 'Integrated coastal zone management in Vietnam: present potentials and future challenges'. *Ocean and Coastal Management*, vol. 48, pp. 813–827.

Sekimoto, Teruo (2003) 'Batik as a commodity and a cultural object'. In Shinji Yamashita and J.S. Eades (eds), *Globalization in Southeast Asia: Local, National and Transnational Perspectives*, New York and Oxford: Berghann Books, pp. 111–125.

Selwyn, Tom (1996) 'Introduction'. In Tom Selwyn (ed.), *The Tourist Image: Myths and Myth Making in Tourism*. Chichester: Wiley.

Shackley, M. (1994) 'When is the past? authenticity and the commoditisation of heritage'. *Tourism Management*, vol. 15, no. 5, pp. 396–397.

Shamsul, A.B. (1999) 'From Orang Kaya Baru to Melayu Baru: cultural constructions of the Malay "new rich"'. In M. Piches (ed.), *Culture and Privilege in Capitalist Asia*. London and New York: Routledge, pp. 86–110.

—— (2001) 'A history of identity, an identity of a history: the idea and practice of "Malayness" in Malaysia reconsidered'. *Journal of Southeast Asian Studies*, vol. 32, no. 3, pp. 355–366.

Shaw, Brian J. and Roy Jones (eds) (1997) *Contested Urban Heritage: Voices from the Periphery*. Aldershot: Ashgate.

Shaw, Brian J. and Rahil Ismail (2006) 'Ethnoscapes, entertainment and 'eritage in the global city: segmented spaces in Singapore's Joo Chiat Road'. *Geojournal*, vol. 66, pp. 187–198.

Shaw, Gareth and Allan M. Williams (2002) *Critical Issues in Tourism: A Geographical Perspective* (second edition), Oxford: Blackwell.

Sheller, Mimi and John Urry (eds) (2004) *Tourism Mobilities: Places to Play, Places in Play.* London: Routledge.

Shenhav-Keller, S. (1995) 'The Jewish pilgrim and the purchase of a souvenir in Israel'. In M.F. Lanfant, J.B. Allcock and E.M. Bruner (eds), *International Tourism: Identity and Change.* London: Sage, pp. 143–158.

Sherwin, M.D. (1981) 'The palace of Sultan Mansur Shah at Malacca', *Journal of the Society of Architectural Historians*, vol. 40, no. 2, pp. 101–107.

Shimotsuma, Kumiko, Herb Stovel and Simon Warrack (2003) *ICCROM–SPAFA Living Heritage Programme: First Strategy Meeting, Summary Report.* ICCROM – Heritage Settlement Unit.

Shipman, A. (2002) *The Globalization Myth.* Cambridge: Icon Books.

Siddique, S. (1990) 'The phenomenology of ethnicity: a Singapore case study'. In J.H. Ong, C.K. Tong and E.S. Tan (eds), *Understanding Singapore Society.* Singapore: Times Academic Press, pp. 107–124.

Silver, I. (1993) 'Marketing authenticity in third world countries'. *Annals of Tourism Research*, vol. 20, no. 2, pp. 302–318.

Simamora, Adianto P. and Bambang Nurbianto (2003) 'S. Sulawesi now shifts priority to local tourists'. *The Jakarta Post*, 2 March 2003 (http://www.kabar-irian.com/pipermail/kabar-indonesia/2003-March/000259.html), accessed 20 June 2003.

Simon, S. (2002) 'The underside of a miracle: industrialization, land and Taiwan's indigenous peoples'. *Cultural Survival Quarterly*, Summer, pp. 66–69.

Sinclair, M.T. and Asrat Tsegaye (1990) 'International tourism and export instability'. *Journal of Development Studies*, vol. 26, no. 3, pp. 487–505.

Singapore Art Museum (2007) 'About us'. Singapore Art Museum homepage, http://www.nhb.gov.sg/SAM/Information/AboutUs, accessed 21 February 2007.

Singapore: Ministry of Information and the Arts (2000) *Renaissance City Report: Culture and the Arts in Renaissance Singapore.* Singapore: Ministry of Information and the Arts.

Singapore: National Heritage Board (1998) *Singapore: Journey into Nationhood.* Singapore: National Heritage Board.

—— (2004) *Annual Report 2003/4.* Singapore: National Heritage Board.

Singapore: National Tourism Plan Committees (1996) *Tourism 21: Vision of a Tourism Capital.* Singapore: Singapore Tourism Promotion Board.

Singapore Tourist Promotion Board (1996) *Destination Singapore, the Arts Experience.* Singapore: Singapore Tourist Promotion Board.

Singapore Tourist Promotion Board and Singapore Ministry of Information and the Arts (1995) *Singapore, Global City for the Arts.* Singapore: Ministry of Information and the Arts and Singapore Tourist Promotion Board.

Singho, M.G. (no date) 'Reclamation and the Portuguese settlement'. In G. Fernandis (ed.), *Save our Portuguese Heritage Conference 1995, Malacca, Malaysia*. Melaka, privately published, pp. 22–30.

Smith, Melanie K. (2003) *Issues in Cultural Tourism Studies*. London and New York: Routledge.

Smith, V. (1996) 'War and its tourist attractions'. In A. Pizam and Y. Mansfeld (eds), *Tourism, Crime and International Security Issues*. Chichester: Wiley.

SERI (Socioeconomic and Environmental Research Institute) (2001) *Penang Economic Report 2001*, vol. 3, issue 12.

—— (2003) *Penang Economic Report 2003*, vol. 5, issue 12.

—— (2004) *Penang Economic Report 2004*, vol. 6, issue 12.

—— (2005a) *Penang Economic Monthly 2005*, vol. 7, issue 8.

—— (2005b) *Penang Economic Monthly 2005*, vol. 7, issue 12.

Soeharto (1975) 'Words of welcome'. In *Apa dan Siapa Indonesia Indah [What and Who in Beautiful Indonesia]*. Jakarta: The Writer's Group, p. 9.

Soeharto, Tien (1975) 'Preface'. In *Apa dan Siapa Indonesia Indah [What and Who in Beautiful Indonesia]*. Jakarta: The Writer's Group, pp. 13–14.

Sofield, Trevor H.B. (2001) 'Rethinking and reconceptualizing social and cultural issues in Southeast and South Asian tourism development'. In Peggy Teo, T.C. Chang and K.C. Ho (eds), *Interconnected Worlds: Tourism in Southeast Asia*. Oxford: Elsevier Science, Pergamon, pp. 103–120.

Sofield, Trevor H.B. and S. Li (1998) 'Tourism development and cultural policies in China'. *Annals of Tourism Research*, vol. 25, no. 2, pp. 362–392.

Sok, An (2001) 'Opening speech at the National Seminar on Cultural Tourism'. Siem Reap-Phnom Penh, 2–3 July 2001, Phnom Penh: Royal Government of Cambodia.

Sørensen, A. (2003) 'Backpacker ethnography'. *Annals of Tourism Research*, vol. 30, no. 4, pp. 847–67.

Sparkes, Stephen (1995) 'Taming nature – controlling fertility: concepts of nature and gender among the Isan of Northeast Thailand'. In Ole Bruun and Arne Kalland (eds), *Asian Perceptions of Nature: A Critical Approach*. Richmond: Curzon Press, NIAS Studies in Asian Topics, Number 18, pp. 64–87.

Spivak, G.C. (1987) *In Other Worlds: Essays in Cultural Politics*. London and New York: Methuen.

Stainton, M. (1999) 'The politics of Taiwan aboriginal origins'. In M.A. Rubinstein (ed.), *Taiwan: A New History*. Armonk: East Gate Books, pp. 27–46.

—— (2002) 'Presbyterians and the aboriginal revitalization movement in Taiwan'. *Cultural Survival Quarterly*, Summer, pp. 63–69.

Stanley, B. (1994) 'Investor breaks ground of luxury hotel at "Hanoi Hilton" prison site'. *The Associate Press*, 29 November 1994.

Stanley, N. (1998) *Being Ourselves for You: The Global Display of Cultures*. London: Middlesex University Press.

Steels, Stephanie (2007) *Borobodur Temple: Tourism and Constructions of Indonesian Culture and Identity*. Unpublished M.A. dissertation, University of Leeds.

Steiner, Christopher B. (1994) *African Art in Transit*. New York: Cambridge University Press.

Stewart, I. (1997) 'Vietnam names "Hanoi Hilton" historical site'. *The Associated Press*, 21 June 1997.

Stewart, Susan (1993) *On Longing: Narratives of the Miniature, the Gigantic, the Souvenir, the Collection*. Durham, N.C.: Duke University Press.

Stockwell, A.J. (1993) 'Early tourism in Malaysia'. In Michael Hitchcock, Victor T. King and Michael J.G. Parnwell (eds), *Tourism in South-East Asia*. London: Routledge, pp. 258–270.

Stoessel, Hans (1997) 'Impact on socioeconomic, cultural and environmental development'. Paper presented to the international conference on 'Sustainable Tourism Development in Vietnam', Hue, Vietnam, 22–23 May 1997.

Stovel, Herb (2003) 'Approaches to managing urban transformation for historic cities'. Paper presented to the UNESCO Macao workshop, 2003.

Suchai Worachananant, Bill Carter and Marc Hockings (2006) 'Recovert and management in Surin Marine National Park, Thailand'. Paper presented to the conference on 'Post-Disaster Assessment and Monitoring of Changes in the Coastal, Ocean and Human Systems in the Indian Ocean and Asian Waters', Phuket, Thailand, 20–23 February 2006.

—— (2007) 'Impacts of the 2004 tsunami on Surin Marine National Park, Thailand'. *Coastal Management*, vol. 35, pp. 399–412.

Suchai Worachananant, R.W. Carter, Marc Hockings, Pasinee Reopanichkul and Thon Thamrongnawasawat (2004) 'Tourism Management in Surin Marine National Park, Thailand'. Paper presented to the conference on 'Coastal Zone Asia Pacific', Brisbane, 5–9 September 2004.

Sundin, Bosse (2005) 'Nature as heritage: the Swedish case'. *International Journal of Heritage Studies*, vol. 11, no. 1, pp. 9–20.

Swain, M.B. (2002) 'Introduction'. In M.B. Swain and J.H. Momsen (eds), *Gender/Tourism/Fun (?)*. New York: Cognizant Communication Corporation, pp. 1–14.

Szerszynski, Bronislaw and John Urry (2006) 'Visuality, mobility and the cosmopolitan: inhabiting the world from afar'. *The British Journal of Sociology*, vol. 57, no. 1, pp. 113–131.

Tai, Hue-Tam Ho (2001) *The Country of Memory: Remaking the Past in Late Socialist Vietnam*. Berkeley: University of California Press.

Tan Chee Beng (1979) 'Baba and Nyonya: a study of ethnic identity of the Chinese Peranakan in Malacca'. Unpublished Ph.D. thesis, Cornell University.

—— (1984) 'Acculturation, assimilation and integration: the case of the Chinese'. In S. Husin Ali (ed.), *Kaum, Kelas dan Pembangunan (Ethnicity, Class and Development)*. Kuala Lumpur: Persatuan Sains Sosial Malaysia, pp. 189–211.

Tan Wan Hin (1991) 'International tourism in Malaysia: development, achievement and problems'. *Malaysian Journal of Tropical Geography*, vol. 22, no. 2, pp. 163–173.

Tang, B.H. (1993) *Chu Dau Ceramics*. Hanoi: Kinh Books.

—— (2004) *Traditional Handicraft Villages of Hai Duong*. Hanoi: Culture–Information Publishing House.

Taylor, Paul Michael (ed.) (1994) *Fragile Traditions: Indonesian Art in Jeopardy*. Honolulu: University of Hawai'i Press, pp. 29–41.

Teague, K. (2000) 'Tourist markets and Himalayan craftsmen'. In Michael Hitchcock and Ken Teague (eds), *Souvenirs: The Material Culture of Tourism*. Aldershot: Ashgate, pp. 194–208.

Teo, Peggy (2002) 'Striking a balance for sustainable tourism: implications of the discourse on globalization'. *Journal of Sustainable Tourism*, vol. 10, no. 6, pp. 459–474.

—— (2003a) 'Global and local interactions in tourism'. *Annals of Tourism Research*, vol. 30, no. 2, pp. 287–306.

—— (2003b) 'The limits of imagineering: a case study of Penang'. *International Journal of Urban and Regional Research*, vol. 27, no. 3, pp. 545–563.

Teo, Peggy, T.C. Chang and K.C. Ho (eds) (2001) *Interconnected Worlds: Tourism in Southeast Asia*. Oxford: Elsevier Science, Pergamon.

Teo, Peggy and S. Huang (1995) 'Tourism and heritage conservation in Singapore'. *Annals of Tourism Research*, vol. 22, no.3, pp. 589–615.

Teo, Peggy and Brenda S.A. Yeoh (1997) 'Remaking local heritage for tourism'. *Annals of Tourism Research*, vol. 24, no. 1, pp. 192–213.

Thamasak Yeemin, Makamas Sutthacheep and Rattika Pettongma (2006) 'Coral reef restoration projects in Thailand'. *Ocean and Coastal Management*, vol. 49, pp. 562–575.

The China Post (2007) '13th indigenous group recognized'. http://www.chinapost.com.tw/news/archives/front/2007118/100283.htm (site accessed 7 August 2007).

Theuns, Theo (1997) 'Vietnam: tourism in an economy in transition'. In F. Go and C. Jenkins (eds), *Tourism and Economic Development in Asia and Australia*. London: Cassell.

Thomas, Nicholas (1997) *In Oceania: Visions, Artifacts, Histories*. Durham, N.C. and London: Duke University Press.

Tilley, Christopher (1997) 'Performing culture in the global village'. *Critique of Anthropology*, vol. 17, no. 1, pp. 67–89.

Timothy, D. (1997) 'Tourism and the personal heritage experience'. *Annals of Tourism Research*, vol. 24, no. 3, pp. 751–754.

Tipton, E.K. (2002) *Modern Japan: A Social and Political History*. London and New York: Routledge.

Tomlinson, John (1999) *Globalization and Culture*. Chicago: University of Chicago Press.

Tourism Malaysia (1998) *Malaysia: A General Guide*. Kuala Lumpur: Ministry of Culture, Arts and Tourism.

—— (2004) *Travel Manual Malaysia Truly Asia*. Malaysia: Tourism Malaysia.

Towner, John (1985) 'The Grand Tour: a key phase in the history of tourism'. *Annals of Tourism Research*, vol. 12, pp. 297–333.

—— (1996) *An Historical Geography of Recreation in the Western World, 1540–1940*. Chichester: Wiley.

Tran Kiem Luu and Mai Kim Dinh (1997) 'Education and training for sustainable tourism development: ASEAN experience – implication for Vietnam'. Paper presented to the international conference on 'Sustainable Tourism Development in Vietnam', Hue, Vietnam, 22–23 May 1997.

Tsurumi, P.E. (1977) *Japanese Colonial Education Taiwan, 1895–1945*. Cambridge: Harvard University Press.

Tu Giang (2001) 'Hanoi old quarter catches land fever'. *The Vietnam Investment Review*, 19 March 2001.

UNESCO (1983) *Conventions concerning the Protection of the World Cultural and Natural Heritage*. Paris: UNESCO.

—— (1992) *World Heritage Nomination – IUCN Summary: 671: Ha Long Bay (Vietnam)*, Paris: UNESCO World Heritage Centre.

—— (1995) *The UNESCO International Campaign for the Safeguarding of the Hue Monuments Complex and World Heritage Site*. Hanoi: Hue–UNESCO Working Group and Vietnam National Commisssion for UNESCO.

—— (1999) *Report of the Nara Seminar on the Development and Integrity of Historic Cities (5–7 March 1999, Nara, Japan)*. Presented at the 23rd session of the World Heritage Committee, Marrakesh.

—— (2003) 'Vietnam: Ha Long Bay'. In UNESCO *State of Conservation of the World Heritage Properties in the Asia–Pacific Region*. Washington: World Heritage Center, pp. 236–242.

—— (2004) *World Heritage Reports 12, The State of World Heritage in the Asia–Pacific Region, 2003*. Paris: UNESCO World Heritage Centre.

UNESCO for the Inter-Governmental Conference on Angkor (1993) *Safeguarding and Development of Angkor*. Tokyo: UNESCO.

UNESCO/Sophie Boukhari (2002) 'Heritage: Angkor's role in the search for a lost unity'. *UNESCO New Source*. Paris: UNESCO.

Urry, John (1990) *The Tourist Gaze: Leisure and Travel in Contemporary Societies*. London: Sage Publications.

—— (1993) 'The tourist gaze "revisited"'. *The American Behavioural Scientist*, vol. 36, no. 2, pp. 172–186.

Utusan Konsumer (2002) 'The Acheen Street Mosque controversy: replacement or revitalisation, revenue or restoration'. Penang, November 2002, pp. 11–12.

van der Borg, J., P. Costa and G. Gotti (1996) 'Tourism in European heritage cities'. *Annals of Tourism Research*, vol. 23, no. 2, pp. 306–321.

Van Vollenhoven, C. (1918) *Het Adatrecht van Nederlandsch-Indië*. Leiden: Brill/KITLV.

Vann, Elizabeth F. (2006) 'The limits of authenticity in Vietnamese consumer markets'. *American Anthropologist*, vol. 108, no. 2, pp. 286–296.

Villalon, A. (2001) 'Cultural heritage preserves our identity'. *Philippine Daily Enquirer*, Monday 7 May 2001 (http://www.inq7.net/lif/2001/may/07/lif_5-1.htm), downloaded 29 August 2001.

Vines, Elizabeth (2005) *Streetwise Asia: a Practical Guide for the Conservation and Revitalization of Heritage Cities and Towns in Asia*. Bangkok: UNESCO and the World Bank.

Vis, I.L. (1982) 'Het Stadthuys te Malacca: een restauratie-plan voor het oudste VOC-gebouw in het verre osten'. *Verstagen en Aanwinsten 1980–1981 van de Stichting Cultuurgeschiedenis Nederlanders Overzee*. Amsterdam, pp. 34–44.

Vladimir, N. (1996) 'Vietnam: respected in life, Ho Chi Minh revered even in death'. *IPS-Inter Press Service*, 17 September 1996.

VNAT (1997) 'War Seeing Tours to Vietnam'. In VNAT, *Vietnam: Travel, Hotel and Restaurant Index*. Vietnam National Administration of Tourism, Ho Chi Minh City, pp. 311–313.

VNAT/UNDP/UNWTO (2001) 'Revised national tourism development plan for Vietnam, 2001–2010'. Vietnam National Administration of Tourism, United Nations Development Programme, United Nations World Tourism Organisation.

Vogel, E. (1979) *Japan As Number One: Lessons for America*. Cambridge, Mass.: Harvard University Press.

Vu Thuy Huong (1999) 'Quarter striving to grow old gracefully'. *The Vietnam Investment Review*, 12 December 1999.

Wade, G. (1997) 'Melaka in Ming Dynasty texts'. *Journal of the Malaysian Branch of the Royal Asiatic Society*, vol. 70, no. 1, pp. 31–69.

Wake, C. (1983) 'Melaka in the fifteenth century: Malay historical traditions and the politics of Islamization'. In K. Sandhu and P. Wheatley (eds), *Melaka: The Transformation of a Malay Capital, 1400–1980*. Kuala Lumpur: Oxford University Press, pp. 128–161.

Wall, Geoffrey and Heather Black (2004) 'Global heritage and local problems: some examples from Indonesia'. In David Harrison and Michael Hitchcock (eds), *Current Issues in Tourism*, special issue on 'The Politics of World Heritage: Negotiating Tourism and Conservation', vol. 7, pp. 436–439.

Walsh, K. (1992) *The Representation of the Past: Museums and Heritage in the Post-modern World*. London: Routledge.

Waterson, Roxanna (1990) *The Living House: An Anthropology of Architecture in Southeast Asia*. Oxford: Oxford University Press.

—— (1995) 'Houses and hierarchies in island Southeast Asia'. In J. Carsten and S. Hugh-Jones (eds), *About the House: Levi-Strauss and Beyond.* Cambridge: Cambridge University Press, pp. 47–68.

Watson, G.L. and J.P. Kopachevsky (1994) 'Interpretations of tourism as commodity'. *Annals of Tourism Research*, vol. 21, no. 3, pp. 643–660.

Watson, Steve (2000) 'Theorising heritage tourism: a review'. In Mike Robinson, Philip Long, Nigel Evans, Richard Sharpley and John Swarbrooke (eds), Tourism and Heritage Relationships: Global, National and Local Perspectives. Sunderland: Centre for Travel and Tourism in association with Business Education Publishers Ltd., pp. 449–465.

Wen, Z. and X. Xiao (eds) (1997) Wulai: A Local History.Taiwan: Wulai Hsiang Office.

Wiedfeldt, O. (2003) 'The Atayal of Taiwan: basic economic, legal and social structures: probing the causes for the stagnation of Atayal culture'. In Shung Ye Taiwan Aborigines Research Group in Japan, Studies of Taiwan Aborigines. (Translated by E. Kaneko and H. Yamada). Tokyo: Fukyo, pp. 4–47.

Winter, Tim (2003) 'Tomb raiding Angkor: a clash of cultures'. In Michael Hitchcock and Victor T. King (eds), *Indonesia and the Malay World,* special issue on 'Tourism and Heritage in South-East Asia', vol. 31, no. 89, pp. 58–68.

—— (2004) 'Landscape, memory and heritage: new year celebrations at Angkor, Cambodia'. In David Harrison and Michael Hitchcock (eds), *Current Issues in Tourism*, special issue on 'The Politics of World Heritage: Negotiating Tourism and Conservation', vol. 7, pp. 330–345.

—— (2007) 'Rethinking tourism in Asia'. *Annals of Tourism Research*, vol. 34, no. 1, pp. 27–44.

Wolters, O. (1970) The Fall of Srivijaya in Malay History. London: Lund Humphries.

Wong, K.F. (2004) 'Entanglements of ethnographic images: Torii Ryuzo's photographic record of Taiwan aborigines (1896–1900)'. Japanese Studies, vol. 24, no. 3, pp. 283–299.

Wong, Tim, Elery Hamilton-Smith, Stuart Chape and Hans Friederich (eds) (2001) 'Proceedings of the Asia–Pacific Forum on Karst Ecosystems and World Heritage', Gunung Mulu National Park World Heritage Area, Sarawak, 26–30 May 2001. Washington: UNESCO World Heritage Centre.

Wood, Robert E. (1984) 'Ethnic tourism, the state and cultural change in Southeast Asia'. *Annals of Tourism Research*, vol. 11, pp. 353–374; also published in *Economic Development and Cultural Change*, vol. 28, pp. 561–581.

—— (1993) 'Tourism, culture and the sociology of development'. In Michael Hitchcock, Victor T. King and Michael J.G. Parnwell (eds), *Tourism in South-East Asia.* London and New York: Routledge, pp. 48–70.

—— (1997) 'Tourism and the state: ethnic options and constructions of otherness'. In Michel Picard and Robert E. Wood (eds), *Tourism, Ethnicity, and the State in Asian and Pacific Societies.* Honolulu: University of Hawai'i Press, pp. 1–34.

Wook, Chui Byung (2004) *Southern Vietnam Under the Reign of Minh Mang (1820–1841): Central Policies and Local Responses*. Ithaca: Cornell University Southeast Asia Program Publications.

Worden, Nigel (2003) 'National identity and heritage tourism in Melaka'. *Indonesia and the Malay World*, vol. 31, pp. 31–43.

World Bank (2006) *Thailand Environment Monitor 2006: Marine and Coastal Resources: Status and Trends*. Bangkok: World Bank.

World Commission on Environment and Development (WCED) (1987) *Our Common Future*. Oxford: Oxford University Press.

Worts, Douglas (2006) 'Transformational encounters: reflections on cultural participation and ecomuseology'. *Canadian Journal of Communication*, vol. 31, no. 1, pp. 127–145.

Wu, A. (1998) 'Taiwanese cultural identity: tourism and museum perspectives'. Unpublished M.A. Thesis, University of North London.

Wulai Township Office (2004) *Population*. http://www.wulia.tpc.gov.tw.proxy.lib.uwaterloo.ca/chinese/main01.html (site accessed 10 July 2006).

Wulandari, Anak Agung Ayu (2005) 'Taman Mini Indonesia Indah: entertainment or education'. Unpublished M.A. Thesis, London Metropolitan University.

Yamamoto, Y. (1999) 'The prohibition of tattooing among the Atayal: history and analysis (1)'. In Shung Ye Taiwan Aborigines Research Group in Japan, *Studies of Taiwan Aborigines*. Tokyo: Fukyo, pp. 3–40.

—— (2000) 'Interference by the bureau of aboriginal affairs and the elimination of tattooing: forbidding the Atayal to apply tattoos (2)'. In Shung Ye Taiwan Aborigines Research Group in Japan, *Studies of Taiwan Aborigines*. Tokyo: Fukyo, pp. 49–70.

Yamashita, Shinji (2003) 'Introduction: "glocalizing" Southeast Asia'. In Shinji Yamashita and J.S. Eades (eds), *Globalization in Southeast Asia: Local, National and Transnational Perspectives*. New York and Oxford: Berghann Books, pp. 1–17.

Yamashita, Shinji, Kadir H. Din and Jeremy S. Eades (eds) (1997) *Tourism and Cultural Development in Asia and Oceania*. Bangi: Penerbit Universiti Kebangsaan Malaysia.

Yao Souchou (ed.) (2001) *House of Glass: Culture, Modernity, and the State in Southeast Asia*. Singapore: Institute of Southeast Asian Studies.

Yeoh, Brenda (1996) *Contesting Space: Power Relations and Urban Built Environment in Colonial Singapore*. Kuala Lumpur: Oxford University Press.

Yeoh, Brenda and Lily Kong (eds) (1995) *Portraits of Places: History, Community and Identity in Singapore*. Singapore: Times Editions.

—— (1996) 'The notion of place in the construction of history, nostalgia and heritage in Singapore'. *Singapore Journal of Tropical Geography*, vol. 17, no. 1, pp. 52–65.

Zubaida, S. (1995) 'Is there a Muslim society? Ernest Gellner's *Sociology of Islam*'. *Economy and Society*, vol. 24, no. 2, pp. 151–88.

Index

bold=extended discussion or term highlighted in the text
[number within square brackets]=oblique reference
f=figure; n=note; t=table

Vietnam: National Strategy for Environ-
mental Protection (2000–2010) 248
Vietnamese Communist Party (VCP)
176–178, 183–184, 197–200, 211,
262–263(n3), 270
Vietnamese Environmental Protection
Agency (1993) 248
villages 63, 76, 79, 122, 231, **238**, 267
Vision 2020 (1991) 144
Voice of America 217–218

Wade, G. 146(n6), 307
Wake, C. 137, 146(n1), 307
Wall, G. ix, **xiii**, 3, 16, 18, **21**, **49–71**, 106,
264, 272, 278, 307
Walsh, K. 9, 307
Wantanee Suntikul ix, **xiii–xiv**, **25**,
202–220
'war tourism' 205–206, 286
Ward, K. 146(n1)
Warisan Dunia 268
Waterson, R. 36, 47, 307–308
Wathen, J. 150
weaving 21, **49–52**, **57–69**, 70–71, 224
Wei Hui–lin 78
Wesner, S. viii, **xiv**, **221–235**
West, the 84, 86, 97
West Asia/Middle East 94–95, 99, 153,
157t, 157
Winter, T. 17, **87–88**, 266, 308
women **50–51**, 164, 180, 194, 226
Wood, R.E. 11–13, 15, 290, 298, 308
Wook Chui Byung 200(n2), 309
Worden, N. ix, **xiv**, **23**, **130–146**, 309
World Commission for Protected Areas
239
world heritage 'fixing' **43–46**, 48(n22)
World Heritage Sites (WHS)
absence 7, 12
community-based approach **124–126**,
129(n40)
comparative research required
272–273

contestation processes 104–145
cultural 4, **5–7**, 8–9t, 10, **33**, 46–
47(n4), 107
'in Danger' 105, 108, 110, 128(n13), 240
'defining role' of tourism 219
definition 32, 46–47(n6)
'double-edged sword' 240–241
emergence 45
global–local interactions **15–20**, 278
miscellaneous viii, ix, 2, 205, 237
mixed 4, 6, **33**
multiple and shifting meanings
32–38
natural 4, **6**, 8–9t, **33**, 47(n4)
'new meeting grounds' 127
opposition to designation 15
'preservation' theme 33–34
processes of change before and after
nomination 103–104
prospective 32–33, 46(n5)
selection criteria 5–6
World Heritage Sites in Southeast Asia
(Ch. 6) 8–9t, **103–129**, 266, 269
chapter purpose **104–105**
shared issues **106–114**, **128(n7–22)**
World Monuments Fund 7
World Tourism Organization 229
World War II 37, 92, 212, 217
World's Greatest Natural Areas (IUCN,
1982) 239
Wulai (Taiwan) **49–71**
'golden era' (tourism) 50–51, 67
international tourism development
64–66
Wulandari, Anak Agung Ayu 80, 82n, 309

Xiamen 141

Yamamoto, Y. 58, 309
Yeang trees 117–118, 129(n17)
Yeoh, B. 149, 309
Yoshimura Mami ix, **xiv**, **21**, **49–71**, 264

Zainal Kling 48(n15), 291